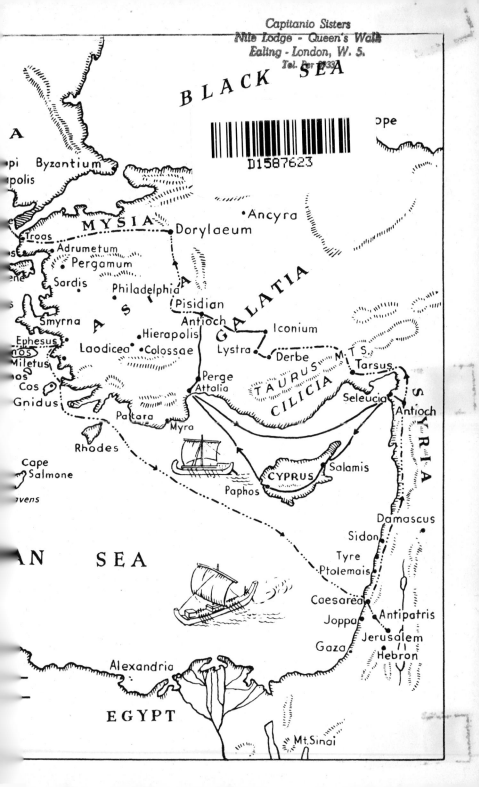

BLACK SEA

ope

D1587623

•Ancyra

MYSIA Dorylaeum

GALATIA

pi Byzantium
polis

Troas
Adrumetum
Pergamum
Sardis
Philadelphia
ene
Pisidian
Antioch
Iconium
Smyrna
Hierapolis
Ephesus
Laodicea •Colossae
Lystra
Derbe
TAURUS MTS.
Tarsus
nos
Miletus
Cos
CILICIA
Seleucia
Gnidus
Perge
Attalia
Antioch

Patara
Myra

Rhodes

Cape
Salmone

Salamis
CYPRUS

avens

SEA

AN

Paphos

Damascus
Sidon
Tyre
Ptolemais
Caesarea
Joppa
Antipatris
Gaza
Jerusalem
Hebron

Alexandria

EGYPT

Mt.Sinai

ASIA

PHRYGIA

SYRIA

IT IS PAUL WHO WRITES

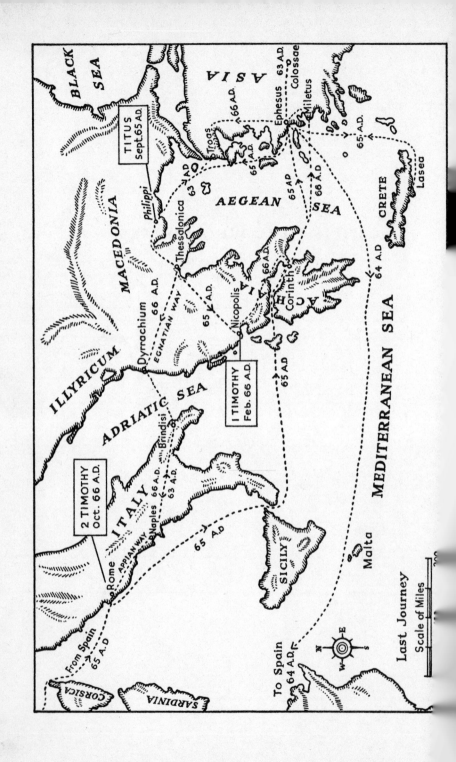

Last Journey

Scale of Miles

IT IS PAUL WHO WRITES

based on the translation of the Epistles of
Saint Paul & of the Acts of the Apostles by
RONALD KNOX

arranged in a continuous narrative
with explanations by
RONALD COX, C.M., S.T.L., S.S.L.

BURNS & OATES   LONDON

IMPRIMI POTEST: N.S. ROSSITER, C.M., D.D.

VISITOR AUSTRALIAN PROVINCE

IMPRIMATUR: ✠ JAMES M. LISTON, D.D.

BISHOP OF AUCKLAND

22 AUGUST 1956

MADE AND PRINTED IN GREAT BRITAIN BY
LOWE AND BRYDONE (PRINTERS) LTD., LONDON, N.W.10, FOR
BURNS OATES AND WASHBOURNE LTD.,
28 ASHLEY PLACE, LONDON, S.W.1

Contents

Contents

Maps

Introduction

This book is a sequel to *The Gospel Story*; it takes up at the point in Scripture where that left off, at the Descent of the Holy Ghost. The layout of both books is the same: on the left-hand page the text of the Acts of the Apostles and the Pauline Letters runs continuously; on the opposite page there is a commentary, paragraph for paragraph. I have made almost no attempt to explain difficult passages but have concentrated on supplying the atmosphere in which St. Paul wrote, and on following his main line of thought.

The New Testament arranges these letters according to their length and importance. I have rearranged them so that they are now read in the order in which they were written; the Letter to the Romans is in sixth place in this book, not first as in the New Testament. Seven of these letters were written during the course of St. Paul's missionary journeys as recorded in the Acts; I have interrupted the narrative of the Acts in order to fit in these letters where they belong. The remaining seven are grouped together at the end of the book; they were all written after the conclusion of the Acts.

For reasons of convenience rather than conviction I have located the Letter to the Hebrews at Caesarea in 60 A.D. The date of writing is uncertain, so I have taken the liberty of placing it where I think the reader will most easily appreciate its message. The events leading up to St. Paul's arrest and imprisonment give the authentic background for the Letter to the Hebrews.

Monsignor Knox's version was made from the Latin Vulgate.

The slight variations in my text arise from the fact that I have corrected his text in accordance with the original Greek; practically all of these corrections were made by Monsignor Knox himself; in the majority of cases they do not alter the meaning of the passage.

In interpreting St. Paul's thoughts I am greatly indebted to Mgr. Knox's *A New Testament Commentary* (Sheed & Ward); most of the paragraph headings and many of the ideas in my commentary have come from this source. For the chronology of St. Paul's life I have followed *A Catholic Commentary on Holy Scripture* (Nelson). For those readers who wish to look up individual verses this book can be highly recommended. But the two classic works on St. Paul are *The Theology of St. Paul* by Fernand Prat (Newman), and *Paul of Tarsus* by Joseph Holzner (Herder). The two large volumes of Prat are the most profound study of St. Paul yet published. Holzner is a more popular presentation of the Life and Letters of St. Paul against the background of his time.

The theme of St. Paul's Letters is the doctrine of the Mystical Body of Christ. He never forgot his dramatic introduction to this truth. On his way to Damascus, a bright light blinded him, and a voice called to him from above: 'Saul, Saul, why are you persecuting *me*?' That last word is the important one. Jesus Christ, seated in glory at the Father's right hand, was complaining of *personal* persecution by Paul. The only conclusion Paul could reach was that Jesus identified himself with each individual Christian. The identity of the Christian with Christ remained St. Paul's central doctrine for the rest of his life.

R. J. COX

HOLY CROSS COLLEGE

MOSGIEL N.Z.

15 AUGUST 1956

SUNDAY AND FEAST-DAY EPISTLES

IT IS PAUL WHO WRITES

"Cor Pauli cor Christi est."
—ST. JOHN CHRYSOSTOM

TEXT OF SCRIPTURE ON LEFT-HAND PAGES.

COMMENTARY ON RIGHT-HAND PAGES.

The Conversion of Paul

When the day of Pentecost came round, while they were all gathered together in unity of purpose, all at once a sound came from heaven like that of a strong wind blowing, and filled the whole house where they were sitting. Then appeared to them what seemed to be tongues of fire, which parted and came to rest on each of them; and they were all filled with the Holy Spirit, and began to speak in strange languages, as the Spirit gave utterance to each.

Among those who were dwelling in Jerusalem at this time were devout Jews from every country under heaven; so, when the noise of this went abroad, the crowd which gathered was in bewilderment; each man severally heard them speak in his own language. And they were all beside themselves with astonishment: 'Are they not all Galileans speaking?' they asked. 'How is it that each of us hears them talking in his own native tongue? There are Parthians among us, and Medes, and Elamites; our homes are in Mesopotamia, or Judea, or Cappadocia; in Pontus or Asia, Phrygia or Pamphylia, Egypt or the parts of Libya round Cyrene; some of us are visitors from Rome, some of us are Jews and others proselytes; there are Cretans among us too, and Arabians; and each has been hearing them tell of God's wonders in his own language.'

So they were all beside themselves with perplexity, and asked one another, 'What can this mean?'

There were others who said, mockingly, 'They have had their fill of sweet wine.'

But Peter, with the eleven apostles at his side, stood there and raised his voice to speak to them: 'Men of Judea,' he said, 'and all you who are dwelling in Jerusalem, I must tell you this;

Palestine and Syria 30-44 A.D.

Descent of the Holy Ghost. On this day our Lord fulfilled his promise made at the Last Supper: 'I will ask the Father, and he will give you another to befriend you, one who is to dwell continually with you for ever.'

It was a spring morning in Jerusalem; great crowds of Jews were making their way to the temple for the Pentecostal ceremonies. Above the noise of talking and the sound of marching feet came a mighty roar in the sky above; it was a loud, rushing sound like a storm of wind; but the air was still; not a tunic fluttered, not a leaf moved on a tree. All eyes looked up; they saw nothing but blue sky and bright sunlight.

It sounded perhaps like a jet aircraft; but it was to have an incomparably more important effect on humanity. It was a sound in the sky, heralding the coming of the Third Person of the Blessed Trinity.

When the Second Person had his birthday as man, there had been angels singing in the sky over Bethlehem. Today was a new birthday, the coming of the Holy Spirit to make his dwelling in the 120 people in the upper room of the Last Supper. Not one body only, like that of the God-Man at Bethlehem, but a union of God with all the descendants of Adam scattered over the face of the earth. The 120 people in the Cenacle were the beginnings of the Church, the Mystical Body of Christ in its infancy: a new, divine organism destined to bring the fruits of redemption to all nations.

Peter's First Sermon. The crowds surging into the temple did not have to wait long for an explanation of the noise in the sky. A compact, united group of a little more than a hundred men and women were making their way through the west door,

listen to what I have to say. These men are not drunk, as you suppose; it is only nine in the morning. This is what was foretold by the prophet Joel: "In the last times, God says, I will pour out my spirit upon all mankind, and your sons and daughters will be prophets. Your young men shall see visions, and your old men shall dream dreams; and I will pour out my spirit in those days upon my servants and handmaids, so that they will prophesy. I will show wonders in heaven above, and signs on the earth beneath, blood and fire and whirling smoke; the sun will be turned into darkness and the moon into blood, before the day of the Lord comes, great and glorious. And then everyone who calls on the name of the Lord shall be saved."

'Men of Israel, listen to this. Jesus of Nazareth was a man duly accredited to you from God; such were the miracles and wonders and signs which God did through him in your midst, as you yourselves well know. This man you have put to death; by God's fixed design and foreknowledge, he was betrayed to you, and you, through the hands of sinful men, have cruelly murdered him. But God raised him up again, releasing him from the pangs of death; it was impossible that death should have the mastery over him. It is in his person that David says: "Always I can keep the Lord within sight; always he is at my right hand, to make me stand firm. So there is gladness in my heart, and rejoicing on my lips; my body, too, shall rest in confidence that you will not leave my soul in the place of death, or allow your faithful servant to see corruption. You have shown me the way of life; you will make me full of gladness in your presence."

'My brethren, I can say this to you about the patriarch David without fear of contradiction, that he did die, and was buried, and his tomb is among us to this day. But he was a prophet, and

chanting the praises of God (probably in words from the psalms). But they were not speaking in Aramaic or Hebrew; each person spoke in a different language, and all were foreign tongues. They were surrounded by an ever-growing crowd of people, many of these from lands outside Palestine. These men were most excited, as they recognized a voice in the apostolic group chanting aloud in the dialect of their adopted country.

Many of the crowd had often seen Jesus walking into this same temple, and had often listened to him speaking in the covered porches. Today they were witnessing a new approach of that same Lord and Master: he had come back in the persons of his followers. He no longer spoke with his own human voice; he used Peter and James and John instead; but it was he who spoke through their lips. He is the head, they are his organs. He could now love with the hearts of all his followers, all 120 of them (and soon many thousands more); the fire of divine love, the Holy Spirit himself, was the force and power making their lips move in praise of the Lord God.

So Peter stood up to address the excited crowd milling round the apostolic band; he spoke with the authority that our Lord had conferred upon him, when he said to him: 'Feed my lambs, shepherd my sheep.' And like his Lord and Master, whom he now represented, he used the same technique that Jesus had so often used here in this same temple during his public life on earth.

First of all he took up what was topical, what they were all interested in: this amazing gift of tongues. In practical commonsense fashion he disposed of an explanation that he had heard given by several voices in the crowd—the charge of drunkenness. No Jew would dream of taking a drink on a feast day before the morning sacrifice, which was not celebrated until nine o'clock.

he knew God had promised him on oath that he would set the sons of his body upon his throne; it was of the Christ he said, foreseeing his resurrection, that he was not left in the place of death, and that his body did not see corruption. God, then, has raised up this man, Jesus, from the dead; we are witnesses of it.

'And now, exalted at God's right hand, he has claimed from his Father his promise to bestow the Holy Spirit; and he has poured out that Spirit, as you can see and hear for yourselves. David never went up to heaven, and yet David has told us: "The Lord said to my Master, 'Sit on my right hand, while I make your enemies a footstool under your feet.' "

'Let it be known, then, beyond doubt, to all the house of Israel, that God has made him Master and Christ, this Jesus whom you have crucified.'

When they heard this, their consciences were stung; and they asked Peter and his fellow apostles, 'Brethren, what must we do?'

'Repent,' Peter said to them, 'and be baptized, every one of you, in the name of Jesus Christ, to have your sins forgiven; then you will receive the gift of the Holy Spirit. This promise is for you and for your children, and for all those, however far away, whom the Lord our God calls to himself.'

And he used many more words besides, urgently appealing to them: 'Save yourselves,' he said, 'from this false-minded generation.'

So all those who had taken his words to heart were baptized, and about three thousand souls were won for the Lord that day. These occupied themselves continually with the apostles' teaching and fellowship, and the breaking of bread, and

Now that Peter had struck a note of commonsense, he proceeded to give the true explanation of this amazing spectacle of 120 people all talking at once, and every one in a different language. Peter announced it as the fulfilment of one of the many Old Testament prophecies; it was exactly as the prophet Joel had foretold.

Peter's third point was to prove that Jesus is still alive, and that this Pentecostal outpouring of his Spirit comes from him, now enthroned in heaven. He quotes psalm 15 in proof. David, using the first person, could not have been speaking in his own name; he certainly did die (his body still lies in his tomb here in Jerusalem), and there is no claim that he ever rose from the dead. But it is just the opposite with Jesus: everyone knows that his tomb by Golgotha is empty.

The First Converts. It was only fifty days (Pentecost in Greek) since our Lord had died on the cross in this very city of Jerusalem. Even on Good Friday many of those present at the crucifixion 'went home beating their breasts.' Then they showed the first signs of sorrow; on hearing Peter's sermon they gave themselves completely to God. It was the beginning of a steady stream of converts to the Church which has never ceased.

Nicodemus must have been a happy man as he watched the first baptismal ceremony, the rite of initiation into the Mystical Body of Christ. Now he would understand our Lord's words to him that night at Bethany: 'Believe me, no man can enter into the kingdom of God unless birth comes to him from water, and from the Spirit.'

Christianity is not merely a set of beliefs; it is a way of life. The life of the early Church was based on the earthly life of

prayers; and every soul was struck with awe, so many were the wonders and signs performed by the apostles in Jerusalem. All the faithful held together, and shared all they had, selling their possessions and their means of livelihood, so as to distribute to all, as each had need. They persevered with one accord, day by day, in the Temple worship, and as they broke bread in this house or that, took their share of food with gladness and simplicity of heart, praising God, and winning favour with all the people. And each day the Lord added to their fellowship others that were to be saved.

Peter and John were going up to the temple at three o'clock in the afternoon, which is an hour of prayer, when a man was carried by who had been lame from birth. Every day he was put down at what is called the Beautiful Gate of the temple, so that he could beg alms from the temple visitors. And he asked Peter and John, as he saw them on their way into the temple, if he might have alms from them.

Peter fastened his eyes on him, as John did too, and said, 'Turn towards us'; and he looked at them attentively, hoping that something would be given him.

Then Peter said to him, 'Silver and gold are not mine to give, I give you what I can. In the name of Jesus Christ of Nazareth, rise up and walk.' So, taking him by his right hand, he lifted him up; and with that strength came to his feet and ankles; he sprang up, and began walking, and went into the temple with them, walking, and leaping, and giving praise to God.

All the people, as they saw him walking and praising God, recognized him for the man who used to sit begging at the Beautiful Gate of the temple, and were full of wonder and bewilderment at what had befallen him. And he would not

our Lord: the close unity of a family with Peter and the apostles as leaders, and the sharing of goods in common. All the time they were studying the living tradition of our Lord's own example as handed down by the apostles.

Our Lord had told his followers in the Sermon on the Mount: 'Do not think that I have come to set aside the law and the prophets; I have not come to set them aside, but to bring them to perfection.' And so the early Christians did not break with Judaism; they continued to frequent divine worship in the temple.

A Lame Man Healed.   Peter and John were together because the Master himself had paired them that way, when he first sent the apostles out to preach 'two and two.' If they were living at the Cenacle, which is in the southwest section of the city, they should not have been entering the temple by the eastern gate, called the Beautiful Gate. Were they doing so because that was the gate most used by the Master when he went into the temple courts? Or had they been paying a visit to the garden of Gethsemani, which is just outside the eastern gate? More likely they were living at Bethany, where Jesus himself used to stay with Lazarus and his two famous sisters; the Cenacle would be a place of meeting, but not all the disciples would be living there.

As they climbed up the marble steps leading from the Court of the Gentiles into the Women's Court, they were walking in the footsteps of the Master; more than that, they were now hands and feet of that Head of the Body; Jesus would now work his wonders of healing only through these limbs of his Mystical Body. The same compassion for misery and suffering that had moved him to heal a cripple, just north of the temple a year before, was now the force and power that made Peter

let go of Peter and John, so that all the crowd gathered about them in what is called Solomon's Porch, beside themselves with wonder.

Peter, when he saw it, addressed himself to the people: 'Men of Israel,' he said, 'why does this astonish you? Why do you fasten your eyes on us, as if we had enabled him to walk through some power or virtue of our own? It is the God of Abraham and Isaac and Jacob, the God of our forefathers, who has thus brought honour to his Son Jesus. You gave him up, and disowned him in the presence of Pilate, when Pilate's voice was for setting him free. You disowned the holy, the just, and asked for the pardon of a murderer, while you killed the author of life. But God has raised him up again from the dead, and we are here to bear witness of it.

'Here is a man you all know by sight, who has put his faith in that name, and that name has brought him strength; it is the faith which comes through Jesus that has restored him to full health in the sight of you all.

'Come then, brethren, I know that you, like your rulers, acted in ignorance; but God has fulfilled in this way what was foretold by all the prophets about the sufferings of his Christ. Repent, then, and turn back to him, to have your sins effaced; so shall the day come when the Lord sees fit to refresh our hearts. Then he will send out Jesus Christ, who is yours by promise, but must have his dwelling-place in heaven until the time when all is restored anew, the time which God has spoken of by his holy prophets from the beginning.

'Thus, Moses said: "The Lord your God will raise up for you a prophet like myself, from among your brethren; to him, to every word of his, you must listen. It is ordained that every-

turn at the sound of the beggar's voice. All the wealth of
heaven was at Peter's disposal; he was the vicar of Christ.

Peter Explains the Miracle. The Master always appealed to
reason and facts; he respected the gift of reason in human beings, and so explained his conduct in such a way as to win a
rational adherence to his claims. Peter, ever mindful of the
methods of his Master, follows the same reasonable approach.

In sight, and towering above the temple colonnades and
porches, was the Fortress Antonia. Within its walls, hardly a
hundred yards to the north, only a few months before, the
Jewish people had disowned Jesus, their only hope of salvation;
so it was this incident of Jesus' trial before Pilate that Peter
now spoke of.

The scene comes alive once more, as Peter recounts the re-
action of the Passover crowd to Pilate's proposal that he release
Jesus their king: 'We want Barabbas released, not this man—
Barabbas! Barabbas!'

When Pilate tried a last time to have the Jews accept Jesus,
they completely disowned their king: 'Away with him, away
with him; crucify him, crucify him.'

'What,' Pilate said to them, 'shall I crucify your king?'

'We have no king,' the chief priests answered, 'except
Caesar.'

But Peter knows, as his Master did, that to convert men it is
as necessary to win their hearts by love as their minds by truth.
With the same charity as that of Jesus nailed to the cross, he
excuses their guilt through ignorance: 'Father, forgive them;
they do not know what it is they are doing.'

The Jews were looking for a military leader to drive out the
Romans; Jesus had come in the way of suffering to drive out

one who will not listen to the voice of that prophet shall be
lost to his people." And all the prophets who spoke to you,
from Samuel onwards, have foretold those days. You are the
heirs of the prophets, and of the covenant which God made
with our fathers, when he said to Abraham, "Every race on
earth shall receive a blessing through your posterity." It is to
you first of all that God has sent his Son, whom he raised
from the dead to bring you a blessing, to turn away every one
of you from his sins.'

Before they had finished speaking to the crowd, they were
interrupted by the priests, the temple superintendent, and
the Sadducees. These, indignant at their teaching the people
and proclaiming the resurrection of Jesus from the dead, laid
hands on them, and put them in prison (for it was already
evening) until the next day. (Meanwhile, many of those who
had listened to their preaching had joined the believers, so
that their numbers had now risen to five thousand men.)

On the next day, there was a gathering of the rulers and
elders and scribes in Jerusalem; the high priest Annas was
there, and Caiphas, and John, and Alexander, and all those
who belonged to the high-priestly family. And they had Peter
and John brought into their presence, and asked them, 'By
what power, in whose name, have such men as you done
this?'

Then Peter was filled with the Holy Spirit, and said to
them: 'Rulers of the people, elders of Israel, listen to me.
If it is over kindness done to a cripple, and the means by
which he has been restored, that we are called in question,
here is news for you and for the whole people of Israel. You
crucified Jesus Christ, the Nazarene, and God raised him from
the dead; it is through his name that this man stands before you
restored. He is that stone, rejected by you, the builders, that

Satan and sin. That the Jews should have fallen into such an error was the consequence of their explaining away, or ignoring, what the prophets had foretold.

Peter probably uses the prophecy of Isaias 53, and Psalm 21, to show that a suffering Messiah was foretold by God in the scriptures. He also quotes from Moses and Abraham to show that salvation can come only through the promised Messiah, Jesus. The time of blessing promised in the Old Testament is now a reality.

Peter and John in Prison.   The shadows lengthened across the temple courts; at last the sun set behind the west wall of the temple, and still Peter talked on. He must have continued speaking and answering questions for three hours or more. (This shows how summary are the records of discourses in the Acts; only the highlights are given.) The temple authorities could ignore him no longer; the evening sacrifice was ended, and instead of going home the crowds increased around Peter.

The temple police were ordered to arrest the two apostles and imprison them for the night in one of the rooms inside the temple area. Peter and John must have recalled, in the long night that followed, another night only a few months before, when they had waited in the courts of Caiphas' house while Jesus was locked up inside. Our Lord in his own human body could no longer be imprisoned; but he could undergo, and was undergoing, the same treatment in the members of his Mystical Body.

Next morning they were brought before the Jewish rulers, in the council chamber of the temple, just as the Master had been arraigned and tried in the house of the high priest: 'A disciple is no better than his master, a servant than his lord; enough that the disciple should fare like his master.' This was

has become the chief stone at the corner. Salvation is not to be found elsewhere; this alone of all the names under heaven has been appointed to men as the one by which we must needs be saved.'

Seeing the boldness of Peter and John, and discovering that they were simple men, without learning, they were astonished, and recognized them now as having been in Jesus' company. They could find no answer to make, with the man who had been healed standing there beside them; so they ordered them out of the council-chamber, and conferred together. 'What are we to do with these men?' they asked. 'It is commonly known among all the people of Jerusalem that a notable miracle has been done by their means, and we are powerless to deny it. But the news must not spread any further; we must deter them by threats from preaching to anybody in this man's name again.'

So they called them in, and warned them not to utter a word or give any teaching in the name of Jesus.

At this, Peter and John answered them, 'Judge for yourselves whether it would be right for us, in the sight of God, to listen to your voice instead of God's. It is impossible for us to refrain from speaking of what we have seen and heard.'

And they, after threatening them further, let them go; they could find no means of punishing them, because all the people were praising God over what had befallen; the man in whom this miracle of healing had taken place was more than forty years old.

Now that they were set free, they went back to their company, and told them all the chief priests and elders had said. And they, when they heard it, uttered prayer to God with one accord: 'Ruler of all, you who are the maker of heaven

not a formal trial like our Lord's before the full council of
seventy; it was only a preliminary enquiry into the incident
leading to their arrest the previous day. Peter again shows that
he is the accepted leader and spokesman.

The Council Warns Peter and John. In the courts of the
temple in Jerusalem there was a school for the training of
teachers in Israel. It was a course of studies similar to those in
our seminaries for the training of priests. Each candidate was
tested in knowledge of the law of Moses and the prophets before he was permitted to preach to the people in the synagogues. Those officially approved were known as rabbis. St.
Paul was one of the most brilliant of such students trained in
Jerusalem. He may even have been present on this occasion.

Our Lord was never trained in this school; he caused amazement in these teachers when he visited the holy city as a boy
of twelve. When he began teaching in Jerusalem, less than a
year before the incident recorded here, the Jews were astonished, and asked: 'How does this man know how to read?
He has never studied.'

Such laymen as Peter and John caused as much amazement
as would a member of the Sunday congregation standing up
after the gospel at Mass, and mounting the pulpit to deliver
the accustomed sermon to the people.

The Council probably remembered the difficulties they had
caused themselves when they denied a similar miracle worked
by our Lord on the blind man (Jn. 9); they decided to handle
this situation more adroitly.

The Church Offers Public Prayer. It was probably back in
the Cenacle that this gathering of Christians took place. The
Church had emerged triumphant from its first testing at the
hands of the Jews. It was not through any power of its own;

and earth and the sea, and all that is in them. You have said
through your Holy Spirit, by the lips of your servant David,
our father, "What means this turmoil among the nations;
why do the people cherish vain dreams? See how the kings
of the earth stand in array, how its rulers make common cause,
against the Lord and his Christ." True enough, in this city
of ours, Herod and Pontius Pilate, with the Gentiles and the
people of Israel to aid them, made common cause against your
holy servant Jesus, so accomplishing all that your power and
wisdom had decreed. Look down upon their threats, Lord,
now as of old; enable your servants to preach your word con-
fidently, by stretching out your hand to heal; and let signs
and miracles be performed in the name of Jesus, your holy
Son.'

When they had finished praying, the place in which they
had gathered rocked to and fro, and they were all filled with
the Holy Spirit, and began to preach the word of God with
confidence.

There was one heart and soul in all the company of believers; none of them called any of his possessions his own,
everything was shared in common. Great was the power with
which the apostles testified to the resurrection of the Lord
Jesus Christ, and great was the grace that rested on them all.
None of them was destitute; all those who owned farms or
houses used to sell them, and bring the price of what they
had sold to lay it at the apostles' feet, so that each could
have what share of it he needed.

There was a Levite, called Joseph, a Cypriot by birth, to
whom the apostles gave the fresh name of Barnabas, which
means, the man of encouragement; he had an estate, which
he sold, and brought the purchase-money to lay it at the
apostles' feet.

it was through divine help from God on high that this first persecution was turned back. So the Mystical Body prayed, as their Master and Head had prayed so often during his earthly life, looking to and acknowledging the Father as its only source of strength in times of trial.

The prayer is based on Psalm 2, a Messianic psalm, narrating the victory of Christ over his enemies. It is applied to present circumstances: first the attack on Jesus himself, and now the attack on his Mystical Body on earth. This type of prayer (a scriptural basis with an application to present needs) has remained the classic prayer form in the Church (as in the collects at Mass).

A miracle similar to that of Pentecost Sunday then took place; it was an obvious manifestation of divine power. Instead of a rushing wind, there was an earthquake: God can show his power in a great variety of ways. These signs of God's power were meant primarily to strengthen the faith of the early Christians.

Death of Ananias and Sapphira. The Cenacle had been a second home to Barnabas; there he and his cousin John Mark had become close friends, during the years that he was a student in the rabbinical school in the temple. In such close contact with the early Church, he was soon converted to the faith. With no loss of time he returned to Cyprus (only 100 miles off the Syrian coast), and sold his property there. He was mindful of the advice of the Master: 'Sell all that belongs to you, and give to the poor; so the treasure you have shall be in heaven; then come back and follow me.'

Barnabas is our first real link with St. Paul, the hero of the early Church. They were probably students together at Jerusalem. Later, Barnabas would take the new convert Paul under his care and introduce him to the Christian community. To-

But there was a man called Ananias, who, with his wife Sapphira, sold an estate, and kept back some of the money, with his wife's knowledge, only bringing a part of it to lay at the feet of the apostles. Whereupon Peter said, 'Ananias, how is it that Satan has taken possession of your heart, bidding you defraud the Holy Spirit by keeping back some of the money that was paid you for the land? Unsold, the property was yours; after the sale, the money was at your disposal; what has put it into your heart so to act? It is God, not man, you have defrauded.'

At these words Ananias fell down and died; and a great fear came upon all those who heard it. So the young men rose up, wrapped him up and carried him out to burial.

It was about three hours later that his wife came in, knowing nothing of what had happened; and Peter said to her, 'Tell me, was it for so much that you sold the estate?'

'Yes,' she said, 'for so much.'

Then Peter said to her, 'What is this conspiracy between you, to put the Spirit of the Lord to the test? Even now I hear at the door the footsteps of those who have been burying your husband; they will carry you out too.'

And all at once she fell at his feet and died; so that when the young men came in they found her a corpse, and carried her out to bury her with her husband. Great fear came upon the church and upon all who heard the story.

And there were many signs and miracles done by the apostles before the people. They used to gather with one accord in Solomon's Porch. No one else dared to join them, although the people held them in high honour, and the number of those who believed in the Lord, both men and women, still increased; they even used to bring sick folk into the streets, and lay them down there on beds and pallets, in the

gether they would start off, with John Mark in their company, on the first missionary journey to Barnabas' homeland, Cyprus.

The Mystical Body of Christ is a continuation and projection in time of our Lord's earthly existence. His members, the first Christians, consciously imitated his earthly life as it was remembered by the apostles. Community life, a sharing of all possessions, was one of the characteristics of Jesus and his twelve. In leading this common life they acted freely, and from the motive of complete dedication to God's service.

In contrast to Barnabas are Ananias and Sapphira. The continuance of good and bad fish in the net, of weeds among the wheat, was foretold by the Master himself. The sin of hypocrisy was especially reprobated by our Lord; this vice of the Pharisees he denounced again and again. And this it was that Peter by inspiration detected in the lies of Ananias and Sapphira.

The Holy Spirit is the soul of the Church; that is why Peter used such strong language of condemnation. Punishment in such spectacular fashion was meant as a warning to others and a proof of God's interest in the moral law. St. Augustine expresses the view of most authorities when he says that the two were not lost eternally.

Second Attempt to Silence the Apostles. 'And they brought to him all those who were in affliction, distressed with pain and sickness of every sort, the possessed, the lunatics, the paralytics; and he healed all their diseases.' That is how the gospels speak of our Lord's ministry in Galilee. That same loving care which he showed while on earth still continues its charitable ministration through his Mystical Body; and he also bequeathed

2

hope that even the shadow of Peter, as he passed by, might fall upon one of them here and there. From neighbouring cities, too, the common people flocked to Jerusalem, bringing with them the sick and those who were troubled by unclean spirits; and all of them were cured.

This roused the high priest and those who thought with him, that is the party of the Sadducees. Full of indignation, they arrested the apostles and shut them up in the common gaol. But, in the night, an angel of the Lord came and opened the prison doors, and led them out: 'Go,' he said, 'and take your stand in the temple; preach fully to the people the message of true life.'

So, at his word, they went into the temple at dawn, and began preaching. Meanwhile the high priest and his followers met, and summoned the Council, with all the elders of the Jewish people; and they sent to the prison-house to have them brought in. When they came to look in the prison, the officers could not find them there; so they went back and reported, 'We found the prison-house locked up with all due care, and the guards at their posts before the door; but when we opened it there was no one to be found within.'

At hearing this, the temple superintendent and the chief priests were at a loss to know what had become of them; until an eye-witness told them, 'The men you put in prison are standing in the temple, teaching the people there.'

So the superintendent and his officers went and fetched them, using no violence, because they were afraid of being stoned by the people; and they brought them in and bade them stand before the Council, where the high priest questioned them. 'We warned you in set terms,' he said, 'not to preach in this man's name, and you have filled all Jerusalem

the same power of miracles to Peter and many other members
of the early Church.

The Jewish leaders showed opposition to our Lord right
from the start; but it was only when the crowds gathered round
him and he began to collect disciples that the Jewish leaders
understood that he was a threat to their own leadership of the
people, and must be destroyed if they themselves were to
survive.

Exactly the same situation had now arisen for his Mystical
Body: the Jewish authorities came up with the same solution
that they had found for disposing of our Lord. The apostles
had been warned by the Master to expect such treatment:
'Men will be laying hands on you and persecuting you; they
will give you up to the synagogues, and to prison, and drag
you into the presence of kings and governors on my account;
that will be your opportunity for making the truth known.'

So Peter took up Jesus' task of proclaiming the truth. Instead of one trouble-maker to deal with, the high priest now
had to silence five thousand: Jesus' tongue and lips are multiplied by the number of his followers, by all the members of
his Mystical Body.

Peter follows the same line of thought made familiar from
our Lord's own discourses: 'I have not come on my own errand; I was sent by one who has a right to send. I consult the
will of him who sent me, not my own.' It is this acting with a
mission to fulfil that makes Peter indifferent to opposition; he
is not seeking to establish a personal reputation, he is acting
for and on behalf of his Master in heaven. He is conscious of
divine assistance, and the truth of his cause; he knows that
final victory always belongs to God.

When our Lord was tempted by the devil in the desert,

with your preaching; you are determined to lay this man's death at our door.'

Peter and the other apostles answered, 'God has more right to be obeyed than men. It was the God of our fathers that raised up Jesus, the man you hung on a gibbet to die. It is God that has raised him up to his own right hand, as the prince and Saviour who is to bring Israel repentance, and remission of sins. Of this, we are witnesses; we and the Holy Spirit God gives to all those who obey him.'

On hearing this they were cut to the quick, and designed to kill them. But now one of the Pharisees in the Council, a lawyer named Gamaliel, who was held in esteem by all the people, rose and bade them send the apostles out for a little; then he said to them, 'Men of Israel, think well what you mean to do with these men. There was Theodas, who appeared in days gone by and claimed to be someone of importance, and was supported by about four hundred men; he was killed, and all his followers were dispersed, and came to nothing. And after him Judas the Galilean appeared in the days of the registration; he persuaded the people to rebel under his leadership, but he too perished, and all his followers were scattered. And my advice is still the same: have nothing to do with these men, let them be. If this is man's design or man's undertaking, it will be overthrown; if it is God's, you will have no power to overthrow it. You would not willingly be found fighting against God.'

And they fell in with his opinion; so they sent for the apostles and, after scourging them, let them go with a warning that they were not on any account to preach in the name of Jesus. And they left the presence of the Council, rejoicing that they had been found worthy to suffer indignity for the sake of Jesus' name. And every day, both in the temple and

'angels came and ministered to him.' When he was in an agony
in Gethsemani, 'he had sight of an angel from heaven, encouraging him.' And so it is with his followers; the angels of
heaven are at the service of his sorely tried members; they give
to them the help they need; help which an angel is quite competent to give. 'What are they,' St. Paul asks about angels,
'all of them, but spirits apt for service, whom God sends out
when the destined heirs of eternal salvation have need of
them?'

Gamaliel Pleads for the Apostles. God can use all means,
and the most unlikely people, to assist those whom he loves.
In this same Council of Israel, a rabbi called Nicodemus had
spoken up for Jesus: 'Is it the way of our law to judge a man
without giving him a hearing first, and finding out what he
is about?' So now Gamaliel rose to defend Christ's members.

He was a grandson of the famous Hillel, the founder of
the liberal party among the Pharisees; and was himself noted
for his knowledge of the law. He is our second contact with
St. Paul: 'I was trained, under Gamaliel, in exact knowledge
of our ancestral law.' His was the most famous name in the
professorial faculty of the rabbinical school in Jerusalem, and
he is remembered in Jewish history as one of their best lawyers.

His advice is that of prudence, not sympathy to the Christian cause. In effect it is: wait and see. And that is not necessarily good advice on all occasions; otherwise error and evil
would be allowed to flourish unopposed. But it gave some
short breathing space to the infant Church, before persecution
came in real earnest.

In the same unemphatic manner as that in which the gospels
record our Lord's scourging ('Then Pilate took Jesus and
scourged him'), St. Luke mentions the punishment of the

from house to house, their teaching and their preaching was continually of Jesus Christ.

At this time, as the number of the disciples increased, complaints were brought against those who spoke Hebrew by those who spoke Greek; their widows, they said, were neglected in the daily administration of relief. So the twelve called together the general body of the disciples, and said, 'It is too much that we should have to forgo preaching God's word, and bestow our care upon tables. Come then, brethren, you must find among you seven men who are well spoken of, full of the Spirit and of wisdom, for us to put in charge of this business, while we devote ourselves to prayer, and to the ministry of preaching.'

This advice found favour with all the assembly; and they chose Stephen, a man who was full of faith and of the Holy Spirit, Philip, Prochorus, Nicanor, Timon, Parmenas, and Nicolas, who was a proselyte from Antioch. These they presented to the apostles, who laid their hands on them with prayer.

By now the word of God was gaining influence, and the number of disciples in Jerusalem was greatly increasing; many of the priests had given their allegiance to the faith. And Stephen, full of grace and power, performed great miracles and signs among the people. There were those who came forward to debate with him, some of the synagogue of the Freedmen (as it is called), and of the Cyreneans and Alexandrians, and of those who came from Cilicia and Asia; but they were no match for Stephen's wisdom, and for the Spirit with which he spoke. Thereupon they employed agents to say they had heard him speaking blasphemously of Moses, and of God. Having thus roused the feelings of the people,

apostles. It was 39 strokes of the rod, a Jewish punishment, not the appalling Roman torture inflicted on Jesus.

The Seven Deacons. There is not yet question of Gentile converts; all are Jews. This distinction is between those native to Palestine and those from other lands (the Dispersion, as they are called). These latter had come to Jerusalem for the feast of Pentecost.

This is the first apostolic ordination ceremony. It shows how the apostles adapted themselves to the circumstances of the times. The Mystical Body was growing fast; there were new needs to be met. There is a hierarchy in the body; each member with his own special function to perform. St. Paul expressed it in this way: 'Are all of us apostles, all prophets, all teachers? The body, after all, consists not of one organ but of many.'

There is a divine side to the Mystical Body; but there is a human side too (remember the story of Ananias and Sapphira). The Hebrew speakers, who were in the majority, gave more attention to their own than to foreigners.

The Deacon Stephen on Trial. With the grace of the sacrament of Holy Orders still fresh upon him, Stephen emerged as an articulate champion of the Christian cause. Jesus now had a new mouth to speak the truth for him; and Stephen did it with a skill and power that resembled that of Jesus himself. There is that same deftness in turning an argument, that same sureness in dealing with objections and difficulties from questioners.

'After this the Pharisees withdrew, and plotted together to make him betray himself in his talk.' The same pattern is followed in the attempt to entangle Stephen; it came mostly from groups of foreign Jews (five are mentioned) who had their

and of the elders and scribes, they set upon him and carried him off, and so brought him before the Council. There they put forward false witnesses, who declared, 'This man is never tired of uttering insults against the holy place, and the law. We have heard him say that the Nazarene, Jesus, will destroy this place, and will alter the traditions which Moses handed down to us.'

And all those who sat there in the Council fastened their eyes on him, and saw his face looking like the face of an angel.

Then the high priest asked, 'Are these charges true?'

And he answered, 'Brethren and fathers, listen to me. When the God of glory appeared to our father Abraham, it was while he was still in Mesopotamia, before he took up his dwelling in Haran. "Leave your country," he said, "and your kindred, and come to the land to which I direct you." So it was that he left the country of the Chaldeans, and lived in Haran; it was only after his father's death that he was bidden to remove thence into this land where you now dwell. There, God gave him no inheritance, not so much as a foot's space; he only promised the possession of it to him and to his posterity after him, although at this time he had no child. And this is what God told him, that his descendants would live as strangers in a foreign land, where they would be enslaved and ill-used for four hundred years. "But I will pass judgment," the Lord said, "on the nation which enslaves them; and at last they will escape, and settle down to worship me here." Then he made a covenant with Abraham, the covenant that ordained circumcision. So it was that he became the father of Isaac, whom he circumcised seven days afterwards, and Isaac of Jacob, and Jacob of the twelve patriarchs.

'The patriarchs, out of jealousy, sold Joseph as a slave,

synagogues in Jerusalem.

When this fails, as it did with our Lord, the opponents of Christianity fall back on their familiar 'frame-up' technique. They show little originality; the same charge is put forward as that against our Lord at his trial before Caiphas: 'We heard him say, "I will destroy this temple that is made with men's hands, and I will build another with no hand of man to help me."' To this they added the crime of opposing the law of Moses; a familiar charge against our Lord during his public ministry.

Stephen's Speech: Does God Live in Palestine? There was a spacious room, to the south of the Holy Place in the temple courts, called the council chamber; it was there that special business of the Council (Sanhedrin) was conducted. Stephen was probably talking in one of the porches inside the temple area when he was arrested and brought before the Council in the nearby council chamber. The Council was ready, waiting to try this new disturber of the established order in Israel.

The previous trial before the Council was that of Jesus. Owing to special circumstances, notably the need for haste, our Lord had been tried in the house of the high priest Caiphas. And it was still Caiphas who presided over the Council of seventy (at least twenty-three were required for a trial) at Stephen's trial.

Our Lord had been silent at his trial. He did not speak because the charge brought against him had failed to secure agreement of two witnesses: 'but even so their accusations did not agree.' Consequently the charge was null and void in Jewish law. At Stephen's trial at least two witnesses did agree on the specific terms of the charge; the Jewish leaders were better prepared this time, and so did not fall into the same mistake that they had made at the trial of Christ.

2*

to be taken to Egypt. In Egypt, God was with him; he rescued him from all his afflictions, and won him favour and a name for wisdom with Pharao, king of Egypt, who made him ruler over Egypt and over all the royal household. And now a famine came upon all Egypt and Canaan, cruelly afflicting them, till our fathers could procure no food. So Jacob, hearing that there was corn in Egypt, sent out our fathers on their first journey; and on their second journey Joseph made himself known to them, and Pharao learned about Joseph's kindred. Then Joseph sent for his father Jacob, and for his family, seventy-five souls in all; and Jacob went down into Egypt, where he and our fathers died. They were removed afterwards to Sichem; and it was in the grave which Abraham had bought for a sum of money from the sons of Hemor, the man of Sichem, that they were buried.

'And when the time drew near for the fulfilment of the promise which God had made to Abraham, the people had increased and multiplied in Egypt. And now a new king arose in Egypt, one who knew nothing of Joseph; this king dealt treacherously with our race, using them so ill that they exposed their children, instead of rearing them. It was at this time that Moses was born, and, finding favour with God, was brought up in his father's house for three months; then, when he had been exposed, he was rescued by Pharao's daughter, who adopted him as her son. Thus Moses was well trained in all the learning of the Egyptians; he was vigorous, too, in speech and in act. And now, when he had reached forty years of age, it came into his mind to visit his brethren, the children of Israel. When he saw one of them being unjustly used, he came to the rescue and avenged the man who was wronged, by killing the Egyptian. He expected them to understand, but they could not understand, that he was the means by which

In contrast to the silence of our Lord is the almost interminable defence speech of Stephen. His purpose is to disprove the validity of the charge brought against him. He uses an historical approach: a résumé of the history of the chosen people from the time of their founder Abraham to king David. He begins with the Book of Genesis, chapter 12. And in his discourse, as in Genesis, the careers of Abraham and his great-grandson Joseph are highlighted. But the account of these two individuals occupies only one-third of this first point of Stephen's speech in defence of his teaching.

The third and most important person is Moses. His story is found in the second book of the Bible, Exodus. Stephen gives two-thirds of his words to the career of Moses, because it was part of the charge against him that he never tired of uttering insults against the law and the traditions which Moses had handed down.

All the facts listed by Stephen in his résumé of Old Testament history were familiar to his hearers; what he does is to give them a Christian interpretation instead of a Jewish one. A crisis had arisen in Jerusalem: was this new organization, the Christian Church, to remain a national Jewish institution, or was it to rise above national barriers and become Catholic?

The Samaritan woman converted by our Lord expressed the Jewish outlook that Stephen is arguing against. She said to our Lord: 'You Jews tell us that the place where men ought to worship is in Jerusalem.' To her Jesus replied: 'Believe me, woman, the time is coming when you will not go to Jerusalem to worship the Father; the time has already come when true worshippers will worship the Father in spirit and in truth.'

That God was worshipped only in the small territory of Palestine, and particularly in the temple, is the Jewish thesis

God was to bring them deliverance. Next day, he came in sight when two of them were quarrelling, and tried to restore peace between them; "Sirs," he said, "you are brethren; why do you inflict injury on one another?"

'Whereupon the man who was doing his neighbour a wrong thrust him aside, asking, "Who made you a ruler and a judge over us? Are you ready to kill me, as you killed the Egyptian yesterday?"

'And at that Moses fled, and lived as an exile in the land of Madian; it was there that two sons were born to him.

'Forty years later, a vision came to him in the wilderness of mount Sinai; a bush had caught fire; and an angel was standing among the flames. Moses saw it, and was astonished at the sight; and as he drew near to look, the voice of the Lord came to him, "I am the God of your fathers, of Abraham, and Isaac, and Jacob." And Moses did not dare to look close; fear made him tremble. Then the Lord said to him, "Take the shoes off your feet; the place on which you stand is holy ground. The affliction of my people in Egypt is before my eyes continually; I have heard their lamenting, and have come down to deliver them. Come now, I have an errand for you in Egypt."

'It was this same Moses, the man whom they had disowned, and asked him, "Who made you a ruler and a judge over us?" that God sent to be their ruler and their deliverer, helped by the angel whom he saw there at the bush. He it was who led them out, performing wonders and signs in Egypt, and at the Red Sea, and in the wilderness, over a space of forty years.

'It was this Moses who said to the children of Israel, "The Lord your God will raise up for you a prophet like myself, from among your own brethren." He it was who took part with the angel that spoke to him on mount Sinai, and with

as outlined by Stephen; he proposes to show that Israel's history does not substantiate that view. He does not argue the details of his own case; he takes the matter back to its fundamentals. Actually he is not concerned with his personal fate; he is out to win converts to the Christian way of thought.

Take the first phase of the history of God's chosen people. God spoke to Abraham, called him out of his own country to begin a new life of service to the Lord. Did this revelation happen in Palestine? Not at all, says Stephen; it was way out in Mesopotamia. God can talk to men anywhere in the wide world.

Take the case of the great hero of the patriarchal period, Joseph the saviour of his people. Where was it that God favoured him with his own divine revelation? Not in Palestine, but in Egypt. Surely men like Abraham and Joseph were true worshippers of God; all his promises and divine favours came to Israel through them.

And Moses, that man whose name is ever on your lips; why, he never set foot in Palestine. He was born in Egypt; lived in the wilderness an exile even from his own people; finally he accompanied them on the wanderings of the Exodus. He was the first to be told the divine name of God, the name Yahweh. This happened, not in Palestine, but in the Sinai desert, at the famous vision of the burning bush. Do not these three men show clearly that God can be known and worshipped outside Palestine? The whole history of the race is one of migration, not of settled occupancy of this small section of the world.

Particularly with regard to Moses, and to some extent with regard to Joseph and Abraham, Stephen emphasizes the rejection by their own people. It seems as though he himself knows that the same fate awaits him; how could he hope to fare better

our fathers, at the meeting in the desert. There he received words of life to hand on to you; and yet our fathers would not give him obedience. They disowned him; they turned their thoughts towards Egypt, and said to Aaron, "Make us gods, to lead our march; as for this Moses, who brought us out of the land of Egypt, there is no saying what has become of him." So they fashioned a calf at this time, making offerings to an idol, and keeping holiday over the works of their own hands. Whereupon God turned away from them, and gave them over to the worship of all the host of heaven; so it is written in the book of the prophets, "Is it true that you brought me victims and sacrifices, you sons of Israel, for forty years in the wilderness? You carried about the tent of Moloch, and the star of your god Rempham, and worshipped them, images of your own fashioning. And now I will send you into exile on the further side of Babylon."

'In the wilderness, our fathers had the tabernacle with them, to remind them of God's covenant; he who spoke to Moses bade him fashion it after the model which had been shown him. And when God dispossessed the Gentiles, to make room for our fathers' coming, our fathers under Joshua brought this tabernacle, as an heirloom, into the land which they conquered. So it was until the time of David. David, who had won favour in God's sight, longed to devise a resting-place for the God of Israel, but in the end it was Solomon that built the house for him. Yet we are not to think that the most High dwells in temples made by men's hands; the prophet says: "Heaven is my throne, and earth is the footstool under my feet. What home will you build for me, says the Lord, what place can be my resting-place? Was it not my hands that made all this?"

than the Master, before this same tribunal?

Stephen had little time to prepare his defence; it is not to be wondered at if his memory fails him here and there in tracing such a long period of history. The two notable discrepancies with the Old Testament account are (1) the burial of the patriarchs at Sichem, (2) the quotation from Amos: 'And now I will send you into exile on the further side of Babylon.'

(1) It is clear from the Book of Genesis that the patriarchs were buried in Hebron, not Sichem; the only exception being Joseph, who was buried at Sichem. (2) The original text of Amos reads Damascus in place of Babylon; there is no evidence for Stephen's change of place name. Stephen was not inspired; he could make mistakes, like any other man. Luke's inspiration, in writing the Acts, consists in recording correctly what Stephen said, even the errors in his discourse.

Stephen's Speech: Does God Live in the Temple? The holiest place on earth was the temple in Jerusalem; there, day after day, true worship was offered to the Lord. But Israel had been a nation for a thousand years before the temple was built. Did they not worship God in a manner pleasing to him during all that time? The tabernacle in the wilderness was made at God's express command, as a place to offer sacrifice to him. And how about the long period of Babylonian exile, when Israel worshipped God not in the temple (it had been destroyed) but in a foreign land?

This should show them that God's presence cannot be restricted to a small building in a single city. True worship is that which comes from perfect love in a man's heart and will: 'The greatest of them all is charity.'

'Stiff-necked race, your heart and ears still uncircumcised, you are for ever resisting the Holy Spirit, just as your fathers did. There was not one of the prophets they did not persecute; it was death to foretell the coming of that just man, whom you in these times have betrayed and murdered; you, who received the law dictated by angels, and did not keep it.'

At hearing this, they were cut to the heart, and began to gnash their teeth at him. But he, full of the Holy Spirit, fastened his eyes on heaven, and saw there the glory of God, and Jesus standing at God's right hand: 'I see heaven opening,' he said, 'and the Son of Man standing at the right hand of God.'

Then they cried aloud, and put their fingers into their ears; with one accord they fell upon him, thrust him out of the city, and stoned him. And the witnesses put down their clothes at the feet of a young man named Saul.

Thus they stoned Stephen; he, meanwhile, was praying: 'Lord Jesus,' he said, 'receive my spirit.'

And then, kneeling down, he cried aloud: 'Lord, do not count this sin against them.' And with that he fell asleep in the Lord.

Saul was one of those who gave their voices for his murder.

The church in Jerusalem was much persecuted at this time, and all except the apostles were scattered over the countryside of Judea and Samaria. Stephen was buried by devout men, who mourned greatly over him. Saul, meanwhile, was making havoc of the church; he made his way into house after house, carrying men and women off and committing them to prison.

Those who had been driven away spread the gospel as

Martyrdom of Stephen. *He is probably interrupted at this point by shouts of abuse from the onlookers. It is obvious to him that a reasoned defence will make no impression on this crowd with hatred in their eyes, intent only on his death. So he uses hard words of condemnation, reminiscent of the language used by Jesus himself of the hypocritical leaders who had failed their people and were leading them to ruin. Stephen would make it clear why he was dying: in defence of truth, and for the sake of Jesus Christ.*

At this climax of his life, he is rewarded with a vision of Jesus standing (not sitting, as is usual in scripture), ready to come to his aid, and in an attitude of welcome. His face radiates the consolation he received from this gracious gesture: 'They saw his face looking like the face of an angel.'

Moved by rage at such blasphemy, the mob gave no thought to getting Roman permission to carry out the death sentence. They rushed Stephen out the east gate down into the Kedron, and there stoned him at a place not far from Gethsemani. A young rabbi with a genius for sizing up a situation, and with ability to lead and organize, took charge of the execution; his name in Hebrew was Saul. This is our third contact with the man we know as St. Paul; soon he will take Stephen's place in the Christian ranks.

Simon the Sorcerer of Samaria. *The murder of Stephen was the beginning of a general persecution of the Church. It was directed at the 5,000 Christian Jews living in Jerusalem; the reason for excepting the twelve apostles was their high standing among the ordinary people; the authorities in Jerusalem had already tried to silence the twelve with threats, but without success. It would be just as effective to destroy their followers, and so leave the apostolic leaders without subjects.*

they went from place to place; and Philip, who had gone down to one of the cities of Samaria, preached Christ there. The people listened with general accord to what Philip said, as their own eyes and ears witnessed the miracles he did. There were many possessed by unclean spirits, and these came out, crying aloud; many, too, were healed of paralysis, and of lameness, and there was great rejoicing in that city.

And there was a man called Simon, who had been in the city before Philip came there, misleading the people of Samaria with sorcery, and pretending to have great powers, so that high and low hung upon his words; 'This,' they said, 'is an angel called the great angel of God.' Long misled by his sorceries, they continued to pay attention to him, until Philip came and preached to them about God's kingdom and the name of Jesus Christ. Then they found faith and were baptized, men and women alike; and Simon, who had found faith and been baptized with the rest, kept close to Philip's side; he was astonished by the great miracles and signs he saw happening.

And now the apostles at Jerusalem, hearing that Samaria had received the word of God, sent Peter and John to visit them. So these two came down and prayed for them, that they might receive the Holy Spirit, who had not, as yet, come down on any of them; they had received nothing so far except baptism in the name of the Lord Jesus.

Then the apostles began to lay their hands on them, so that the Holy Spirit was given them, and Simon, seeing that the Holy Spirit was granted through the imposition of the apostles' hands, offered them money; 'Let me too,' he said, 'have such powers that when I lay my hands on anyone he will receive the Holy Spirit.'

Whereupon Peter said to him, 'Take your wealth with you to perdition, you who have told yourself that God's free

Our Lord had shown by his own conduct and teaching how his followers should act in time of persecution: 'If they persecute you in one city, take refuge in another.' Within one day's walk of Jerusalem, to the north, lay the Samaritan country; there the high priest and his fellow persecutors had no authority. Those who were so fortunate as to get out of Jerusalem before Saul called at their house made their way to Samaria, delaying only to collect a few personal belongings.

The Church of its very nature must grow: 'You must go out and make disciples of all nations.' This persecution did not produce a group of idle settlers in Samaria; they immediately began to preach the gospel there. Among the most successful preachers was another deacon, like Stephen. His name was Philip, and he operated probably in the city of Sichem, the most ancient city of Samaria (Abraham had first settled there when he arrived in the promised land), and the real centre of Samaritan life.

The people of Sichem were not completely ignorant of Christianity. At the beginning of his public ministry Jesus had spent two days there, on the occasion of his meeting with the woman at Jacob's well; and 'many of the Samaritans from that city came to believe in him.'

But it was the presence of a dealer in black magic that gave a dramatic touch to Philip's preaching in Sichem. He watched Philip with professional interest; he soon saw such wonders as he could not match—making the blind see, giving hearing to the deaf, casting out devils. It would seem that he became a Christian because of the miracles he saw, rather than to gain eternal life.

Peter and John came to administer confirmation (a deacon is restricted to the sacrament of baptism); in those early days of Christianity, the Pentecostal gift of tongues, the sound of

gift can be bought with money. There is no share, no part for you in these doings; your heart is not true in the sight of God. Repent of this baseness of yours, and pray to God, in the hope of finding pardon for the thought which your heart has conceived. I see plainly that a bitter poison has taken hold of you; you are the bondsman of iniquity.'

And Simon answered, 'Pray for me to the Lord, that none of this harm you have spoken of may fall upon me.'

So, when they had borne their full witness and preached the word of the Lord, they began their journey back to Jerusalem, carrying the gospel into many Samaritan villages. Meanwhile, Philip was commanded by an angel of the Lord, 'Rise up, and go south to meet the road which leads from Jerusalem to Gaza; this is desert country.'

So he rose up and went; and found there an Ethiopian. This man was a eunuch, a courtier of Candace, queen of Ethiopia, and had charge of all her wealth; he had been up to worship at Jerusalem, and was now on his way home, driving along in his chariot and reading the prophet Isaias.

The Spirit said to Philip, 'Go up to that chariot and keep close by it.'

And Philip, as he ran up, heard him reading the prophet Isaias, and asked, 'Can you understand what you are reading?'

'How could I,' said he, 'without someone to guide me?' And he entreated Philip to come up and sit beside him.

The passage of scripture which he was reading was this: 'He was led away like a sheep to be slaughtered; like a lamb that is dumb before its shearer, he would not open his mouth. He was brought low, and all his rights taken away; who shall tell the story of his age? His life is being cut off from the earth.'

a loud rushing wind, and often the rocking of the building as in an earthquake accompanied the conferring of the sacrament. When Simon saw these amazing effects, he could not conceal his eagerness to possess such power. Imagine what a success he would have, could he produce such a spectacle!

His attempt to buy this spiritual power with money has immortalized his name (like that of Pontius Pilate); his crime is still known as simony.

Philip and the Ethiopian. It is probably still the same year, 30 A.D., as that of the first Pentecost, possibly the feast of Tabernacles in September. A rich Sudanese (Ethiopia stands for the headwaters of the Nile in Southern Egypt), the finance minister of Candace (a royal title like Pharao), probably of black skin, is driving along the road south from Jerusalem; he is reading aloud in Greek the prophecy of Isaias. Distracted by the jolting of the chariot, his mind is unable to cope with the deep mysteries of the book.

Had he only known it, he had just passed through the birthplace of the Man he was reading about; he could not have been far beyond Bethlehem when a running figure overtook the slow-moving chariot and jogged along beside it, obviously interested in its passenger. He kept on with his task of reading Isaias; and then on a sudden Philip bent his head towards the open door and asked him if he needed a skilled interpreter.

The chapter of the prophet Isaias the Sudanese was reading was the classic text in the Old Testament on the suffering Messiah. It was undoubtedly one of the texts interpreted by our Lord in similar circumstances on the road to Emmaus, on the first Easter afternoon. Philip is now the voice of Jesus, carrying on the same teaching. He probably quotes the words

And the eunuch turned to Philip, and said, 'Tell me, about whom does the prophet say this? Himself, or some other man?'

Then Philip began speaking, and preached to him about Jesus, taking this passage as his theme.

As they went on their way, they came to a piece of water, and the eunuch said, 'See, there is water here; why may I not be baptized?'

So he had the chariot stopped, and both of them, Philip and the eunuch, went down into the water, and Philip baptized him there. But when they came up from the water, Philip was carried off by the spirit of the Lord, and the eunuch did not see him any longer; he went on his way rejoicing. As for Philip, he was next heard of at Azotus; and from there he went preaching all round the villages, until he reached Caesarea.

Saul, with every breath he drew, still threatened the disciples of the Lord with massacre; and now he went to the high priest and asked him for letters of commendation to the synagogues at Damascus, so that he could arrest all those he found there, men and women, who belonged to the Way, and bring them back to Jerusalem. Then, on his journey, when he was nearly at Damascus, a light from heaven shone suddenly about him. He fell to the ground, and heard a voice saying to him, 'Saul, Saul, why do you persecute me?'

'Who are you, Lord?' he asked.

And he said, 'I am Jesus, whom Saul persecutes; rise up, and go into the city, and there you shall be told what your work is.'

His companions stood in bewilderment, hearing the voice speak, but not seeing anyone. When he rose from the ground he could see nothing, although his eyes were open, and they

of John the Baptist when that herald of Christ pointed him out to his disciples: 'Look, this is the Lamb of God, who takes away the sin of the world.'

After the baptism of the Sudanese, Philip was miraculously removed from his presence. His work finished, he was taken further up the Mediterranean coast from Gaza to Azotus; he finally came to Caesarea, where we find him again thirty years later.

There are at least three roads from Jerusalem to Gaza. I have presumed that the chariot followed the main south road to Hebron, and then west to Gaza. The point of the angel's remark, 'this is desert country,' seems to be that he was re-assuring Philip on the safety of his person in such territory; it was uninhabited country, and far from the danger zone of persecution in Jerusalem.

The Conversion of Paul. The small group of persecutors under the leadership of Saul was camped for the night on the hills to the north of the lake of Galilee. Further north loomed the massive bulk of mount Hermon, 9,000 feet high; to the south the lake lay smooth as glass. The white houses of Capharnaum caught the last rays of the sun. But Saul had no eye for the beauty and grandeur of the view; his thoughts were on the Christians who had escaped from Galilee and taken refuge in Syria. Tomorrow he would be in Damascus, and he would hunt them out from their hiding places. In Saul's mind there was only one solution of the Christian problem—complete extermination: the treatment that Stephen had received.

As they approached the south gate of Damascus at midday, a light brighter than the sun, as bright as that which had shone from Jesus' face at the Transfiguration on nearby Hermon,

had to lead him by the hand, to take him into Damascus. Here for three days he remained without sight, and neither ate nor drank.

There was, in Damascus, a disciple named Ananias; to him the Lord called in a vision, 'Ananias.'

'Here I am, Lord,' he answered.

And the Lord said to him, 'Rise up and go to the road called Straight Street; and enquire at the house of Judas for a man of Tarsus, named Saul. Even now he is at his prayers; and he has had a vision of a man called Ananias coming in and laying hands on him, to cure him of blindness.'

At this, Ananias answered, 'Lord, many have told me about this man, and all the hurt he has done to your saints at Jerusalem; and he has come here with authority from the chief priests to imprison all those who call upon your name.'

But the Lord said to him, 'Go on your errand; this is a man I have chosen to be the instrument for bringing my name before the heathen and their rulers, and before the people of Israel too. I have yet to tell him, how much suffering he will have to undergo for my name's sake.'

So Ananias set out; and as soon as he came into the house he laid his hands upon him, and said, 'Brother Saul, I have been sent by that Lord Jesus who appeared to you on your way as you came here; you are to recover your sight, and be filled with the Holy Spirit.'

And with that, a kind of film fell away from his eyes, and his sight was recovered. He rose up, and was baptized; and now, when he had taken food, his strength returned to him. For some days he lived with the disciples at Da scus, and from the first, in the synagogues, he preached that Jesus was the Son of God. All those who heard it were amazed; 'Why,' they said, 'is not this the man who brought ruin on all those

enveloped the persecution party. As suddenly as that, Saul was changed from a persecutor to an apostle. The face of Stephen, so persistently before Saul's eyes, suddenly became the face of Jesus; the compassionate, compelling eyes of the Master looked deep into those of Saul, and claimed him for his own chosen instrument for the winning of the heathen world; from now on he is dedicated to the Christian cause.

It was not Christians he was persecuting; it was Christ himself. The basic doctrine of the Mystical Body was presented to him right at the start; he had learned the meaning of Jesus' words: 'Believe me, when you did it to one of the least of my brethren here, you did it to me.' He will never forget this first lesson in Christian living; it will come up again and again in his letters: 'All you who have been baptized in Christ's name have put on the person of Christ . . . You are Christ's body . . . There is nothing but Christ in any of us.'

There is another aspect of the doctrine of the Mystical Body: not only is the Christian, the other man, identified with Christ, but Paul himself must put on the person of Christ. He must permit Christ to take full possession of his whole being; his mind, his will, his voice, all his actions are the instruments through which the Lord will influence the world around him. The more perfect the instrument, the more Jesus can use this new disciple in the conversion of the world.

Our Lord summed up his own life, and the way of life for all members of his Mystical Body, in the words: 'If any man has a mind to come my way, let him renounce self, and take up his cross and follow me.'

All the complicated procedure surrounding Ananias is meant to show Saul that from now on it is only God's will that matters; he must trample on self, his own plans and ambitions;

who invoked this name, when he was in Jerusalem; the man who came here for the very purpose of arresting such people and presenting them to the chief priests?'

But Saul was inspired with ever greater strength, and silenced the Jews who lived at Damascus by showing them clearly that this was the Christ.

So many days passed, and then the Jews plotted against his life. Saul was aware of the plot; and since they kept watch over the gates, day and night, to make an end of him, his disciples contrived to let him down by night along the face of the wall, lowering him to the ground in a hamper. So he reached Jerusalem, where he tried to attach himself to the disciples; but they could not believe he was a true disciple, and all avoided his company. Whereupon Barnabas took him by the hand and brought him in to the apostles, telling them how, on his journey, he had seen the Lord and had speech with him, and how at Damascus he had spoken boldly in the name of Jesus. So he came and went in their company at Jerusalem, and spoke boldly in the name of the Lord. He preached, besides, to the Jews who talked Greek, and disputed with them, till they set about trying to take his life. As soon as they heard of this, the brethren took him down to Caesarea, and put him on his way to Tarsus.

Meanwhile, all through Judea and Galilee and Samaria, the church enjoyed peace and became firmly established, guided by the fear of the Lord; and it grew in numbers through the encouragement of the Holy Spirit.

And now Peter, as he visited the saints everywhere, came down to see those who dwelt at Lydda. There he found a man called Aeneas, who had not left his bed for eight years, being

his food must be to do the will of him who now rules his life. And the Lord's own special technique for the perfection of his members is the cross. Calvary occupied the supreme place in Jesus' mortal life; it must be equally prominent in the lives of his followers: 'With Christ I hang upon the cross.'

Paul in Jerusalem.   *It was still 30 A.D.*, the year of the crucifixion, when St. Paul was baptized at Damascus. But it was not till three years later that he made his first visit to Jerusalem as a Christian. This he tells us in his letter to the Galatians 1, 16-18: 'My first thought was not to hold any consultations with any human creature; I did not go up to Jerusalem to see those who had been apostles longer than myself; no, I went off into Arabia, and when I came back it was to Damascus. Then, when three years had passed, I did go up to Jerusalem, to visit Kephas, and I stayed a fortnight there in his company.' This is the visit here recorded by St. Luke in the Acts; it was a busy two weeks given to preaching the gospel mainly in Greek to the Jews of the Dispersion.

St. Paul's three years in the desert east of Damascus ('Arabia') served the same purpose as our Lord's forty days in the desert: it was a time of preparation for his public ministry of healing and teaching.

Peter Visits Aeneas and Dorcas.   The most effective way to stop a persecution is to convert the persecutor. It began suddenly with the murder of Stephen, and died just as suddenly and dramatically; with Saul a Christian all enthusiasm departed from the Jewish leaders. There could be no better testimony to the dynamic personality of Paul than this dominant position he held both in Jewish and in Christian circles.

paralysed. And Peter said to him, 'Aeneas, Jesus Christ sends you healing; rise up, and make your bed'; whereupon he rose up at once. All those who dwelt at Lydda and Sharon came to see him, and their hearts turned to the Lord.

And there was a disciple at Joppa called Tabitha, which means the same as Dorcas, a gazelle. She abounded in acts of charity and in almsdeeds; and it so happened that at this time she fell sick, and died, and they washed the body and laid it in an upper room. Since Lydda was close to Joppa, the disciples, hearing that Peter was there, sent two men to find him; 'Come to us,' they urged him, 'without delay.' So Peter rose and went with them; and when he came there they took him into the upper room, where all the widows stood round him in tears, showing him the coats and cloaks which Dorcas used to make while she was among them. Peter sent them all out, and went on his knees to pray; then, turning to the body, he said, 'Tabitha, rise up'; and she opened her eyes and looked at Peter, and sat up on the bed. So he gave her his hand, and raised her to her feet; and then, calling in the saints and the widows, he showed her to them alive. This became known all over Joppa, and many learned to believe in the Lord. He stayed in Joppa a number of days after this, lodging with a tanner whose name was Simon.

There was, at Caesarea, a centurion named Cornelius, belonging to what is called the Italian cohort, a pious man who worshipped the true God, like all his household, gave alms freely to the people, and prayed to God continually. He, about three o'clock in the afternoon, had a vision, in which he clearly saw an angel of God come in and address him by name.

'What is it, Lord?' he asked, gazing at him in terror.

And he answered, 'Your prayers and almsdeeds are recorded

Christianity had not been at a standstill during the persecution period; converts were being made throughout Palestine. It is not surprising to find converts in Galilee, seeing that our Lord spent almost two years of his public life preaching to them. The Acts record no detail of their conversion, and only a passing mention of converts in Judea and Samaria (which shows how fragmentary is the record in Acts).

Peter is the shepherd, the vicar of Christ, the rock on which the Church is built; it is only fitting that he should visit and strengthen his flock. But the real source of Christian life is not human agencies; the Holy Spirit himself is the vital power of the Church. St. Paul was later to put it in his memorable fashion: 'It was for me to plant the seed, for Apollo to water it, but it was God who gave the increase.'

'A man's body is all one, though it has a number of different organs; and all this multitude of organs goes to make up one body; so it is with Christ.' These words of St. Paul are well illustrated by Dorcas, the first Sister of Charity. There is need for members to work at menial and unnoticed duties of charity, as well as for the more spectacular works of healing cripples and raising the dead to life.

An Angel Appears to Cornelius. This Italian soldier knew nothing of Jewish religion until one day he came across a copy of their Sacred Writings, written in Greek. He made his first contact with the God of the Hebrews, whose name is Yahweh. According to the Jews he was the only real God; all the others, so familiar to Cornelius, such as Jupiter, Mars, Venus, were only invented by the imagination of men; in the world of reality they did not exist. Yahweh reigned alone.

in God's sight. And now he would have you send men to Joppa, to bring here one Simon, who is surnamed Peter; he lodges with a tanner, called Simon, whose house is close to the sea.'

So the angel visitor left him, and thereupon he summoned two of his servants, and one of the soldiers who were in attendance on him, a man of piety; he told them all that had passed, and sent them on their way to Joppa.

Next day, while these were on their journey, and were drawing near the city, Peter went up to the housetop about noon, to pray there. He was hungry, and waiting for a meal; and while they were preparing it, he fell into a trance. He saw heaven opening, and a bundle, like a great sheet, let down by its four corners on to the earth; in it were all kinds of four-footed beasts, and things that creep on the earth, and all the birds of heaven.

And a voice came to him, 'Rise up, Peter, lay about you and eat.'

'It cannot be, Lord,' answered Peter; 'never in my life have I eaten anything profane, anything unclean.'

Then the voice came to him a second time, 'It is not for you to call anything profane, which God has made clean.'

Three times this happened, and then the bundle was drawn up again into heaven. Peter was still puzzling in his mind over the meaning of his vision, when Cornelius' messengers, who had now found their way to Simon's house, were seen standing at the gate; where they called out and asked if Simon, who was also called Peter, lodged there.

To Peter, as he was turning over the vision in his mind, the Spirit said, 'Here are some men asking for you; rise and go down, and accompany them without misgiving; it is I who have sent them.'

Yahweh ruled all nations, not Jews only, with justice and charity. He was not capricious and unpredictable like the Roman gods. He took a personal and loving interest in all men; man could return his affection by living according to the laws Yahweh had revealed; God had even told man the manner in which he wished true worship to be offered to his name. Cornelius had come to believe in and submit his life to Yahweh.

Peter Has a Vision. The picture of animals marching into Noah's ark two by two is not quite correct. There were two camels and two donkeys, but fourteen sheep and a like number of cattle. Here are God's words to Noah: 'Take seven pairs of all the clean animals with you, male and female, and one pair of all the animals that are unclean' (Gen. 7, 2).

This distinction of clean (kosher is the Hebrew word) and unclean animals was a continual reminder to the Jews that they were a people set apart, as the Lord God himself was apart and above all heathen gods; they must not let themselves be contaminated by eating food that was abominable for either sanitary or religious reasons. It was a call to perfection, just as our Lord told his followers in the Sermon on the Mount: 'You are to be perfect, as your heavenly Father is perfect.'

The list of kosher foods, and the basis for the distinction, is found in Leviticus 11. Five groups of living things are considered; though only three of them are listed in Peter's vision in the Acts.

Quadrupeds that chew the cud and have cloven hoofs are kosher. This excludes the camel, which has an undivided hoof, and the pig, which does not chew the cud. Fish must have fins and scales. The distinction among birds is that non-carrion are clean; doves and pigeons are the principal kosher birds.

So Peter went down to the men; 'Here I am,' he said, 'the man you are looking for; what is your errand?'

'The centurion Cornelius,' they said, 'a man who worships the true God and keeps his law, as all the Jewish people will testify, has received a revelation from one of the holy angels; he was to have you brought to his house, and listen to what you would say.'

Thereupon Peter bade them come in, and made them welcome; and next day he set out with them, accompanied by some of the brethren from Joppa.

The day after that, they reached Caesarea, where Cornelius was awaiting them; he had gathered his kinsmen and his closest friends about him. And as soon as Peter had entered, he was met by Cornelius, who fell at his feet and did reverence to him; but Peter raised him up; 'Stand up,' he said, 'I am a man like yourself.'

So he went in, still conversing with him, and found a great company assembled. 'You know well enough,' he told them, 'that a Jew is contaminated if he consorts with one of another race, or visits him; but God has been showing me that we ought not to speak of any man as profane or unclean; and so, when I was sent for, I came without demur. Tell me then, why you have sent for me.'

And Cornelius said, 'Three days ago, at this very time, I was making my afternoon prayer in my house, when suddenly I saw a man standing before me, in white clothes, who said to me, "Cornelius, your prayer has been heard, your almsdeeds have won remembrance in God's sight. You are to send to Joppa, and summon thence that Simon who is also called Peter; he is lodging with a tanner called Simon, close to the sea." I lost no time, therefore, in sending for you, and you have done me a favour in coming. Now you see us assembled

The only winged insects that were clean were those 'which have the hinder legs longer, and leap from one spot to another.' These are grasshoppers, the food of John the Baptist. All 'things that creep on the earth' were unclean; snakes are the main members of this classification.

The kosher legislation was familiar to every Jew, just as fish on Friday is to a Catholic. He was reminded of it every time he went to the market to buy food or reclined at table for his daily meals.

Peter Visits Cornelius. Peter should have been used to working out the hidden meanings of visions and parables; he had been trained in it by Jesus himself. Actually, this very matter of kosher regulations had been treated by our Lord at Capharnaum, for the special benefit of the apostles: 'Do you not observe that any uncleanness which finds its way into a man's mouth has no means of defiling him, because it travels, not into his heart, but into his belly? Whereas all that comes out of his mouth comes from the heart, and it is that which makes a man unclean.' And St. Peter (who was the original author of St. Mark's Gospel) comments: 'Thus he declared all meat to be clean' (Mk. 7, 19).

The ten men walking the thirty miles up the plain of Sharon from Joppa to Caesarea were making history. For the first time in the history of the Church, the faith was being brought directly to the Gentiles.

Caesarea was the headquarters of the Roman procurator, still Pontius Pilate (presuming that this incident took place before Pilate's recall in 36 A.D.). It was a modern city, only 50 years old, with Roman buildings, a fine port, about 5,000 soldiers, and in all its ways and culture Roman to the core. By

3

in God's presence, ready to listen to whatever charge the Lord
has given you.'

Thereupon Peter began speaking; 'I see clearly enough,' he
said, 'that God makes no distinction between man and man;
he welcomes anybody, whatever his race, who fears him and
does what piety demands. He has sent his word to the sons
of Israel, giving them news of peace through Jesus Christ, who
is Lord of all. You have heard the story, a story which ran
through the whole of Judea, though it began in Galilee, after
the baptism which John proclaimed; about Jesus of Nazareth,
how God anointed him with the Holy Spirit and with power,
so that he went about doing good, and curing all those who
were under the devil's tyranny, with God at his side. We are
witnesses of all he did in the country of the Jews, and in
Jerusalem. And they killed him, hanging him on a gibbet; but
on the third day God raised him up again, and granted the
clear sight of him, not to the people at large, but to us the witnesses whom God had appointed beforehand; we ate and
drank in his company after his rising from the dead. And he
gave us a commission to preach to the people, and to bear
witness that he, and none other, has been chosen by God to
judge the living and the dead. All the prophets bear him this
testimony, that everyone who has faith in him is to find remission of sins through his name.'

Before Peter had finished speaking to them thus, the Holy
Spirit fell on all those who were listening to his message. The
faithful who had come over with Peter, holding to the tradition of circumcision as they did, were astonished to find that
the free gift of the Holy Spirit could be lavished upon the
Gentiles, whom they heard speaking with tongues, and proclaiming the greatness of God. Then Peter said openly, 'Who
will grudge us the water for baptizing these men, that have

invading this Gentile stronghold, Peter was preparing for the
capture of Rome itself.

The First Gentile Converts. Amidst the sound of marching
feet on the cobblestones outside Cornelius' house, and the
pounding of surf on the breakwater of the port of Caesarea,
Peter began his first instruction class for the reception of
heathen converts. The family of Cornelius was made up of
his wife and children, the domestic servants and his batman.
The scene surely recalled to Peter the famous Domine, non
sum dignus centurion of Capharnaum, whose servant Jesus
had healed. Cornelius was of a similar type, and was worthy
of the same praise which the Master gave to that other one:
'Believe me, I have not found faith like this, even in Israel.'

Peter's plan of instruction was simple. The Master himself
had said: 'I am the way; I am truth and life.' So Peter told the
story of Jesus' life; he was the Lord God (Yahweh) incarnate.
Cornelius had only to believe in him, and eternal life was his.

As he searched his memory for the outstanding facts of
Jesus' life on earth, he began that selection of incidents which
later became the basis of all Christian narrative about the
Master, and which was written down in the four gospels; par-
ticularly the Gospel of St. Mark, which is often called the
Memoirs of Peter.

It did not include the Infancy Story, but began with John
the Baptist (the baptism of our Lord was the true beginning
of his public life), and finished with the Resurrection. To find
out what Peter said to Cornelius, it is only necessary to read
St. Mark.

Peter was dramatically interrupted before he could conclude
his instructions. Suddenly, unexpectedly, Cornelius and the
members of his household were on their feet, ecstatically

received the Holy Spirit just as we did?' And he gave orders
that they should be baptized in the name of Jesus Christ.
And after this, they asked him to stay on some days with
them.

And now the apostles and brethren in Judea were told how
the word of God had been given to the Gentiles. And when
Peter came up to Jerusalem, those who held to the tradition
of circumcision found fault with him; 'Why did you pay a
visit,' they asked, 'to men who are uncircumcised, and eat
with them?'

Whereupon Peter told them the story point by point from
the beginning; 'I was in the city of Joppa,' he said, 'at my
prayers, when I fell into a trance and saw a vision. A bundle,
like a great sheet, came down from heaven, lowered by the
four corners, till it reached me. I looked closely to find out
what it was, and there I saw four-footed creatures of earth,
and wild beasts, and creeping things, and the birds that fly in
heaven. And I heard a voice saying to me, "Rise up, Peter,
lay about you and eat."

'So I answered, "It cannot be, Lord; nothing profane or
unclean has ever crossed my lips."

'And a second utterance came from heaven in answer, "It
is not for you to call anything profane, which God has made
clean."

'Three times this happened, and then all was drawn up
again into heaven. And at that very moment three men appeared at the door of the house where we were, with a message to me from Caesarea. The Spirit bade me accompany
them without misgiving; so these six brethren came with me,
and together we entered the man's home. There he told us
how he had had a vision of an angel in his house; this angel
stood before him, and said, "Send to Joppa, and bid Simon,

praising God in foreign tongues. It was the Pentecostal manifestation all over again; the Holy Ghost had come down upon
them, and that even before they were baptized Christians.

Peter Justifies His Action.   The first Christians kept up their
Jewish way of life by frequenting the temple and assisting at
the synagogue services. They had the Master's own example
and express words to follow: 'Do not think that I have come
to set aside the law and the prophets; I have not come to set
them aside, but to bring them to perfection. Believe me,
heaven and earth must disappear sooner than one jot, one
flourish disappear from the law; it must all be accomplished.'

But our Lord himself had observed that the new vitality of
the Church could not be contained in the ancient observances
of Israel; he hinted at this in his reference to patching up an
old garment with a piece from a new cloak, and to putting
new wine into old skins. And in the parable of the Prodigal
Son, Jesus pointed out the true solution of the Jew-Gentile
problem: both the older brother (Jewry) and the younger
prodigal (Gentiles) were to live in amity in the Father's
house.

The Holy Spirit performed his part in this deeper understanding of Jesus' words, and their application to the new
problems that confronted the infant Church. At the Last
Supper our Lord had outlined the Holy Spirit's function: 'I
have still much to say to you, but it is beyond your reach as
yet. It will be for him, the truth-giving Spirit, to guide you
into all truth; and he will make plain to you what is still to
come.'

The vision at Caesarea left no doubt in Peter's mind; it was
definite guidance from the Holy Spirit. As head of the Church,

who is also called Peter, come to you. He will have such a message for you as will bring salvation to you and to all your household." And then, when I had set about speaking to them, the Holy Spirit fell upon them, just as it was with us at the beginning. Then I was reminded of what the Lord said to us: "John's baptism was with water, but there is a baptism with the Holy Spirit which you are to receive." And now, if God has made them the same free gift, which he made to us when faith in the Lord Jesus had gone before it, who was I, what power had I, to stay God's hand?'

At these words they were content, and gave glory to God; 'Why then,' they said, 'it seems God has granted life-giving repentance of heart to the Gentiles too.'

Meanwhile, those who had been dispersed owing to the persecution that was raised over Stephen had travelled as far away as Phoenicia and Cyprus and Antioch, without preaching the word to anyone except the Jews. But there were some of them, men of Cyprus and Cyrene, who, when they found their way to Antioch, spoke to the Greeks as well, preaching the Lord Jesus to them. And the Lord's power went with them, so that a great number learned to believe, and turned to the Lord.

The story of this came to the ears of the Church at Jerusalem, and they sent Barnabas on a mission to Antioch. When he came there and saw what grace God was bestowing on them, he was full of joy, and encouraged them all to remain true to the Lord with steady purpose of heart, like the good man he was, full of the Holy Spirit, full of faith; a great number of people were thus won over to the Lord. He went on to Tarsus, to look for Saul, and when he found him, brought him back to Antioch. For a whole year after this they were made welcome in the Church there, teaching a great multi-

it was now Peter's office to see that the hierarchy of the Church understood and accepted this decision, which had come from God himself.

It was Peter who laid down the principle; but it was Paul who played the dominant role in putting it into practice. This is how he speaks of it to the Ephesians: 'It was never made known to any human being in past ages, as it has now been revealed by the Spirit to his holy apostles and prophets, and it is this: that through the gospel preaching the Gentiles are to win the same inheritance, to be made part of the same body, to share the same divine promise, in Christ Jesus. On me he has bestowed this privilege of publishing to the world the plan of this mystery' (Ephes. 3, 5-9).

Paul and Barnabas at Antioch. Three years in the desert, and ten years more at home in Tarsus, is a long time of inactivity for a man who has seen Jesus face to face and is burning with zeal to spread his kingdom. Yet that is what God planned for Paul: a period of preparation that is surely based on the earthly life of our Lord. Paul was to be the greatest of all missionaries, and he must prepare for his public life by a long period of prayer; because that is what Jesus did.

Antioch, the capital of the province of Syria, was the fourth city of the Roman empire; a city that has been rightly named Queen of the East. It was the ambition of every Roman to be posted to Antioch. Built on the river Orontes, surrounded by wooded mountains, having a climate that would satisfy a modern Californian, it was as fashionable and pleasure-loving as Hollywood. The main street ran for over four miles, paved with marble and flood-lit at night. There were race courses, theatres, night clubs, swimming pools, central heating, and plumbing.

The open-door policy adopted at the conversion of Cor-

tude. And Antioch was the first place in which the disciples were called Christians.

At this time, some prophets from Jerusalem visited Antioch; and one of these, Agabus by name, stood up and prophesied through the Spirit that a great famine was to come upon the whole world, as it did in the reign of the emperor Claudius. Thereupon it was decided that each of the disciples should contribute according to his means, to send relief to the brethren who lived in Judea. And so they did; and in sending it to the presbyters they entrusted it to the hands of Barnabas and Saul.

It was at this same time that Herod exerted his authority to persecute some of those who belonged to the Church. James, the brother of John, he beheaded, and then, finding that this was acceptable to the Jews, he went further, and laid hands on Peter too. It was the time of unleavened bread; and he imprisoned Peter, after arresting him, with a guard of four soldiers, relieved four times a day; when paschal-time was over, he would bring him out in the presence of the people. Peter, then, was well guarded in prison, but there was a continual stream of prayer going up to God from the church on his behalf. And now the day was coming when Herod was to bring him out; that night, Peter was sleeping with two chains on him, between two soldiers, and there were warders at the door guarding his prison. Suddenly an angel of the Lord stood over him, and a light shone in his cell. He smote Peter on the side, to rouse him; 'Quick,' he said, 'rise up'; and thereupon the chains fell from his hands.

Then the angel said to him, 'Gird yourself up, and put on your shoes'; and when he had done this, 'Throw your cloak over you, and follow me.'

So he followed him out, unaware that what the angel had

nelius had its first great success at Antioch; the Church there was almost entirely Gentile. It was the people of Antioch who coined a name for this new religion; the name that has lasted down to the present day. The Jews used the word Nazarenes, the Christians themselves usually referred to each other as saints, or brethren.

Paul's second visit to Jerusalem was a mission of relief; the church at Antioch began its new life with an expression of the key Christian virtue—charity.

Peter Delivered from Prison. At Rome in 41 A.D. the emperor Caligula fell dead with more than thirty dagger wounds in his body. In the confusion that followed, a young prince of the house of Herod was the person responsible for placing on the throne the new emperor Claudius. This prince was Agrippa 1, a grandson of the slayer of the Holy Innocents, Herod the Great. He was rewarded by Claudius with the king-ship of Palestine. The procurators were withdrawn, and Agrippa arrived at Caesarea to restore the splendours of his grandfather's kingdom.

The apostles were no longer immune from persecution. The policy of permitting free access to their ranks on the part of the Gentiles had alienated Jewish popular opinion. And Agrippa, with the shrewdness that characterized the Herodian house, saw an opportunity of winning favour with his Jewish subjects.

The first martyr from the ranks of the twelve was James, the brother of John. In the week before our Lord's death, the mother of these two apostles had made this request: 'Grant that in your kingdom one may take his place on your right hand and the other on your left.' Our Lord granted their

3*

done for him was true; he thought he was seeing a vision. Thus they passed one party of guards, then a second, and reached the iron gate which leads out into the city; this opened for them of its own accord. They came out, and as soon as they passed on up one street, the angel left him.

At this, Peter came to himself. 'Now I can tell for certain,' he said, 'that the Lord has sent his angel, to deliver me out of Herod's hands, and from all that the people of the Jews hoped to see.'

After some thought, he made for the house belonging to Mary the mother of John, also called Mark. Here many had gathered for prayer; a girl named Rhoda came to answer, when he knocked at the porch door, and she, recognizing Peter's voice, was too overjoyed to open the gate for him; she ran in, and told them that Peter was standing at the gate. 'You are mad,' they told her, but she still insisted that it was so; and then they said, 'It must be his guardian angel.'

Meanwhile, Peter went on knocking; so they opened, and found him there, and stood astonished. Calling for silence by a gesture of his hand, he told them how the Lord had delivered him from prison; 'Give news of this,' he said, 'to James and the rest of the brethren.' And so he left them, and went elsewhere.

When day broke, there was a great to-do among the soldiers, to know what had become of Peter. Herod, after searching for him without avail, questioned the warders and had them punished. Then he went down from Judea to Caesarea, and spent his time there. He was much out of humour with the people of Tyre and Sidon; and these, since their country depended on the king's country for supplies, waited upon him by common consent, and tried (by winning over Blastus, the

request, in symbolic language that was beyond their understanding at that time: 'You shall indeed drink of the cup I
am to drink, and be baptized with the baptism I am to be
baptized with.' The martyrdom of James is regarded as the
fulfilment of our Lord's prophecy. Much later John's turn
would come, when he was thrown into a cauldron of boiling
oil in Rome; but he was delivered unharmed by a miracle.

It was probably in fortress Antonia that Peter was locked
up and securely guarded; he had been in gaol before and had
escaped from it.

The Church knew where her power lay. There was no plan
to rescue Peter by breaking into the fortress; instead, all the
members of the Christian community went down on their
knees in prayer. Paul's metaphor of the body expresses this
perfectly: 'If one part is suffering, all the rest suffer with it.
There was to be no want of unity in the body; all the different
parts of it were to make each other's welfare their common
care.'

St. Peter made directly for the Cenacle, the headquarters
of the Church in Jerusalem. All the apostles were either in
hiding or had left Jerusalem. James, the cousin of our Lord,
was bishop of Jerusalem. Peter left word for him at the Cenacle
and, it is most likely, went north to the security of the Antioch
community.

Death of Herod Agrippa 1. The big celebration at Caesarea
was probably to honour Claudius' conquest of Britain. The
historian Josephus adds a macabre detail to Luke's account:
as the morning rays of the summer sun shone on the silver
robes of Agrippa, suddenly an owl hooted in a nearby tree;
this was an omen of death.

After a reign of only three years, Agrippa died; he was the
last king of the Jews; procurators ruled again in Judea. Agrippa

royal chamberlain), to make their peace. So, on an appointed day, Herod put on his royal finery and sat down on a raised dais to harangue them; whereupon the people cried out in applause, 'It is no man, it is a god that speaks.' And immediately the angel of the Lord smote him, for not referring the glory to God; and he was eaten up by worms, and so died.

And still the word of God grew strong and spread wide. Barnabas and Saul returned from Jerusalem, their mission of relief fulfilled, and took John, also called Mark, in their company.

First Missionary Journey

The Church at Antioch had as its prophets and teachers Barnabas, and Simon who was called Niger, and Lucius of Cyrene, and Manahen, foster-brother of Herod the tetrarch, and Saul. These were offering worship to God and fasting, when the Holy Spirit said, 'I must have Barnabas and Saul dedicated to the work to which I have called them.' Thereupon they fasted and prayed and laid hands on them, and so took leave of them. And they, sent on their travels by the Holy Spirit, went down to Seleucia, and from there took ship for Cyprus. So they reached Salamis, where they preached God's word in the Jewish synagogues; they had John, too, to help them. And when they had been through the whole island up to Paphos, they encountered there a magician who claimed to be a prophet, a Jew named Bar-Jesus. He was in the company of the governor, Sergius Paulus, a man of good sense, who had sent for Barnabas and Saul and asked if he might hear the word of God. And Elymas, the magician (that is what his name means when translated), opposed them, trying to turn the governor away from the faith.

left a son of the same name, a boy of seventeen, and two younger daughters, Bernice and Drusilla. All three will return to the story sixteen years later, when Paul is a prisoner at Caesarea.

The sudden and unexpected lifting of persecution was as dramatic as the removal of the first persecutor, Saul. The hand of the Lord was certainly stretched out to protect the Mystical Body. With the joy of gratitude in their hearts, Paul, Barnabas, and John Mark, the future author of the Second Gospel and the son of Mary of the Cenacle, followed Peter to Antioch.

Cyprus and Galatia 45-47 A.D.

Paul and the Magician in Cyprus. Peter had just finished Mass when one of the congregation rose to his feet and spoke; it was the Holy Spirit manifesting the divine will through a member of the Mystical Body. The message was to inaugurate the foreign missions of the Church; Barnabas and Paul were selected to pioneer this new activity which was to convert the world.

Just visible on the horizon, 100 miles out to sea, are the mountains of the copper-mining island of Cyprus (the name is Latin for copper). It was Barnabas' homeland; he was the leader of the expedition. They arrived at the eastern port of Salamis and covered the whole island from east to west, a distance of 60 miles along a paved road. Salamis was the commercial capital; Paphos the centre of Roman administration.

At Paphos, Paul worked his first miracle. By it he demonstrated that Christianity is not a mere pale system of thought; it has power to lay all magic in the dust. Elymas represented that Oriental mysticism and black magic which held the pagan world in its spell. The man to deal with it was Paul, not Barna-

Then Saul, whose other name is Paul, filled with the Holy Spirit, fastened his eyes on him, and said: 'Child of the devil, versed in all trickery and cunning, enemy of all honest dealing, will you never have done with trying to twist the straight paths of the Lord? See, then, if the hand of the Lord does not fall upon you now. You shall become blind, and see the sun no more for a while.'

At this, a dark mist fell upon him, and he had to go about looking for someone to lead him by the hand. And now the governor, seeing what had happened, and overcome with awe at the Lord's teaching, learned to believe.

After this Paul and his companions took ship from Paphos and made for Perge in Pamphylia; here John left them, and went back to Jerusalem. They passed on from Perge, and reached Pisidian Antioch, where they went and took their seats in the synagogue on the sabbath day. When the reading of the law and the prophets was finished, the rulers of the synagogue sent a message to them to say, 'Brethren, if you have in your hearts any word of encouragement for the people, let us hear it.'

Then Paul stood up, and made a gesture with his hand to claim audience. 'Listen,' he said, 'men of Israel, and all you who worship the true God. The God of this people of Israel chose out our fathers, and made his people great at the time when they were strangers in the land of Egypt, stretching out his arm to deliver them from it. For forty years he bore with their hard hearts in the wilderness; then he overthrew seven nations in the land of Canaan, whose lands he gave them for an inheritance. By now, some four hundred and fifty years had passed; and after this he appointed judges over them, up to the time of the prophet Samuel. Then they asked for a king, and God gave them Saul, son of Kish, a man of the

bas; and that is why we find the role of leader taken over by him; from now on it is always Paul who leads the way.

For the first time St. Luke abandons the Jewish name Saul; from now on it is always the Roman civic name, Paul, that he uses. It came spontaneously to Paul's lips when the governor asked him his name. It best expresses his position as apostle of the Gentiles. He is no longer a Hebrew, an alien in the Roman world; he belongs to it as a citizen; he is a herald of the Catholic Church, above all divisions of race and speech.

Paul Preaches at Pisidian Antioch. As the ship crossed the 60 miles of water between Cyprus and the mainland of Asia Minor (now Turkey), Paul could see the vast bulk of the Taurus Mountains lost in the clouds to the north. This range ran 500 miles from east to west, and rose up as high as 12,000 feet. It was familiar scenery to Paul; Tarsus lies to the south of it, at its eastern end. Paul had often crossed it in imagination; he was now to make the hazardous 100-mile journey through rugged canyons, in peril from robbers, cold and hunger, to the Roman capital of Galatia.

With his instinct for big cities and main highways, Paul came to Pisidian Antioch on the main trade route from Ephesus to Syrian Antioch. Had not the Master said: 'What has been whispered in your ears in secret chambers, you are to proclaim on the housetops'? Paul had sensed that Cyprus was off the map; here in Pisidian Antioch he was in his first really Roman city

He opens his sermon in the same fashion as Stephen did before the Council in Jerusalem; an apt beginning by one who has now to speak for Stephen as well as Jesus. He summarizes the history of the chosen people till the time of David, listing

tribe of Benjamin, who reigned forty years; but afterwards dispossessed him, and raised up David to be their king. To him, he gave this testimony, "I have found in David, son of Jesse, a man after my own heart, who will accomplish all that is my will."

'It is out of this man's posterity, according to the promise made to him, that God has brought us a Saviour, Jesus. John had prepared the way for his coming, by proclaiming a baptism in which all the people of Israel were to repent; but John himself, when he was coming to the end of his life's course, told them, "I am not what you suspect me to be; look rather for one who comes after me; I am not worthy to untie the shoes on his feet."

'Brethren, you who are sons of Abraham, and you others who fear God, this message of salvation is sent to us. The people at Jerusalem, like their rulers, did not recognize Jesus for what he was; unwittingly they fulfilled, by condemning him, those utterances of the prophets which they had heard read, sabbath after sabbath. And although they could find no capital charge against him, they petitioned Pilate for his death. So, when they had fulfilled all that had been written about him, they took him down from the cross and laid him in a tomb.

'And God raised him from the dead. He was seen, over a space of many days, by the men who had come up with him from Galilee to Jerusalem; it is they who now bear witness of him before the people. And this is the message we preach to you: there was a promise made to our forefathers, and this promise God has redeemed for us, their children, by raising Jesus to life. Thus, it is written in the second Psalm, "You are my son; I have begotten you this day." And this is how he describes raising him from the dead, never to return to corruption again, "I will grant you the privileges I have promised to David"; to which purpose he says in another

the four main periods, that of the Exodus, the Judges, Saul, and David. His point seems to be that God is always making new departures in his care of his chosen people, thus preparing them for the new Christian message.

Jesus is the Messiah. There was a thousand years of history between David and Christ; but Paul is not interested in it. David represented the climax of the Old Testament; he lived at Israel's most prosperous period; his kingdom was the dominant power in the Near East; the Messiah would be the true son of this great king. Even though there were many kings after David, the Messiah is never referred to as son of any of them; it is always Son of David. That is why Paul stopped at him; his name immediately suggested that of the Messiah.

Like Peter in his speech on Pentecost Sunday, Paul spoke mainly of our Lord's crucifixion and resurrection. And the words he used were almost identical with those of Peter, showing that at this early stage the story of our Lord's life was taking a set pattern, in which it would eventually be written down in the gospels (it is possible that Matthew's Aramaic Gospel may have been written already; his Greek text came later).

The facts of Jesus' condemnation and death had already spread throughout the Jewish world; but the details and vividness of Paul's narrative held his audience spellbound. Writing later to these same Galatians, Paul told them: 'With Christ I hang upon the cross.' His daily meditation on the crucified Lord, the hardships and sufferings of his missionary life, gave a vitality and unction to his words; it was as though the audience themselves were actually present at the death of Jesus.

To prove that Jesus was not still lying in his grave, Paul appealed to the witness of those apostles who had seen him,

psalm, "You will not allow your faithful servant to see corruption." David saw corruption; he served God's purpose in his own generation, and then fell asleep, and rested with his fathers; but he whom God raised to life saw no corruption at all.

'Here is news for you, then, brethren; remission of your sins is offered to you through him. There are claims from which you could not be acquitted by the law of Moses, and whoever believes in Jesus is quit of all these. Beware, then, of incurring the prophet's rebuke: "Look upon this, you scornful souls, and lose yourselves in astonishment. Such wonders I am doing in your days, that if a man told you the story you would not believe him." '

As they left, they were implored to preach the same message there on the next sabbath. And when the synagogue broke up, many Jews and many who worshipped the true God as proselytes followed Paul and Barnabas; and they preached to them, urging them to be true to the grace of God.

On the following sabbath almost all the city had assembled to hear God's word. The Jews, when they saw these crowds, were full of indignation, and began to argue blasphemously against all that Paul said. Whereupon Paul and Barnabas told them roundly, 'We were bound to preach God's word to you first; but now, since you reject it, since you declare yourselves unfit for eternal life, be it so; we will turn our thoughts to the Gentiles. This, after all, is the charge the Lord has given us, "I have appointed you to be a light for the Gentiles, that you may bring salvation to the ends of the earth." '

The Gentiles were rejoiced to hear this, and praised the word of the Lord; and they found faith, all those of them who were destined to eternal life. And the word of the Lord spread far and wide all through the country. But the Jews used

spoken with him, and eaten with him. But for Jews, it was primarily the witness of God's inspired word, the Holy Scriptures, that had the strongest appeal as proof. If God said so, then it must be true. So, Paul argues mainly from Psalm 15 (just as Peter did): 'You will not allow your faithful servant to see corruption.' When David wrote those words, he could not have been speaking of himself; he was speaking of Jesus the Messiah, who now reigns with the Father.

The approach to God is now solely through Jesus; he is the only way of salvation. This is the theme of Galatians: 'It is through faith in Jesus Christ, not by obeying the law, that a man is justified.'

Apostle of the Gentiles. Paul was a tentmaker by trade; he found lodging with a family of this occupation and instructed the crowds of converts who came to him while he worked, and often long into the night; he followed this procedure for the remainder of his missionary life: 'We toiled and laboured, all the time we were preaching God's gospel to you, working day and night so as not to burden you with expense.'

The majority of his converts were descendants of the Roman soldiery who had been settled here fifty years before; this was Rome's practical solution of the bandit problem on the main highways of the empire. To these level-headed men, used to dealing with cold facts, Paul's presentation of the Lord Jesus appealed strongly. This Saviour, unlike the vague, shadowy gods they were used to, had lived in a part of the empire, only sixteen years before. Paul gave place and time for every incident of his life. And the climax of his life, his crucifixion, had been acted out in the presence of the Roman governor of Palestine, Pontius Pilate.

The reaction of the Jewish leaders of the synagogue was

influence with such women of fashion as worshipped the
true God, and with the leading men in the city, setting on
foot a persecution against Paul and Barnabas and driving
them out of their territory; so they shook off the dust from
their feet as they left them, and went on to Iconium. The
disciples, meanwhile, were filled with rejoicing, and with the
Holy Spirit.

While they were at Iconium, they went into the Jewish
synagogue together, and preached in such a way that a great
number both of Jews and of Greeks found faith, although the
Jews who would not believe stirred up trouble among the
Gentiles and poisoned their minds against the brethren. For
a long time, then, they remained there, speaking boldly in
the Lord's name, while he attested the preaching of his grace
by allowing signs and wonders to be performed by their means;
the common folk of the city were divided in opinion, some
taking part with the Jews, and some with the apostles. Then,
when both Gentiles and Jews, in concert with their rulers,
made a movement to assault and stone them, they thought it
best to take refuge in the Lycaonian cities, Lystra and Derbe,
and the country round them; and they preached the gospel
there.

There was a lame man sitting at Lystra, crippled from birth,
so that he had never walked, who listened to Paul's preaching;
and Paul, looking closely at him, and seeing there was saving
faith in him, said aloud, 'Stand upright on your feet'; whereupon he sprang up, and began to walk.

The crowds, seeing what Paul had done, cried out in the
Lycaonian dialect, 'It is the gods, who have come down to us
in human shape.' They called Barnabas Jupiter, and Paul
Mercury, because he was the chief speaker; and the priest of
Jupiter, Defender of the City, brought out bulls and wreaths

the same as that shown to the preaching of Jesus himself: they rejected Paul, just as they had rejected his Master. Under the guiding influence of the Holy Spirit, Paul spoke strong words in his second sermon at Pisidian Antioch: 'We will turn our thoughts to the Gentiles.' It was a dramatic and momentous decision that would influence the rest of his life.

A Lame Man Healed at Lystra. Iconium, the commercial centre of this region of Galatia, lay 65 miles south-east of Pisidian Antioch. It is the only one of these Galatian cities visited by Paul that still exists. Iconium was a free Greek city, whereas Pisidian Antioch and Lystra were Roman colonies. The Jews at Pisidian Antioch had worked on the Roman city fathers through their wives, a number of whom were probably of Jewish origin. Here in Iconium the Jews again opposed Paul; but this time they stirred up a genuine popular riot, in accordance with the democratic atmosphere of Iconium.

According to a very early tradition, Paul converted a young woman called Thecla on his first visit to Iconium. The picturesque and dramatic story of this girl saint, and the various attempts to make a martyr of her, has come down to us in 'The Acts of Paul and Thecla,' an historical novel of the second century. It is of special interest because it contains the earliest description of St. Paul: 'A man of little stature, thin-haired upon the head, crooked in the legs, of good state of body, with eyebrows joining, and nose somewhat hooked, full of grace; sometimes he appeared like a man, and sometimes he had the face of an angel.'

At Lystra, only 25 miles from Iconium, Paul made a convert of a young man whose name far overshadowed that of Thecla. He was Timothy, destined to be Paul's most intimate

to the gates, eager, like the crowd, to do sacrifice.

The apostles tore their garments when they heard of it; and both Barnabas and Paul ran out among the crowd crying aloud: 'Sirs, why are you doing all this? We too are mortal men like yourselves: the whole burden of our preaching is that you must turn away from follies like this to the worship of the living God, who made sky and earth and sea and all that is in them. In the ages that are past, he has allowed Gentile folk everywhere to follow their own devices; yet even so he has not left you without some proof of what he is: it is his bounty that grants you rain from heaven, and the seasons which give birth to your crops, so that you have nourishment and comfort to your heart's desire.' With words like this they persuaded the people, not easily, to refrain from offering sacrifice to them.

But some of the Jews from Antioch and Iconium had followed them; these won over the crowd to their side, and they stoned Paul and dragged him out of the city, leaving him there for dead. But the disciples formed a ring about him, and soon he rose up and went back into the city; next day he left, with Barnabas, for Derbe. In that city too they preached, and made many disciples; then they returned to Lystra, Iconium and Antioch, where they fortified the spirits of the disciples, encouraging them to be true to the faith, and telling them that we cannot enter the kingdom of heaven without many trials. Then, with fasting and prayer, they appointed presbyters for them in each of the churches, and commended them to the care of the Lord in whom they had learned to believe. So they passed through Pisidia, and reached Pamphylia. They preached the word in Perge, and went down to Attalia, taking ship there for Antioch, where they had been committed to God's grace for the work they had now achieved.

disciple. His conversion was far more important than the miraculous healing of the lame man which caused such a disturbance in the city.

The story of Jupiter and Mercury coming down to earth incognito, and being refused shelter until they were taken in by an old couple who alone were saved by them from a flood that swamped the country, is told in Ovid. This story is what prompted the people to make such a demonstration for Paul and Barnabas.

Paul's speech to this pagan crowd takes up this error: the gods are mere fictional beings. This does not mean that God is wanting in care for his children; his divine Providence does take care of men, through the laws of nature—the rain that makes their crops grow, the renewal of life in spring, the heat of summer.

Paul Returns to Antioch. According to an early tradition, Barnabas, Timothy, his mother, Eunice, and his grandmother, Lois, went out at night to carry back the body of Paul; but the Lord had more work, and more sufferings too, for him; they found him still alive.

Thirty miles from Lystra, on the eastern border of Galatia, was another Roman colony. There, to Derbe, the wounded Paul was taken, probably to the house of Gaius, later a disciple of Paul on his missionary tours. This seems to have been the only place where he did not meet with trouble and opposition from the Jews.

Almost three years had passed since Paul had left on this Galatian journey; Tarsus was only 125 miles further on, and Antioch not far beyond. But instead of taking this easy way home, Paul decided to return through the recently won territory, over the wild, stony plain that stood almost 4,000 feet above sea level.

On their arrival, they called the Church together, and told the story of all God had done to aid them, and how, through faith, he had left a door open for the Gentiles. And they stayed there for a considerable time with the disciples.

Letter to the Galatians

Paul, an apostle not holding his commission from men, not appointed by man's means, but by Jesus Christ, and God the Father who raised him from the dead, sends his greeting, and greeting from all the brethren who are with him, to the churches of Galatia. Grace and peace be yours from God, the Father, and from the Lord Jesus Christ. He it is who has given himself up for our sins, to rescue us from the evil world that surrounds us, according to the will of God, who is our Father; to him be glory for ever and ever, Amen.

I am astounded that you should have been so quick to desert one who called you by the grace of Christ, and go over to another gospel; this can only mean, that certain people are causing disquiet among you, in their eagerness to pervert the gospel of Christ. Friends, though it were we ourselves, though it were an angel from heaven that should preach to you a gospel other than the gospel we preached to you, a curse upon him! I repeat now the warning we gave you before it happened: if anyone preaches to you what is contrary to the tradition you received, a curse upon him! Do you think it is man's favour, or God's, that I am trying to win now? Shall I be told, now, that I am courting the good will of men? If, after all these years, I were still courting the favour of men, I should not be what I am, the slave of Christ.

His main reason for this was to appoint priests and bishops to govern the province conquered for Christ, to consolidate his hard-won victory. Paul was not only a genius at winning converts, he was a master organizer as well; he was the perfect missionary.

On Christian Freedom

Within twelve months of the mission to the Galatians, trouble had come upon these churches. Paul's anxiety mounted as traveller after traveller reported the turmoil in Pisidian Antioch, Iconium, Lystra, and Derbe. Paul was up to his eyes in work at Antioch; he could not possibly visit these churches in the near future. Under inspiration from the Holy Ghost, he decided to solve their problems by means of a circular letter. So he began the first of fourteen letters that have come down to us.

Defection of the Galatians. People dictated letters in those days, and a scribe wrote as they spoke. Paul's anxiety and indignation made him go straight to the point without spending much time on greetings; his thoughts came tumbling out one on top of the other.

There was a Jewish element in the Church which did not approve of Paul's free welcome of Gentiles as converts; these people thought that the heathen should go through a preparatory course of instruction in Judaism; that they should be circumcised before they were baptized. These Christian missionaries, Paul declares in strong terms, are perverting Christ's true gospel. He coins a new name for them, which has stuck; it is Judaizers. One of their chief objectives was to discredit Paul, his apostolic office and his motives.

Let me tell you this, brethren: the gospel I preached to you is not a thing of man's dictation: it was not from man that I inherited or learned it, it came to me by a revelation from Jesus Christ. You have been told how I bore myself in my Jewish days, how I persecuted God's Church beyond measure and tried to destroy it, going further in my zeal as a Jew than many of my own age and race, so fierce a champion was I of the traditions handed down by my forefathers. And then, he who had set me apart from the day of my birth, and called me by his grace, saw fit to make his Son known in me, so that I could preach his gospel among the Gentiles. My first thought was not to hold any consultations with any human creature; I did not go up to Jerusalem to see those who had been apostles longer than myself; no, I went off into Arabia, and when I came back, it was to Damascus. Then, when three years had passed, I did go up to Jerusalem, to visit Kephas, and I stayed a fortnight there in his company; but I did not see any of the other apostles, except James, the Lord's brother. Such is my history; as God sees me, I am telling you the plain truth. Afterwards, I travelled into other parts of the world, Syria and Cilicia; and all the time I was not even known by sight to the Christian churches of Judea; they only knew by hearsay, 'The man who used to persecute us is now preaching the faith he once tried to destroy,' and they praised God for what he had done in me.

Then, after an interval of fourteen years, once again I went up to Jerusalem with Barnabas, and Titus also accompanied me. I went up in obedience to a revelation, and there I communicated to them (only in private, to men of repute) the gospel I always preach among the Gentiles; was it possible that the course I had taken and was taking was useless? And

Paul's Apostolate from Christ. Paul, said the Judaizers, does not rank with Peter, John, James the Less, and the rest of the Twelve; he did not get his knowledge of Christ at first hand, he only picked it up from others. And so he is unreliable, a mere disciple of apostles; one has to go to the immediate followers of Jesus, to drink from the spring of knowledge at its source.

To this Paul replies that he is an apostle of the same standing as Peter and the rest: 'Paul an apostle' is how he starts off his letter. But he had not known our Lord during his life on earth; how, then, could he make this claim to apostleship? To prove his claim he narrates the story of his conversion; he saw Jesus Christ on the Damascus Road: 'Am I not an apostle, have I not seen our Lord Jesus?' Paul had fallen in the dust, not only a convert but an apostle with full apostolic powers, conferred there and then by the risen Master; the same powers that our Lord had given to the twelve when he called them by the Lake of Galilee.

To show that his knowledge of the Christian revelation came from Christ directly, and not through any of the leaders in Jerusalem, Paul explains that his first visit to Jerusalem was not to find out the truths of Christianity; it was merely a courtesy visit to Peter. (Paul calls him by the Aramaic equivalent, Kephas.) Paul, the former persecutor, was not a welcome visitor among Christians.

Approval of the Apostles. Paul did go a second time to Jerusalem; but this was not a journey of his own choosing. The prophet Agabus had received a revelation from God that a famine was coming soon. (Agabus was living at Antioch, where Paul was residing after his ten years at home in Tarsus.) A collection was taken up for the mother church at Jerusalem; Paul

it is not even true to say that they insisted on my companion Titus, who was a Greek, being circumcised; we were only thinking of those false brethren who had insinuated themselves into our company so as to spy on the liberty which we enjoy in Jesus Christ, meaning to make slaves of us. To these we did not give ground for a moment by way of obedience: we were resolved that the true principles of the gospel should remain undisturbed in your possession. But as for what I owe to those who were of some repute—it matters little to me who or what they were, God makes no distinction between man and man—these men of repute, I say, had nothing to communicate to me. On the contrary, those who were reputed to be the main support of the Church, James and Kephas and John, saw plainly that I was commissioned to preach to the uncircumcised, as Peter was to the circumcised; he whose power had enabled Peter to become the apostle of the circumcised, had enabled me to become the apostle of the Gentiles. And so, recognizing the grace God had given me, they joined their right hands in fellowship with Barnabas and myself; the Gentiles were to be our province, the circumcised theirs. Only we were to remember the poor; which was the very thing I had set myself to do.

Afterwards, when Kephas came to Antioch, I opposed him openly; he stood self-condemned. He had been eating with the Gentiles, until we were visited by certain delegates from James; but when these came, he began to draw back and hold himself aloof, overawed by the supporters of circumcision. The rest of the Jews were no less false to their principles; Barnabas himself was carried away by their insincerity. So, when I found that they were not following the true path of the gospel, I said to Kephas in front of them all, 'Since

and Barnabas were chosen to carry this gift.

At that time, about 44 A.D., Agrippa's persecution was raging in Jerusalem; this persecution was directed mainly at the apostles, who went into hiding. So the monetary gift was handed over to the presbyters (Acts 11, 27-30); this group of non-apostolic rulers are here referred to by Paul as 'men of repute.' Paul did see three of the apostles briefly, and they gave their approval to his policy of receiving Gentiles without obliging them to observe the Jewish law.

The case of Titus had been quoted freely by Paul's adversaries as proof that he was inconsistent, and so could not be trusted: one day he preached that there was no need for circumcision, and the next he had Titus circumcised. To this Paul replied that no one compelled him to circumcise Titus. While still uncircumcised, this Gentile Christian had eaten with the Jewish leaders in Jerusalem, and not one of them had objected.

It was true that Titus had been circumcised since then. But this was done freely by Paul for the sake of the Judaizing agitators, without prejudice to the liberty of the Galatian converts; soon he would do the same to Timothy.

Peter and Paul at Antioch. This incident probably took place between Paul's return from the Galatian mission and the writing of his letter to them. It was the most recent proof that Paul had not altered his views about circumcision as a result of pressure from headquarters. Although conscious of his audacity in openly rebuking the prince of the apostles and the acknowledged vicar of Christ, Paul is forced to bring the incident forward because of the charge of inconsistency by the Judaizing agitators (Judaizer is the Greek word translated in the last five

you, who are a born Jew, follow the Gentile, not the Jewish
way of life, by what right do you bind the Gentiles to live
like the Jews?'

We are Jews by right of nature, we do not come from the
guilty stock of the Gentiles; yet we found out that it is through
faith in Jesus Christ, not by obeying the law, that a man is
justified. We, like anyone else, had to learn to believe in
Jesus Christ, so that we might be justified by faith in Christ,
not by observance of the law. Observance of the law cannot
win acceptance for a single human creature.

By putting our hopes of justification in Christ, we took our
rank as guilty creatures like the rest. Does that mean that
Christ brings us guilt? That is not to be thought of; do I put
myself in the wrong, when I destroy and then rebuild?
Through the law, my old self has become dead to the law, so
that I may live to God; with Christ I hang upon the cross,
and yet I am alive; or rather, not I; it is Christ that lives in
me. True, I am living, here and now, this mortal life; but
my real life is the faith I have in the Son of God, who loved
me, and gave himself for me. I do not spurn the grace of
God. If we can be justified through the law, then Christ's
death was needless.

Senseless Galatians, who is it that has cast a spell on you,
before whom Jesus Christ has been exposed to view on his
cross? Let me be content with asking you one question: Was
it from observance of the law that the Spirit came to you, or
from obeying the call of faith? Are you so far out of your
right senses? You dedicated your first beginnings to the spirit;
and can you now find your completion in outward things?
Was it to no purpose that you went through so much? Since
it seems it was to no purpose. When God lavishes his Spirit on
you and enables you to perform miracles, what is the reason for

words of Paul's speech, 'To live like the Jews').

During the past four years since Peter had come to Antioch from Jerusalem, he had been preaching the gospel in this centre of Gentile converts. His vision and the reception of the Gentile Cornelius into the Church had convinced him that the Jewish observances were no longer part of the Christian way of life; but the Church was still in a transition stage, and it was part of Peter's office as head to keep unity and peace. Paul, with his Galatian experience still fresh, saw that such acts on the part of the Christian leaders would endanger the faith of the Gentile converts.

The dogma in danger was basic to the Christian cause: the efficacy of our Lord's redemptive death. Not only the Gentiles, but the Jews as well, including Peter and Paul, were justified by Christ on Calvary, not by observing the Mosaic law. The Jews outlawed the crucified Jesus; and since the Christians, as members of the Mystical Body, are united with their Head, the Jewish law had no more claim on them: 'Well, brethren, you too have undergone death, as far as the law is concerned, in the person of Christ crucified.'

Justification Comes from Faith. A deadening gloom has settled down on the Galatian churches with the arrival of new missionaries after the departure of Paul. These men had different ideas: even the Gentile converts must follow precisely the law of Moses; the kosher food regulations, the hand washings, the strict sabbath, isolation from their pagan friends, were all imposed as part of the Christian way of life.

How Timothy longed to hear once more Paul's words about the crucified and risen Jesus; persecution and hardships had seemed of no account when undergone for love of the cruci-

it? Your observance of the law, or your obedience to the call
of faith? Remember how Abraham put his faith in God, and
it was reckoned virtue in him.

You must recognize, then, that Abraham's real children
are the children of his faith. There is a passage in Scripture
which, long beforehand, brings to Abraham the good news,
'Through you all the nations shall be blessed'; and that passage looks forward to God's justification of the Gentiles by
faith. It is those, then, who take their stand on faith that share
the blessing Abraham's faithfulness won. Those who take
their stand on observance of the law are all under a curse;
'Cursed be everyone,' we read, 'who does not persist in carrying out all that this book of the law prescribes.' And indeed,
that the law cannot make a man acceptable to God is clear
enough; 'It is faith,' we are told, 'that brings life to the just
man'; whereas the law does not depend on faith; no, we are
told 'it is the man who carries out the commandments that
will find life in them.' From this curse invoked by the law
Christ has ransomed us, by himself becoming, for our sakes,
an accursed thing; we read that, 'There is a curse on the man
who hangs on a gibbet.' Thus, in Christ Jesus, the blessing of
Abraham was to be imparted to the Gentiles, so that we,
through faith, might receive the promised gift of the Spirit.

Brethren, let me take an argument from common life. A
valid legal disposition made by an ordinary human being
cannot afterwards be set aside; no one can make fresh provisions in it. The promises you know of were made to Abraham and his offspring; (it does not, by the way, say, 'To your
descendants,' as if it meant a number of people; it says, 'To
your offspring,' in the singular, meaning Christ). And this
is my contention: The law, coming into being four hundred

fied Master. The supernatural life had come to them through the redeeming death of Christ; the miracles of Paul and his converts, the Christians standing up in the assembly and praising God in foreign tongues, had all come from baptism, not from carrying out the burdensome prescriptions of the law.

The authentic words of Paul read out in the Christian meeting places brought hope and joy once more to the Galatians. All could follow his first argument: it was based on the experience of each one of them.

Paul's second argument is from the story of Abraham. This was directed at the Jewish section of the community; Jews looked to Abraham as the founder of their race; all prided themselves on following closely in the footsteps of their father. Our Lord made reference to this same filial quality: 'If you are Abraham's true children, it is for you to follow Abraham's example.'

Instead of being the support of the Judaizing party, Paul shows that Abraham is the classic example of his own teaching: justification by faith, not by the works of the law. This is clear from Genesis: 'Abraham put his faith in God, and it was reckoned virtue in him.' And in this, he is not only father to the Jews but to the Gentiles too: 'Through you all the nations shall be blessed.'

The Law is Inferior to the Promises. In the Old Testament two persons crystallize the Jew-Gentile controversy; they are Abraham and Moses (referred to in this paragraph as 'spokesman'). Abraham is the champion of the Gentiles; the promise made by God to him was that the Gentiles would be blessed, and so find salvation in the Messiah, the offspring of Abraham. Their way of entering into this promised blessing is through faith.

4

and thirty years afterwards, cannot unmake the disposition which God made so long ago, and cancel the promise. If our inheritance depends on observing the law, then it is not the inheritance secured to us by promise; that was promised to Abraham as a free gift.

What, then, is the purpose of the law? It was brought in to make room for transgression, while we waited for the coming of that posterity, to whom the promise had been made. Its terms were dictated by angels, acting through a spokesman; (a spokesman represents more than one, and there is only one God).

Is the law an infringement, then, of God's promises? That is not to be thought of. Doubtless, if a law had been given that was capable of imparting life to us, it would have been for the law to bring us justification. But in fact Scripture represents us as all under the bondage of sin; it was faith in Jesus Christ that was to impart the promised blessing to all those who believe in him.

Until faith came, we were all being kept in bondage to the law, waiting for the faith that was one day to be revealed. So that the law was our tutor, bringing us to Christ, to find in faith our justification. When faith comes, then we are no longer under the rule of a tutor; through faith in Jesus Christ you are all now God's sons. All you who have been baptized in Christ's name have put on the person of Christ; no more Jew or Gentile, no more slave and freeman, no more male and female; you are all one person in Jesus Christ. And if you belong to Christ, then you are indeed Abraham's children; the promised inheritance is yours.

Consider this: One who comes into his property while he is still a child has no more liberty than one of the servants, though all the estate is his; he is under the control of guard-

In contrasting Abraham and Moses, or faith and the law, Paul first of all makes a point of chronology: the time lag between the two is a long period of 430 years. God would be going back on his promise to Abraham if, centuries later, he demanded observance of a newly instituted law, of which Abraham knew nothing.

The second point of contrast is the manner in which God made his promise to Abraham: it was direct and personal. In giving the law to Moses he did not intervene personally; he used his angels, and they, being numerous, could not all speak at once; so they used Moses as spokesman to promulgate the law to the chosen people.

The law was only a secondary thought on God's part; it was a temporary expedient until men could find life by faith in Jesus Christ. The ten commandments, the essential part of the law, served to make men conscious that they were sinful transgressors of a positive law; they did not give men grace to observe the law.

Galatians are God's Sons. For St. Paul the entire history of the human race before Christ is man's minority; man is but a child undergoing the discipline and acquiring the knowledge imparted in the schoolroom. The Messianic promises will one day belong to him; they are his inheritance held in trust until he comes of age. Jew and Gentile are alike in this, with one exception: the Jews have the law to prepare them. St. Paul looks on the law as a combination of nurse, servant, and tutor; it can feed him, lead him by the hand to school, and impart some of the elementary lessons of a primary school. It cannot give him access to the Father's wealth; that can come from Christ alone.

A child's change from boyhood to manhood was official when he put on grown-up clothes (toga virilis was the Roman

ians and trustees, until he reaches the age prescribed by his
father. So it was with us; in those childish days of ours we
toiled away at the schoolroom tasks which the world gave us,
till the appointed time came. Then God sent out his Son
on a mission to us. He took birth from a woman, took birth
as a subject of the law, so as to ransom those who were subject to the law, and make us sons by adoption. To prove that
you are sons, God has sent out the Spirit of his Son into our
hearts, crying out in us, 'Abba, Father.' No longer, then, are
you a slave, you are a son; and because you are a son, you
have a son's right of inheritance.

Formerly you had no knowledge of God; you lived as slaves
of deities who were in truth no deities at all. Now you have
recognized the true God, or rather, the true God has recognized you. How is it that you are going back to those old
schoolroom tasks of yours, so abject, so ineffectual, eager to
begin your drudgery all over again? You have begun to observe special days and months, special seasons and years. I
am anxious over you; has all the labour I have spent on you
been useless?

Stand by me; I have taken my stand with you. I appeal to
you, brethren. You have never treated me amiss. Why, when
I preached the gospel to you in the first instance, it was, you
remember, because of outward circumstances which were
humiliating to me. Those outward circumstances of mine
were a test for you, which you did not meet with contempt
or dislike; you welcomed me as God's angel, as Christ Jesus.
What has become now of the blessing that once was yours?
In those days, I assure you, you would have plucked out your
eyes, if you had had the chance, and given them to me. Have
I made enemies of you, then, by telling you the truth? Oh,

name). Mankind attained its spiritual majority not by putting on Christian clothes but by putting on Christ. By baptism man is incorporated into the Mystical Body of Christ as a living organ. Christ is the Son of God; so the Christian becomes a son of God too, with all the rights of inheritance that belong to a son. To go back again to the observance of the Mosaic law would be the same as for a grown-up man to abandon his freedom and return to school and start at his sums again.

Until the coming of Christ the world was divided; there were racial distinctions (Jew-Gentile), social distinctions (slave-freeman), and family distinctions (male-female). There is no room for any distinctions in a Christian world; by building all men into his own body, the Church, Christ raised them to a new plane, a sharing in his own life of the Blessed Trinity.

This is why men should no longer have the outlook of servants and slaves; they are sons of the divine family who address God the Father with the warm intimacy and spontaneous affection of sons; moved by the indwelling Spirit, they speak the words 'Pater Noster.'

Paul's Motherly Anxiety. Paul here speaks with that tender affection which our Lord himself expressed for the misguided Jewish people: 'Jerusalem, Jerusalem, how often have I been ready to gather your children together, as a hen gathers her chickens under her wings.' It shows the gentleness and maternal affection of this fearless apostle; he attacks his opponents and rebukes his flock, but it is love which moves him to act so.

Paul contrasts the present coolness of his beloved Galatians with their affectionate reception when he first came to them; the opposition and persecution of the Jews in Pisidian Antioch, Iconium, and Lystra did not deter them from listening to him

they are jealous over you, but for a dishonourable purpose; their aim is to shut you out from their company, so that you may be jealous of them. Your jealousy should be for the honourable gifts you see in a man of honour; always, not only when I am at your side. My little children, I am in travail over you afresh, until I can see Christ's image formed in you! I wish I were at your side now, and could speak to you in a different tone; I am bewildered at you.

Tell me, you who are so eager to have the law for your master, have you never read the law? You will find it written there, that Abraham had two sons; one had a slave for his mother, and one a free woman. The child of the slave was born in the course of nature; the free woman's, by the power of God's promise. All that is an allegory; the two women stand for the two dispensations. Agar stands for the old dispensation, which brings up its children to bondage, the dispensation which comes to us from mount Sinai (after all, Sinai is a mountain in Arabia). Agar has the same meaning in the allegory as Jesrusalem, the Jerusalem which exists here and now; an enslaved city, whose children are slaves. Whereas our mother is the heavenly Jerusalem, a city of freedom. So it is that we read, 'Rejoice, you barren woman that have never borne child, break out into song and cry aloud, you that have never known travail; the deserted one has more children than she whose husband is with her.'

It is you, brethren, that are children of the promise, as Isaac was. Now, as then, the son who was born in the course of nature persecutes the son whose birth is a spiritual birth. But what does our passage in scripture say? 'Rid yourself of the slave and her son; it cannot be that the son of a slave should divide the inheritance with the son of a free woman.'

and being baptized into the Christian community.

He now appeals to the Galatian Church not to listen to the new teaching of the Judaizers. Their purpose is dishonourable: they wish to exclude the Gentiles from the Church unless they agree to observe all the prescriptions of the Mosaic law. The Galatians must be firm in Paul's absence, just as when he was present.

Jewish Slavery and Christian Freedom.   It is hardly likely that the Gentile converts of Galatia were familiar enough with the story of Abraham to appreciate the details from Genesis 16 and 21 which Paul here applies to the Jewish-Christian problem. It is rather meant as ammunition for his disciples in their arguments with the Judaizers, who would squirm in their seats as they listened to their own scriptural texts being turned against them. It was not for nothing that Paul had sat at the feet of Gamaliel in Jerusalem.

An allegory is a story with a deeper, hidden meaning, after the style of our Lord's parables. Paul sees in the story of Abraham's two wives, Sara and Agar, and their sons, Isaac and Ishmael, a providential foretelling of the present relations between the slavery of Jewish observance and the freedom which Christianity brings. Ishmael represents the Jewish agitators in bondage to the law; Isaac the freedom of the Christian dispensation, the true heir of the promise made to Abraham: 'All the races of the world shall find a blessing through your posterity.'

Paul complicates the historical parallel by introducing two geographical details. He links Ishmael with mount Sinai, where the law was given to Moses; Arabia is the right place for the Ishmaelite slaves to live, because it was the cradle of the Mosaic law. And the present city of Jerusalem, the home of Jewish

You see, then, brethren, that we are sons of the free woman, not of the slave; such is the freedom Christ has won for us. Stand fast, and do not let yourselves be caught again in the yoke of slavery.

The word of Paul is your warrant for this; if you are for being circumcised, Christ is of no value to you at all. Once again I would warn anyone who is accepting circumcision that he thereby engages himself to keep all the precepts of the law. You who look to the law for your justification have cancelled your bond with Christ, you have forfeited grace. All our hope of justification lies in the spirit; it rests on our faith; once we are in Christ, circumcision means nothing, and the want of it means nothing; the faith that finds its expression in love is all that matters.

Till now, you had been shaping your course well; who is it that has come between you and your loyalty to the truth? Not he who called you; this pressure comes from elsewhere. It takes but a little leaven to leaven the whole batch. I am fully confident in the Lord that you will be of the same mind with me, leaving the disturbers of your peace, be they who they may, to answer for it. As for myself, brethren, if it is true that I preach the need of circumcision, why am I persecuted? If I did, the preaching of the cross would no longer give offence. I would rather they should lose their own manhood, these authors of your unrest.

Yes, brethren, freedom claimed you when you were called. Only, do not let this freedom give a foothold to corrupt nature; you must be servants still, serving one another in a spirit of charity. After all, the whole of the law is summed up in one phrase, 'You shall love your neighbour as yourself'; if

observance, an earthly city, must not be confused with the true, heavenly Jerusalem, 'that holy city, all clothed in readiness, like a bride who has adorned herself to meet her husband.'

Circumcision Repudiates Grace. It seems that Paul's circumcision of his disciple Titus was at the back of this Judaizing plea for circumcision. They made a distinction between the Mosaic law and circumcision, which originated with Abraham and was the mark of a member of the chosen race. Paul seemingly had admitted this distinction when he had Titus circumcised. They now proposed a compromise solution of the Jew-Gentile division of the Christian community: surely the mere removal of a small collar of skin from the male organ of generation (circumcision) was a triviality which ought not to be an obstacle to Christian unity.

But Paul saw the subtlety and danger of this error; it was leaven working in the dough, and finally changing the Christian doctrine of justification through faith in Christ; he knew that such a compromise only obscured the real point at issue —Moses or Jesus. Circumcision was more than a surgical operation leaving a mark on the body; it was an act by which a person bound himself to observe the Mosaic law; for a Christian this meant denial of the efficacy of the grace of Christ. A pity such people did not use the knife further and make themselves incapable of reproducing their kind.

Live by the Spirit in Charity. As this letter was read aloud to the Galatian churches in city after city, the reaction of the Gentiles was one of elation; Paul had defended the cause of freedom in masterly fashion; he was devastating in the way he exposed the errors of the Jewish agitators. They now had a

4*

you are always backbiting and worrying each other, it is to be feared you will wear each other out in the end.

Let me say this: learn to live and move in the spirit; then there is no danger of your giving way to the impulses of corrupt nature. The impulses of nature and the impulses of the spirit are at war with one another; either is clean contrary to the other, and that is why you cannot do all that your will approves. It is by letting the spirit lead you that you free yourselves from the yoke of the law. It is easy to see what effects proceed from corrupt nature; they are such things as adultery, impurity, incontinence, idolatry, witchcraft, feuds, quarrels, jealousies, outbursts of anger, rivalries, dissensions, factions, spite, drunkenness, and debauchery. I warn you, as I have warned you before, that those who live in such a way will not inherit God's kingdom. Whereas the spirit yields a harvest of love, joy, peace, patience, kindness, generosity, faith, gentleness, temperateness. No law can touch lives such as these; those who belong to Jesus Christ have crucified nature, with all its passions, all its impulses. Since we live by the spirit, let the spirit be our rule of life; we must not indulge in vain ambitions, envying one another and provoking one another to envy.

Brethren, if a man is found guilty of some fault, you, who are spiritually minded, ought to show a spirit of gentleness in correcting him. Have an eye upon yourself; you, too, will perhaps encounter temptation. Bear the burden of one another's failings; then you will be fulfilling the law of Christ. The man who thinks he is of some worth, when in truth he is worth nothing at all, is merely deluding himself. Everyone should examine his own conduct; then he will be able to take the measure of his own worth; no need to compare himself with others. Each of us, then, will have his own load to carry.

document in their possession which would silence any further arguments that might be brought against their right to live the Christian life without all those wearisome, burdensome obligations of the Mosaic law.

But even a Christian cannot look at the errors and faults of others without danger of complacency. Jesus had given a warning in his parable of the Pharisee and the Publican: it is a common human failing to see the sins of others and be blind to one's own.

It is easier to defeat an opponent in combat than to live a complete Christian life. The Galatians, both those of Gentile and those of Jewish origin, must now take a look at themselves. They will find a twofold principle at work within their own souls; what Paul calls 'nature' and 'spirit.' The first is human nature wounded by original sin: man with a darkened intellect, a weakened will, and a tendency to evil. The second is mankind redeemed by Christ, raised to the supernatural life of grace, living a life of holiness, directed by the indwelling Holy Spirit. This is to live by the spirit.

In his Sermon on the Mount, our Lord gave a test by which a man can tell whether he is living according to nature or according to the spirit: 'The test of the tree is in its fruit; it is by their fruit that you will know them.'

Paul lists fifteen fruits which proceed from nature, and nine (of the twelve in the Vulgate, three are double translations) which come from the spirit; eight of the fifteen vices are breaches of charity, six of the nine virtues are different aspects of charity. Such emphasis is in accord with the Master's teaching: 'The mark by which all men will know you for my disciples will be the love you bear one another.'

In his priestly prayer after the Last Supper, our Lord asked his Father: 'That they should all be one, as we are one.' This

Your teachers are to have a share in all that their disciples
have to bestow. Make no mistake about it; you cannot cheat
God. A man will reap what he sows; if nature is his seed-
ground, nature will give him a perishable harvest, if his seed-
ground is the spirit, it will give him a harvest of eternal life.
Let us not be discouraged, then, over our acts of charity; we
shall reap when the time comes, if we persevere in them. Let
us practise generosity to all, while the opportunity is ours;
and above all, to those who are of one family with us in the
faith.

Here is some bold lettering for you, written in my own
hand. Who are they, these people who insist on your being
circumcised? They are men, all of them, who are determined
to keep up outward appearances, so that the cross of Christ
may not bring persecution on them. Why, they do not even
observe the law, although they adopt circumcision; they are
for having you circumcised, so as to make a display of your
outward conformity. God forbid that I should make a display
of anything, except the cross of our Lord Jesus Christ, through
which the world stands crucified to me, and I to the world.
Circumcision means nothing, the want of it means nothing;
there has been a new creation. Peace and pardon to all those
who follow this rule, to God's true Israel. Spare me, all of you,
any further anxieties; already I bear the scars of Jesus printed
on my body. Brethren, the grace of our Lord Jesus Christ be
with your spirit. Amen.

divine unity of the Church was in grave danger in Galatia owing to the recent Jew-Gentile controversy. Argument led to ill-will, pride, and contentiousness; breaches of charity were a too frequent result of the animated disputes that were raging in every meeting of the Christian community. The only way to peace and harmony in Galatia was for each Christian to behave with kindness, consideration, and meekness: 'Order your lives in charity, upon the model of that charity which Christ showed to you.'

Last Warning Against Agitators. This teaching on how to live on peaceful terms with their opponents should not blind the Gentiles to the errors of the Judaizers. To make sure that he is perfectly understood Paul takes the pen from his secretary and writes this last paragraph with his own hand. To make it more emphatic, he writes in large, block letters: under no circumstances must the cause of Christian freedom be compromised.

Paul was born a Jew, just as these agitators were. But he no longer prided himself on his Jewish blood and the circumcision mark on his body. In the brief course of his missionary life he had acquired other marks, the scars of scourging and stoning; they were the brand on his body demonstrating that he now belonged to Jesus. If he wanted to boast of anything, it was this conformity to Christ crucified; for him the cross had ceased to be a symbol of shame; it was his standard of victory.

The Decree on Gentile Converts

But now some visitors came down from Judea, who began to tell the brethren, 'You cannot be saved without being circumcised according to the tradition of Moses.' Paul and Barnabas were drawn into a great controversy with them; and it was decided that Paul and Barnabas and certain of the rest should go up to see the apostles and presbyters in Jerusalem about this question. So the church saw them on their way, and they passed through Phoenicia and Samaria, relating how the Gentiles were turning to God, and so brought great rejoicing to all the brethren. When they reached Jerusalem, they were welcomed by the church, and by the apostles and presbyters; and they told them of all that God had done to aid them. But some believers who belonged to the party of the Pharisees came forward and declared, 'They must be circumcised; we must call upon them to keep the law of Moses.'

When the apostles and presbyters assembled to decide about this matter there was much disputing over it, until Peter rose and said to them, 'Brethren, you know well enough how from early days it has been God's choice that the Gentiles should hear the message of the gospel from my lips, and so learn to believe. God, who can read men's hearts, has assured them of his favour by giving the Holy Spirit to them as to us. He would not make any difference between us and them; he had removed all the uncleanness from their hearts when he gave them faith. How is it, then, that you would now call God in question, by putting a yoke on the necks of the disciples, such as we and our fathers have been too weak to bear? It is by the grace of the Lord Jesus that we hope to be saved, and they no less.'

Jerusalem 49 A.D.

Visitors were all welcome at Antioch. The small party of Christians from Jerusalem was treated with special warmth and affection; after all, they came from the very city where Jesus had died for all mankind and opened the door of salvation to the Gentiles. In contrast to the openhearted welcome at Antioch was the cold, disturbing message from Judea; it was delivered with the definiteness of a dogmatic statement.

Fortunately Paul, the hero of the Antioch community, was at home to defend his beloved Gentiles. He had all the arguments at his finger tips; he had just set them all down in writing in his Letter to the Galatians. Now it was time to have the question settled once for all by the leaders of the Church. Peter, the vicar of Christ, was at the moment in Jerusalem; both sides agreed to submit the matter to his judgment.

Peter Asserts the Liberty of the Gentiles.   There were two sources of information from which Peter could draw in making a decision on the questions submitted to him: the words and deeds of Jesus and the revelation of the Holy Spirit since Pentecost Sunday.

He chose to base his argument on the vision he had received from the Holy Spirit some fifteen years before; it had been meant expressly for such a crisis as this. It was that vision of the unclean animals lowered from heaven in a sheet; it had been followed by the conversion of the first Gentile, the centurion Cornelius.

Peter was content with this one illustration: it showed clearly that salvation came from faith in Christ, independent of the Mosaic law. The only uncleanness that man has to worry about

Then the whole company kept silence, and listened to Barnabas and Paul describing all the signs and wonders God had performed among the Gentiles by their means.

And when they had finished speaking, James answered thus: 'Listen, brethren, to what I have to say. Simon has told us, how for the first time God has looked with favour on the Gentiles, and chosen from among them a people dedicated to his name. This is an agreement with the words of the prophets, where it is written: "Afterwards, I will come back, and build up again David's tabernacle that has fallen; I will build up its ruins, and raise it afresh; so that all the rest of mankind may find the Lord, all those Gentiles among whom my name is named, says the Lord, who makes this known from all eternity." And so I give my voice for sparing the consciences of those Gentiles who have found their way to God; only writing to bid them abstain from what is contaminated by idolatry, from fornication, and from meat which has been strangled or has the blood in it. As for Moses, ever since the earliest times he has been read, sabbath after sabbath, in the synagogues, and has preachers in every city to expound him.'

Thereupon it was resolved by the apostles and presbyters, with the agreement of the whole church, to choose out some of their own number and despatch them to Antioch with Paul and Barnabas; namely, Judas who was called Barsabbas, and Silas, who were leading men among the brethren. And they sent, by their hands, this message in writing: 'To the Gentile brethren in Antioch, Syria and Cilicia, their brethren the apostles and presbyters send greeting. We hear that some of our number who visited you have disquieted you by what they said, unsettling your consciences, although we had given them no such commission; and therefore, meeting together

is sin, not that uncleanness defined by the multitudinous prescriptions of the law; it is the grace of Christ that removes sin,
and nothing else matters.

James Proposes a Decree. Jerusalem was worlds apart from
Antioch; and its bishop, James the cousin of our Lord, was a
strict observer of the Mosaic law, as were all the other members of his flock. It is likely that he had been cited by the
Judaizing party as their patron and as the shining example of
what a good Christian should be. He realized his delicate position in the controversy; while defending the freedom of the
Gentiles, he tried to smooth the way to a better understanding
and a more harmonious way of life between Jew and Gentile.

   To prove the truth of Gentile freedom, James quotes from
the scriptures; the text he uses is from Amos, but he could have
chosen dozens in similar strain. But, for the cause of Christian
unity, he suggests certain restrictions to be observed by the
Gentiles. There is no need, suggests James, to remind Jewish
Christians of these obligations; they will not be likely to forget
them, seeing that they listen to the Mosaic law every week.

Wording of the Decree. After discussion this decree was
framed, under guidance of the Holy Spirit. The leaders of the
Church clearly stated that the Judaizing party had no support
from them. They also gave full approval to Paul, his missionary
activity, and his doctrine on the liberty of Gentile converts.
Though Galatia is not specifically mentioned in the decree, it
is sufficiently indicated under the name Cilicia. The same conditions prevailed in these two provinces, which were alongside
each other; they were separated only by the Taurus Mountains.
   The first two prescriptions of the decree deal with kosher

with common purpose of heart, we have resolved to send you chosen messengers, in company with our well-beloved Barnabas and Paul, men who have staked their lives for the name of our Lord Jesus Christ. We have given this commission to Judas and Silas, who will confirm the message by word of mouth. It is the Holy Spirit's pleasure and ours that no burden should be laid upon you beyond these, which cannot be avoided; you are to abstain from what is sacrificed to idols, from blood-meat and meat which has been strangled, and from fornication. If you keep away from such things, you will have done your part. Farewell.'

So they took their leave and went down to Antioch, where they called the people together and delivered the letter to them; and they, upon reading it, were rejoiced at this encouragement. Judas and Silas, for they were prophets too, said much to encourage the brethren and establish their faith; they stayed there for some time before the brethren let them go home, in peace, to those who had sent them.

Second Missionary Journey

Paul and Barnabas waited at Antioch, teaching and preaching God's word, with many others to help them; and then, after some days, Paul said to Barnabas, 'Let us go back and visit the brethren in all the cities where we have preached the word of the Lord, to see how they are doing.' And Barnabas was for taking John, also called Mark, with them. But Paul said, here was a man who left them when they reached Pamphylia, and took no part with them in the work; it was not right to admit such a man to their company. So sharp

food regulations. They are meant to preserve unity and charity, to save embarrassment when the mixed communities of Jews and Gentiles sit down to their common meal. It would be easier for the Gentiles to adopt the Jewish methods of preparing and eating food than for the Jews to change such venerable customs.

The third prescription, 'fornication,' seems completely out of place alongside the other two. The most probable explanation is that the Greek refers to an entirely different matter, to marriage within the forbidden degrees of affinity and consanguinity, as set down in the Mosaic law: 'It is not for you to live by the customs of the Egyptians, or to imitate the men of Canaan, and follow their observances. It is my laws, my decrees you must keep. And it is I, the Lord, who tell you that no man is to betake himself to a woman who is near of kin to him, and mate with her' (Lev. 18). It is Jewish law, not Roman law or local custom, that must guide Christians in determining what are and what are not irregular relations in their marriage cases.

From Antioch to Corinth 50-51 A.D.

Paul and Barnabas Separate. As soon as the snow began to melt on the Taurus Mountains and the passes were open to traffic after the winter, Paul was anxious to be on his way into Galatia; he wanted them to know the contents of the Jerusalem Decree.

Seemingly Paul objected to taking Mark, as one who had abandoned the missionary expedition at the sight of the rugged mountains and unexplored tracks into Galatia on the first journey; he had no time for such weaklings. Mark eventually

was their disagreement, that they separated from each other; Barnabas took Mark with him, and sailed off to Cyprus, while Paul chose Silas for his companion and went on his journey, commended by the brethren to the Lord's grace. And he travelled all through Syria and Cilicia, establishing the churches in the faith.

So he reached Derbe, and Lystra. Here he met a disciple, named Timothy, son of a believer who was a Jewess and a Gentile father. He was well spoken of by the brethren at Lystra and Iconium, and Paul resolved to take him as a companion on his journey. But he was careful to circumcise him; he was thinking of the Jews living in those parts, who all knew that Timothy's father was a Gentile. As they passed from city to city, they recommended to their observance the decree laid down by the apostles and presbyters at Jerusalem. They found the churches firmly established in the faith, and their numbers daily increasing. Thus they passed through the Phrygian region of Galatia; the Holy Spirit prevented them from preaching the word in Asia. Then, when they had come as far as Mysia on their journey, they planned to enter Bithynia; but the Spirit of Jesus would not allow it. So they crossed Mysia, and went down to the sea at Troas.

Here Paul saw a vision in the night; a certain Macedonian stood by him in entreaty, and said, 'Come over into Macedonia, and help us.' That vision once seen, we were eager to sail for Macedonia; we concluded that God had called us there to preach to them. So we put out from Troas, made a straight course to Samothrace, and next day to Neapolis. Thence we reached Philippi, which is a Roman colony and the chief city in that part of Macedonia; in this city we remained for some days, passing the time. On the sabbath day

won back Paul's esteem; he was with him during both Roman imprisonments. Finally he became bishop of Alexandria in Egypt.

Barnabas spent the rest of his life preaching the gospel in Cyprus, his homeland; his work there has earned him the title of apostle of that island.

Timothy Joins Paul. The friendship between these two reminds us of the friendship between our Lord and his beloved disciple St. John. They are closely associated during the next seventeen years. Timothy is mentioned eighteen times throughout eleven of St. Paul's fourteen letters: 'I have no one else who shares my thoughts as he does; he has shared my task of preaching the gospel like a son helping his father.'

Although Timothy had been baptized only a couple of years earlier, by Paul on his first journey to Galatia, he was probably ordained a priest at Lystra before setting out with Paul and Silas (see 1 and 2 Timothy).

'With the Jews I lived like a Jew, to win the Jews.' That is the basic reason for the circumcision of Timothy. It would win the good will of the Jews everywhere and make Timothy acceptable in their synagogues; otherwise his assistance to Paul would have been restricted.

Luke Joins the Expedition. Paul had not planned to come to Troas; it was the Holy Spirit who directed him there. Originally he intended to follow the highroad through Galatia west to Ephesus; when God told him to take the road north from Pisidian Antioch, Paul thought of going into the rich province of Bithynia; but at Dorylaeum his steps were directed west to Troas.

This beautiful city was the port for Europe: only a few miles inland across the flat plains were the ruins of Troy, im-

we went out beyond the city gates, by the riverside, a meeting-place, we were told, for prayer; and we sat down and preached to the women who had assembled there. One of those who were listening was a woman called Lydia, a purple-seller from the city of Thyatira, and a worshipper of the true God; and the Lord opened her heart, so that she was attentive to Paul's preaching. She was baptized, with all her household; and she was urgent with us; 'Now you have decided that I have faith in the Lord,' she said, 'come to my house and lodge there'; and she would take no denial.

And now, as we were on our way to the place of prayer, we chanced to meet a girl who was possessed by a divining spirit; her predictions brought in large profits to her masters. This girl used to follow behind Paul and the rest of us, crying out, 'These men are the servants of the most high God; they are proclaiming to us the way of salvation.' And when she had done this for a number of days, Paul was distressed by it; he turned round and said to the spirit: 'I command you to come out of her, in the name of our Lord Jesus Christ'; and there and then it came out of her.

Her masters, who saw that all their hopes of profit had vanished, took hold of Paul and Silas and dragged them off to justice in the market-place. When they brought them before the magistrates, they said, 'These men, Jews by origin, are disturbing the peace of our city; they are recommending customs which it is impossible for us, as Roman citizens, to admit or to observe.' The crowd gathered round, to join in the accusation; and the magistrates, tearing their clothes off them, gave orders that they should be beaten; then, when they had inflicted many lashes on them, put them in prison, and bade the gaoler keep them in safe custody. Thus instructed, he put them in the inner ward, and secured their

mortalized by the poet Homer. Paul was about to make an assault on Europe: he was leaving the oriental atmosphere of Asia and Jewry for the home of Graeco-Roman culture. The details of God's guidance had been preparing him for this step; and finally a vision settled any doubts left in his mind.

Luke, the author of the Acts and the Third Gospel, tells his story in the third person; but here, for the first of three times, he breaks into the first person plural (the 'we-sections' they are called); it announces his arrival on the scene.

Tradition has it that he was a brother of Titus, already a disciple of Paul but not with him at this time. Both were natives of Antioch; Luke was already a Christian, and well known to Paul (possibly he even studied at Tarsus). He may have been practising his profession of doctor in Troas when Paul arrived there. He ranks next to Timothy in close association with Paul, who calls him 'my beloved Luke, the physician.'

Greek seamen sailed by landmarks and travelled only by day. It would take two days to Philippi, with the island mountain peak of Samothrace as a guide.

Freed By An Earthquake. When our Lord entered the pagan district of Samaria, his first contact with the people was through a woman who came to draw water at Jacob's well. In like manner, Paul made contact with his first European converts through a wealthy widow by the riverside at Philippi. She was not a Jewess but observed the Jewish law as a proselyte, like the centurion Cornelius. Two other women, Evodia and Syntyche, are known to us from Paul's Letter to the Philippians; they were probably members of the same prayer group as Lydia.

When Paul drove the evil spirit out of the possessed girl, he hit the representatives of paganism where it hurt most— in their pockets. They fought back fiercely. Their technique

feet in the stocks. At midnight, Paul and Silas were at their prayers, praising God, while the prisoners listened to them. And all at once there was a violent earthquake, so that the foundations of the prison rocked; whereupon every door opened, and every man's chains were undone. The gaoler, who had been awakened, saw the prison doors open, and drew his sword as if to kill himself, thinking the prisoners had escaped; but Paul cried with a loud voice, 'Do no hurt to yourself; we are all here.'

And so, when he had called for a light, he came running in and fell at the feet of Paul and Silas, all trembling; 'Sirs,' he asked, as he led them out, 'what am I to do, to save myself?'

'Have faith,' they said to him, 'in the Lord Jesus; there lies salvation for you, and for your household.'

Then they preached the word of the Lord to him, and to all that were in his house; and he, there and then, at dead of night, took them away to wash their wounds, and without delay he and all his were baptized. So he led them to his home, where he put food before them, and he and all his household made rejoicing at having found faith in God.

When day came, the magistrates sent their officers to say, 'Those men are to be discharged.' And the gaoler reported the message to Paul: 'The magistrates have sent ordering your discharge; it is time you should come out, and go on your way in peace.'

But Paul said to them, 'What, have they beaten us in public, without trial, Roman citizens as we are, and sent us to prison, and now would they let us out secretly? That will not serve; they must come here themselves, and fetch us out in person.'

was the same as that employed at Pisidian Antioch, and for the same reason: Philippi was a new Roman colony with an exaggerated show of loyalty to the emperor. They saw Christianity as a threat to established order.

Paul and Silas, as Roman citizens, were exempt from the jurisdiction of local magistrates. Maybe the confusion of a noisy, shouting crowd gave them no chance to make this fact known; possibly Paul made no attempt, knowing that he had to endure much suffering in order to establish the kingdom of God. Scourging and imprisonment only made him more like the Master himself.

The earthquake was a providential intervention of God. Locks in those days were mere wooden bars let into sockets in the doors; a good shake would swing the doors wide open. The chains would fall from the gaping holes in the walls. The gaoler preferred suicide to execution; he was responsible for prisoners with his own life.

Paul, the zealous missionary, wasted no time in instructing the gaoler and his family. In the early summer light, around the fountain in the courtyard, he baptized them. Full instruction would be given later by Luke, who was left here as bishop of Philippi.

Paul Demands An Apology. Justice was the symbol of Roman rule. Paul was not acting in an unchristian spirit when he insisted on his rights. The Master before him, on the night of his trial before Caiphas, had done the same. When one of the soldiers struck Jesus, he said: 'If there was harm in what I said, tell us what was harmful in it; if not, why do you strike me?'

Lydia's house became the first church in Philippi. Luke was left in charge as its first bishop; he remained there for seven years, rejoining Paul towards the end of his third missionary

When the officers gave this message to the magistrates, they were alarmed by this talk of Roman citizenship; so they came and pleaded with them, urging them, as they brought them out, to leave the city. On leaving the prison, they went to Lydia's house, where they saw the brethren and gave them encouragement; then they set out on their journey.

They continued their journey through Amphipolis and Apollonia, and so reached Thessalonica. Here the Jews had a synagogue, and Paul, as his custom was, paid them a visit there. Over a space of three sabbaths he reasoned with them out of the scriptures, expounding these and bringing proofs from them that the sufferings of Christ and his rising from the dead were foreordained; 'The Christ,' he said, 'is none other than the Jesus whom I am preaching to you.' Some of them were convinced, and threw in their lot with Paul and Silas; a great number too, of those Gentiles who worshipped the true God, and not a few of the leading women. The Jews were indignant at this, and they found confederates among the riff-raff of the market-place, to make a disturbance and throw the city into an uproar. Then they made a sudden descent on Jason's house, in the hope of bringing Paul and Silas out into the presence of the people; but, as they could not find them, they dragged Jason and some of the brethren before the city council, crying out, 'Here they are, the men who are turning the world upside down; they have come here too; and Jason has given them hospitality. All these folk defy the edicts of Caesar; they say there is another king, Jesus.' Both the crowd and the city council took alarm at hearing this, and they demanded bail from Jason and the others before they would let them go.

journey. Clement is mentioned in the Letter to the Philippians; he was probably Luke's chief assistant in establishing the Church; scholars dispute whether this was the Clement who became fourth pope of Rome. Of all Paul's foundations, Philippi was his favourite; it never caused him the least worry, and it alone contributed to his material needs.

The Jews Stir Up a Riot. The 100 miles west from Philippi to Thessalonica was easy going along the most famous road yet trodden by Paul. It was called the Egnatian Way and was the main artery linking Greece with Rome. It ran from Philippi to Dyrrachium; a short journey by ship across the Adriatic brought the traveller to Brindisi, and there the road continued to Rome, with a still more famous name, the Appian Way.

Thessalonica was an important commercial port; and so it had a large colony of Jewish traders and merchants. A year earlier its population had increased by a large number of Jews expelled from Rome by the emperor Claudius. Among them was a Christian, Jason. As a convert of Peter's, Jason was delighted to meet and give hospitality to the apostle Paul.

There is always noise in any busy city; but the convert class assembled in Jason's house was alarmed at the shouting and yelling outside in the street this summer afternoon. It was Paul's name they picked up first, then the dangerous word, treason. As Paul was directed to a hiding place upstairs, he must have recalled how the pattern of Jesus' life was taking shape in his. His mind went back to the trial scene before Pilate on Good Friday morning, and the shouts of another crowd: 'We have no king . . . no king, except Caesar.'

Thereupon the brethren sent Paul and Silas away by night to Beroea; where, as soon as they arrived, they made their way to the Jewish synagogue. These were a better breed than the Thessalonians; they welcomed the word with all eagerness, and examined the Scriptures, day after day, to find out whether all this was true; so that many of them learned to believe, as certain Greek women of fashion did, and not a few of the men as well. But now some of the Thessalonian Jews, hearing that the word of God had been preached by Paul at Beroea too, came on there, to upset and disturb the minds of the people; whereupon the brethren sent Paul away, to continue his journey up to the coast; Silas and Timothy remained there still.

Those who were escorting Paul on his journey saw him as far as Athens, and then left him, with instructions for Silas and Timothy to rejoin him as soon as possible. And while Paul was waiting for them in Athens, his heart was moved within him to find the city so much given over to idolatry, and he reasoned, not only in the synagogue with Jews and worshippers of the true God, but in the marketplace, with all he met. He encountered philosophers, Stoics and Epicureans, some of whom asked, 'What can his drift be, this dabbler?' while others said, 'He would appear to be proclaiming strange gods'; because he had preached to them about Jesus and Resurrection. So they took him by the sleeve and led him up to the Areopagus. 'May we ask,' they said, 'what this new teaching is you are delivering? You introduce terms which are strange to our ears; pray let us know what may be the meaning of it.' (No townsmen of Athens, or stranger visiting it, has time for anything else than saying something new, or hearing it said.)

That night the three missionaries moved out under cover of darkness, escorted by two converts, Aristarchus and Secundus. They left the Egnatian Way and went southwest to an out-of-the-way town, Beroea, a distance of fifty miles. It was some weeks before the malevolent Thessalonian Jews found out their hiding place.

It is usually presumed that Paul went by ship directly to Athens. But Mgr. Knox has put a brilliant case for a different itinerary; it is based mainly on Paul's two Letters to the Thessalonians. Paul doubled back to the Egnatian Way, journeying 'up to the coast' at Dyrrachium; that is, he went to the Adriatic not the Aegean Sea. He intended to go back to Thessalonica but was prevented. It was several months before he arrived at Athens.

Paul At Athens.   Athens was the second city of the Empire, surpassed only by Rome itself. It was the richest and most beautiful city in which Paul had yet set foot. It was the intellectual, artistic, and religious centre of the Roman world. Though its glory had faded when Paul visited it, it still had no equal in intellectual leadership; no Roman considered himself educated unless he had studied at Athens.

The city was dominated by the Acropolis, a vast bulk of rock which rose up hundreds of feet above the buildings in the centre of the city. And on top of the Acropolis stood the cream-coloured Parthenon, a temple in the sky, poised lightly as a bird after flight. And rising high above the Parthenon was the great wooden statue of Athena, the goddess of wisdom. It was seventy feet high and covered with ivory and gold plates that shone and flashed in the sunlight; the gilded point of Athena's spear was the first thing sailors saw, coming into port.

So Paul stood up in full view of the Areopagus, and said, 'Men of Athens, wherever I look I find you scrupulously religious. Why, in examining your monuments as I passed by them, I found among others an altar which bore the inscription, "To the unknown God." And it is this unknown object of your devotion that I am revealing to you. The God who made the world and all that is in it, that God who is Lord of heaven and earth, does not dwell in temples that our hands have made; no human handicraft can do him service, as if he stood in need of anything, he, who gives to all of us life and breath and all we have. It is he who has made, of one single stock, all the nations that were to dwell over the whole face of the earth. And he has given to each the cycles it was to pass through and the fixed limits of its habitation, leaving them to search for God; would they somehow grope their way towards him? Would they find him? And yet, after all, he is not far from any one of us; it is in him that we live, and move, and have our being; thus, some of your own poets have told us, "For indeed, we are his children." Why then, if we are the children of God, we must not imagine that the divine nature can be represented in gold, or silver, or stone, carved by man's art and thought. God has shut his eyes to these passing follies of ours; now, he calls upon all men, everywhere, to repent, because he has fixed a day when he will pronounce just judgment on the whole world. And the man whom he has appointed for that end he has accredited to all of us, by raising him up from the dead.'

When resurrection from the dead was mentioned, some mocked, while others said, 'We must hear more from you about this.' So Paul went away from among them. But there were men who attached themselves to him and learned

Paul's Speech to the Philosophers.   *There were many temples and buildings on the Acropolis; an open-air auditorium on the western slope not far from the Parthenon was known as the Areopagus; it was the meeting place for the university education board. It was before this ruling body, and many undergraduates, that Paul delivered his speech.*

The Christian attitude to idols is given in Paul's First Letter to the Corinthians: 'A false god has no existence in the order of things; there is one God, and there can be no other. Whatever gods may be spoken of as existing in heaven or on earth, for us there is only one God, the Father who is the origin of all things, and the end of our being; only one Lord, Jesus Christ, the creator of all things, who is our way to him.'

The greater part of Paul's speech is concerned with the nature of God, particularly his qualities of creator and father. Both these qualities were absent from the pagan picture of the supreme being. They had a vast collection of gods, each with his or her own restricted field of activity; these were all aloof and indifferent to what happened among men on earth.

Paul skilfully builds up a different picture: God is a pure spirit, the creator of all the matter which makes up the world seen by human eyes. God is interested in and cares for all men, since all are made to his image and likeness, and are all descended from one man. God is the only true father worthy of that name.

The great vice of the Athenians was intellectual pride. This audience expressed the reaction of the city to the Christian message. Athens was almost the last city in the Roman Empire to accept Christ; and it took almost 500 years for it to become Christian.

According to an early legend, Dionysius became bishop of

to believe, among them Dionysius the Areopagite; and so did a woman called Damaris, and others with them.

Paul left Athens after this, and went to Corinth. Here he met a Jew named Aquila, born in Pontus, who, with his wife Priscilla, had lately come from Italy, when Claudius decreed that all Jews should leave Rome. He paid them a visit: then, since they were brothers of the same craft (both were tent-makers), he stayed and worked with them. Every sabbath he held a disputation in the synagogue, trying to convince both Jews and Greeks. Just at the time when Silas and Timothy arrived from Macedonia, Paul was much occupied with preaching, while he bore witness to the Jews that Jesus was the Christ. But they set their faces against it and talked blasphemy, until he shook the dust out of his garments, and said to them, 'Your blood be upon your own heads; I am clear of it; I will go to the Gentiles henceforward.' So he left them, and went to the house of one Titius Justus, a worshipper of the true God, who lived next door to the synagogue. But Crispus, the ruler of the synagogue, learned to believe in the Lord, and so did all his household; and by now many of the Corinthians listened and found faith, and were baptized. And the Lord said to Paul in a vision at night, 'Do not be afraid, speak out, and refuse to be silenced; I am with you, and none shall come near to do you harm; I have a great following in this city.' So he remained there a year and six months, preaching the word of God among them.

Paris and is the patron of that city, having suffered martyrdom there for the faith.

Paul At Corinth. Forty miles to the west of ancient, so-phisticated Athens was the modern cosmopolitan port of Corinth. For Paul it was a journey into another world (like leaving Oxford one day and being in Port Said the next). Corinth had been built a hundred years before on a narrow neck of land extending between the Adriatic and the Aegean seas; the bulk of east-west trade passed through this port. Light vessels were dragged the few miles overland to the eastern port of Cenchrae; or else the cargo was unloaded and transported by waggon from one port to the other. This saved vessels the dangerous two hundred mile detour around the dreaded Cape Malea.

Among the refugees from Rome was a Christian couple, Aquila, an Asiatic Jew, and his Gentile wife, the Roman Priscilla (Paul calls her Prisca); they became Paul's closest friends outside the intimate group of his disciples. We shall find them later at Ephesus, then at Rome, and finally back at Ephesus.

It took a vision to convince Paul that God wanted him to work in this corrupt city of Corinth; he was anxious to get back to his Macedonian converts, to whom God had called him—back at Troas. Later, Paul will write two letters to Corinth; from these we know a dozen of the first Christians by name and can learn more of their way of life than from any other early document.

First Letter to the Thessalonians

Paul and Silvanus and Timothy, to the church assembled at Thessalonica in God the Father and the Lord Jesus Christ, grace and peace be yours. We give thanks to God always for all of you, making mention of you continually in our prayers; such memories we have of your active faith, your unwearied love, and that hope in our Lord Jesus Christ which gives you endurance, in the sight of him who is our God and Father. Brethren, God loves you, and we are sure that he has made choice of you. Our preaching to you did not depend upon mere argument; power was there, and the influence of the Holy Spirit, and an effect of full conviction; you can testify what we were to you and what we did for you. And on your side, you followed our example, the Lord's example. There was great persecution, and yet you welcomed our message, rejoicing in the Holy Spirit; and now you have become a model to all the believers throughout Macedonia and Achaia. Yes, the Lord's message has echoed out from you, and not only in Macedonia and Achaia; your faith in God has overflowed everywhere, so that we do not need to speak a word; our friends themselves tell the story of our journey, and how we first came among you. They describe how you have turned away from idolatry to the worship of God, so as to serve a living God, a God who really exists, and to wait for the appearing of his Son from heaven, Jesus, whom he raised from the dead, our Saviour from the vengeance that is to come.

Yes, brethren, you yourselves can testify that when we arrived among you, it proved to be no fruitless visit. We had been ill treated and insulted, as you know, at Philippi,

Persevere under Persecution

A Model to All Believers. It was late afternoon when Timothy and Silas (Paul always refers to him as Silvanus, the Roman equivalent of Silas) made their way to the workshop of Aquila. Six months had passed since Paul had last seen these two disciples of his; that had been a hurried farewell at night in Beroea as Paul escaped from the Jews. So they had much to talk of, mostly the state of the church in Thessalonica.

The Thessalonian converts had undergone a savage persecution from the Jews there; they had hoped day after day for their father and champion, Paul, to return to their aid. Paul saw that a visit in the near future was impracticable; the converts were crowding round him in great numbers. He must stay at Corinth; but he would write a letter of consolation, as he had done in similar circumstances to his Galatians.

Seeing that this church owed its existence as much to Timothy and Silas as to himself, Paul includes them not only in the opening salutation but throughout the letter; the plural 'we' occurs 65 times in the course of the letter. In all his other letters, except the two to the Thessalonians, Paul uses the first person singular as his normal mode of address.

It is a tender, intimate letter of a father who is proud of these children of his. He thanks God for their faith, hope, and charity, their endurance under persecution, and their zeal for the conversion of others.

Paul's Memories of His Visit. A note of defence clearly underlies this whole paragraph. Paul's enemies, in this instance the Thessalonian Jews, had spread an insidious slander about

but our God gave us courage to preach the divine gospel
to you amid much opposition. Our appeal to you was not
based on any false or degraded notions, was not backed by
cajolery. We have passed God's scrutiny, and he has seen
fit to entrust us with the work of preaching; when we speak,
it is with this in view; we would earn God's good opinion, not
man's, since it is God who scrutinizes our hearts. We never
used the language of flattery, you will bear us out in that,
nor was it, God knows, an excuse for enriching ourselves; we
have never asked for human praise, yours or another's, although, as apostles of Christ, we might have made heavy
demands on you. No, you found us gentle in your midst;
no nursing mother ever cherished her children more; in our
great longing for you, we desired nothing better than to offer
you our own lives, as well as God's gospel, so greatly had we
learned to love you. Brethren, you can remember how we
toiled and laboured, all the time we were preaching God's
gospel to you, working day and night so as not to burden you
with expense. Both you and God can witness how upright
and honest and faultless was our conduct towards you believers; it is within your knowledge that we treated every
one of you as a father treats his children, encouraging you,
comforting you, imploring you to lead a life worthy of
the God who now invites you to the glory of his kingdom.
This is why we give thanks to God unceasingly that, when we
delivered the divine message to you, you recognized it for
what it is, God's message, not man's; it is God, after all,
who manifests his power in you that have learned to believe. You took for your model, brethren, the churches
of God which are assembled in Judea in the name of Jesus
Christ. You were treated by your fellow countrymen as
those churches were treated by the Jews, the men who killed
the Lord Jesus and the prophets, and persecuted us; the men

the reason for Paul's not returning to his Thessalonian foundation. Paul, so the Jews said, was a man who loved to be made
a fuss of; he sought only praise and adulation. Consequently
his treatment by the converts at Thessalonica had displeased
him; they had not played up to his love of flattery.

Paul was intent only on making money. He had come to
the rich port of Thessalonica only for the sake of gain. When
he found that no substantial payments were being made him,
he soon left them and went elsewhere to more profitable fields.
That was the substance of the Jewish accusation: Paul had not
come back to a place where he had received neither praise nor
pay.

To disprove this slander, Paul recalls to his converts his way
of life, his conduct and his motives, when he first came among
them six months before. Like his Master before him, his one
concern was to do God's will, 'to earn God's opinion, not
man's.' He had acted toward them with the tender love of a
mother and the firm guiding hand of a father: 'He will not
snap the staff that is already crushed, or put out the wick that
still smoulders,' as the prophet Isaias foretold of Jesus.

On the question of support, Paul was most sensitive. He
insisted on working at his trade of tentmaker (as he was doing
at the moment in Corinth), so as not to be a burden on his
converts. He will later recall to the Corinthians his touchiness
on this same point. The only exception he made was to accept money from Philippi (probably at the insistence of the
dominant Lydia), during his stay at Thessalonica: 'not once
but twice, when I was at Thessalonica, you contributed to my
needs.'

Paul was acutely aware of the animosity of the Jews. He had
personal knowledge of it from his own days of persecuting
Christians; he had just experienced it again here in Corinth.

who displease God and show themselves the enemies of mankind, when they try to hinder us from preaching salvation
to the Gentiles. They must always be filling up the measure
of their sins, and now it is God's final vengeance that has
fallen upon them.

Finding ourselves separated from you, brethren, even for
a little while, though only in person, not in spirit, we conceived an overwhelming desire to visit you in person, such
was our longing for you; and we planned a journey to you,
I myself, Paul, more than once; but Satan has put obstacles
in our way. What hope or delight have we, what prize to
boast of before our Lord Jesus when he comes, if not you?
All our pride, all our delight is in you. At last we could not
bear it any longer, and decided to remain at Athens by ourselves, while we sent our brother Timothy, who exercises
God's ministry in preaching the gospel of Christ, to confirm
your resolutions, and give you the encouragement your faith
needed. There must be no wavering amidst these trials; you
know well enough that this is our appointed lot. Indeed,
when we visited you we told you that trials were to befall
us; now you can see for yourselves that it was true. That was
my reason for sending him, when I could bear it no longer,
to make sure of your faith; it might be that the tempter
of souls had been tempting you, and that all our labour would
go for nothing. Now that Timothy has come back to us from
seeing you, and told us about your faith and love, and the kind
remembrance you have of us all the while, longing for our
company as we long for yours, your faith has brought us
comfort, brethren, amidst all our difficulties and trials. If
only you stand firm in the Lord, it brings fresh life to us.
What thanks can we return to God for you, to express all
the joy we feel in rejoicing over you in the presence of our

It was an implacable hatred at the sight of Gentiles being accepted as the true heirs of Abraham; in punishment God had allowed them to become hardened in their unbelief; that is 'God's final vengeance that has fallen upon them.'

The Mission of Timothy.   Contrary to the Jewish picture of an indifferent Paul, unconcerned with what was happening to the Thessalonian foundation, we see him here as a loving shepherd anxious and worried over the fierce persecution of his flock at Thessalonica. In this section he gives an account of the difficulties that he encountered every time he planned to return to Thessalonica. It covers a period of about six months, which Luke has passed over in silence in his record in the Acts.

When Paul left Beroea, he was uncertain of his future movements. He would come back and collect Silas and Timothy as soon as he could. As it turned out, he was prevented by obstacles put in his way by Satan; this was most probably the opposition of his Jewish enemies from Thessalonica; they did not relax their watch over his movements even for a single day.

While Silas and Timothy remained in Beroea, expecting Paul's return any day, he continued his work of preaching the gospel along the Egnatian Way to Dyrrachium. From there he went north into Illyricum (he mentions this in Rom. 15, 19); then, finding the Thessalonian Jews still keeping an eye on him, he doubled back south to Apollonia and Nicopolis. On his arrival at Athens, where the Acts take over the story once more, he sent off his Macedonian guides, Aristarchus and Secundus of Thessalonica and Sopater of Beroea. They were to tell Timothy to return with them from Beroea to Thessalonica; as soon as Timothy found out the state of the church

God, as we pray more than ever, night and day, for the opportunity of seeing you face to face, and making good whatever your faith still lacks? May he himself, our God and our Father, may our Lord Jesus speed us on our journey to you; and as for you, may the Lord give you a rich and an ever richer love for one another and for all men, like ours for you. So, when our Lord Jesus comes with all his saints, may you stand boldly before the presence of God, our Father, in holiness unreproved.

And now, brethren, this is what we ask, this is our appeal to you in the name of the Lord Jesus. We gave you a pattern of how you ought to live so as to please God; live by that pattern, and make more of it than ever. You have not forgotten the warnings we have handed on to you by the command of the Lord Jesus. What God asks of you is that you should sanctify yourselves, and keep clear of fornication. Each of you must learn to control his own body, as something holy and held in honour, not yielding to the promptings of passion, as the heathen do in their ignorance of God. None of you is to commit transgression, and defraud his brother in this matter. For all such wrong-doing God exacts punishment; we have told you so already, in solemn warning. The life to which God has called us is not one of incontinence, it is a life of holiness, and to despise it is to despise, not man, but God, the God who has implanted his Holy Spirit in you. As for love of the brethren, there is no need to send you any message; you have learned for yourselves God's lesson about the charity we ought to show to one another, or you could not practise it as you do towards all the brethren throughout Macedonia. We would only ask you, brethren, to make more of it than ever. Let it be a point of honour with you to keep calm and to go on looking after your

at Thessalonica, he was to pick up Silas and rejoin Paul at Athens. But when these two did arrive at Athens, Paul had already gone off to Corinth; it is there that the meeting takes place.

Timothy's report brought comfort to Paul: they were standing up courageously under persecution. As a true disciple of Jesus, Paul had warned them that they must expect such trials: 'Blessed are you when men revile you, and persecute you, and speak all manner of evil against you falsely, because of me.'

On Purity, Charity, and Honest Work. The Christian mission to the heathen world around them is clearly defined by our Lord himself: 'Your light must shine so brightly before men that they can see your good works, and glorify your Father who is in heaven.' Timothy brought back to Paul a report on some aspects of Christian life in Thessalonica which showed that they were not giving a good example to their pagan neighbours.

Sexual morals were low in all pagan communities; but in seaports like Thessalonica and Corinth the standards were notoriously the worst in the Empire. Paul had need to remind both communities (1 Cor. 6) of the gravity of sins of sexual indulgence; there was always the danger of poorly instructed converts returning to pagan ways.

Possibly the earthquake at Philippi had been only one of many in that region; in any case there was plenty of opportunity for practical charity to people in poverty and distress. Paul's mention of the extent of the charity practised by the Thessalonians shows that a considerable time must have elapsed since their conversion.

The earthquake disasters had left an atmosphere of anxiety and near panic in Macedonia. This had led to one very serious social upset: a number of Christians considered it frivolous to

5*

affairs, working with your hands as we bade you; thus your life will win respect from the world around you, and you will not need to depend on others.

Make no mistake, brethren, about those who have gone to their rest; you are not to lament over them, as the rest of the world does, with no hope to live by. We believe, after all, that Jesus underwent death and rose again; just so, when Jesus comes back, God will bring back those who have found rest through him. This we can tell you as a message from the Lord himself: those of us who are still left alive to greet the Lord's coming will not reach the goal before those who have gone to their rest. No, the Lord himself will come down from heaven to summon us, with an archangel crying aloud and the trumpet of God sounding; and first of all the dead will rise up, those who died in Christ. Only after that shall we, who are still left alive, be taken up into the clouds, be swept away to meet the Lord in the air, and they will bear us company. And so we shall be with the Lord for ever. Tell one another this for your consolation.

There is no need, brethren, to write to you about the times and the seasons of all this; you are keeping it clearly in mind, without being told, that the day of the Lord will come like a thief in the night. It is just when men are saying, 'All quiet, all safe,' that doom will fall upon them suddenly, like the pangs that come to a woman in travail, and there will be no escape from it. Whereas you, brethren, are not living in the darkness, for the day to take you by surprise, like a thief; no, you are all born to the light, born to the day; we do not belong to the night and its darkness. We must not sleep on, then, like the rest of the world, we must watch and keep sober; night is the sleeper's time for sleeping, the drunkard's time for drinking; we must keep sober, like men of

be working, when the end of the world might come at any moment. Far better to look to the good of their souls, to be engaged in prayer when the Lord Jesus came in judgment.

The Dead Will Rise At Christ's Coming. Our knowledge of what will happen when the world comes to an end is very meagre; God's revelation on this point is contained in the Creed: 'He shall come to judge the living and the dead.' The extent to which the detail provided in Matthew 24, 2 Peter 3, and Thessalonians is meant to be a description of things as they will actually happen is not agreed on by the experts.

It would seem that the trumpet, archangel, and clouds are only scenic properties meant to provide an atmosphere of awe in the presence of divine intervention in human affairs; they probably come from God's manifestation of power and majesty at Mt. Sinai, as recorded in the Book of Exodus; our Lord used the same terminology in describing the fall of Jerusalem (Mt. 24, 29-31).

The Thessalonians probably pictured the return of Christ at the end of the world as similar to the triumphal procession of the emperor on a state visit to their city. One matter was worrying them: Would not those who had died miss the pageant of Christ's triumphal return? It would all be over before they rose again from the grave. This was the question sent back by Timothy.

In answer, Paul quotes words of Jesus unrecorded elsewhere in Scripture: The resurrection will precede the last judgment. This satisfied the Thessalonians, but it has raised two more problems for modern readers.

Did Paul mean that those who would be alive on the last day would be glorified without first undergoing death? Yes. In 1 Corinthians 15, 51 he states it explicitly: 'We shall not all fall asleep, but we shall all be changed.'

the daylight. We must put on our breastplate, the breastplate of faith and love, our helmet, which is the hope of salvation. God has not destined us for vengeance; he means us to win salvation through our Lord Jesus Christ, who has died for our sakes, that we, waking or sleeping, may find life with him. Go on, then, encouraging one another and building up one another's faith.

Brethren, we would ask you to pay deference to those who work among you, those who have charge of you in the Lord, and give you directions; make it a rule of charity to hold them in special esteem, in honour of the duty they perform. Maintain unity among yourselves. And, brethren, let us make this appeal to you: warn the vagabonds, encourage the faint-hearted, support the waverers, be patient towards all. See to it that nobody repays injury with injury; you must aim always at what is best, for one another and for all around you. Joy be with you always. Never cease praying. Give thanks upon all occasions; this is what God expects of you all in Christ Jesus. Do not stifle the utterances of the Spirit, do not hold prophecy in low esteem; and yet you must scrutinize it all carefully, retaining only what is good, and rejecting all that has a look of evil about it. So may the God of peace sanctify you wholly, keep spirit and soul and body unimpaired, to greet the coming of our Lord Jesus Christ without reproach. The God who called you is true to his promise; he will not fail you. Brethren, pray for us. Greet all the brethren with the kiss of saints. I adjure you in the Lord's name to see that this letter is read out to all our brethren. The grace of our Lord Jesus Christ be with you.

Did Paul think he would live until judgment day? No. He knew no more of the time of Christ's coming than any other human being: 'It is known to none, not even to the angels in heaven' (Mt. 24, 36). But with his Mystical Body outlook he could identify himself with those Christians who would be alive, just as the Master had identified himself with those Christians Paul had been persecuting: 'Saul, Saul, why do you persecute me?'

Directions To Church Authorities. Jason was probably the leader of the Thessalonian community; together with the other priests and deacons he would be the recipient of Paul's letter, delivered by some Christian making the journey from Corinth. It was his duty to see that this letter was read publicly to his flock and to make provision for its advice to be carried out.

There is no close sequence in this final paragraph. Paul moves from one point to another, giving practical counsels of conduct. Most of these are concerned with the two main lines of thought already treated: the persecution raging against the Christians and their anxiety over the return of the Lord. Paul warns them against the danger of despondency; they must be strong not faint-hearted in face of persecution. They must not be vindictive against their persecutors.

His reference to 'utterances of the Spirit' indicates that the Thessalonian church enjoyed these special gifts of the Holy Ghost, such as speaking in foreign tongues, reading men's hearts, and miraculous powers of healing, which we find recounted in great detail later in the Corinthian church (1 Cor., 12-14). Paul warns them that Satan can disguise himself as an angel of light.

Second Letter to the Thessalonians

Paul and Silvanus and Timothy, to the church assembled at Thessalonica in God our Father, and the Lord Jesus Christ; from God, our Father, and the Lord Jesus Christ, grace be yours and peace. We owe a constant debt of thanksgiving to God, brethren, on your behalf; we have good reason for it, when your faith thrives so well, and your love for one another exceeds all measure; our own boasting, as we visit the churches of God, is of your perseverance and your faith amidst all the persecutions and trials which you have to endure. It will be a proof of the just award God makes, when he finds you worthy of a place in his kingdom, the kingdom for which you are prepared to suffer. Or do you doubt that there is justice with God, to repay with affliction those who afflict you, and you, the afflicted, with that rest which will be ours too? But that is for the day when the Lord Jesus appears from heaven, with angels to proclaim his power; with fire flaming about him, as he pours out vengeance on those who do not acknowledge God, on those who refuse obedience to the gospel of our Lord Jesus. The presence of the Lord, and the majesty of his power, will condemn them to eternal punishment, when he comes to show how glorious he is in his saints, how marvellously he has dealt with all the faithful, that our witness should have reached you Gentiles, and found belief! Yes, there will be justice when that day comes. It is with this in view that we are always praying for you, praying that God may find you worthy of your vocation, and ripen by his influence all your love of well-doing, all the activity of your faith. So may the name of our Lord Jesus be glorified in you, and you glorified in him, through the grace given by our God and by the Lord Jesus Christ.

But there is one entreaty we would make of you, brethren, as you look forward to the time when our Lord Jesus Christ

The Second Coming of Christ

God's Justice On Judgment Day.   Paul had not remained in Corinth after writing the First Letter to the Thessalonians. He set off to the north to visit the churches of Nicopolis, Apollonia, and Dyrrachium. It was probably about three months before he returned to Corinth. He had kept away from Thessalonica, so as not to stir up a more violent outburst from the Jews there. He surely did not expect to find such perturbing news of that church awaiting him at Corinth.

Communication between Corinth and Thessalonica was frequent both by land and sea. Some Corinthian merchants were just back from Thessalonica and lost no time in informing Paul of the disturbing picture there: Christians were sitting round idle, expecting the end of the world at any moment. They had become so despondent over the persecution that they had almost lost faith in a just judge who would redress their wrongs.

It is this last point that Paul takes up first: he describes what will take place at the last judgment. His teaching is that of Jesus: 'Will not God give redress to his elect, when they are crying out to him, day and night? Will he not be impatient with their wrongs? I tell you, he will give them redress with all speed.'

A modern audience would expect a reference to the particular judgment at death, rather than the more remote general judgment. Paul's line of thought shows how preoccupied the world was with expectancy of the end of the world; it was the mood of the moment. The emphasis was on the corporate existence of the Mystical Body, not on the fate of the individual. It was the atmosphere in which people of those times lived; with us the emphasis has shifted to personal retribution.

Why the Second Coming is Delayed.   Paul's rebel, 'the champion of wickedness,' is better known as Antichrist (a title

will come, and gather us in to himself. Do not be terrified out of your senses all at once, and thrown into confusion, by any spiritual utterance, any message or letter purporting to come from us, which suggests that the day of the Lord is close at hand. Do not let anyone find the means of leading you astray. The apostasy must come first; the champion of wickedness must appear first, destined to inherit perdition. This is the rebel who is to lift up his head above every divine name, above all that men hold in reverence, till at last he enthrones himself in God's temple, and proclaims himself as God. Do not you remember my telling you of this, before I left your company? At present there is a power (you know what I mean) which holds him in check, so that he may not show himself before the time appointed to him; meanwhile, the conspiracy of revolt is already at work; only, he who checks it now will be able to check it, until he is removed from the enemy's path. Then it is that the rebel will show himself; and the Lord Jesus will destroy him with the breath of his mouth, overwhelming him with the brightness of his presence. He will come, when he comes, with all Satan's influence to aid him; there will be no lack of power, of counterfeit signs and wonders; and his wickedness will deceive the souls that are doomed, to punish them for refusing that fellowship in the truth which would have saved them. That is why God is letting loose among them a deceiving influence, so that they give credit to falsehood; he will single out for judgment all those who refused credence to the truth, and took their pleasure in wrong-doing.

We must always give thanks in your name, brethren whom the Lord has so favoured. God has picked you out as the firstfruits in the harvest of salvation, by sanctifying your spirits and convincing you of his truth; he has called you, through

found only in John's Epistles), the beast of the sea whose number is 666 (Apoc. 13). Paul, and John's Apocalypse, present Antichrist as an individual, but our Lord, and John's Epistles, as a collectivity: 'Many false teachers have appeared in the world; here is the deceiver you were warned against, here is Antichrist' (2 Jn. 7; 1 Jn. 2, 18-22; 4, 3; Mk. 13, 22). So that many commentators think Paul is personifying a thing (just as he personifies Sin in Romans 6), that Antichrist is merely the personification of the forces of evil perpetually at war with Christ and his Church.

The Bible is full of battles, the imagery of war runs through all its pages; the victory of Christ over sin is pictured as a battle. But this biblical imagery is not to be taken literally; our Lord's victory will be spiritual not material. That this final battle is not imminent, Paul proves by a reference to some obstacle which was well known to the Thessalonians; but we today are uncertain, and can only guess at its identity.

Holzner takes the obstacle to be Roman law and order checking the rebel and his revolt. Prat thinks that the archangel Michael is the power in the path of Antichrist, the tool of Satan. Knox holds that the obstacle in the way of Christ's Coming is the unbelief of the Jews. In favour of this is Romans 11, 25-26, where Paul states that the Jews must be converted before Christ returns. It is a condition easily verifiable by the Thessalonians: the Jewish persecution now raging there shows how far the Jews are from conversion to the faith.

The Grace Of Faith. This rather frightening picture of the end of the world, all the discussion about the proximity of the day of judgment, has given a wrong emphasis to the Thessalonians' spiritual life. So Paul here recalls them to the mes-

our preaching, to attain the glory of our Lord Jesus Christ.
Stand firm, then, brethren, and hold by the traditions you
have learned, in word or in writing, from us. So may our
Lord Jesus Christ himself, so may God, our Father, who has
shown such love to us, giving us unfailing comfort and welcome hope through his grace, encourage your hearts, and
confirm you in every right habit of action and speech.

And now, brethren, let us have your prayers, that the
word of the Lord may run its course trimphantly with us,
as it does with you; and that we may be preserved from
malicious interference; the faith does not reach all hearts.
But the Lord keeps faith with us; he will strengthen you,
and keep you from all harm. We are sure of you in the Lord,
sure that you are doing and will do as we bid you; may the
Lord direct you where the love of God and the patience of
Christ show you the way.

Only, brethren, we charge you in the name of our Lord
Jesus Christ to have nothing to do with any brother who
lives a vagabond life, contrary to the tradition which we
handed on; you do not need to be reminded how, on our
visit, we set you an example to be imitated; we were no vagabonds ourselves. We would not even be indebted to you for
our daily bread, we earned it in weariness and toil, working
with our hands, night and day, so as not to be a burden to
any of you; not that we are obliged to do so, but as a model
for your own behaviour; you were to follow our example. The
charge we gave you on our visit was that the man who refuses
to work must be left to starve. And now we are told that there
are those among you who live in idleness, neglecting their
own business to mind other people's. We charge all such, we
appeal to them in the Lord Jesus Christ, to earn their bread
by going on calmly with their work. For yourselves, brethren,

sage he originally preached to them; he puts things in their right proportion again. The really important element in the Christian picture of life is their belief in a loving Father who has chosen them out, the first among all pagans in this part of the world; it is the gifts of faith, hope, and charity that supply life to their souls, and motivation to act according to God's divine will.

And it is not a healthy sign for them to be always thinking of themselves and the trials they are undergoing. The power to stand firm under assault comes from Christ, who was patient when insulted; it does not depend on their own strength. As members of the Mystical Body they should have the welfare of other churches in their prayers. By this appeal for prayers, Paul takes their minds off their own trials and encourages them to assist the Corinthians, now under assault from the Jews.

Go On Calmly With Daily Work. This strike among the Christian dockworkers of Thessalonica must be the most unusual in history. The space given it by Paul seems to indicate that it was widespread: workmen in every trade were idle, waiting for the day of judgment to dawn; they were a drain on the community. Spiritually it was worse still: our Lord taught his followers how to endure and profit from persecution, but there is no Christian way of sanctifying idleness.

Paul reminds these stop-workers of his own persistent toil in their midst; they are to model their conduct on his way of life, just as he took the labouring Carpenter of Nazareth as the pattern of his own life.

Paul is also a realist; and he gives two practical means of restoring these idlers to their right senses. Do not give them anything to eat; let the pinch of hunger bring them back to a saner view of things. Show displeasure at their conduct by

never weary of doing good. If anybody refuses to listen to what we have said in our letter, he is to be a marked man; avoid his company till he is ashamed of himself, correcting him like a brother, not treating him as an enemy. And may the Lord of peace grant you peace at all times and in all ways; the Lord be with you all.

Here is Paul's greeting in his own hand; the signature which is to be found in all my letters; this is my handwriting. The grace of our Lord Jesus Christ be with you all.

Second Missionary Journey
continued

Then, when Gallio was proconsul of Achaia, the Jews made a concerted attack on Paul, and dragged him before the judgment seat. 'This fellow,' they said, 'is persuading men to worship God in a manner the law forbids.' Paul was just opening his mouth to speak, when Gallio said to the Jews, 'It would be only right for me to listen to you Jews with patience, if we had here some wrong done, or some malicious contrivance; but the questions you raise are a matter of words and names, of the law which holds good among yourselves. You must see to it; I have no mind to try such cases.' And he drove them away from the judgment seat. Thereupon there was a general onslaught upon Sosthenes, the ruler of the synagogue, who was beaten before the judgment seat; but all this caused Gallio no concern.

Paul stayed on many days yet, then took leave of the brethren and sailed off to Syria; before he left Cenchrae he shaved his head, since he was under a vow. He took Priscilla

cutting them off from the Christian community; the absence of social life and contact with normal Christian living may wake them up to the folly of their present line of conduct.

Paul took the pen from Silas and added the last few lines in his own handwriting; this was his usual custom at the end of his letters. It was all the more necessary in this letter, because of the spurious documents being circulated in his name.

From Corinth to Jerusalem 52 A.D.

Paul Dragged Before Gallio.   The Jews watched with hostile eyes the growing Christian Church at Corinth; converts were flowing into it from all classes of society, but especially from the dockworkers. Paul's enemies waited patiently for the opportune moment. The arrival of a new governor seemed the right time to close in on Paul and present him as an opponent of religion.

Gallio was a cultured Roman gentleman, a brother of the famous Seneca, then tutor to Nero, the next emperor. What the Jews did not know was that Gallio shared his brother's dislike for the Jewish race. So the attack on Paul misfired and turned into an anti-Semitic demonstration. The extra number of Jews at Corinth since their expulsion from Rome two years before had caused tension in the Jew-Gentile situation. The Gentiles took this opportunity to show their resentment by beating up the leader of the Jews. It did him good too; we find him a disciple of Paul before long.

and Aquila with him, but left them behind when he reached Ephesus. He himself went to the synagogue and reasoned with the Jews, who asked him to make a longer stay. But he would not consent; he said, as he took leave of them, 'I will come back to you again, if it is God's will,' and departed from Ephesus by sea.

Third Missionary Journey

On landing at Caesarea, he went up from there to greet the church, then went down again to Antioch, where he spent some time; he left it to make an orderly progress through the Phrygian region of Galatia, where he established the disciples in the faith.

Meanwhile a Jewish visitor came to Ephesus, Apollo by name; he was born in Alexandria, and was an eloquent man, well grounded in the scriptures. He had had instruction in the way of the Lord; and, with a spirit full of zeal, used to preach and teach about the life of Jesus accurately enough, although he knew of no baptism except that of John. So he began to speak out boldly in the synagogue, whereupon Priscilla and Aquila, who had been listening, made friends with him, and explained the way of God to him more particularly. He was meaning to continue his journey into Achaia; in this the brethren encouraged him, and wrote asking the disciples there to welcome him who had had the grace to believe. His visit was a welcome reinforcement to the believers; he spared no pains to refute the Jews publicly, proving from the scriptures that Jesus was the Christ.

It was while Apollo was away at Corinth that Paul finished

Paul left for Jerusalem by ship from the eastern port of Corinth, called Cenchrae. We know the name of only one person there, a devout church worker, Phoebe. Paul would carry part of the hair of his shaven head up to Jerusalem to be burnt on the altar there; it was the fulfilment of a Nazirite vow (Num. 6).

From Antioch to Ephesus 53-57 A.D.

Apollo Instructed About Baptism. Although the name of Jerusalem does not occur here in the narrative, there is no doubt that Paul went there from the seaport of Caesarea. Despite flourishing Christian foundations in Galatia, Macedonia, and Achaia, Paul still venerated the mother church of the Cenacle; not only the place but the Jewish community who worshipped the Lord there ranked high in Paul's esteem.

While waiting out the winter in Antioch, Paul made some rearrangements in the group of disciples to accompany him on his third missionary journey. Silas, a former disciple of Peter, rejoined the prince of the apostles; ten years later he is still with Peter at Rome (1 Pet. 5, 12). His place was taken by Titus, a brother of Luke whom Paul had left in charge at Philippi. Luke never mentions his own name or Titus in the Acts; it was bad literary form for a writer of those times to speak of himself or his family. Timothy stayed with Paul as his right hand and closest disciple. The group was joined by Gaius at Derbe, on the road to Ephesus.

It was probably not till 54 A.D. that Paul arrived at Ephesus. He could not have left Antioch till about June (the passes over the Taurus Mountains were closed until early summer);

his journey through the inland country, and came to Ephesus. He met some disciples there and asked them, 'Was the Holy Spirit given to you, when you learned to believe?'

'Why,' they said, 'nobody even mentioned to us the existence of a Holy Spirit.'

'What baptism, then, did you receive?' Paul asked.

And they said, 'John's baptism.'

So Paul told them, 'John baptized to bring men to repentance; but he bade the people have faith in one who was to come after him, that is, in Jesus.'

On hearing this, they received baptism in the name of the Lord Jesus; and when Paul laid his hands upon them, the Holy Spirit came down on them, and they spoke with tongues, and prophesied. In all, these men were about twelve in number.

And now he went into the synagogue, and for three months spoke boldly there, reasoning with them and trying to convince them about the kingdom of God; but since there were some who hardened their hearts and refused belief, discrediting the Way in the eyes of the people, he left them, and withdrew his own disciples, holding disputations daily in the school of Tyrannus. This lasted for two years, so that the Lord's word came to the ears of all those who lived in Asia, both Jews and Greeks. And God did miracles through Paul's hands that were beyond all wont; so much so, that when handkerchiefs or aprons which had touched his body were taken to the sick, they got rid of their diseases, and evil spirits were driven out.

Some of the wandering Jewish exorcists took it upon themselves to invoke the name of the Lord Jesus over those who were possessed by evil spirits, with the words, 'I conjure you in the name of Jesus, the name that is preached by Paul.'

it would take the rest of the year to visit his Galatian churches. He had not to search for lodgings in Ephesus; Aquila and Priscilla were waiting, ready to give him a warm welcome.

They could hardly wait to tell him of a most unusual and distinguished visitor who had come in one day on a ship from Alexandria in Egypt, and had now gone on to Corinth. His name was Apollo. A pity Paul had missed him; he was a most learned gentleman.

Paul soon came across some results of Apollo's work in Ephesus—twelve poorly instructed converts. The incident is given at length because of the Apollo-Paul factions in Corinth. Luke wished to show that Paul was justified in rebaptizing Apollo's converts; 'John's baptism' was not the Christian sacrament at all.

Paul's Victory Over Black Magic. Paul's three years at Ephesus is his longest stay at any of his missionary centres. It corresponds in Paul's life to the Galilean ministry of our Lord: large crowds, miracles, continual preaching, and a strategic location. Ephesus, even more than the lake of Galilee, was on the crossroads of the world. It was the capital of Asia, the most populous province in the Roman Empire; roads branched out from this busy port to more than 500 cities and towns of Asia.

For the first time in his career, Paul found that the private homes of his converts were inadequate to hold the crowds that were streaming in for instruction. His first convert was Epaenetus, 'the first offering Asia made to Christ' (Rom. 16, 5); he was the herald of a mighty army that forced its way into the kingdom at Ephesus. To cope with this, Paul gave public classes of instruction in the hall of a philosopher convert, Tyrannus. An early tradition says he lectured daily from just

Among these were the seven sons of Skeva, one of the Jewish chief priests. And the evil spirit answered, 'Jesus I recognize, Paul I know well enough; but you, what are you?' And with that, the man who was possessed by the evil spirit ran at them and got the better of them, defying the power of both; so that they fled from the house naked and wounded.

This came to the ears of every Jew and Greek living at Ephesus; fear fell upon them all, and the name of the Lord Jesus was held in great honour. Many believers came forward, confessing their evil practices and giving a full account of them; and a number of those who followed magic arts made their books into a heap and burned them in public; the value of these was reckoned up, and proved to be fifty thousand silver pieces. So, irresistibly, the word of the Lord spread and prevailed.

When all this was over, the thought in Paul's heart was to go to Jerusalem, first travelling through Macedonia and Achaia: 'When I have been there,' he said, 'I must go on and see Rome.' And he sent on two of those who ministered to him, Timothy and Erastus, into Macedonia, but waited for a while himself in Asia.

First Letter to the Corinthians

Paul, whom the will of God has called to be an apostle of Jesus Christ, and Sosthenes, who is their brother, send greetings to the church of God at Corinth, to those who have been sanctified in Jesus Christ, and called to be holy; with all those who invoke the name of our Lord Jesus Christ, in every dependency of theirs, and so of ours. Grace and peace be yours from God, who is our Father, and from the Lord Jesus Christ.

before midday until mid-afternoon; which means that he worked all through the daily siesta period.

Ephesus was also a holy city, like Athens and Jerusalem. It was the home of Asiatic magic, and all the vice and mystery that went with the magic of the Orient. An incident is recorded by Luke to show how powerful the names of both Jesus and Paul became in the war with demons and black magic. It eventually led to a public burning of much of the occult literature of Ephesus.

In writing to the Corinthians from Ephesus Paul tells them of both his amazing success for Christ and of the fierce opposition he encountered: 'A great and promising opportunity lies open to me, and strong forces oppose me; death is daily at my side.' His flourishing congregation in Asia will come back into the picture of his life in five of his remaining letters—Ephesians, Colossians, Philemon, 1 and 2 Timothy. After his Roman imprisonment he will send his favourite disciple to represent him at Ephesus. This city is also famous as the home of St. John the apostle, in his later days; his three Letters and the Fourth Gospel were written here.

Problems of Christian Living

There was no convert class tonight at the home of Aquila and Priscilla on the Ephesian waterfront. Sosthenes was seated at a table, pen in hand, as Paul paced up and down the room; the Holy Spirit was there too, enlightening the mind of Paul so that he would dictate only what God wanted him to tell the church at Corinth.

This was not the first letter to Corinth; Paul had sent off a

I give thanks to my God continually in your name for that grace of God which has been bestowed upon you in Jesus Christ; that you have become rich, through him, in every way, in eloquence and in knowledge of every sort; so fully has the message of Christ established itself among you. And now there is no gift in which you are still lacking; you have only to look forward to the revealing of our Lord Jesus Christ. He will strengthen your resolution to the last, so that no charge will lie against you on the day when our Lord Jesus Christ comes. The God, who has called you into the fellowship of his Son, Jesus Christ our Lord, is faithful to his promise.

Only I entreat you, brethren, as you love the name of our Lord Jesus Christ, use, all of you, the same language. There must be no divisions among you; you must be restored to unity of mind and purpose. The account I have of you, my brethren, from Chloe's household, is that there are dissensions among you; each of you, I mean, has a cry of his own, 'I am for Paul, I am for Apollo, I am for Kephas, I am for Christ.' What, has Christ been divided up? Was it Paul that was crucified for you? Was it in Paul's name that you were baptized? Thank God I did not baptize any of you except Crispus and Gaius; so that no one can say it was in my name you were baptized. (Yes, and I did baptize the household of Stephanas; I do not know that I baptized anyone else.)

Christ did not send me to baptize; he sent me to preach the gospel; not with an orator's cleverness, for so the cross of Christ might be robbed of its force. To those who court their own ruin, the message of the cross is but folly; to us, who are on the way to salvation, it is the evidence of God's

previous note (1 Cor. 5, 9), but it has not come down to us. Actually he wrote four letters to Corinth; a second lost letter seems to be referred to in 2 Corinthians 2, 4 and 7, 8. The two surviving letters are really the Second and Fourth Letters to the Corinthians.

Sosthenes is probably the same man who persecuted Paul in Corinth; most likely he is a convert of Apollo, at this moment also in Ephesus. Paul associates Sosthenes with himself to show that there is no real rivalry between himself and Apollo. The reason why he does not use Apollo's name is probably that Apollo was unco-operative; he would not submit to Paul's authority.

Rival Parties of Paul and Apollo. Our Lord's final prayer at the Last Supper was that his Church should manifest the same unity as that possessed by Father, Son, and Holy Ghost: 'That they should all be one, as we are one.' It was as essential to the life of the Corinthian church as it was to the life of the Blessed Trinity.

The seamless robe of Christ was split right down the middle in Corinth; there were the converts of Paul and the converts of Apollo, and they were like two parties at war with each other instead of brothers living in peace and unity. The Paulines had a second champion in Paul's brother apostle, Peter (Paul refers to him by his Aramaic name, Kephas); the party of Apollo, not to be outdone, claimed Christ as their champion.

Preaching of Paul and Apollo Contrasted. With his Christ-like charity Paul does not mention Apollo by name in this paragraph; but there seems little doubt that it is Apollo's presentation of Christianity that he opposes when he speaks of human wisdom and philosophy. There is only one gospel, and

power. So we read in scripture, 'I will confound the wisdom of wise men, disappoint the calculations of the prudent.' What has become of the wise men, the scribes, the philosophers of this age we live in? Must we not say that God has turned our worldly wisdom to folly? When God showed us his wisdom, the world, with all its wisdom, could not find its way to God; and now God would use a foolish thing, our preaching, to save those who will believe in it. Here are the Jews asking for signs and wonders, here are the Greeks intent on their philosophy; but what we preach is Christ crucified; to the Jews, a discouragement, to the Gentiles, mere folly; but to us who have been called, Jew and Gentile alike, Christ the power of God, Christ the wisdom of God. So much wiser than men is God's foolishness; so much stronger than men is God's weakness.

Consider, brethren, the circumstances of your own calling; not many of you are wise, in the world's fashion, not many powerful, not many well born. No, God has chosen what the world holds foolish, so as to abash the wise, God has chosen what the world holds weak, so as to abash the strong. God has chosen what the world holds base and contemptible, nay, has chosen what is nothing, so as to bring to nothing what is now in being; no human creature was to have any ground for boasting, in the presence of God. It is from him that you take your origin, through Christ Jesus, whom God gave us to be all our wisdom, our justification, our sanctification, and our atonement; so that the scripture might be fulfilled, 'If anyone boasts, let him make his boast in the Lord.'

So it was, brethren, that when I came to you and preached God's message to you, I did so without any high pretensions to eloquence, or to philosophy. I had no thought of bringing you any other knowledge than that of Jesus Christ, and of him as crucified. It was with distrust of myself, full of anxious

*it is centred on the historical fact of the crucifixion. If any-
one tampered with this essential message, Paul spoke out in
no uncertain terms:* 'Though it were we ourselves, though it
were an angel from heaven that should preach to you a gospel
other than the gospel we preached to you, a curse upon him!'

Apollo was not a heretic, but his language and ideas were
borrowed from the Jewish scriptures and Greek philosophy.
His picture of Christ was coloured by the Old Testament
rather than the happenings in Galilee and Jerusalem; Jesus
was presented as a victorious king, not a crucified redeemer.
The atmosphere of his sermons was not the shouting mob in
Pilate's palace, it was that of Psalm 109: 'The Lord will make
your empire spring up like a branch out of Sion. From birth
princely state shall be yours, holy and glorious; you are my
son, born like the dew before the day-star rises. At your right
hand, the Lord will beat down kings in the day of his vengeance: he will pass sentence on the nations.'

For Paul, the crucified Master was the model of Christian
living: 'With Christ I hang upon the cross.' Apollo was inclined to neglect the cross and present Christianity as an easy
way of life. Take the problem of food offered to idols, in
chapter 8. Apollo would solve the problem by saying that an
idol has no real existence; the food offered to it is no different
from any other food. Where Apollo made an ingenious distinction, Paul saw the person of Christ in the scrupulous Christian:
'When you sin against your brethren, by injuring their doubtful consciences, you sin against Christ.'

The Corinthians were, for the most part, slaves and dockworkers; such people were hardly the right material to be made
into philosophers by Professor Apollo. Not that this should
bother them, seeing that our Lord's followers were simple

fear, that I approached you; my preaching, my message depended on no persuasive language, devised by human wisdom, but rather on the proof I gave you of spiritual power. God's power, not man's wisdom, was to be the foundation of your faith.

There is, to be sure, a wisdom which we make known among those who are fully grounded; but it is not the wisdom of this world, or of this world's rulers, whose power is to be abrogated. What we make known is the wisdom of God, his secret, kept hidden till now; so, before the ages, God had decreed, reserving glory for us. (None of the rulers of this world could read his secret, or they would not have crucified him to whom all glory belongs.) So we read of, 'Things no eye has seen, no ear has heard, no human heart conceived, the welcome God has prepared for those who love him.' To us, then, God has made a revelation of it through the Spirit; there is no depth in God's nature so deep that the Spirit cannot find it out. Who else can know a man's thoughts, except the man's own spirit that is within him? So no one else can know God's thoughts, but the Spirit of God. And what we have received is no spirit of worldly wisdom; it is the Spirit that comes from God, to make us understand God's gifts to us; gifts which we make known, not in such words as human wisdom teaches, but in words taught us by the Spirit, matching what is spiritual with what is spiritual. Mere man with his natural gifts cannot take in the thoughts of God's Spirit; they seem mere folly to him, and he cannot grasp them, because they demand a scrutiny which is spiritual. Whereas the man who has spiritual gifts can scrutinize everything, without being subject, himself, to any other man's scrutiny. 'Who has entered into the mind of the Lord, so as to be able to instruct him?' And Christ's mind is ours.

men and women, with no pretensions to human wisdom. Christian greatness does not come from learning, but by union with Christ crucified; he is himself the source of all wisdom and knowledge, surpassing and reducing all human learning to nothing.

True Divine Wisdom. Aristotle, the greatest of all Greek philosophers, defined wisdom as the knowledge of principles and first causes. It yielded its secrets only to those who engaged in a long, arduous process of reasoning; it gave an imperfect knowledge of the Deity through the study of created things. But it did not bring man to union with God; that is not the result of intellectual activity; that comes only through charity, the unifying love that springs from man's will. This is true wisdom, a Christian philosophy of life far surpassing the worldly wisdom of the Greeks.

A man does not have to be learned to acquire this Christian wisdom; it is accessible to slaves and stevedores, which most of the Corinthians were. Understanding of its secrets comes from the indwelling of the Holy Spirit, through the gift of sanctifying grace. As the Third Person of the Blessed Trinity, the Holy Spirit reveals divine wisdom to the Christian, and inspires him in the expression of divine truths and principles.

But the great secret of divine wisdom, not revealed to anyone in past times, is that man shares in the life of God himself by membership in the Mystical Body of Christ. Our Lord's life on this earth did not end with his Ascension; he still speaks with the tongues of his followers, heals with the touch of their hands, and sees the things of this world with their eyes. The Christian no longer thinks with his own intellect alone; he has the use of Christ's mind too. It is not mere imitation; it is a real living of Christ's own life.

6

And when I preached to you, I had to approach you as men with natural, not with spiritual thoughts. You were little children in Christ's nursery, and I gave you milk, not meat; you were not strong enough for it. You are not strong enough for it even now; nature still lives in you. Do not these rivalries, these dissensions among you show that nature is still alive, that you are guided by human standards? When one of you says, 'I am for Paul,' and another, 'I am for Apollo,' are not these human thoughts? Why, what is Apollo, what is Paul? Only serving-men, who have brought you faith, brought it to each of you in the measure God granted. It was for me to plant the seed, for Apollo to water it, but it was God who gave the increase. And if so, the man who plants, the man who waters, count for nothing; God is everything, since it is he who gives the increase. This man plants, that man waters; it is all one. And yet either will receive his own wages, in proportion to his own work. You are a field of God's tilling, a structure of God's design; and we are only his assistants.

With what grace God has bestowed on me, I have laid a foundation as a careful architect should; it is left for someone else to build upon it. Only, whoever builds on it must be careful how he builds. The foundation which has been laid is the only one which anybody can lay; I mean Jesus Christ. But on this foundation different men will build in gold, silver, precious stones, wood, grass, or straw, and each man's workmanship will be plainly seen. It is the day of the Lord that will disclose it, since that day is to reveal itself in fire, and fire will test the quality of each man's workmanship. He will receive a reward, if the building he has added on stands firm; if it is burnt up, he will be the loser; and yet he himself will be saved, though only as men are saved by passing through fire.

Teachers Only Lay The Foundations. Only men of mature judgment are able to profit by a highly intellectual and philosophical presentation of Christian truths. Paul now demonstrates how unsuitable such an approach would be to the Corinthians, seeing that they still have the immature outlook of children. The importance they have assigned to himself and Apollo shows that they do not possess a true sense of proportion; they have jumbled up and distorted the true Christian way of life.

What makes the Christian live is not the teaching of Paul or Apollo; it is a vital power communicated to him from God, a sharing in the life of the Trinity. Paul vividly presents the doctrine under the metaphor of a growing plant: all effort on the part of teachers is only secondary; it is God who makes the plant grow.

To illustrate two other aspects of Christian life, Paul changes his metaphor from agriculture to building. It is essential to the permanence of any structure that it have solid foundation; and Paul has clearly shown in his preaching to the Corinthians that the Christian edifice, the Church, has no foundation but Christ. Any attempt to build on worldly wisdom could only raise a tottering structure that would fall when 'the rain fell and the floods came and the winds blew.'

And finally, the Christian himself must make his contribution; man must use the grace put at his disposal by God. This he does by good works, by building up his own personal life in the society where divine providence has placed him. How well each man builds will be tested on judgment day: just as fire tests the materials of a house, so God's scrutiny will test man's deeds. If his spiritual life stands the test, he will be rewarded with heaven; if it does not, he may escape hell by passing through the purifying flames of purgatory.

Do you not understand that you are God's temple, and that God's Spirit has his dwelling in you? If anybody desecrates the temple of God, God will bring him to ruin. It is a holy thing, this temple of God which is nothing other than yourselves. You must not deceive yourselves, any of you, about this. If any of you thinks he is wise, after the fashion of his fellow-men, he must turn himself into a fool, so as to be truly wise. This world's wisdom, with God, is but folly. So we read in scripture, 'I will entrap the wise with their own cunning.' And again, 'The Lord knows the thoughts of the wise, and how empty they are.' Nobody, therefore, should repose his confidence in men. Everything is for you, whether it be Paul, or Apollo, or Kephas, or the world, or life, or death, or the present, or the future; it is all for you, and you for Christ, and Christ for God.

That is how we ought to be regarded, as Christ's servants, and stewards of God's mysteries. And this is what we look for in choosing a steward; we must find one who is trustworthy. Yet for myself, I make little account of your scrutiny, or of any human audit-day; I am not even at pains to scrutinize my own conduct. My conscience does not, in fact, reproach me; but that is not where my justification lies; it is the Lord's scrutiny I must undergo. You do ill, therefore, to pass judgment prematurely, before the Lord's coming; he will bring to light what is hidden in darkness, and reveal the secrets of men's hearts; then each of us will receive his due award from God.

All this, brethren, I have applied to myself and to Apollo, but it is meant for you. The lesson you must learn from our example is, not to go beyond what is laid down for you, one slighting another out of partiality for someone else. After all, friend, who is it that gives you this pre-eminence? What

Dissension Destroys Church Unity. A temple is not a private house but a community building where all the people assemble to worship God. Both the holiness of its members and their unity as a society come from the divine Being whose dwelling place the temple is. By their disputes over Paul and Apollo the Corinthians have so concentrated on the human elements in the Church that they have lost sight of its divine nature. Instead of a society united by the bonds of divine charity, they have made it into two factions at enmity.

Paul's sermons on Christ crucified, Apollo's eloquent discourses on Christian living, are only means put at their disposal to lead them through Christ into the life of God. The Christian temple, the Church, can carry out its true function only when it is centred on God.

Leave Judgment To God. Paul has not come to the people of Corinth in his own name; he is merely a servant of Christ; he is Christ's voice preaching divine truths. All his gifts come from God, the source of all his power to win their souls; and it is to God alone that he must give an account of his stewardship.

In correcting the division that has sprung up at Corinth, he has been forced to compare his own preaching of the gospel with that of Apollo. This does not mean that he has been trying to win them away from Apollo to follow himself; what he really wants is that they shall learn to look to God as the source of all their natural and supernatural gifts. On judgment day they will appear before the divine judge; it is their relation to him that is important, not their adherence to the party of either Paul or Apollo.

It is time the Corinthians examined their consciences and saw the error of their ways. Their partisanship over Paul and

powers have you, that did not come to you by gift? And if
they came to you by gift, why do you boast of them, as if
there was no gift in question?

Well, you are already fully content; already you have grown
rich; already you have come into your kingdom, without waiting for help from us. Would that you had come into your
kingdom indeed; then we should be sharing it with you. As it
is, it seems as if God had destined us, his apostles, to be in
the lowest place of all, like men under sentence of death; such
a spectacle do we present to the whole creation, men and
angels alike. We are fools for Christ's sake, you are so wise;
we are so helpless, you so stout of heart; you are held in honour,
while we are despised. Still, as I write, we go hungry and
thirsty and naked; we are mishandled, we have no home to
settle in, we are hard put to it, working with our own hands.
Men revile us, and we answer with a blessing, persecute us,
and we make the best of it, speak ill of us, and we fall to
entreaty. We are still the world's refuse; everybody thinks
himself well rid of us. I am not writing this to shame you;
you are my dearly loved children, and I would bring you to
a better mind. Yes, you may have ten thousand school-masters
in Christ, but not more than one father; it was I that begot
you in Jesus Christ, when I preached the gospel to you. Follow my example, then, I entreat you.

That is why I have sent Timothy to you, a faithful and
dearly loved son of mine in the Lord; he will remind you
of the path I tread in Christ, the lessons I give to all churches
alike. Some of you have grown contemptuous, thinking that
I would never come to visit you. But I shall be coming to see
you soon, if the Lord is willing, and then I will test, not the
fine words of those who hold me in contempt, but the powers

Apollo has led them into pride and uncharitable criticism: a true Christian should be concerned only with how he stands with God.

A Father Corrects His Children. The Christians at Corinth had a high opinion of the healthy spiritual condition of their young and flourishing church. According to the report they had made in a letter to Paul, they were 'rich in eloquence and in knowledge of every sort.' This is a reference to spiritual gifts, specifically the gift of tongues and wisdom; some spoke foreign tongues in spiritual ecstasy, others stood up and translated these words into Greek, others had an amazing ability to understand and expound the deepest mysteries (1 Cor. 12-14). And they considered these gifts a sign of the spiritual well-being of the church.

To correct this error, Paul goes back to his favourite theme, the Mystical Body of Christ. There must be unity in the body: members must live the same life as that of their head, and they must not be at variance among themselves. The self-satisfied picture of a rich, highly honoured and esteemed community painted by the Corinthians is just the opposite to the life of suffering, humiliation, and danger of death that is the lot of Paul and most of the Christian world. The Master did not predict comfort and honours for his followers: 'If any man has a mind to come my way, let him renounce self, and take up his cross daily, and follow me.'

These words come from the paternal heart of Paul; the Corinthians are his wayward children; his one concern is to win them back to the imitation of their father in Christ; he is not a harsh schoolmaster; his words are inspired by his love for them. But his love does not blind him to their faults; and

they can show. It is power that builds up the kingdom of God, not words. Choose, then; am I to come to you rod in hand, or lovingly, in a spirit of forbearance?

Why, there are reports of incontinence among you, and such incontinence as is not practised even among the heathen; a man taking to himself his father's wife. And you, it seems, have been contumacious over it, instead of deploring it, and expelling the man who has been guilty of such a deed from your company. For myself, though I am not with you in person, I am with you in spirit; and, so present with you, I have already passed sentence on the man who has acted thus. Call an assembly, at which I will be present in spirit, with all the power of our Lord Jesus, and so, in the name of our Lord Jesus, hand over the person named to Satan, for the overthrow of his corrupt nature, so that his spirit may find salvation in the day of the Lord. This good conceit of yourselves is ill grounded. Have you never been told that a little leaven is enough to leaven the whole batch? Rid yourselves of the leaven which remains over, so that you may be a new mixture, still uncontaminated as you are. Has not Christ been sacrificed for us, our paschal victim? Let us keep the feast, then, not with the leaven of yesterday, that was all vice and mischief, but with unleavened bread, with purity and honesty of intent.

In the letter I wrote to you, I told you to avoid the company of fornicators; not meaning everyone in the world around you who is debauched, or a miser and an extortioner, or an idolater; to do that, you would have to cut yourselves off from the world altogether. No, my letter meant that if anyone who is counted among the brethren is debauched, or a miser, or an idolater, or bitter of speech, or a drunkard, or an ex-

he would be unfaithful to his trust and paternal obligations
if he did not threaten to use the stick on those who still hold
out against his apostolic authority.

A Public Sinner Excommunicated. For the good of its members and to preserve its unity, our Lord gave to his Church
the authority to exclude unworthy members: 'If he will not
listen to the church, then count him all one with the heathen
and the publican.' It is this formal act of excommunication in
the name of and with the power of Christ that Paul now pronounces with all the weight of his apostolic authority.

As well as a punishment for his crime against the marriage
laws of the Church, the sentence was also meant as a corrective; by exclusion from the graces of the Mystical Body,
the sinner would learn by experience the need his soul has for
union with Christ, the head, and that Satan cannot satisfy
his spiritual needs. And so he would be moved to repent and
return to his true home, just as the Prodigal Son did.

The crime for which he was being punished was an offence
against the marriage laws of affinity: he had married his step-
mother (his father was probably dead). In the lax moral atmosphere of Corinth, Paul saw danger to the young Christian community in tolerating this scandal. He took a topical illustration
from the current feast of Easter, when all leaven (yeast) was
put out of the houses; leaven was a symbol of corruption.

There is a link with the preceding chapters in Paul's rebuke
to the church authorities in Corinth; they had disregarded his
apostolic authority when he had written, in a previous letter,
ordering the expulsion of the public sinner from the church.
He also corrects a wrong interpretation of his words; some

6*

tortioner, you must avoid his company; you must not even sit at table with him. Why should I claim jurisdiction over those who are without? No, it is for you to pass judgment within your own number, leaving God to judge those who are without. Banish, then, the offender from your company.

Are you prepared to go to law before a profane court, when one of you has a quarrel with another, instead of bringing it before the saints? You know well enough that it is the saints who will pass judgment on the world; and if a world is to abide your judgment, are you unfit to take cognizance of trifling matters? You have been told that we will sit in judgment on angels; how much more, then, over the things of common life? What, when you have these common quarrels to decide, would you appoint as judges men who go for nothing in the Church? That I say to humble you. What, have you really not a single man among you wise enough to decide a claim brought by his own brother? Must two brethren go to law over it, and before a profane court? And indeed, it is a defect in you at the best of times, that you should have quarrels among you at all. How is it that you do not prefer to put up with wrong, prefer to suffer loss? Instead of that you commit wrong, you inflict loss, and at a brother's expense. Yet you know well enough that wrong-doers will not inherit God's kingdom. Make no mistake about it; it is not the debauched, the idolaters, the adulterous, it is not the sinners against nature, the misers, the drunkards, the bitter of speech, the extortioners that will inherit the kingdom of God. That is what some of you once were; but now you have been washed clean, now you have been sanctified, now you have been justified in the name of our Lord Jesus Christ, by the Spirit of the God we serve.

thought he meant that they should avoid the company of all sinners, whether Christian or pagan. But such is not the nature and function of the Church; it must mix with pagans in order to influence and convert them: 'I have come to save the world, not to pass sentence on the world.'

Lawsuits Before Pagan Courts.   The reference to judging, at the end of the previous paragraph, leads Paul to mention here another scandal in Corinth. He finds the solution of this problem of Christian litigation in the doctrine of the Mystical Body: a Christian lives with the life of Christ and shares in all his activities. He not only hangs with Christ on the cross; he dies with him, rises again with him, ascends with him and sits enthroned with him above the heavens. At his Second Coming, our Lord will demonstrate his authority to judge the living and the dead, both men and angels. The Christian as a member of Christ also enjoys this judicial power; it is his duty to exercise it, and not submit Christian cases to the judgment of heathen courts.

But Paul is not content to leave it there; he goes to the cause of these quarrels among Christians (whom he refers to as 'saints' and 'brethren'). He traces it all back to their self-interest and want of the virtue of charity. They have forgotten the teaching of their head and master: 'Blessed are the patient; blessed are the merciful; blessed are the peace-makers, they shall be counted the children of God. . . If a man strikes you on your right cheek, turn the other cheek also towards him; if he is ready to go to law with you over your coat, let him have it and your cloak with it. . . Do good to those who hate you; bless those who curse you, and pray for those who treat you insultingly.'

'I am free to do what I will'; yes, but not everything can be done without harm. 'I am free to do what I will,' but I must not abdicate my own liberty. 'Food is meant for our animal nature, and our animal nature claims its food'; true enough, but then, God will bring both one and the other to an end. But your bodies are not meant for debauchery, they are meant for the Lord, and the Lord claims your bodies. And God, just as he has raised our Lord from the dead, by his great power will raise us up too. Have you never been told that your bodies belong to the body of Christ? And am I to take what belongs to Christ and make it one with a harlot? God forbid. Or did you never hear that the man who unites himself to a harlot becomes one body with her? 'The two,' we are told, 'will become one flesh.' Whereas the man who unites himself to the Lord becomes one spirit with him. Keep clear, then, of debauchery. Any other sin a man commits, leaves the body untouched, but the fornicator is committing a crime against his own body. Surely you know that your bodies are the shrines of the Holy Spirit, who dwells in you. And he is God's gift to you, so that you are no longer your own masters. A price was paid to ransom you; glorify God in your bodies.

As for the questions raised in your letter; a man does well to abstain from all commerce with women. But, to avoid the danger of fornication, let every man keep his own wife, and every woman her own husband. Let every man give his wife what is her due, and every woman do the same by her husband; he, not she, claims the right over her body, as she, not he, claims the right over his. Do not starve one another, unless perhaps you do so for a time, by mutual consent, to have more freedom for prayer; come together again, or Satan will tempt

Liberty Does Not Mean Licence. Paul was the great champion of Christian liberty. In the Letter to the Galatians, he defended the freedom of his Gentile converts from the ceremonial prescriptions of the Mosaic law, particularly the rite of circumcision: 'You see, then, brethren, that we are sons of the free woman, not of the slave; such is the freedom Christ has won for us.' But some of his converts in Corinth pushed his teaching too far; they considered that they were free from all moral restraint, that they were no longer bound by any law at all. They even quoted Paul's words to prove it.

In correcting this error, Paul does not appeal to the sanctity and permanence of the moral law; he argues from the sanctity of the human body. At the Incarnation, 'the Word was made flesh'; the Second Person of the Trinity was not united to a human soul only, he took a human body as well. Just as he needed human organs, such as a tongue and hands, to preach and heal with, so his Mystical Body is made up of men, without whom it could not come into contact with and convert mankind, and these men have bodies as well as souls. The whole physical and emotional life of a Christian now belongs to Christ; all his actions are Christ's own actions: he must not profane the body of Christ.

Marriage Is Right and Natural. At this point, Paul begins his reply to the Corinthian letter brought to him at Ephesus by Stephanas, Fortunatus, and Achaicus. The letter contained a number of problems, mostly to do with Christian living, which are answered in the rest of this First Letter to the Corinthians (probably carried back to Corinth by the same three).

The first question was: Is marriage part of the Christian scheme? A rather unexpected question from the lax moral

you, weak as you are. I say this by way of concession; I am
not imposing a rule on you. I wish you were all in the same
state as myself; but each of us has his own endowment from
God, one to live in this way, another in that. To the unmarried, and to the widows, I would say that they will do well
to remain in the same state as myself, but if they have not
the gift of continence, let them marry; better to marry than to
feel the heat of passion. For those who have married already,
the precept holds which is the Lord's precept, not mine; the
wife is not to leave her husband (if she has left him, she
must either remain unmarried, or go back to her own husband
again), and the husband is not to put away his wife.

To those others, I give my own instructions, not the Lord's.
If any of the brethren has a wife, not a believer, who is well
content to live with him, there is no reason why he should
put her away, nor is there any reason for a woman to part with
her husband, not a believer, if he is content to live with
her. The unbelieving husband has shared his wife's consecration, and the unbelieving wife has shared in the consecration of one who is a brother. Were it otherwise, their offspring
would be born under a stain, whereas in fact it is holy. On
the other hand, if the unbelieving partner is for separating, let
them separate; in such a case, the brother or the sister is
under no compulsion. It is in a spirit of peace that God's
call has come to you. There is no knowing whether you, the
wife, will save your husband, whether you, the husband, will
save your wife. No, the part which God has assigned, the
vocation which God has bestowed, is to be the rule in each
case. That is the direction which I am giving all through the
churches.

atmosphere of Corinth; but it is well known that laxity and rigorism can flourish side by side.

Paul's sublime teaching on Christian marriage as a sacramental union based on that of Christ and the Church is given in Ephesians 5: 'You who are husbands must show love to your wives, as Christ showed love to the Church.' But here, to the Corinthians, he is content to point out that there are two vocations in the Church: the married life and the celibate. Both are good, and each has its function to perform in the activities of the body of Christ. The state in life chosen by each individual depends on the graces given him by God; the fact that Paul himself is unmarried does not mean that the state of marriage is not a Christian institution.

Social Status Unchanged By Christianity. By baptism the convert entered a new world; he became a new man with beliefs and practices that set him apart from the pagan world in which he had lived. Paul himself expressed the decisiveness of the break with heathenism: 'You must not consent to be yokefellows with unbelievers. What has innocence to do with lawlessness? What is there in common between light and darkness?'

Applying this general principle to the family, some Corinthians thought that a convert should leave his heathen wife and family. In reply, Paul points out that both wife and children are in close contact with the supernatural graces enjoyed by the believing husband: there is usually a good chance of their conversion.

Starting from this marriage case, Paul proceeds to lay down a general principle: The primary objective of the Church is to save souls, not to change their social condition. The racial and social distinctions, such as slavery, which men think so

If a man is already circumcised when he is called, he is not to disguise it; if he is uncircumcised, he is not to undergo circumcision. There is no virtue either in circumcision or in the want of it; it is keeping the commandments of God that signifies. Everyone has his own vocation, in which he has been called; let him keep to it. Have you been called as a slave? Do not let it trouble you; and if you have the means to become free, make all the more use of your opportunity. If a slave is called to enter Christ's service, he is Christ's freedman; just as the free man, when he is called, becomes the slave of Christ. A price was paid to redeem you; do not enslave yourselves to human masters. Each of you is to remain, brethren, in the condition in which he was called.

About virgins, I have no command from the Lord; but I give you my opinion, as one who is, under the Lord's mercy, a true counsellor. This, then, I hold to be the best counsel in such times of stress, that this is the best condition for men to be in. Are you yoked to a wife? Then, do not go about to free yourself. Are you free of wedlock? Then do not go about to find a wife. Not that you commit sin if you marry; nor, if she marries, has the virgin committed sin. It is only that those who do so will meet with outward distress. But I leave you your freedom. Only, brethren, I would say this; the time is drawing to an end; nothing remains, but for those who have wives to behave as though they had none; those who weep must forget their tears, and those who rejoice their rejoicing, and those who buy must renounce possession; and those who take advantage of what the world offers must not take full advantage of it; the fashion of this world is soon to pass away. And I would have you free from concern. He who is unmarried is concerned with the Lord's claim, asking how he is

important in daily life, are only of secondary importance in the life of the Church. A slave can be united to Christ by membership in his Mystical Body, just as easily as a free man; the Jewish mark of circumcision, of which he is so proud, does not help him at all in putting on the person of Christ.

Paul's statement, 'If the unbelieving partner is for separating, let them separate,' is known as the Pauline Privilege; it is canon 1120 of the Code of Canon Law. In virtue of this privilege, a marriage between pagans can be dissolved if one of them is converted and the other party refuses to live peaceably. The privilege bears Paul's name, because he promulgated it by act of apostolic authority, and not as originating from our Lord during his life on earth.

Virginity Better Than Marriage.   When God chose a virgin to be the mother of his Son he did so with a purpose: he was making known to the world that the state of virginity is superior to that of marriage. By this preference he went against the accepted standards of all antiquity (with the exception of a Jewish sect known as the Essenes); for the pre-Christian world, marriage was the superior state of life. Through the perfect life of a virgin Mother and Son, God wished to restore the right proportion between soul and body; fallen mankind was to be reminded that union with God, the perfect act of love, is in man's soul, not in his body.

The state of virginity not only reminds men of the superiority of spiritual over material things, it also provides a better set of conditions in which the Christian can devote himself entirely to the service of God. By freeing him from the ties of wife and family, he has opportunity for a life of prayer and meditation; he is more suited to missionary work away from home, and can give himself more fully in charitable and edu-

to please the Lord; whereas the married man is concerned with the world's claim, asking how he is to please his wife; and thus he is at issue with himself. So a woman who is free of wedlock, or a virgin, is concerned with the Lord's claim, intent on holiness, bodily and spiritual; whereas the married woman is concerned with the world's claim, asking how she is to please her husband. I am thinking of your own interest when I say this. It is not that I would hold you in a leash; I am thinking of what is suitable for you, and how you may best attend on the Lord without distraction.

And if anyone considers that he is behaving unsuitably towards the girl who is in his charge, on the ground that she is now past her prime, and there is no way of avoiding it, why, let him please himself; there is nothing sinful in it; let them marry. Whereas, if a man remains fixed in his resolution, and makes up his mind to keep the girl who is in his charge unwed, although there is no necessity for it, and he is free to choose for himself, such a man is well advised. Thus, a man is well advised to give his ward in marriage, and still better advised not to give her in marriage.

As for a wife, she is yoked to her husband as long as he lives; if her husband is dead, she is free to marry anyone she will, so long as she marries in the Lord. But more blessed is she, if she remains as she is, in my judgment; and I, too, claim to have the Spirit of God.

And now about meat that has been used in idolatrous worship. We all know, to be sure, what is the truth about it: but knowledge only breeds self-conceit, it is charity that binds the building together. If anyone claims to have superior knowledge, it means that he has not yet attained the knowledge

cational works for the good of the community. In itself a celibate life can be selfish and ill-spent; a religious motive of dedication to the Lord is what raises it to such a high position in the life of the Mystical Body.

Our Lord himself made it clear that a life of virginity is a special vocation: 'It cannot be taken in by everybody, but only by those who have the gift' (Mt. 19, 11). Paul also goes to some trouble to make his teaching clear: no one is forced to adopt a celibate life; it is a matter of counsel, not of obligation.

There is a background of peril to Paul's advice about virginity; he writes as though there were difficult times ahead for the Christians of Corinth; and the dangers he visualizes seem to be beyond the normal problems of Christians in a pagan society. He seems to share that sense of expectancy of the closeness of the Second Coming that was so prominent in early Christian circles; a man unfettered by family ties would be better able to cope with the trying days soon to come.

It would seem that many of the Corinthian girls remained unmarried for this very reason. They were fast becoming a community of old maids. Since husbands were chosen for girls by their parents in ancient times, these parents now enquired what they should do about their aging daughters. Paul allows them to act as they wish; but virginity is preferable.

Meat Sacrificed to Idols. This is the second moral problem submitted to Paul by the Corinthians; it was a daily worry to the housewife as she went about her shopping. The joints of mutton, beef, and pork on display in the butchers' shops had been offered up to one of the various heathen gods in the

which is true knowledge; it is only when a man loves God that God acknowledges him. About meat, then, used in idolatrous worship, we can be sure of this, that a false god has no existence in the order of things; there is one God, and there can be no other. Whatever gods may be spoken of as existing in heaven or on earth (and there are many such gods, many such lords), for us there is only one God, the Father who is the origin of all things, and the end of our being; only one Lord, Jesus Christ, the creator of all things, who is our way to him. But it is not everybody who has this knowledge; there are those who still think of such meat, while they eat it, as something belonging to idolatrous worship, through being accustomed to false gods; their conscience is not easy, and so incurs guilt. And it is not what we eat that gives us our standing in God's sight; we gain nothing by eating, lose nothing by abstaining; it is for you to see that the liberty you allow yourselves does not prove a snare to doubtful consciences. If any of them sees you, who are better instructed, sitting down to eat in the temple of a false god, will not his conscience, all uneasy as it is, be emboldened to approve of eating idolatrously? And thus, through your enlightenment, the doubting soul will be lost; your brother, for whose sake Christ died. When you thus sin against your brethren, by injuring their doubtful consciences, you sin against Christ. Why then, if a mouthful of food is an occasion of sin to my brother, I will abstain from flesh meat perpetually, rather than be the occasion of my brother's sin.

Am I not free to do as I will? Am I not an apostle, have I not seen our Lord Jesus? Are not you yourselves my achievement in the Lord? To others I may not be an apostle, but to you at least I am; why, you are the sign-manual of my

local temples before being put up for sale in the market; this was the general custom of the pagans with all meat used for food. Only a small portion of the meat was burnt in sacrifice; the rest of the carcass was either eaten at a sacrificial banquet there and then in the temple of the god or sold to one of the butchers for the public market.

Apollo had probably been asked about this same matter. With his philosophical approach, he had pointed out that an idol was not a real being; meat offered to a piece of painted wood or carved marble was not changed by such an act; it was exactly the same piece of beef after the heathen sacrifice as it was before. A Christian with such knowledge was in a different position from the ignorant heathen who knew no better: and so he could eat the sacrificial meat with a clear conscience.

While admitting the truth of this argument, Paul does not approve of it as a guide to Christian conduct; for him it is charity, not reason alone, that decides how he acts. Among the slaves and dockers of Corinth there would surely be some who would not follow Apollo's reasoning on the non-existence of heathen gods. Even if there is only one Christian whose conscience is troubled by eating such sacrificial food, that one is enough to make Paul give up his liberty to eat, and even to become a vegetarian for the rest of his life. Paul always remembered his first instruction in the mystery of the Mystical Body on the road to Damascus: any hurt done to a Christian is an attack on Christ himself.

Paul's Right to Maintenance. Paul has not finished with the subject of meat sacrificed to idols. Even though he makes no mention of it in this paragraph, he has not gone on to some other subject. He is illustrating a principle of conduct

apostleship in the Lord. This is the answer I make to those who call me in question. Have we not a right to be provided with food and drink; nay, have we not the right to travel about with a woman who is a sister, as the other apostles do, as the Lord's brethren do, and Kephas? Must I and Barnabas, alone among them, be forbidden to do as much? Why, what soldier ever fought at his own expense? Who would plant a vineyard, and not live on its fruits, or tend a flock, and not live on the milk which the flock yields? This is not a plea of man's invention; the law declares it. When we read in the law of Moses, 'You shall not muzzle the ox that treads out the corn,' must we suppose that God is making provision for oxen? Is it not clear that he says it for our sakes? For our sakes it was laid down that the ploughman has a right to plough, and the thrasher to thrash, with the expectation of sharing in the crop. Here are we, who have sown in you a spiritual harvest; is it much to ask, that we should reap from you a temporal harvest in return? If others claim a share of such rights over you, have not we a better claim still? And yet we have never availed ourselves of those rights; we bear every hardship, sooner than hinder the preaching of Christ's gospel. You know, surely, that those who do the temple's work live on the temple's revenues; that those who preside at the altar share the altar's offerings. And so it is that the Lord has bidden the heralds of the gospel live by preaching the gospel. Yet I have not availed myself of any such right.

I am not writing thus in the hope of being treated otherwise; I would rather die than have this boast taken from me. When I preach the gospel, I take no credit for that; I act under constraint; it would go hard with me indeed if I did not preach the gospel. I can claim a reward for what I do of my own choice; but when I act under constraint, I am only

set down in the last paragraph: a Christian must be prepared to give up some of his rights for the good of his neighbour. In this illustration, from his own life, Paul gets off the subject of idolatrous meat; but his digression is part of the general instruction on the need for charity in Christian conduct.

Paul never deviated from his policy of working for his keep. At Thessalonica, Corinth, and Ephesus he worked daily at weaving goat hair for tents: 'We would not even be indebted to you for our daily bread, we earned it in weariness and toil, working with our own hands, night and day, so as not to be a burden to any of you.' But some Corinthians put a different interpretation on Paul's policy; they said he had to work because he was not an apostle, and so did not share in the apostolic privilege of being supported by the churches. That is why Paul shows so much indignation at these false accusations; the opposition at Corinth touched him on a tender spot.

The preachers of the gospel had the example of our Lord's own conduct and his express words as well in support of their right to receive maintenance from their converts. A group of women travelled with Jesus and his followers, and 'ministered to them with the means they had.' Our Lord handed on the same right to his disciples when he told the twelve: 'The labourer has the right to his maintenance' (Mt. 10, 10).

Paul elaborates this main argument by seven additional proofs of his thesis. He covers a wide range of ways of life— soldier, vinedresser, shepherd, ploughman, harvester, priest— and adds the example of the ox, quoting from the Mosaic law which prohibited the muzzling of the beasts trampling the ears of wheat on the threshing floor that would prevent them from taking a mouthful as they worked. God is much more concerned with the welfare of his children than with the rest of his creation, as our Lord told his followers: 'If God so

executing a commission. What title have I, then, to a reward? Why, that when I preach the gospel I should preach the gospel free of charge, not making full use of the rights which gospel preaching gives me. Thus nobody has any claim on me, and yet I have made myself everybody's slave, to win more souls. With the Jews I lived like a Jew, to win the Jews; with those who keep the law, as one who keeps the law (though the law had no claim on me), to win those who kept the law; with those who are free of the law, like one free of the law (not that I recognized no divine law, but it was the law of Christ that bound me), to win those who were free of the law. With the scrupulous, I behaved myself like one who is scrupulous, to win the scrupulous. I have been everything by turns to everybody, to bring salvation to some by all and every means.

All that I do, I do for the sake of the gospel promises, to win myself a share in them. You know well enough that when men run in a race, the race is for all, but the prize is for one; run, then, for victory. Every athlete must keep all his appetites under control; and he does it to win a crown that fades, whereas ours is imperishable. So I do not run my course like a man in doubt of his goal; I do not fight my battle like a man who wastes his blows on the air. I buffet my own body, and make it my slave; or I, who have preached to others, may myself be rejected as worthless.

Let me remind you, brethren, of this. Our fathers were hidden, all of them, under the cloud, and found a path, all of them, through the sea; all alike, in the cloud and in the sea, were baptized into Moses' fellowship. They all ate the same prophetic food, and all drank the same prophetic drink, watered by the same prophetic rock which bore them com-

clothes the grasses of the field, will he not be much more ready to clothe you, men of little faith?'

In giving up this right to maintenance, Paul is thinking only of the good of souls; his motive is charity. In this he is following closely in the footsteps of his Master: 'The Son of Man did not come to have service done him; he came to serve others, and to give his life as a ransom for the lives of many.' The example of Jesus going about through Palestine doing good is the pattern of Paul's life among the Corinthians, Ephesians, Galatians, and Thessalonians. He accommodates himself to the people with whom he is dealing; he is considerate of their way of life, their ideas and outlook: he knows how to treat Jew and Gentile, and he is tender and gentle in adapting himself to the scruples of his latest convert.

The Danger of Apostasy. The subject under discussion is still food sacrificed to idols. Paul is engaged in the task of forming a Christian conscience in his converts at Corinth. In the previous paragraph, he emphasized the part played by charity in determining how a Christian should act; here he treats of the virtue of prudence, of the need to look to one's own welfare. When dealing with things used in pagan worship, there is danger of a Christian falling back into pagan ways, of being contaminated by the heathenism he has renounced.

He takes an illustration first from athletics—running and boxing, sports familiar to the Greeks (the people who originated the Olympic Games). A Christian can learn from an athlete to make his body his slave, to mortify and control its appetites so that it will carry him to victory; he must avoid anything that stands in the way of his objective, the imperishable crown that does not fade.

pany, the rock that was Christ. And for all that, God was ill
pleased with most of them; see how they were laid low in the
wilderness. It is we that were foreshadowed in these events.
We were not to set our hearts, as some of them set their
hearts, on forbidden things. You were not to turn idolatrous,
as some of them did; so we read, 'The people sat down to
eat and drink, and rose up to take their pleasure.' We were
not to commit fornication, as some of them committed
fornication, when twenty-three thousand of them were killed
in one day. We were not to try the patience of the Lord, as
some of them tried it, the men who were slain by serpents; nor
were you to complain, as some of them complained, till the
destroying angel slew them. When all this happened to them,
it was a symbol; the record of it was written as a warning
to us, in whom history has reached its fulfilment; and it
means that he who thinks he stands firmly should beware
of a fall. So far, no temptation has befallen you that is beyond
man's strength. Not that God will play you false; he will not
allow you to be tempted beyond your powers. With the
temptation itself, he will ordain the issue of it, and enable
you to hold your own.

Keep far away, then, my well beloved, from idolatry. I am
speaking to you as men of good sense; weigh my words for
yourselves. We have a cup that we bless; is not this cup we
bless a participation in Christ's blood? Is not the bread we
break a participation in Christ's body? The one bread makes
us one body, though we are many in number; the same bread
is shared by all. Or look at Israel, God's people by nature;
do not those who eat their sacrifices associate themselves with
the altar of sacrifice? I am not suggesting that anything can
really be sacrificed to a false god, or that a false god has any
existence; I mean that when the heathen offer sacrifice they

The second illustration is from a different world; it is a lesson from the Exodus in the Old Testament. Paul presumes that his Corinthians are familiar with this scripture story. It was probably a scene well known from the preaching of Apollo, 'a man well grounded in the scriptures.' This was the type of instruction favoured by that eloquent Alexandrian; Paul demonstrates his skill in the same medium of Old Testament typology.

The Exodus is a lesson in Christian living. The Jews on the way out of Egypt received unusual divine favours that foreshadowed the two great sacraments of Baptism and the Blessed Eucharist; the water of the Red Sea symbolized Baptism, the manna and water from the rock symbolized the Eucharistic food and drink. But these favoured men and women fell down in worship to the golden calf at Sinai; they incurred the divine anger and failed to reach the Promised Land. The same thing can happen to baptized communicants; if the Corinthians presume on divine grace and consider themselves secure from all danger of contamination from pagan sacrifices, they can fall from divine grace. Thank God it has not happened yet; but a prudent man will heed the warning of history.

Practical Rules About Sacrificial Food. After laying down his two principles of charity to others and a prudent estimation of the dangers to oneself, Paul now proceeds to give practical instructions on conduct. He considers three different occasions when a Christian could come face to face with the problem of sacrificial food. First of all, in the temple of the god at the banquet following the actual sacrifice. To eat there, says Paul, is a formal act of idolatry, and so forbidden. It is not right for a Christian, united to Christ by Holy Communion, to share in a sacrificial meal with devils; that is what a heathen sacrifice really is—devil worship.

are really offering it to evil spirits and not to a God at all.
I have no mind to see you associating yourselves with evil
spirits. To drink the Lord's cup, and yet to drink the cup of evil
spirits, to share the Lord's feast, and to share the feast of
evil spirits, is impossible for you. Are we, then, to provoke
the Lord to jealousy? Have we powers greater than his?

'I am free to do what I will'; yes, but not everything can
be done without harm. 'I am free to do what I will,' but
some things disedify. Each of you ought to study the well-
being of others, not his own. When things are sold in the open
market, then you may eat them, without making any enquiries
to satisfy your consciences: 'This world and all that is in it
belongs to the Lord.' If some unbeliever invites you to his
table, and you consent to go, then you need not ask questions
to satisfy your consciences, you may eat whatever is put before
you. But if someone says to you, 'This has been used in
idolatrous worship,' then, for the sake of your informant,
you must refuse to eat it; it is a matter of conscience; his
conscience, I mean, not yours. There is no reason why I
should let my freedom be called in question by another man's
conscience. I can eat such food and be grateful for it; why
should I incur reproach for that over which I say grace? In
eating, in drinking, in all that you do, do everything as for
God's glory. Give no offence to Jew, or to Greek, or to God's
church. That is my own rule, to satisfy all alike, studying
the general welfare rather than my own, so as to win their
salvation. Follow my example, then, as I follow the example of
Christ.

I must needs praise you for your constant memory of me,
for upholding your traditions just as I handed them on to you.

In contrasting the Blessed Eucharist to pagan and Jewish sacrifices, Paul quite clearly assumes that the Mass is a true sacrifice. He also teaches that Communion means union with each other through our common union with Christ; it is the sacrament of unity in the Mystical Body. Christians at Corinth and at Ephesus all eat of the one same bread; an impossibility unless the bread has been changed into the body of Christ. We are all one in Christ because we all live by his life.

Much of the meat sacrificed to the gods eventually finished at the butchers' to be sold to the general public. Christians may buy and eat this without scruple of conscience; it is taken away from the idol, and is once more the property of the Lord.

The third case considered by Paul is that of invitations to dine with pagan friends. A Christian may eat whatever is served, unless the food is specified as having been an idol-offering; in this case alone he must abstain on the principle of charity. To eat would be to give scandal to his unbelieving host.

Eight years earlier, at the Council of Jerusalem, the apostles had decided against Gentiles eating sacrificial food: 'You are to abstain from what is sacrificed to idols' (Acts 15, 29). Paul was present on that occasion, and actually promulgated the decree at Antioch; yet he does not even mention it to the Corinthians. The reason he acts so is that the conditions in Corinth were completely different from those visualized in the decree. The Jerusalem decree was only temporary and dealt with the Jew-Gentile problem in Syria and Galatia.

Women Must Not Pray Unveiled. In the next four chapters, Paul corrects some abuses that have crept into the litur-

And here is something you must know. The head to which a wife is united is her husband, just as the head to which every man is united is Christ; so, too, the head to which Christ is united is God. And whereas any man who keeps his head covered when he prays or utters prophecy brings shame upon his head, a woman brings shame upon her head if she uncovers it to pray or prophesy; she is no better than the woman who has her head shaved. If a woman would go without a veil, why does she not cut her hair short too? If she admits that a woman is disgraced when her hair is cut short or shaved, then let her go veiled. A man has no need to veil his head; he is God's image, the pride of his creation, whereas the wife is the pride of her husband. (The woman takes her origin from the man, not the man from the woman; and indeed, it was not man that was created for woman's sake, but woman for man's.) And for that reason the woman ought to have authority over her head, for the angels' sake. (Not that, in the Lord's service, woman has her place apart from man, or man his apart from woman; if woman takes her origin from man, man equally comes to birth through woman. And indeed all things have their origin in God.) Judge for yourselves; is it fitting that a woman should offer prayer to God unveiled? Does not nature itself teach you that, whereas it is a disgrace to a man to wear his hair long, when a woman grows her hair long, it is an added grace to her? That is because her hair has been given her to take the place of a veil. And if anyone is prepared to argue the matter, he must know that no such custom is found among us, or in any of God's churches.

And here is a warning I have for you. I can give you no praise for holding your assemblies in a way that does harm, not

gical life of the Corinthian church. The first of these concerns the status of women in public worship. In 14, 34 he makes a sweeping prohibition: 'Women are to be silent in the churches; utterance is not permitted to them.' He does the same in this paragraph, but in a more tactful manner. By forbidding women to cast aside their veils, he is in fact preventing them from speaking; the heavy oriental veil (the yashmak still worn by Moslem women) hanging down over the face was an efficient barrier to clear speech in public.

In his diplomatic approach to this explosive problem of silencing women, Paul tries five lines of thought in his attempt to demonstrate the secondary status of woman. (1) The narrative of Genesis makes it clear that man was created first; Eve was not an independent creation of God; she was made from Adam to help and complete him in founding the human race. Man is the head and primary being of God's created universe. (2) The angels, who are the guardians of divine worship, were the only witnesses of the creation of woman in her subordinate status; reverence for them should make women retain the veil as a sign of subordination to their husbands. (3) St. Paul sees a mystic parallel between the creation of Adam and Eve and the Incarnation: Christ came from God, but his divinity is veiled or hidden in our Lord; so too woman came from man, but the humanity is veiled in her. Women wear veils to honour the Incarnation of their Saviour. (4) The natural symbolism of hair: the veil is natural to woman as the extension of her long hair (only slaves and courtesans wore their hair short). (5) The custom of the rest of Christendom prohibits this novelty.

Charity and the Blessed Eucharist. This letter was written less than thirty years after the death of our Lord Jesus Christ.

good. From the first, when you meet in church, there are divisions among you; so I hear, and in some measure believe it. Parties there must needs be among you, so that those who are true metal may be distinguished from the rest. And when you assemble together, there is no opportunity to eat a supper of the Lord; each comer hastens to eat the supper he has brought for himself, so that one man goes hungry, while another has drunk deep. Have you no homes to eat and drink in, that you should show contempt to God's church, and shame the poor? Praise you? There is no room for praise here.

The tradition which I received from the Lord, and handed on to you, is that the Lord Jesus, on the night when he was being betrayed, took bread, and gave thanks, and broke it, and said: 'This is my body, given up for you. Do this for a commemoration of me.' And so with the cup, when supper was ended: 'This cup,' he said, 'is the new testament, in my blood. Do this, whenever you drink it, for a commemoration of me.' So it is the Lord's death that you are heralding, whenever you eat this bread and drink this cup, until he comes; and therefore, if anyone eats the bread or drinks the cup of the Lord unworthily, he will be held to account for the Lord's body and blood. A man must examine himself first, and then eat of the bread and drink of the cup; he is eating and drinking damnation to himself if he eats and drinks, not recognizing the Lord's body for what it is. That is why many of your number want strength and health, and not a few have died. If we recognized our own fault, we should not incur these judgments; as it is, the Lord judges us and chastises us, so that we may not incur, as this world incurs, damnation.

So, brethren, when you assemble to eat together, wait for one another; those who are hungry had best eat at home, for

Within that period, the Mass had become a familiar and essential part of Christian worship. Each Saturday night at Corinth the faithful assembled in the house of one of their number (there were no dedicated buildings at this early date) for the celebration of Mass. It had not yet taken its present form but was based closely on the Last Supper; essentially this was a banquet, which culminated in the consecration of the bread and wine. The banquet was usually protracted till midnight, because that was the accepted time for the sacrifice of the Mass to commence.

The division of the church at Corinth into two factions, the followers of Paul and the followers of Apollo, showed itself at this sacred ceremony; the two parties kept apart; there was no community spirit, no sharing of food. And a worse abuse was the division between rich and poor; that social division in the community manifested itself even at the Christian mysteries. This state of affairs was directly opposed to the nature of the Blessed Eucharist, the sacrament of fraternal charity and unity in the Mystical Body of Christ.

Paul reminds them of the sacredness of the act they perform at Mass by identifying it with both the Last Supper and the Crucifixion. The manner of celebrating Mass is the same as that used by our Lord at the Last Supper (that is, the consecration of bread and wine into his own body and blood). Though different in manner, it is really the sacrificial death of Christ on the cross that is commemorated at each Mass.

It is not fitting that the Corinthians prepare for the coming of their Lord and Master by mere bodily eating and drinking; they should see that they have right dispositions of soul, particularly charity. The abuses here corrected by Paul were eventually responsible for the abolition of the banquet in the

7

fear that your meeting should bring you condemnation. The other questions I will settle when I come.

And now about spiritual gifts; I would not willingly leave you in doubt about these. While you were still heathen, as you can remember well enough, you let yourselves be led away wherever men would lead you, to worship false gods that gave no utterance. That is why I am telling you of this. Just as no one can be speaking through God's Spirit if he calls Jesus accursed, so it is only through the Holy Spirit that anyone can say, 'Jesus is the Lord'; and yet there are different kinds of gifts, though it is the same Spirit who gives them, just as there are different kinds of service, though it is the same Lord we serve, and different manifestations of power, though it is the same God who manifests his power everywhere in all of us. The revelation of the Spirit is imparted to each, to make the best advantage of it. One learns to speak with wisdom, by the power of the Spirit, another to speak with knowledge, with the same Spirit for his rule; one, through the same Spirit, is given faith; another, through the same Spirit, powers of healing; one can perform miracles, one can prophesy, another can test the spirit of the prophets; one can speak in different tongues, another can interpret the tongues; but all this is the work of one and the same Spirit, who distributes his gifts as he will to each severally.

A man's body is all one, though it has a number of different organs; and all this multitude of organs goes to make up one body; so it is with Christ. We too, all of us, have been baptized into a single body by the power of a single Spirit, Jews and Greeks, slaves and free men alike; we have all been given drink at a single source, the one Spirit. The body, after all, con-

fourth century; they also played a part in introducing the fast before Communion.

Holy Spirit Author of All Spiritual Gifts.   After his resurrection, our Lord promised his apostles: 'Where believers go, these signs shall go with them; they will cast out devils in my name, they will speak in tongues that are strange to them; they will take up serpents in their hands, and drink poisonous draughts without harm; they will lay their hands upon the sick and make them recover.' These spectacular, miraculous gifts came to the infant Church at Pentecost; they flourished in all newly founded Christian communities.

To the heathen, for the most part illiterate and unacquainted with the Jewish scriptures, they were a powerful apologetic; any pagan could see for himself the divine power that worked in the Christian Church. The pagan deities, Paul reminds his Corinthian converts from paganism, were separate and divided gods; they contradicted and opposed each other in their teaching and objectives. In Christianity there is unity and harmony; that is because the Holy Spirit is the origin of all these gifts. The Church is one precisely because the three persons of the Blessed Trinity are one God; the different manifestations of divine power, now appearing in the Corinthian assemblies, all come from the same source. None of these gifts is authentic if it denies the divinity of Christ.

Harmony Among Members of the Body.   These strange gifts were a passing phase of the life of the early Church; they were special spiritual helps given to establish the Church in new territory, and they did not help the individual become holier. For the sanctity of each Christian, God provides sanctifying grace and the virtues that accompany it; for building up the

sists not of one organ but of many; if the foot should say, 'I am not the hand, and therefore I do not belong to the body,' it does not belong to the body any the less for that. If the ear should say, 'I am not the eye, and therefore I do not belong to the body,' it does not belong to the body any the less for that. Where would the power of hearing be, if the body were all eye? Or the power of smell, if the body were all ear? As it is, God has given each one of them its own position in the body, as he would. If the whole were one single organ, what would become of the body? Instead of that, we have a multitude of organs, and one body. The eye cannot say to the hand, 'I have no need of you,' or the head to the feet, 'I have no need of you.'

On the contrary, it is those parts of our body which seem most contemptible that are necessary to it; what seems base in our bodies, we surround with special honour, treating with special seemliness that which is unseemly in us, whereas that which is seemly in us has no need of it. Thus God has established a harmony in the body, giving special honour to that which needed it most. There was to be no want of unity in the body; all the different parts of it were to make each other's welfare their common care. If one part is suffering, all the rest suffer with it; if one part is treated with honour, all the rest find pleasure in it.

And you are Christ's body, organs of it depending upon each other. God has given us different positions in the church; apostles first, then prophets, and thirdly teachers; then come miraculous powers, then gifts of healing, works of mercy, the management of affairs, and speaking with different tongues. Are all of us apostles, all prophets, all teachers? Have all miraculous powers, or gifts of healing? Can all speak with tongues, can all interpret?

Christian community, he provided an extra help through these spiritual gifts. They are defined by Prat as: 'Gratuitous, supernatural and transitory gifts, conferred for the general good and for the building up of the Mystical Body of Christ.'

In the previous paragraph, Paul lists nine of these gifts; at the end of this paragraph he lists eight; four from the first list are repeated in the second, leaving a total of thirteen. This is just half of the total number (twenty-seven) found in all the Pauline letters. The thirteen mentioned here may be divided into three groups. (1) Graces for those holding office: apostles, prophets, teachers. (2) Strikingly miraculous powers: faith (that can move mountains), healing, miracles, tongues. (3) Powers to enable ordinary duties to be carried out in a more perfect way: wisdom, knowledge, works of mercy, management of affairs, testing prophets, interpreting tongues.

The second group, particularly the gift of tongues, was rated highest in Corinthian circles. So much so that the familiar party system of Paul and Apollo took sides for their respective champions; they despised all other gifts; they wanted nothing else at their assemblies but the spectacular gift of tongues. The unity and harmony of the Corinthian church was endangered; pride and jealousy were dominating their spiritual life.

Paul recalled them to their senses by comparing the Church to a human body; the various organs are all necessary to the welfare and harmony of the body, hands as well as feet, sight as well as hearing. Far from despising the inferior organs (organs of sex, which Paul calls base and contemptible), man treats them with special honour by always keeping them covered. So it should be with the Mystical Body of Christ: every member has its own special function in the harmonious whole; all are necessary for its completeness.

Prize the best gifts of heaven. Meanwhile, I can show you a way which is better than any other. I may speak with every tongue that men and angels use; yet, if I lack charity, I am no better than echoing bronze, or the clash of cymbals. I may have powers of prophecy, no secret hidden from me, no knowledge too deep for me; I may have utter faith, so that I can move mountains; yet if I lack charity, I count for nothing. I may give away all that I have, to feed the poor; I may give myself up to be burnt at the stake; if I lack charity, it goes for nothing.

Charity is patient, is kind; charity feels no envy; charity is never boastful or proud, never insolent; does not claim its rights, cannot be provoked, does not brood over an injury; takes no pleasure in wrongdoing, but rejoices at the victory of truth; sustains, believes, hopes, endures, to the last.

The time will come when we shall outgrow prophecy, when speaking with tongues will come to an end, when knowledge will be swept away; we shall never have finished with charity. Our knowledge, our prophecy, are only glimpses of the truth; and these glimpses will be swept away when the time of fulfilment comes. (Just so, when I was a child, I talked like a child, I had the intelligence, the thoughts of a child; since I became a man, I have outgrown childish ways.) At present, we are looking at a confused reflection in a mirror; then, we shall see face to face; now, I have only glimpses of knowledge; then, I shall recognize God as he has recognized me. Meanwhile, faith, hope and charity persist, all three; but the greatest of them all is charity.

Make charity your aim, the spiritual gifts your aspiration, and, by preference, the gift of prophecy. The man who talks

Charity the Greatest of All Gifts. The life of Christ is summed up in one phrase: 'You shall love the Lord your God with the love of your whole heart . . . and your neighbour as yourself.' The Mystical Body must keep that same estimation of the importance of its various activities; to live the life of the Head, it must see things with the eyes of Christ. The spiritual gifts, so valued by the Corinthians, are all valueless without the theological virtue of charity. Paul illustrates his thesis by taking five of the most important gifts: tongues, prophecy, knowledge, faith and works of mercy.

Next he lists fifteen qualities of charity. In choosing these particular aspects of the virtue, he has his eye on the Christian community at Corinth; their disputes and jealousy over the possession of spiritual gifts have led them into loss of temper, ill-feeling, angry words, feelings of revenge. If charity dominated their assemblies, none of these evils would be present.

In the final section, Paul no longer is concerned with love of the neighbour; he passes on to the primary objective of charity, the love of God himself. The supremacy of charity over spiritual gifts is evident: it unites man to God directly, completely, and permanently; all other gifts yield only indirect, incomplete, and transitory contacts with God. In the fulfilment of his destiny in the beatific vision, man shall possess only one gift—charity; all the rest will cease at death. The obscure glimpses of God's own inner life obtained through the gifts of knowledge, prophecy, and faith are like dull reflections in a piece of polished metal.

Tongues Less Valuable Than Prophecy. When the Holy Spirit came down upon the 120 followers of Jesus on Pente-

in a strange tongue is talking to God, not to men; nobody understands him, he is holding mysterious converse with his own spirit; whereas the prophet speaks to edify, to encourage, to comfort his fellow men. By talking in a strange tongue, a man may strengthen his own faith; by prophesying he can strengthen the faith of the church. I would gladly see you all speaking with strange tongues, but I would rather you should prophesy, because the prophet ranks higher than the man who speaks with strange tongues. It would be different if he could translate them, to strengthen the faith of the church; but as things are, brethren, what good can I do you by coming and talking to you in strange languages, instead of addressing you with a revelation, or a manifestation of inner knowledge, or a prophecy, or words of instruction? Senseless things may be vocal, a flute, for example, or a harp; but even with these, there must be distinctions between the sounds they give, or how can we recognize what melody flute or harp is playing? If a trumpet, for that matter, gives out an uncertain note, who will arm himself for battle? So it is with you, how can it be known what your message is, if you speak in a language whose accents cannot be understood? Your words will fall on empty air. No doubt all these different languages exist somewhere in the world, and each of them has its significance; but if I cannot understand what the language means, the effect is that I am a foreigner to the man who is speaking, and he is a foreigner to me. So the case stands with you. Since you have set your hearts on spiritual gifts, ask for them in abundant measure, but only so as to strengthen the faith of the church; the man who can speak in a strange tongue should pray for the power to interpret them.

If I use a strange tongue when I offer prayer, my spirit is

cost Sunday, 'they all began to speak in strange languages, as the Spirit gave utterance to each.' This was the same gift of tongues, now so popular among the Corinthians, which Paul here attempts to restrain. The speakers did not understand the language in which they spoke. They were not preaching to the people either; they were proclaiming God's wonders in a form of ecstatic prayer. For preaching the gospel, the Holy Spirit inspired Peter to stand up and talk to the assembled crowd in their native tongue, Aramaic. He proved the divinity of Christ from the Resurrection, and so converted 3,000 people.

And that is the real distinction between tongues and prophecy: in tongues the inspired utterance is addressed to God, in prophecy it is addressed to men. This is how Prat defines them. TONGUES: The supernatural ability to pray or to praise God in a strange language with an enthusiasm bordering on ecstasy. PROPHECY: Any inspired, unpremeditated utterance in the language of the congregation for their supernatural guidance.

To prove the superiority of prophecy over tongues, Paul considers their value to each of four divisions of the Corinthian assemblies: the faithful, the speakers, the catechumens, and the unbelievers. (1) The faithful are the Mystical Body at Corinth; the value of any gift one of their members possesses must be decided in terms of its usefulness to the whole body. Prophecy certainly fulfils the essential purpose of all spiritual gifts; it builds up the faith of the church: 'The prophet speaks to edify, to encourage, to comfort his fellow men.' Tongues, on the other hand, unless they are translated, are mere empty sounds; the faithful cannot receive spiritual help from words they cannot understand; a foreign language serves its purpose in the country where it is spoken, but Greek is the tongue spoken all over Corinth. A foreign tongue is no better than

7*

praying, but my mind reaps no advantage from it. What, then, is my drift? Why, I mean to use mind as well as spirit when I offer prayer, use mind as well as spirit when I sing psalms. If you pronounce a blessing in this spiritual fashion, how can one who takes his place among the uninstructed say Amen to your thanksgiving? He cannot tell what you are saying. You, true enough, are duly giving thanks, but the other's faith is not strengthened. Thank God, I can speak with tongues more than any of you; but in the church, I would rather speak five words which my mind utters, for your instruction, than ten thousand in a strange tongue. Brethren, do not be content to think childish thoughts; keep the innocence of children, with the thoughts of grown men. We read in the law, 'I will speak to this people with an unknown tongue, with the lips of strangers, and even so they will not listen to me, says the Lord.' Thus, talking with a strange tongue is a sign given to unbelievers, not to the faithful; whereas prophecy is meant for the faithful, not for unbelievers. And now, what will happen if the uninstructed or the unbelievers come in when the whole church has met together, and find everyone speaking with strange tongues at once? Will they not say you are mad? Whereas, if some unbeliever or some uninstructed person comes in when all alike are prophesying, everyone will read his thoughts, everyone will scrutinize him, all that is kept hidden in his heart will be revealed; and so he will fall on his face and worship God, publicly confessing that God is indeed among you.

What am I urging, then, brethren? Why, when you meet together, each with a psalm to sing, or some doctrine to impart, or a revelation to give, or ready to speak in strange tongues, or to interpret them, see that all is done to your

random notes without melody played on a flute, harp, or trumpet.

(2) The speaker sometimes spoke his prayer to God, sometimes chanted it after the Christian custom of singing the psalms; in either case he was raised to a state of ecstasy. He did not understand a word of what he was saying; the divine impulse ('spirit') was working within him, moving him to utter his praise of God, but his mind was inactive. It would be far better if he could interpret what he was saying; then both his mind and his spirit would join in worshipping God.

(3) The catechumens are called 'the uninstructed.' These people were unable to participate in the prayer coming from the lips of the speaker in strange tongues; instead of voicing their approval by saying Amen, they had to sit lost and isolated—hardly a satisfactory preparation for membership in the Mystical Body!

(4) The unbelievers are pagan enquirers. Tongues would seem to be more important to them than prophecy; but even here, Paul contends, they are inferior to prophecy. Just as on Pentecost Sunday, tongues excite the curiosity of the unbelievers but do not convert them; they lead the pagans to the Christian meeting-place; it is then that prophecy takes over and wins them for Christ. From Paul's argument it is clear that prophecy was sometimes more than an inspired utterance; it took on a miraculous quality by manifesting knowledge of secret thoughts hidden away in the conscience of unbelievers.

Rules for Orderly Procedure at Meetings. Sosthenes, Stephanas, Fortunatus, Achaicus, Crispus, Gaius, Lucian, Jason, Sosipater, Tertius, Quartus, Erastus, Chloe: those are thirteen Corinthians mentioned in Paul's letters. Just imagine

spiritual advantage. If there is speaking with strange tongues, do not let more than two speak, or three at the most; let each take his turn, with someone to interpret for him, and if he can find nobody to interpret, let him be silent in the church, conversing with his own spirit and with God. As for the prophets, let two or three of them speak, while the rest sit in judgment on their prophecies. If some revelation comes to another who is sitting by, let him who spoke first keep silence; there is room for you all to prophesy one by one, so that the whole company may receive instruction and comfort; and it is for the prophets to exercise control over their own spiritual gifts. God is the author of peace, not of disorder; all the churches of the saints give proof of it.

And women are to be silent in the churches; utterance is not permitted to them; let them keep their rank, as the law tells them: if they have any question to raise, let them ask their husbands at home. That a woman should make her voice heard in the church is not seemly.

Tell me, was it from you that God's word was sent out? Are you the only people it has reached? If anybody claims to be a prophet, or to have spiritual gifts, let him prove it by recognizing that this message of mine to you is the Lord's commandment. If he does not recognize it, he himself shall receive no recognition.

Set your hearts, then, my brethren, on prophesying; and as for speaking with strange tongues, do not interfere with it. Only let us have everything done suitably, and with right order.

Here, brethren, is an account of the gospel I preached to you. It was this that was handed on to you; upon this your faith rests; through this (if you keep in mind the tenor of its

the confusion if all of them spoke at once in the assembly at Chloe's house; it would be a babel of competing voices. That is the situation Paul has to deal with here. His solution is that the spiritual advantage of the whole church must be their primary concern, and not a demonstration of each individual's personal eminence in the possession of spiritual gifts.

Two new facts about spiritual gifts come to light in this paragraph. First, some of the gifts were not genuine; there were bogus speakers in tongues, and prophets too. Second, these gifts were subject to the control of the speaker; he could stop at will, or even resist the impulse to speak in the first place.

Paul gives five practical rules for conducting their meetings in an orderly fashion. (1) Only one person is to speak at one time; they are to take turns in addressing the congregation. (2) Not more than half a dozen are to speak at each meeting. (3) The gift of tongues is not to be exercised unless there is someone present to translate the message into Greek; there was a special gift of interpreting tongues. (4) Prophets are not to be allowed to speak without some control on the genuineness of their utterances; there was also a special gift for testing the authenticity of prophets. (5) Women are not to speak at all; this is a more direct prohibition than that contained in their veiling (11, 5-6).

The Corinthians, so rich in spiritual gifts, should be able to recognize these prescriptions as coming from the Lord himself through his minister Paul.

Evidence for Christ's Resurrection. Paul's preaching concentrated on three events of our Lord's life, his death, resurrection, and second coming. Just as Peter based his first sermon on

preaching) you are in the way of salvation; unless indeed your belief was ill founded. The chief message I handed on to you, as it was handed on to me, was that Christ, as the scriptures had foretold, died for our sins; that he was buried, and then, as the scriptures had foretold, rose again on the third day. That he was seen by Kephas, then by the twelve apostles, and afterwards by more than five hundred of the brethren at once, most of whom are alive at this day, though some have gone to their rest. Then he was seen by James, then by all the apostles; and last of all, I too saw him, like the last child, that comes to birth unexpectedly. Of all the apostles, I am the least; nay, I am not fit to be called an apostle, since there was a time when I persecuted the church of God; only, by God's grace, I am what I am, and the grace he has shown me has not been without fruit; I have worked harder than all of them, or rather, it was not I, but the grace of God working with me. That is our preaching, mine or theirs as you will; that is the faith which has come to you.

If what we preach about Christ, then, is that he rose from the dead, how is it that some of you say the dead do not rise again? If the dead do not rise, then Christ has not risen either; and if Christ has not risen, then our preaching is groundless, and your faith, too, is groundless. Worse still, we are convicted of giving false testimony about God; we bore God witness that he had raised Christ up from the dead, and he has not raised him up, if it is true that the dead do not rise again. If the dead, I say, do not rise, then Christ has not risen either; and if Christ has not risen, all your faith is a delusion; you are back in your sins. It follows, too, that those who have gone to their rest in Christ have been lost. If the hope we have

Pentecost Sunday on the resurrection of Christ, so Paul began his instructions to new converts by proving that Christ had risen from the dead; it was the main apologetic of the apostles, and the foundation of the Christian faith.

The evidence for our Lord's resurrection was factual; it was given by men who had actually seen the risen Master, talked and eaten with him. All four gospels follow the same pattern of proof. Paul here presents six witnesses; only three of these are mentioned in the gospels, Peter (Kephas) and the two appearances to the apostles. The 500 brethren incident probably took place by the lake of Galilee; it may be the scene mentioned in Matthew 28, 16. Paul selects these witnessses, rather than Mary Magdalen and the two disciples of Emmaus, because they were people he had personally met.

All these saw our Lord between his resurrection and ascension; Paul saw him much later on the road to Damascus (Acts 9, 3-6); it gave him the right to add his voice to the witness of the other apostles.

Our Resurrection Depends on Christ's. For converts from paganism, the hardest doctrine in the Apostles' Creed was the article: 'I believe in the resurrection of the body.' Theoretically they knew that man has an immortal soul which survives death; but for most of the ordinary people this was a vague, shadowy sort of existence, somewhat after the manner of a ghost. That man would see again with his eyes, and touch things with his hands was a fact so new and startling that their minds found it hard to take it in.

Paul's audience of intellectuals at Athens had openly laughed at him when he mentioned this doctrine; so he was used to Gentile reaction to the resurrection, and he had developed a

learned to repose in Christ belongs to this world only, then we are unhappy beyond all other men. But no, Christ has risen from the dead, the firstfruits of all those who have fallen asleep; a man had brought us death, and a man should bring us resurrection from the dead; just as all have died with Adam, so with Christ all will be brought to life. But each must rise in his own rank; Christ is the firstfruits, and after him follow those who belong to him, when he comes. Full completion comes after that, when he places his kingship in the hands of God, his Father, having first dispossessed every other sort of rule, authority, and power; his reign must continue until 'he has put all his enemies under his feet,' and the last of those enemies to be dispossessed is death. 'God has put all things in subjection under his feet'; that is, all things have been made subject to him, except indeed that power which made them his subjects. And when that subjection is complete, then the Son himself will become subject to the power which made all things his subjects so that God may be all in all.

Tell me, what can be the use of being baptized for the dead, if the dead do not rise again? Why should anyone be baptized for them? Why do we, for that matter, face peril hour after hour? I swear to you, brethren, by all the pride I take in you in the name of our Lord Jesus Christ, that death is daily at my side. When I fought against beasts at Ephesus with all my strength, of what use was it, if the dead do not rise again? 'Let us eat and drink, since we must die tomorrow.' Do not be led into such errors: 'Bad company can corrupt noble minds.' Come back to your senses, like right-minded men, and sin no longer; there are some, I say it to your shame, who lack the knowledge of God.

line of argument best suited to convince the sceptics. That is why first of all he established the fact of Jesus' resurrection from the dead; to deny the possibility of resurrection is a denial of an historical event that is the very basis of the Christian faith. But the fact of Christ's resurrection proves only that he, Christ, rose from the dead. How about us?

Paul here introduces his favourite doctrine, the Mystical Body of Christ. Just as resurrection was the completion of our Lord's historical existence, so it must be the final perfection of his members. We are organs belonging to a glorified head; how could such a body be perfect if the organs did not share that glory?

To clinch the argument, Paul compares Adam and Christ: what Adam lost for the human race, Christ regained; death as well as sin resulted from Adam's transgression; so our Lord won back for mankind bodily immortality as well as sanctifying grace. This right to glorification of the body will not be realized for mankind until the Second Coming of Christ; when that day comes, the Mystical Body will have grown to full perfection; there will be no longer a Church militant on earth, only the Church triumphant of glorified humanity in heaven.

Paul's final appeal is to two concrete realities of daily life, one from their experience, the other from his. The first is the Corinthian practice of a friend's receiving baptism on behalf of an unbaptized catechumen; the second is Paul's indifference to death amidst the perils of Ephesus. These two facts do not prove a belief in resurrection, only a belief in survival after death. Paul is probably thinking now of a second error: some thought that only those living at the last day would be glorified; those already dead would miss the resurrection.

But perhaps someone will ask, 'How can the dead rise up? What kind of body will they be wearing when they appear?' Poor fool, when you sow seed in the ground, it must die before it can be brought to life; and what you sow is not the full body that is one day to be, it is only bare grain, of wheat, it may be, or some other crop; it is for God to embody it according to his will, each grain in the body that belongs to it. Nature is not all one; men have one nature, the beasts another, the birds another, and fishes another; so, too, there are bodies that belong to earth and bodies that belong to heaven; and heavenly bodies have one kind of beauty, earthly bodies another. The sun has its own beauty, the moon has hers, the stars have theirs, one star even differs from another in its beauty. So it is with the resurrection of the dead. What is sown corruptible, rises incorruptible; what is sown unhonoured, rises in glory; what is sown in weakness, is raised in power; what is sown a natural body, rises a spiritual body. If there is such a thing as a natural body, there must be a spiritual body too. Mankind begins with the Adam who became, as scripture tells us, 'a living soul'; it is fulfilled in the Adam who has become a life-giving spirit. It was not the principle of spiritual life that came first; natural life came first, then spiritual life; the man who came first came from the earth, fashioned of dust, the man who came afterwards came from heaven. The nature of that earth-born man is shared by his earthly sons, the nature of the heaven-born man, by his heavenly sons; and it remains for us, who once bore the stamp of earth, to bear the stamp of heaven. What I mean, brethren, is this; the kingdom of God cannot be enjoyed by flesh and blood; the principle of corruption cannot share a life which is incorruptible.

Here is a secret I will make known to you: we shall not

Bodily Resurrection Not Against Reason. A few days before Jesus' death, some Sadducees confronted him with their insoluble case of the woman with seven husbands (Mt. 22, 23). They visualized life in the resurrected state exactly as life is here on earth: a resurrected body exactly the same as that of Lazarus come back from the tomb. Our Lord corrects this misrepresentation of glorified bodies by pointing out they are immortal; marriage will be unnecessary once death has been destroyed.

Paul here demonstrates the reasonableness of Christian teaching on the resurrection. First he illustrates from the world of nature. In vegetable life there is a close parallel with man's body: the vast difference between a grain of wheat and its final development into stalk, leaf, and ear; both wheat and man must undergo the corruption of death before rising to a new perfection. The variety of bodies in the animal world, the shining brilliance of the sun by day, of the moon and stars by night, prepare man's imagination for a new kind of body, the glorified beauty of a resurrected body.

In addition to immortality, Paul lists four other qualities of a resurrected body: incorruptibility, glory, power, and spirituality. Just how they will affect the way of life of men after the resurrection on the last day can best be seen by examining our Lord's life after his resurrection. He was free from pain and all physical needs, such as the need for food and sleep; he ate with his apostles to convince them of the reality of his body, not to satisfy his hunger. In his face there was a new glory and beauty, which made it difficult for his followers to recognize him at first sight; he possessed the power to move from place to place just by willing to be wherever he wanted to go; and he could pass through solid objects, such as doors, in a miraculous manner.

all fall asleep, but we shall all be changed. It will happen in
a moment, in the twinkling of an eye, when the last trumpet
sounds; the trumpet will sound, and the dead will rise again,
free from corruption, and we shall find ourselves changed;
this corruptible nature of ours must be clothed with incorruptible life, this mortal nature with immortality. Then, when
this corruptible nature wears its incorruptible garment, this
mortal nature its immortality, the saying of scripture will
come true, 'Death is swallowed up in victory. Where then,
death, is your victory; where, death, is your sting?' It is sin
that gives death its sting, just as it is the law that gives sin its
power; thanks be to God, then, who gives us victory through
our Lord Jesus Christ. Stand firm, then, my beloved brethren,
immovable in your resolve, doing your full share continually
in the task the Lord has given you, since you know that your
labour in the Lord's service cannot be spent in vain.

And now about the collection which is being made for the
saints; follow the plan which I have prescribed for the Galatian churches. Each of you should put aside, on the first day
of the week, what he can afford to spare, and save it up, so
that there may be no need for a collection at the time of my
visit; and when I am with you I will despatch your envoys,
with letters of recommendation from you, to convey your
charity to Jerusalem. If I find it worthwhile to make the
journey myself, they shall travel with me. I shall be coming
to you as soon as I have made the round of Macedonia (I
mean to go round Macedonia), and perhaps stay with you or
even pass the winter with you; it will be for you to put me
on my way to my next stage, whatever it be. This is no occasion for a mere passing visit to you; I hope to spend some

Christ is the Second Adam, the representative and head of the human race. The first Adam was made of nothing from the dust of the earth; the second Adam, incarnate in time, had existed eternally in the glory of his divine nature. To the members of his Mystical Body, he communicates his own life: 'He will form this humbled body of ours anew, moulding it into the image of his glorified body.'

In his treatment of resurrected bodies, Paul is thinking only of the good, not of the damned. It seems at times that he is consoling those Christians who thought that only the living would share in Christ's triumph on the last day, and that the dead would not rise from the tomb. He had reassured the Thessalonians on this same matter (Thess. 4, 12-17). He leaves no doubt, in this final section of 1 Corinthians 15, that death has been conquered: 'He leaps and tramples on the prostrate form of death, singing aloud the song of triumph.'

Final Directions and Future Plans. Paul has finished the body of his letter; his usual practice is to conclude with some practical advice, personal information, and greetings. So this paragraph is in the nature of a postscript. It is no trouble for Paul to come down from the heights of mystical speculation on the resurrected body to the routine matters of finance.

Twelve years before, he and Barnabas had brought a monetary contribution from the Christians at Antioch to the mother church at Jerusalem (Acts 11, 27-30). And from the start of his first missionary journey to Galatia he began the practice of collecting from the Gentile churches and sending money to Jerusalem. It was an act of charity to the poorer mother church, a sign of unity of the members of the Mystical Body and a standing proof that his championing of the Gen-

time with you, if the Lord will let me. Till Pentecost, I shall be staying at Ephesus; a great and promising opportunity lies open to me, and strong forces oppose me. If Timothy comes, be sure to make him free of your company; he is doing the Lord's work as I am. He is not to be treated with disrespect; put him on his way in peace so that he reaches me safely; I am awaiting him here with the brethren. As for our brother Apollo, I have urged him strongly to accompany the brethren on their journey to you; but no, he will not consent to visit you yet, he will come when he has leisure.

Be on the watch, stand firm in the faith, play the man, be full of courage. And let everything you do be done in a spirit of charity.

This appeal, brethren, I must make to you. You know that the household of Stephanas was the first offering Achaia gave; you know how they have devoted themselves to supplying the needs of the saints; you must show deference to such persons, to everyone who shares in the labours of our ministry. I am glad that Stephanas and Fortunatus and Achaicus are here; they have made up for your absence, bringing relief to my mind as well as yours. Such men deserve your recognition. A greeting to you from all the churches of Asia, and many greetings, in the Lord's name, from Aquila and Priscilla, as well as the church in their household. All the brethren greet you; greet one another with the kiss of saints. I send you my greetings in my own handwriting, PAUL. If there is anyone who has no love for the Lord, let him be held accursed; the Lord is coming. The grace of the Lord Jesus be with you; and my love be with you all in Christ Jesus.

tiles did not cut him off from his Jewish heritage. Paul develops this thought in his moving charity sermon in 2 Corinthians 8-9.

Paul had been three years at Ephesus, the longest time he ever stayed in the one city. Corinth was only three hundred miles west across the Aegean Sea; boats were going and coming daily. Seemingly he had thought of a quick voyage to Corinth several times, but was prevented by the demands of his apostolic ministry at Ephesus. So now he makes a promise that he will make a longer stay when he does come overland through Macedonia, later in the year. Actually he did eventually spend the winter of 57-58 A.D. at Corinth, where he wrote the Letter to the Romans. In the meantime he tells them of Timothy's expected arrival in the near future (he and a Corinthian, Erastus, were on their way through Macedonia, Acts 19, 22). Timothy had been only a boy when he was at Corinth with Paul five years before; they must remember that he is now a mature missionary and is to be treated with due reverence.

Stephanas, Fortunatus, and Achaicus had probably brought the Corinthian letter to Paul; with Sosthenes, who served as Paul's secretary for 1 Corinthians, they would carry back Paul's reply. Paul had high hopes that the influence of these loyal followers would help solve the problem of the distressing party spirit in Corinth. It would seem that Paul wanted Apollo to accompany them; he, however, had not yet acquired full Christian perfection and would not co-operate with Paul in putting an end to the divisions in the Corinthian community.

Aquila and Priscilla are mentioned because they had lived for some time at Corinth (Acts 18, 2).

Third Missionary Journey
continued

It was just at this time that the Way was the cause of a notable disturbance. There was a silversmith called Demetrius, who used to make silver models of Diana's temple, and so gave plentiful employment to the craftsmen. And now he called a meeting of these, and of the workmen who were in the same trade, and spoke thus: 'Friends, you all know that our prosperity depends upon this business of ours. And you can see and hear for yourselves that this Paul has persuaded a whole multitude to change their allegiance, not only at Ephesus but over most of Asia, by telling them that gods made by men's hands are no gods at all. It is not only that we are in danger of finding this work of ours discredited. The temple of the great goddess Diana will count for nothing, she will be shorn of her greatness, the goddess whom Asia and all the world reveres.'

At these words, they were all overcome with rage, and began to shout: 'Great is Diana of Ephesus.' The uproar filled the whole city, as they ran by common consent to the theatre, carrying with them Gaius and Aristarchus, who were companions of Paul from Macedonia. When Paul had a mind to show himself before the people, his disciples tried to prevent it; and some of the delegates of Asia, who were his friends, sent a message to him, imploring him not to risk his life in the theatre.

Meanwhile some cried this, some that; the meeting was all in confusion, and most of them could not tell what had brought them together. The Jews thrust Alexander forward, and some of the crowd brought him down with them; so Alexander made a gesture with his hand, and tried to give an account of himself before the people; but as soon as they

From Ephesus to Philippi 57 A.D.

Riot of the Silversmiths. Every four years the month of May was a public holiday at Ephesus. There were sacrifices daily in the temple of Diana, athletics in the amphitheatre, processions through the streets, and dancing at night. The whole city became one big fair; there was a spirit of celebration and revelry for a month. The whole of Asia, the most populous province of the Empire, sent delegates, particularly to the Games, which were the biggest in Asia. The normal population of 35,000 increased to at least a million people in the city of Ephesus for the Diana festival.

This was the 'great and promising opportunity' that Paul told the Corinthians he was waiting for. Earlier during his stay at Ephesus, he had won a notable victory over black magic by having most of the books on this occult science publicly burned. He had stayed on, despite urgent calls to other missionary centres. The vast concourse of people that would assemble at Ephesus for this big festival meant a heaven-sent opportunity to preach the gospel to the heathen.

Paul knew the difficulties and dangers of the situation. He was opposing paganism in one of its strongest centres and its holiest city. He had told the Corinthians: 'Strong forces oppose me.' On this occasion it was one of the wealthy merchants engaged in the production of statuettes of Diana that caused trouble. His name was Demetrius, and he spoke for the thousands of silversmiths engaged in the statue trade. In his speech he cleverly mixed appeals to the motives of gain, religion, and patriotism.

The fanatical crowd that soon gathered in the temple went in search of Paul. Fortunately he was not at the home of Aquila and Priscilla (he was probably instructing converts in

found out that he was a Jew, a single cry came from every mouth, and for some two hours they kept on shouting: 'Great is Diana of Ephesus.'

Then the town clerk restored quiet among the crowd: 'Ephesians,' he said, 'as if there were anyone who does not know that the city of Ephesus is the acolyte of the great Diana, and of the image that fell down from the sky! Since this is beyond dispute, you had best be quiet, and do nothing rashly. These men you have brought here have not robbed the temples; they have not used blasphemous language about your goddess. And if Demetrius and his fellow craftsmen have any charge to bring against them, why, we have our court days, we have proconsuls; let the two parties go to law. If, on the other hand, you have any further question to raise, it can be settled by lawful assembly. We may easily be called to account for today's proceedings, and there is no grievance which will enable us to account for this riot.' With these words he broke up the meeting.

When the tumult was over, Paul summoned his disciples, to rally their spirits and bid them farewell, and set out on his journey to Macedonia.

Second Letter to the Corinthians

From Paul, by God's will an apostle of Jesus Christ, and Timothy, who is their brother, to the Church of God which is at Corinth and to all the saints in the whole of Achaia; grace and peace be yours from God, our Father, and from the Lord Jesus Christ. Blessed be the God and Father of our Lord Jesus Christ, the merciful Father, the God who gives all encouragement. He it is who comforts us in all our trials; and

the school of Tyrannus). So the mob picked up two of his disciples, Gaius and Aristarchus, and swept on through the Jewish quarter to the theatre, with its seating capacity of 25,000.

The Jews, wishing to disassociate themselves from the Christians, persuaded one of their number, Alexander, to speak to the crowd; but they shouted him down. After two hours' shouting, the crowd was exhausted. The town clerk, who was the city's representative before the imperial authorities, seized the opportunity and made a common-sense appeal to reason and self-interest.

Sadly Paul decided to leave Ephesus, visit some of the churches of Asia, continue north to Troas, and cross by sea to Philippi. With him were Titus, soon to be sent with another letter to Corinth, Gaius and Aristarchus.

In 431 A.D. a general council of the Church was held at Ephesus. On that occasion the doctrine that Mary is the Mother of God was defined as an article of faith. Paul's gospel at last found acceptance at Ephesus: in the city that shouted for Diana, Mary was acclaimed.

Conflict Without, Anxiety Within

Comfort in Suffering with Christ. Paul went by land from Ephesus in a northerly direction, possibly to Smyrna; he probably spent several months visiting the churches on the road north to Troas; Sardis, Pergamum and Adrumetum all had flourishing Christian communities. But again he met with persecution, probably at the hands of the Jews in these cities; this is the Asian trial he refers to. Added to his recent experi-

it is this encouragement we ourselves receive from God which enables us to comfort others, whenever they have trials of their own. The sufferings of Christ, it is true, overflow into our lives; but there is overflowing comfort, too, which Christ brings to us. Have we trials to endure? It all makes for your encouragement, for your salvation. Are we comforted? It is so that you may be comforted. And the effect of this appears in your willingness to undergo the sufferings we too undergo; making our hopes of you all the more confident; partners of our sufferings, you will be partners of our encouragement too.

Make no mistake, brethren, about the trial which has been befalling us in Asia; it was something that overburdened us beyond our strength, so that we despaired of life itself. Indeed, for ourselves we could find no outcome but death; so God would have us learn to trust, not in ourselves, but in him who raises the dead to life. It is he who has preserved us, and is preserving us, from such deadly peril; and we have learned to have confidence that he will preserve us still. Only you, too, must help us with your prayers. So thanks will be given by many on our behalf, and in the name of many persons, for the favour God has shown to us.

It is our boast, made in all good conscience, that we have behaved in the world, and towards you especially, with a holiness that was sincere in God's sight, not using human wisdom, but the light of God's grace. And we mean by our letters nothing else than what you read in them, and understand us to mean. I hope that you will come to understand us better, as you do already in some measure; are we not your chief pride, as you are our chief pride, in the day when our Lord Jesus comes? It was with this confidence in you that I had made up my mind to give you a double opportunity of

ence at Ephesus, during the riot of the silversmiths, it almost overburdened the human powers of the strong-willed Paul.

Even in this first paragraph there is a hint that all was not well at Corinth; the details will be filled in as the letter progresses. It is the second element that contributed to Paul's mental anxiety: he not only had to endure opposition in Asia, he had also to cope with the disloyalty of some of the Corinthian converts. These two sources of worry give the tone and theme of the Second Letter to the Corinthians. It is the most personal and autobiographical of Paul's letters and has been called the Epistle of Paul's Passion.

With his Mystical Body outlook, Paul sees in these sufferings, both physical and mental, his own likeness to the suffering Head. Like our Lord in the garden of Gethsemani, Paul looks to the Father as the source of strength to endure and conquer. A favourite word to express this is 'comfort' and 'encouragement.' It is the Greek word familiar to us as the new name of the Holy Ghost, Paraclete—the Comforter. It occurs nine times in this paragraph, and 28 times in Second Corinthians; it is not used nearly so frequently in any other letter. It expresses Paul's reaction to the situation.

Paul Refutes Charge of Inconsistency. When Paul first preached the gospel in Corinth, six years before, his pagan converts enjoyed the freedom of God's children for the first time in their lives; 'I am free to do what I will' were familiar words on his lips. But when he wrote the First Letter to them from Ephesus, earlier this year, he severely criticized their abuse of Christian freedom. He quoted three examples: the man married to his father's wife, lawsuits before pagans, and food offered to idols. Their reaction was: How could you trust a man who said one thing to your face, then contradicted him-

spiritual profit, coming to you first, then passing through
Corinth to Macedonia, and so from Macedonia back to you;
and you were to put me on my way to Judea. When I thus
made up my mind, do you suppose I did it lightly? Can it
be said of me that the plans I form are formed by motives of
human prudence, so that it is first, 'Yes, I will,' and then,
'No, I will not,' with me? As God is faithful, the message we
delivered to you is not one which hesitates between Yes and
No. It was Jesus Christ, the Son of God, that I, that Silvanus
and Timothy preached to you; and that preaching did not
hesitate between Yes and No; in him all is affirmed with cer-
tainty. In him all the promises of God become certain; that
is why, when we give glory to God, it is through him that we
say our Amen. It is God who gives both us and you our cer-
tainty in Christ; it is he who has anointed us, just as it is he
who has put his seal on us, and given us the foretaste of his
Spirit in our hearts.

With my soul as the forfeit I call this God to witness that
if I did not, after all, visit you at Corinth, it was to give you
a fresh chance. (Not that we would domineer over your faith;
rather, we would help you to achieve happiness. And indeed,
in your faith you stand firm enough.) On this I was resolved
in my own mind, that I would not pay you a second visit on
a sad errand. Was I to make you sorry? It meant bringing
sorrow on those who are my own best source of comfort. And
those were the very terms in which I wrote: I would not
come, if it meant finding cause for sorrow where I might
have expected to find cause for happiness. I felt confidence
in you all, I knew that what made me happy would make you
happy too. When I wrote to you, I wrote in great anguish
and distress of mind, with many tears. I did not wish to bring
sorrow on you, only to assure you of the love I bear you, so

self when he wrote later from a safe distance? Such actions were signs of inconsistency and even cowardice.

His change of travel plans was another illustration of this Yes today and No tomorrow attitude. During Paul's three-year stay at Ephesus, he had promised to make the short few days' voyage across the Aegean to Corinth; but he had not come to them. He had gone back on his first promise by a casual notification in writing at the end of his First Letter: 'I shall be coming to you as soon as I have made the round of Macedonia' (1 Cor. 16, 5).

In reality travel plans are not so important; the person of our Lord is what really matters; and he is never far from Paul's thoughts. When Paul preached to them, when he wrote to them, his teaching was about Jesus crucified. There is no room for changing views and opinions about the Son of God; Paul's teaching has always been a constant affirmation of unchanging truth.

Disciplined Man Restored to Full Fellowship. *I* have assumed with Mgr. Knox that Paul is here referring to a lost letter written between 1 and 2 Corinthians. I have surmised that Timothy arrived from Corinth shortly after the riot at Ephesus and joined Paul in one of the nearby Asian cities. Timothy had been in Corinth when Paul's First Letter arrived there; and as Paul's closest friend and disciple he had been subjected to some insult on the part of the man corrected by Paul in 1 Corinthians 5. Possibly he had been physically assaulted by this man, who belonged to the rival Apollo party.

Deeply distressed by this incident, Paul wrote a short but stinging rebuke to the Corinthian community; from his own description of this letter it is often called the Epistle of Tears. He immediately sent off this new letter with Titus as

abundantly. Well, if someone has caused distress, it is not myself that he has distressed but, in some measure, all of you, so that I must not be too hard on him. This punishment inflicted on him by so many of you is punishment enough for the man I speak of, and now you must think rather of showing him indulgence, and comforting him; you must not let him be overwhelmed by excess of grief. Let me entreat you, then, to give him assurance of your good will. The reason why I wrote to you, after all, was to test your loyalty, by seeing whether you would obey me in full. If you show indulgence to anybody, so do I too; I myself, wherever I have shown indulgence, have done so in the person of Christ for your sakes, for fear that Satan should get the advantage over us; we know well enough how resourceful he is.

I went to Troas, then, to preach Christ's gospel there, and found a great opportunity open to me in the Lord's service; but still I had no peace of mind, because I had not yet seen my brother Titus; so I took leave of them all, and pressed on into Macedonia. I give thanks to God, that he is always exhibiting us as the captives in the triumph of Christ, and through us spreading abroad everywhere, like a perfume, the knowledge of himself. We are Christ's incense offered to God, making manifest both those who are achieving salvation and those who are on the road to ruin; as a deadly fume where it finds death, as a lifegiving perfume where it finds life. Who can prove himself worthy of such a calling? We do not, like so many others, adulterate the word of God, we preach it in all its purity, as God gave it to us, standing before God's presence in Christ.

messenger (2 Cor. 7 seems to require this). He demanded strong measures to be taken against the offender; they were to carry out the original sentence of excommunication; he appealed to their loyalty to him as their apostle to right the wrong done. Writing 2 Corinthians from Philippi, five months later, Paul has heard Titus' report on his Corinthian visit: the Epistle of Tears had been well received and the sinner disciplined. He must now be restored to full sacramental life.

Paul's tears recall the Master himself weeping over Jerusalem, his beloved city. Jesus wept because his people were rejecting God, and their only true Saviour; Paul saw the Corinthian rebellion as a rejection of apostolic authority, which comes from God. Our Lord felt sorrow for his people because he loved them so much; it was love not revenge that moved Paul to act as he did.

Christ's Apostles Are His Heralds Everywhere. Paul begins to explain the circumstances of his meeting with Titus, on the latter's return from Corinth; then suddenly breaks off his geographical description. The reader will have to wait until 7, 5 before Paul takes up again the story of his meeting with Titus.

The Corinthians had already accused Paul of changing his travel plans without divine guidance; seeing himself running into a similar difficulty over his journey to meet Titus, Paul breaks off the narrative and gives a homily on the apostolate. The image is from a triumphal procession; Paul is a captive led here, there, everywhere by Jesus. Then he is incense on the coals of the thurifers in the procession, wafted about by every wind. The effect he has on his hearers depends on their dispositions; let the Corinthians look into their consciences.

8

You will say, perhaps, that we are making a fresh attempt to recommend ourselves to your favour. What, do we need letters of recommendation to you, or from you, as some others do? Why, you yourselves are the letter we carry about with us, written in our hearts, for all to recognize and to read. You are an open letter from Christ, promulgated through us; a message written not in ink, but in the Spirit of the living God, with human hearts, instead of stone, to carry it. Such, through Christ, is the confidence in which we make our appeal to God. Not that, left to ourselves, we are able to frame any thought as coming from ourselves; all our ability comes from God, since it is he who has enabled us to promulgate his new law to men. It is a spiritual, not a written law; the written law inflicts death, whereas the spiritual law brings life. We know how that sentence of death, engraved in writing upon stone, was promulgated to men in a dazzling cloud, so that the people of Israel could not look Moses in the face, for the brightness of it, although that brightness soon passed away. How much more dazzling, then, must be the brightness in which the spiritual law is promulgated to them! If there is a splendour in the proclamation of our guilt, there must be more splendour yet in the proclamation of our acquittal; and indeed, what once seemed resplendent seems by comparison resplendent no longer, so much does the greater splendour outshine it. What passed away passed in a flash of glory; what remains, remains instead in a blaze of glory.

Such is the ground of our confidence, and we speak out boldly enough. It is not for us to use veiled language, as Moses veiled his face. He did it, so that the people of Israel might not go on gazing at the features of the old order, which was passing away. But in spite of that, dullness has crept over

Glory of the Christian Ministry.   There are three distinct
lines of thought in this and the next paragraph: (1) Moses, the
minister of the Old Covenant; this image serves as the theme
which unites both paragraphs. (2) Paul's mystic outlook on the
grandeur of the ministry of the New Covenant. (3) The Corinthian background of insinuations and accusations against Paul's
conduct; just what these charges were has to be surmised from
Paul's reply. Paul can talk one moment of sublime spiritual
truths, and in the next descend to practical matters.

Possibly Apollo returned to Corinth after the riot at
Ephesus; the comparison of Paul and Moses sounds very much
like his style of Old Testament allegory. The dazzling cloud,
symbol of the divine presence on mount Sinai when Moses received the Ten Commandments, was a scene far surpassing in
grandeur Paul's own personal meeting with the Lord on the
road to Damascus. The purpose of the comparison was to put
Paul in his rightful position of inferiority among God's ministers.

Paul's reply is to neglect the persons concerned and concen-
trate on the message preached by them. The glory of a minister
of the New Covenant far surpasses that of the Old for three
reasons: (1) The New Law is spiritual, the Old was material.
That is, the Old was written on stone tablets, the New comes
directly from Christ to the hearts of believers. (2) The New
brings acquittal from sin, the Old only made men more aware
of their guilt. (3) The New lasts forever, the Old has passed
away.

Gospel Preachers Do Not Veil the Light.   Paul knew his Old
Testament even more thoroughly than did Apollo. He now
proceeds to take up their Mosaic comparison and turn it
against them. He introduces a new detail from the story of
Moses, the veil worn over his face (Exod. 34, 29-35). For a

their senses, and to this day the reading of the old law is muffled with the same veil; no revelation tells them that it has been abrogated in Christ. To this day, I say, when the law of Moses is read out, a veil hangs over their hearts. There must be a turning to the Lord first, and then the veil will be taken away. The Spirit we have been speaking of is the Lord; and where the Lord's Spirit is, there is freedom. It is given to us, all alike, to catch the glory of the Lord as in a mirror, with faces unveiled; and so we become transfigured into the same likeness, borrowing from that glory, as the Spirit of the Lord enables us.

Being entrusted, then, by God's mercy with this ministry, we do not play the coward; we renounce all shamefaced concealment, there must be no crooked ways, no falsifying of God's word; it is by making the truth publicly known that we recommend ourselves to the honest judgment of mankind, as in God's sight. Our gospel is a mystery, yes, but it is only a mystery to those who are on the road to perdition; those whose unbelieving minds have been blinded by the god this world worships, so that the glorious gospel of Christ, God's image, cannot reach them with the rays of its illumination. After all, it is not ourselves we proclaim; we proclaim Christ Jesus as Lord, and ourselves as your servants for Jesus' sake. The same God who bade light shine out of darkness has kindled a light in our hearts, whose shining is to make known his glory as he has revealed it in the features of Jesus Christ.

We have a treasure, then, in our keeping, but its shell is of perishable earthenware; it must be God, and not anything in ourselves, that gives it its sovereign power. For ourselves, we are being hampered everywhere, yet still have room to breathe, are hard put to it, but never at a loss; persecution does not leave us unbefriended, nor crushing blows destroy

moment Paul is distracted from his argument as he recalls the symbolism of the veil: it represents Jewish blindness to the light of the gospel; the Jews are still walking round with a bandage over their eyes.

For the rest of this paragraph he develops a twofold contrast: he compares the veiled features of Moses and the unveiled face of Christ at the Transfiguration; and secondly he compares the veiled Moses with his own open, unveiled, straightforward language.

Paul's basic doctrine of the Mystical Body leads him naturally to think of our Lord. The incident of Jesus' mortal life that comes to mind is the Transfiguration, because of the parallel with Moses' dazzling features on mount Sinai. The glory of the Second Person of the Blessed Trinity shone out on Jesus' face at the Transfiguration; the members of Christ are like mirrors catching that divine light and reflecting it in their lives and in their preaching of the gospel truths.

Paul's preaching must not be considered apart from Christ; the message from God, delivered through Christ, is the same that Paul gave to the Corinthians. There is no veiling of this message, no subterfuge, no dishonesty; it is as open and straightforward as Christ himself. The cause of all the trouble is among the listeners; those who are honest and sincere see and understand; those who are badly disposed are blinded by Satan ('the god this world worships') and oppose the truth.

Paul Undaunted by Mortal Dangers. The opposition party of Apollo at Corinth put forward a plausible explanation of Paul's change in teaching: he was afraid of the Jews; he was a coward who would not stand up to his principles when pressure was applied. When he first preached at Corinth, he proclaimed the gospel of freedom from the burdensome prescrip-

us; we carry about continually in our bodies the dying state
of Jesus, so that the living power of Jesus may be manifested
in our bodies too. Always we, alive as we are, are being given
up to death for Jesus' sake, so that the living power of Jesus
may be manifested in this mortal nature of ours. So death
makes itself felt in us, and life in you. 'I spoke my mind,' says
the scripture, 'with full confidence,' and we too speak our
minds with full confidence, sharing that same faith, and knowing that he who raised the Lord Jesus from the dead will
raise us, too, and summon us, like you, before him. It is all
for your sakes, so that grace made manifold in many lives may
increase the sum of gratitude which is offered to God's glory.
No, we do not play the coward; though the outward part of
our nature is being worn down, our inner life is refreshed
from day to day. This light and momentary affliction brings
with it a reward multiplied every way, loading us with everlasting glory; if only we will fix our eyes on what is unseen,
not on what we can see. What we can see, lasts but for a
moment; what is unseen is eternal.

Once this earthly tent-dwelling of ours has come to an end,
God, we are sure, has a solid building waiting for us, a dwelling
not made with hands, that will last eternally in heaven. And
indeed, it is for this that we sigh, longing for the shelter of
that home which heaven will give us, if death, when it comes,
is to find us sheltered, not defenceless against the winds. Yes,
if we tent-dwellers here go sighing and heavy-hearted, it is
not because we would be stripped of something; rather, we
would clothe ourselves afresh; our mortal nature must be
swallowed up in life. For this, nothing else, God was preparing
us, when he gave us the foretaste of his Spirit. We take heart,
then, continually, since we recognize that our spirits are exiled
from the Lord's presence so long as they are at home in the

tions of the Mosaic law; but when he wrote to them from distant places, he gave way cravenly under fear of Jewish persecution. He retracted his doctrine of freedom and imposed restrictions such as Jewish marriage laws (1 Cor. 5) and Jewish outmoded kosher food regulations (1 Cor. 8-10).

In reply Paul appeals to the constant opposition and persecution of the Jews wherever he set foot. If he were trying to please the Jews by his teaching, why did they persecute him continually? It is true that Paul is human; he carries the treasure of Christ's revelation in his frail, perishable, mortal frame. But trials and troubles, instead of crushing and cowing him, only serve to remind him of his membership in the Mystical Body. The two essential acts of Jesus' life on earth were his death on the cross and his resurrection; Paul knows that it is through suffering that each member must imitate and relive the Passion of our Lord; this dying state is the only entry into the resurrected life. A passing trial is rewarded by eternal life with God.

The Feast of Tabernacles was held each year in October; for a whole week Paul and his disciples had moved out of Lydia's comfortable home to live in tents, just as the chosen people had done during the Exodus (Lev. 23, 34-44). The contrast between these two standards of living supplied Paul, the tentmaker, with a picturesque illustration of his sublime thoughts on life and death. For most men there is no greater danger than death. But that is not how Paul sees it; for him death is merely giving up the cold, unpleasant life in a tent out in the open for the warmth and comfort of a stone house, such as Lydia's. The temporary exile on earth is exchanged for the life of an eternal, heavenly home.

When Paul is summoned before the divine judge, there are

body, with faith, instead of a clear view, to guide our steps. We take heart, I say, and have a mind rather to be exiled from the body, and at home with the Lord; to that end, at home or in exile, our ambition is to win his favour. All of us have a scrutiny to undergo before Christ's judgment seat, for each to reap what his mortal life has earned, good or ill, according to his deeds.

It is, then, with the fear of the Lord before our minds that we try to win men over by persuasion; God recognizes us for what we are, and so, I hope, does your better judgment. No, we are not trying to recommend ourselves to your favour afresh; we are showing you how to find material for boasting of us, to those who have so much to boast of outwardly, and nothing inwardly. Are these wild words? Then take them as addressed to God. Or sober sense? Then take them as addressed to yourselves. With us, Christ's love is a compelling motive, and this is the conviction we have reached; as one man died on behalf of all, then all thereby became dead men; he died for us all, so that being alive should no longer mean living with our own life, but with his life who died for us and has risen again; and therefore, henceforward, we do not think of anybody in a merely human fashion; even if we used to think of Christ in a human fashion, we do so no longer; it follows, in fact, that when a man becomes a new creature in Christ, his old life has disappeared, everything has become new about him. This, as always, is God's doing; it is he who, through Christ, has reconciled us to himself, and allowed us to minister this reconciliation of his to others. Yes, God was in Christ, reconciling the world to himself, establishing in our hearts his message of reconciliation, instead of holding men to account for their sins.

two possibilities: he may still be in his tent (alive at the Second Coming), or he may be stripped of his tent (already dead). The early Christians were constantly thinking of the likelihood of their survival till the end of the world; it has already been mentioned twice in Paul's letters (1 Thess. 4, 15; 1 Cor. 15, 51). In either case Paul will welcome his homecoming to the vision of God and the glorification of his body.

The Ambassador of Christ. The thought of death and judgment, about which Paul has just been writing, is the link with the previous paragraph. These considerations should be sufficient guarantee to the Corinthians that Paul does not act despotically without thinking of the divine Judge, and that all his words of correction are uttered in sincerity, without subterfuge.

But fear is not the dominant motive in Paul's life; he acts from the highest of all motives, love; and he cannot speak of love without speaking of Christ. In quoting our Lord's example, it is rather surprising that Paul does not make use of some of the incidents in the Gospels; Jesus correcting his disciples, especially Peter, would have served him admirably in this context. But Paul is interested in only one incident of our Lord's life, and that is his death. By baptism a Christian undergoes a mystical death with Christ; the energy with which he lives, the breath he breathes, is the life of Christ. Such is the power and vitality of this new life that it is called a new creation; all distinctions between individuals disappear; no man is superior or inferior to another when all have been raised up with Christ.

Probably Paul is thinking of the taunt of the opposition party in Corinth, that he was not an apostle like the Twelve (1 Cor. 9). So he replies that knowing our Lord personally dur-

8*

We are Christ's ambassadors, then, and God appeals to you through us; we entreat you in Christ's name, make your peace with God. Christ never knew sin, and God made him into sin for us, so that in him we might be turned into the holiness of God. And now, to further that work, we entreat you not to offer God's grace an ineffectual welcome. ('I have answered your prayer,' he says, 'in a time of pardon, I have brought you help in a day of salvation.' And here is the time of pardon; the day of salvation has come already.) We are careful not to give offence to anybody, lest we should bring discredit on our ministry; as God's ministers, we must do everything to make ourselves acceptable. We have to show great patience, in times of affliction, of need, of difficulty; under the lash, in prison, in the midst of tumult; when we are tired out, sleepless, and fasting. We have to be pure-minded, enlightened, forgiving and gracious to others; we have to rely on the Holy Spirit, on unaffected love, on the truth of our message, on the power of God. To right and to left we must be armed with innocence, now honoured, now slighted, now traduced, now flattered. They call us deceivers, and we tell the truth; unknown, and we are fully acknowledged; dying men, and see, we live; punished, yes, but not doomed to die; sad men, that rejoice continually; beggars, that bring riches to many; disinherited, and the world is ours.

We are speaking freely to you, Corinthians; we throw our hearts wide open to you. It is not our fault, it is the fault of your own affections, that you feel constraint with us. Pay us back in the same coin (I am speaking to you as to my children); open your hearts wide too. You must not consent to be yokefellows with unbelievers. What has innocence to do with lawlessness? What is there in common between light

ing his earthly life ('in a human fashion') is no claim to superiority; in the Mystical Body a Christian does not merely live in Christ's company; Christ lives in and acts through him.

It was Christ's death on the cross that won this life for mankind; this redemption from sin comes to men through membership in his Mystical Body. In God's plan, our Lord did not remain on earth to bring the fruits of his redemptive death to the human race; he left that to his ambassadors. And in this official capacity Paul is appealing to his erring Corinthians to allow free entry to the grace of God now coming to them through his ministry; this demands immediate attention.

Finally, in a most moving and eloquent passage, Paul fills in the picture of the ideal ambassador. Though he uses the plural, it is quite clear that he is speaking of himself; it will help the Corinthians to make up their minds whether Paul or the opposition party under Apollo's name is the true ambassador of Christ. The emphasis is on Paul's humiliations, surely the most certain sign that he is following in the footsteps of his crucified Master (a matter he will develop at greater length in chapter 11). His closing list of criticisms is selected from the accusations and charges of the Corinthian opposition; they are the very things that might have been brought up by the Jews against Jesus.

Idolatry Must Be Shunned. There was something radically wrong in the Corinthian community; Paul betrays his anxiety throughout this letter. But he is so cautious in his treatment of the subject that it is difficult to decide just what has gone wrong there. He seems afraid of making the situation worse by speaking out too openly. In this paragraph he gives a clue why he is writing so circumspectly: he was confronted with the

and darkness? What harmony between Christ and Belial? How can a believer throw in his lot with an infidel? How can the temple of God have any commerce with idols? And we are the temple of the living God; God has told us so: 'I will live and move among them, and be their God, and they shall be my people. Come out, then, from among them, the Lord says, separate yourselves from them, and do not even touch what is unclean; then I will make you welcome. I will be your father, and you shall be sons and daughters to me, says the Lord, the Almighty.' Such are the promises, beloved, that await us. Why then, let us purge ourselves clean from every defilement of flesh and of spirit, achieving the work of our sanctification in the fear of God. Be generous with us; it is not as if any of you could say that we had wronged him, or done him harm, or taken undue advantage of him. I am not finding fault when I say this; I have told you before now, we hold you so close in our hearts that nothing in life or in death can part us from you.

With what confidence I speak to you, what pride I take in you! I am full of encouragement, nay, I cannot contain myself for happiness, in the midst of all these trials of mine. By the time we had reached Macedonia, our human weakness could find no means of rest; all was conflict without, all was anxiety within. But there is one who never fails to comfort those who are brought low; God gave us comfort, as soon as Titus came. It was not only that he came; he inspired us with that courage he had derived from you. He told us how you longed for my presence; how you grieved over what had happened, how you took my part, till I was more than ever rejoiced. Yes, even if I caused you pain by my letter, I am not sorry for it. Perhaps I was tempted to feel sorry, when I saw how my letter had caused you even momentary pain,

danger of a return of his Corinthians to paganism.

Most of the friends and relatives of the young Corinthian community were still pagans; they lived in a pagan society where problems of adjustment arose daily. One that they had asked Paul about in 1 Corinthians 8-10 was the question of eating food offered to idols. It seems quite likely that many of the Corinthians had not been impressed by Paul's warning against the danger of idolatry; they had continued to frequent the temple banquets, and this had led them back into the pagan way of life they had abandoned for Christ.

It is with the paternal love of a father for his wayward children that Paul again warns them of the grave danger of such conduct; there can be no compromise between Christ and Satan ('Belial'). If only they would acknowledge their guilt and repent, the constraint they now feel would immediately disappear, and they would once again be on friendly terms with their apostle.

Paul's Joy at Good News Brought by Titus. In chapter 2 of this letter, Paul began to discuss the return of Titus to him at Philippi after delivering the lost Letter of Tears. But other matters took his mind off this subject, and it is only here (five chapters later) that he comes back to Titus. This Letter of Tears had been sent by Paul shortly after leaving Ephesus; it was almost six months since Titus had departed with it for Corinth. Paul in the meantime had arrived at Philippi, and there was still no news of Titus. When he did arrive, and brought good news of the Corinthian acceptance of his rebuke in the Letter of Tears, all Paul's anxiety vanished; he was overjoyed at the success of Titus' mission.

The satisfaction Paul displays in this paragraph is in contrast to the anxious tone of the rest of the letter. The general im-

but now I am glad; not glad of the pain, but glad of the repentance the pain brought with it. Yours was a supernatural remorse, so that you were not in any way the losers through what we had done. Supernatural remorse leads to an abiding and salutary change of heart, whereas the world's remorse leads to death. See what devotion has been bred in you now by this supernatural remorse; how you disowned the guilt; the indignation you felt, the fear that overcame you; how you missed me, how you took my part, how you righted the wrong done. You have done everything to prove yourselves free from guilt in this matter. So, then, I had written you a letter, and it was neither the wrongdoer nor the injured party that was to be the gainer by it; it was to have the effect of showing you your devotion to our welfare in God's sight. It was this that brought us comfort; and besides this comfort, we had still greater cause for rejoicing in the joy which Titus felt, with his heart refreshed by the welcome you all gave him. I had boasted to Titus of the confidence I felt in you, and you did not play me false; no, the boast I had made to Titus proved true, as true as the message which I had delivered to you. He bears a most affectionate memory of you, of the submissiveness you all showed, of the anxious fear with which you received him. I am rejoiced that I can repose such full confidence in you.

And now, brethren, we must tell you about the grace which God has lavished upon the churches of Macedonia: how well they have stood the test of distress, how abundantly they have rejoiced over it, how abject is their poverty, and how the crown of all this has been a rich measure of generosity in them. I can testify that of their own accord they undertook to do all they could, and more than they could; they begged

pression left on the reader of 2 Corinthians is that all is not well at Corinth, and that Paul is most displeased and saddened at the danger signs only too obvious in the community there. Probably the true explanation of this seeming contradiction is that Paul goes out of his way to praise his erring converts in this one matter, because it is the only bright spot in the whole picture. In praising their ready obedience, he hopes to be able to coax them into a saner and more repentant frame of mind concerning the rest of their wayward conduct.

Quite clearly Paul had made the Letter of Tears a test case of his authority; he tells them so explicitly in 2 Corinthians 2, 9: 'The reason why I wrote to you, after all, was to test your loyalty, by seeing whether you would obey me in full.' That is why he waited for Titus' return with such anxiety; if he failed in this, then his authority over the Corinthians was doomed; the rival Apollo party would take complete control of that community.

The spontaneous joy manifested by Paul springs from the same source as that of our Lord at the repentance of the prodigal son, or the return of the lost sheep; as a member of Christ's Mystical Body, Paul shares the compassionate love of the Shepherd for the strayed sheep: 'He rejoices more over that one than over the ninety-nine which never strayed from him.'

The Collection for Jerusalem.   Twelve years before, Paul had gone up from Antioch to Jerusalem, in company with Barnabas; they were carrying a gift of money from the Gentile churches to the mother community in Judea (Acts 11, 27-30). This was right at the beginning of Paul's missionary life, just before the First Journey into Galatia. He never forgot this incident, and made it a practice to send back monetary assistance during

us, most urgently, to allow them the privilege of helping to supply the needs of the saints. And their gift went beyond our hopes; they gave their own services to the Lord, which meant, as God willed, to us; so that we were able to ask Titus to visit you again, and finish this gracious task he had begun, as part of his mission. You excel in so much already, in faith, in power of utterance, in knowledge of the truth, in devotion of every kind, in the love we have awakened in you; may this gracious excellence be yours too. I say this, not to lay any injunction on you, but only to make sure that your charity rings true by telling you about the eagerness of others. (You do not need to be reminded how gracious our Lord Jesus Christ was; how he impoverished himself for your sakes, when he was so rich, so that you might become rich through his poverty.) I am only giving you my advice, then, in this matter; you can claim that as your due, since it was you who led the way, not only in acting, but in proposing to act, as early as last year. It remains for you now to complete your action; readiness of the will must be completed by deeds, as far as your means allow. We value a man's readiness of will according to the means he has, not according to the means he might have, but has not; and there is no intention that others should be relieved at the price of your distress. No, a balance is to be struck, and what you can spare now is to make up for what they want; so that what they can spare may, in its turn, make up for your want, and thus the balance will be redressed. So we read in scripture, 'He who had gathered much had nothing left over, and he who had gathered little, no lack.'

I thank God for inspiring the heart of Titus, your representative, with the same eagerness. He has accepted our invitation; but indeed, of his own choice he was eager to visit

the whole course of his missionary journeys.

It was not merely an act of charity from rich to poor; it was a matter of great dogmatic importance to Paul. For him it was a demonstration of the unity of all members of the Mystical Body; it showed that the Church was catholic. This was of great importance at this period of the Church's existence, because there was a widening gap between Jews and Gentiles. As the apostle of the Gentiles, Paul was regarded with hostility by a great number of the Jewish converts. These collections served to tighten the bonds of unity; they were a continual reminder of the charitable interest the scattered Gentile churches had for the mother church at Jerusalem.

It would seem from Paul's approach that the Corinthians were rather slow in taking up the collection. So Paul emphasizes the generous way that the Macedonian churches (he was writing from the capital city, Philippi) were undertaking their collection. It is an appeal to the natural instinct in men not to be outdone by others; emulation can be a powerful motive moving men to act when otherwise they would have stood idle.

But that is only a natural motive. Paul raises their minds to a much higher reason for giving—the example of Christ himself. He speaks of the Incarnation as a gracious act by which the Second Person of the Trinity, possessing the riches of a heavenly existence, yet embraced the poverty of human life. The picture of the divine baby in the poverty of the stable at Bethlehem is a powerful motive to inspire the Corinthians to give generously; it is a sharing in God's own charity.

Titus Will Take Up the Collection. There was a critical minority in Corinth eager for any opportunity to discredit Paul. That is why he takes such care to avoid suspicion of

you. And we are sending with him that brother of ours who has won the praise of all the churches by his proclamation of the gospel; he, too, is the man whom the churches have appointed to be our companion in this gracious ministry of ours, to further the glory of the Lord himself and our own resolve. They were anxious that no suspicion should be aroused against us, with these great sums to handle; it is not only in the Lord's sight, but in the sight of men, that we have to study our behaviour. And, to accompany these, we are sending a brother of whose eagerness we have had good proof, in many ways and upon many occasions; now he is more eager than ever, such is the confidence he feels in you. As for Titus, he is my partner and has shared my work among you; as for these brethren of ours, they are the envoys of the churches, the glory of Christ: give them proof, then, of your charity, and of the good reason we have to be proud of you, for all the churches to see.

And indeed, to write and tell you about the collection for the saints would be waste of time; I know well your eagerness, which has made me boast to the Macedonians that Achaia has been ready ever since last year, and this challenge of yours has stirred up others besides yourselves. If I am sending the brethren, it is only for fear that the boast we made of you should prove false in this particular; as I told you, I would have you quite ready; or else, when some of the Macedonians come with me and find you unprepared, we, and you too for that matter, will be put to the blush over this confidence of ours. That is why I have thought it necessary to ask the brethren to visit you first, and see that the free offering you have already promised is prepared beforehand. Only it is to be a free offering, not a grudging tribute. I would

dishonesty in handling the relief fund for Jerusalem; he appoints not one or two, but three Christians of repute to collect the Corinthian money.

According to an early tradition, the first of the unnamed companions of Titus is his brother Luke, at that time the bishop of Philippi (these verses are still used as the epistle of the Mass for his feast day). But it is based on a faulty interpretation of the word 'gospel'; in the text the word refers to preaching the good news, rather than to a written document. Actually at this time Luke had not yet written his Gospel.

Most modern commentators think that Paul did name the two companions of Titus (there would be no point in giving a character reference to two nameless persons), but that their names were stricken out because of later defection from the faith. Demas is suggested as one of the names; he is the only one of Paul's disciples that we know to have lost the faith (2 Tim. 4, 9).

The Blessings of Open-Handed Generosity. The headquarters for the Christian community at Philippi was the home of Lydia, a rich and generous convert made by Paul seven years before. The Philippian community was the only church that contributed money to Paul's needs during his missionary journeys (Phil. 4, 15-17). In such surroundings Paul could not help comparing the generous Philippians with the difficult Corinthians; though there was more wealth in Corinth, the members of that church were not so eager to part with it. It is also probable that the opposition party at Corinth had made insinuations about Paul's handling of money; he shows great indignation and touchiness on this point (1 Cor. 9).

That is why he studiously avoids mentioning money in these

remind you of this: He who sows sparingly will reap sparingly; he who sows freely will reap freely too. Each of you should carry out the purpose he has formed in his heart, not with any painful effort; it is 'the cheerful giver God loves.' God has the power to supply you abundantly with every kind of blessing, so that, with all your needs well supplied at all times, you may have something to spare for every work of mercy. So we read, 'He has spent largely, and given to the poor; his charity lives on for ever.' He who puts grain into the sower's hand, and gives us food to eat, will supply you with seed and multiply it, and enrich the harvest of your charity; so that you will have abundant means of every kind for all that generosity which gives proof of our gratitude towards God. The administration, remember, of this public service does more than supply the needs of the saints; it yields, besides, a rich harvest of thanksgiving to God. This administration makes men praise God for the spirit of obedience which you show in confessing the gospel of Christ, and the generosity which you show in sharing your goods with these and with all men; and they will intercede, too, on your behalf, as the abundant measure of grace which God bestows on you warms their hearts towards you. Thanks be to God for his unutterable bounty to us.

And now, here is Paul, 'the man who is so diffident when he meets you face to face, and deals so boldly with you at a distance,' making an appeal to you by the gentleness and courtesy of Christ. What I ask is, that you will not force me to deal boldly with you when we meet. I have my own grounds for confidence, and with these I may well be counted a match for those who think we rely on merely human powers. Human indeed we are, but it is in no human strength that we fight

two chapter (2 Cor. 8-9). It must be the most unusual charity sermon ever delivered: fifteen times he refers to the collection, but not once does he mention the very thing about which he is writing—money. In the Greek text there are seven different words used by Paul in referring to the collection. A study of these seven words reveals four different lines of thought in Paul's appeal for funds for Jerusalem.

The word most frequently used is 'grace . . . gracious task . . . gracious ministry . . . gracious excellence': it is a privilege, a favour granted by God. By contributing to the needy in Jerusalem, the Corinthians are sharers in God's gracious act of taking our poverty on himself by the Incarnation; they also share in God's own creative act of providing and distributing material goods so necessary for human life on this earth.

It is a 'public service,' a liturgical act of divine worship, as in the Mass. It is also an act of 'charity . . . work of mercy . . . sharing': it contributes to the well-being of other members of the Mystical Body, the needy members in Jerusalem, who in turn will pray for the donors. And finally it is a 'free offering': this it is that makes their giving a meritorious act in God's sight. In this way Paul relates the collection to God, to the neighbour, and to the donors themselves.

Paul Threatens the Agitators. The next four chapters are Part Three of 2 Corinthians; this section shows Paul in a most stern and forceful mood. It is a stinging attack on the hard core of opposition in Corinth; Paul is determined to use the full power of his apostolic authority in order to destroy this rebellious minority. In this he is acting as the Master himself acted; he has appealed to them with gentleness and persuasion; it is only after they have rejected his appeal that he decides

our battles. The weapons we fight with are not human weapons; they are divinely powerful, ready to pull down strongholds. Yes, we can pull down the conceits of men, every barrier of pride which sets itself up against the true knowledge of God; we make every mind surrender to Christ's service, and are prepared to punish rebellion from any quarter, once your own submission is complete.

Wait and see what happens when we meet. There may be someone who takes credit to himself for being the champion of Christ; if so, let him reflect further that we belong to Christ's cause no less than himself; and indeed, I might boast of the powers I have, powers which the Lord has given me so as to build up your faith, not so as to crush your spirits, and I should not be put in the wrong. It must not be thought that I try to overawe you when I write. 'His letters,' some people say, 'are powerful and carry weight, but his presence in person lacks dignity, he is but a poor orator.' I warn those who speak thus that, when we visit you, our actions will not belie the impression which our letters make when we are at a distance.

It is not for us to intrude, or challenge comparison with others who take credit to themselves, content to take their own measure and compare themselves with their own standard of achievement. As for us, we may boast, but our boasting will not be disproportionate; it will be in proportion to the province which God has assigned to us, one which reaches as far as you. Nobody can say that we are encroaching, that you lie beyond our orbit; our journeys in preaching Christ's gospel took us all the way to you. Ours, then, is no disproportionate boasting, founded on other men's labours; on the contrary, as your faith bears increase, we hope to attain still

to threaten them with the divinely powerful weapon of authority given him by the Lord.

This final outburst of Paul is unexpected at this stage of his letter. The natural place for it would have been in the first seven chapters. For this reason some authors think that it does not belong to 2 Corinthians, which would finish more naturally with the Charity Sermon. They suggest that it is the lost Letter of Tears, written before 2 Corinthians, and later accidentally tacked on here. Others are of the opinion that Paul had really finished writing the letter at chapter 9, when some fresh information arrived from Corinth, indicating a deterioration in the situation there; deeply moved, Paul immediately decided on an all-out attack on his enemies, and so wrote these last four chapters as an appendix to the letter. But more likely Paul's mercurial temperament is sufficient explanation of this last attack on the rebellious minority; reading over his letter, he saw that it was not forceful enough; he decided to make a stronger attack, and so bring his enemies to repentance.

Paul Claims to be the Apostle of Corinth. In the preceding paragraph, Paul addressed his words directly to the rebellious element at Corinth; for the rest of the letter, he is speaking to the rank and file, the majority in the community who were wavering in their allegiance to him because of the specious arguments directed against his authority. Corinth was a city of slogans and rival parties, as is clear from 1 Corinthians 1-4; it would seem that the group united round the name of Apollo are the rebels attacking Paul, against whom he is arguing in these chapters.

To appreciate the point of Paul's reply it is necessary to find

further vantage-points through you, without going beyond our province, and preach the gospel further afield, without boasting of ready-made conquests in a province that belongs to another. 'He who boasts, should make his boast in the Lord'; it is the man whom the Lord accredits, not the man who takes credit to himself, that proves himself to be true metal.

If you would only bear with my vanity for a little! Pray be patient with me; after all, my jealousy on your behalf is the jealousy of God himself; I have betrothed you to Christ, so that no other but he should claim you, his bride without spot, and now I am anxious about you. The serpent beguiled Eve with his cunning; what if your minds should be corrupted, and lose that spotless innocence which is yours in Christ? Some newcomer preaches to you a different Jesus, not the one we preached to you; he brings you a spirit other than the spirit you had from us, a gospel other than the gospel you received; you would do well, then, to be patient with me.

I claim to have done no less than the very greatest of the apostles. I may be unexperienced in speaking, but I am not so in my knowledge of the truth; everybody knows what we have been in every way to you. Unless perhaps you think I did wrong to honour you by abasing myself, since I preached God's gospel to you at no charge to yourselves? Why, I impoverished other churches, taking pay from them so as to be at your service. I was penniless when I visited you, but I would not cripple any of you with expenses; the brethren came from Macedonia to relieve my necessities; I would not, and I will not, put any burden on you. As the truth of Christ lives in me, no one in all the country of Achaia shall silence this boast of mine. Why is that? Because I have no love for you? God knows I have. No, I shall continue to do as I have done, so as to cut away the ground from those who would

out what argument of the adversaries he is replying to. Since Paul is demonstrating his sole right to be called the apostle of Corinth, it seems that the Apollo party were arguing from Paul's long absence from Corinth. Did this not prove a lack of interest in them? It was hardly the conduct to be expected from one who claimed to be their sole guardian and protector. Paul's first argument is to go back to his original visit to Corinth: he came there to an entirely pagan field, sent directly by God to found the Corinthian church. Even though he has moved elsewhere to preach the gospel, no one can take from him the demonstrable historical fact that he founded the church in Corinth. This gives him a right and an authority above all other teachers and preachers; this is the basis of his claim to be Corinth's apostle.

What annoys Paul most of all is that these newcomers, intruders in the field of his labours, are not preaching the true spirit of Christianity (he is probably thinking of their emphasis on Greek wisdom instead of on the person of Jesus, 1 Cor. 1). It is not their want of allegiance to his own person that worries him; it is their want of allegiance to Christ, their bridegroom. As the bridegroom's friend, he feels anxiety at their consorting with the enemies of Christ. This image of marriage between the Lord and his chosen race is frequent in the Old Testament; it reminds Paul of another scriptural incident that had such disastrous effects on the whole human race—the fall from grace of our first parents, Adam and Eve, when tempted to sin by the devil.

Paul's only interest in Corinth, said the rebels there, was in extracting money from them. Instead of a personal visit, he merely wrote, or sent envoys to collect their hard-earned savings. Is that the action of a loving father, of their own special apostle? In reply, Paul again reminds them of the details of his

gladly boast that they are no different from myself. Such men are false apostles, dishonest workmen, that pass for apostles of Christ. And no wonder; Satan himself can pass for an angel of light, and his servants have no difficulty in passing for servants of holiness; but their end will be what their life has deserved.

Once more I appeal to you, let none of you think me vain; or, if it must be so, give me a hearing in spite of my vanity, and let me boast a little in my turn. When I boast with such confidence, I am not delivering a message to you from the Lord; it is part of my vanity if you will. If so many others boast of their natural advantages, I must be allowed to boast too. You find it easy to be patient with the vanity of others, you who are so full of good sense. Why, you let other people tyrannize over you, prey upon you, take advantage of you, vaunt their power over you, browbeat you! I say this without taking credit to myself, I say it as if we had had no power to play such a part; yet in fact—here my vanity speaks—I can claim all that others claim. Are they Hebrews? So am I. Are they Israelites? So am I. Are they descended from Abraham? So am I. Are they Christ's servants? These are wild words; I am something more. I have toiled harder, spent longer days in prison, been beaten so cruelly, so often looked death in the face. Five times the Jews scourged me, and spared me but one lash in the forty; three times I was beaten with rods, once I was stoned; I have been shipwrecked three times, I have spent a night and a day as a castaway at sea. What journeys I have undertaken, in danger from rivers, in danger from robbers, in danger from my own people, in danger from the Gentiles; danger in cities, danger in the wilderness, danger in the sea, danger among false brethren! I have met with toil

visit to them, seven years before (Acts 18, 1-11). These are facts they all can verify, and which most of them should remember from personal experience. He lived with Aquila and Priscilla and worked at this tentmaker's trade together with his hosts. When he needed money, it was Philippi (Macedonia) not Corinth that supplied his needs.

Paul Boasts of His Humiliations. Apollo was a man of imposing appearance, an eloquent orator, learned in the scriptures, and highly skilled in the philosophy of the Greeks. The party in Corinth who claimed him as their champion boasted of these outstanding qualities of his, so superior to those of the unimpressive Paul: 'His presence in person lacks dignity, he is but a poor orator' (2 Cor. 10, 10). Their estimation of success was based on merely human standards of excellence; such things as Jewish blood, the number of converts, the spectacular gift of tongues were the tests they applied to decide who was the most authentic apostle of Jesus Christ.

So Paul takes them up on their own ground; he will play the actor on the stage and boast of his own qualifications as an apostle. But for Paul there is only one standard of excellence, and that is a man's likeness to Christ. The scene always in Paul's mind was Golgotha: 'With Christ I hang upon the cross' (Gal. 2, 19). The Master himself, both by word and example, left no doubt what it is that makes men great: 'If any man has a mind to come my way, let him renounce self, and take up his cross, and follow me' (Mt. 16, 24).

Paul had now been a follower of Christ for 27 years, engaged in preaching the gospel in Cyprus, Galatia, Asia, Macedonia, and Greece for the past 12 years. Here, he briefly summarizes the sufferings and humiliations he underwent for

and weariness, so often been sleepless, hungry and thirsty; so often denied myself food, gone cold and naked. And all this, over and above something else which I do not count; I mean the burden I carry every day, my anxious care for all the churches; does anybody feel a scruple? I share it; is anyone's conscience hurt? I am ablaze with indignation. If I must needs boast, I will boast of the things which humiliate me; the God who is Father of the Lord Jesus, blessed be his name for ever, knows that I am telling the truth. When I was at Damascus, the agent of king Aretas was keeping guard over the city of the Damascenes, intent upon seizing me, and to escape from his hands I had to be let down through a window along the wall, in a hamper.

If we are to boast (although boasting is out of place), I will go on to the visions and revelations the Lord has granted me. There is a man I know who was carried out of himself in Christ, fourteen years since; was his spirit in his body? I cannot tell. Was it apart from his body? I cannot tell; God knows. This man, at least, was carried up into the third heaven. I can only tell you that this man, with his spirit in his body, or with his spirit apart from his body, God knows which, not I, was carried up into Paradise, and heard mysteries which man is not allowed to utter. That is the man about whom I will boast; I will not boast about myself, except to tell you of my humiliations. It would not be vanity, if I had a mind to boast about such a man as that; I should only be telling the truth. But I will spare you the telling of it; I have no mind that anybody should think of me except as he sees me, as he hears me talking to him. And indeed, for fear that these surpassing revelations should make me proud, I was given a sting to distress my outward nature, an angel of Satan

the name of Jesus. His list shows how incomplete is the record in the Acts. Of the details here narrated by Paul, only three have been told in the Acts: the stoning at Lystra (Acts 14, 18), the beating with rods by the Roman authority at Philippi (Acts 16, 22), and the escape over the wall in a hamper (Acts 9, 23-25). In Acts 27, Luke will tell of another shipwreck, making four in all; we have no details of any of the three ship-wrecks Paul mentions here.

This paragraph is the most impassioned outburst in the Pauline letters; it gives an insight into the intimate thoughts of Paul. It shows what a strain the life of a missioner was in those days of the first preaching of the faith. It brings Paul close as a man like ourselves, a person with human emotions and feelings.

Paul's Visions and a Constant Humiliation.   The Corinthians held spiritual gifts in high esteem (1 Cor. 12-14); they were greatly impressed by some claim to divine revelations on the part of Paul's rivals. So Paul was forced to boast of his visions. Five such are recorded in the Acts, and it is quite likely that the ecstasy mentioned here is the same as that of Acts 22, 17-18. This was probably the occasion of his visit to Jerusalem recorded in Acts 11, 27-30 and Galatians 2, 1; the date would be 44 A.D., fourteen years before the writing of 2 Corinthians. Paul does not like having to boast, and he tries to hide his identity in the phrase 'there is a man I know'; but there is no doubt that it is Paul who experienced this revelation. It seems to have been an almost direct contemplation of God, and most likely accompanied by bodily ecstasy.

But it is humiliations that are the real badge of Christ. So Paul mentions his most trying cross, something permanent and persistent throughout his life: 'A sting to distress my out-ward nature.' The Vulgate translation 'stimulus carnis' en-

sent to rebuff me. Three times it made me entreat the Lord
to rid me of it; but he told me, 'My grace is enough for you;
my strength finds its full scope in your weakness.' More than
ever, then, I delight to boast of the weaknesses that humiliate
me, so that the strength of Christ may enshrine itself in me.
I am well content with these humiliations of mine, with the
insults, the hardships, the persecutions, the times of difficulty
I undergo for Christ; when I am weakest, then I am strongest
of all.

I have given way to vanity; it was you that drove me to it;
you ought to have given me credentials, instead of asking for
them. No, I have done no less than the very greatest of the
apostles, worthless as I am; I have earned the character of
apostleship among you, by all the trials I have undergone, by
signs and wonders and deeds of miracle. What injustice did
I do you, as compared with the other churches, except that
to you, of my own choice, I refused to make myself a burden?
Forgive me, if I wronged you there. This is the third time
I have made preparations for visiting you, and I do not intend
to cripple you with expenses: what I claim is yourselves, not
anything you can give; it is the parents that should save for
their children, not the children for their parents. For my own
part, I will gladly spend and be spent on your souls' behalf,
though you should love me too little for loving you too well.
Ah, you say, that may be; I did not lay any charge on you myself, but I preyed upon you by roundabout means, like the
knave I am. What, those envoys I sent you, did I take advantage of you through any of them? I asked Titus to visit you,
and there was the brother I sent with him; did Titus take any
advantage of you? Did we not all follow the same course, and
in the same spirit?

You have been telling one another, all this while, that we

couraged the opinion that this was sensual temptation. But this is a false rendering of the Greek; and most modern commentators understand it as some chronic physical ailment, such as a nervous disorder, malaria, or an eye disease (Gal. 4, 13-15). St. Chrysostom, followed by Knox, held that it was the continual persecution of Paul by his own flesh and blood, the Jews. Biblical language (Num. 33, 55) supports this interpretation of 'sting.'

Defence of Past Conduct and Coming Visit. Paul returns to the question of money; the prominence given to this topic in 2 Corinthians indicates that Paul's enemies at Corinth were making quite a noise about it. So Paul here enumerates the three occasions in the past when his conduct in money matters aroused annoyance amongst his Corinthian adversaries.

When Paul first came to Corinth in 50 A.D. he refused to take any monetary assistance from his new converts. This was not owing to any lack of affection for or confidence in the Corinthians; it was a basic principle of Paul's not to be a burden on the churches he founded; children should not have to support their parents. He repudiates the charge that his disinterestedness with regard to money was only a pretence, that he was but preparing the ground for a later grand collection. The envoys he sent with First Corinthians, and then Titus with the Letter of Tears, did not collect any money to take back to Paul; they merely reminded the Corinthians of their expressed intention of collecting money to be sent by their own envoys to the Jerusalem community.

Paul is not looking forward to his coming visit. Throughout 2 Corinthians he has shown his anxiety over the way they are living and their attitude to himself. Right at the beginning

are defending our conduct to you. Rather, we have been uttering our thoughts as in God's presence, in Christ; yet always,
beloved, so as to build up your faith. I have the fear that
perhaps, when I reach you, I shall find in you unwelcome
hosts, and you in me an unwelcome visitor; that there will
be dissension, rivalry, ill humour, factiousness, backbiting,
gossip, self-conceit, disharmony. I have the fear that on this
new visit my God has humiliation in store for me when we
meet; that I shall have tears to shed over many of you, sinners
of old and unrepentant, with a tale of impure, adulterous and
wanton living.

This will be the third time I have been on my way to see
you. 'Every question,' we read, 'must be settled by the voice
of two or three witnesses.' I give you now, still absent, the
warning of my second visit; I have told you before, and tell
you now, both those who have sinned already and all the rest
of you, that I will show no leniency next time I come. Must
you have proof that it is Christ who speaks through me? In
him at least you will find no weakness; he still exerts his power
among you. Weakness brought him to the cross, but the
power of God brought him life; and though it is in our weakness that we are united to him, you will find us too, as he is,
alive with God's power. It is your own selves you should be
testing, to make sure you are still true to your faith; it is your
own selves you must put to the proof. Surely your own conscience will tell you that Jesus Christ is alive in you, unless,
somehow, you fail at the test; I think you will recognize that
we have not failed at ours. When we pray God to keep you
from wrong, it is not that we wish to prove successful; our
desire is that you should do what is right, even though we
seem to have failed. The powers we have are used in support
of the truth, not against it; and we are best pleased when we

of 1 Corinthians (1-4), he drew their attention to the rival factions at work in Corinth; it would seem from his list of eight vices in this paragraph that the disunity among the Corinthians was still the main evil to be remedied; the unity that Jesus prayed for (Jn. 17) was far from being realized in the Corinthian church. The second evil, already mentioned in both letters, was the danger of a return to pagan ways. This was emphasized by the conduct of the incestuous man (1 Cor. 5), who had already figured prominently in an attack on Paul's disciple, Timothy (2 Cor. 2).

Last Warning to the Unrepentant. The commentators are divided as to whether Paul paid a visit to Corinth during his three years at Ephesus. His language in 2 Corinthians 1-2 reads more naturally if he did not make this proposed visit. So I have followed Knox in assuming that the visit Paul is about to make to Corinth from his base at Philippi is really his second (his first took place seven years before). Though he had twice made preparations for a visit, circumstances had forced him on both occasions to change his plans.

Paul's long absence has been in great part the consequence of the evils prevailing at Corinth, especially the rebellious element opposed to his apostolic authority. Like the Master himself, Paul has patiently endured the attacks of his enemies; but the time has now come, when, like the resurrected Christ, he will demonstrate his power. In his dealings with the Corinthians he has been imitating Christ crucified; but from now on he will act with the power of the risen Christ. The time for leniency has passed; unless they set their house in order, he will come all sternness and severity. Not that he likes doing this; but it is the only means left to destroy evil and build up their spiritual life.

9

have no power against you, and you are powerful yourselves. That is what we pray for, your perfection. I write this in absence, in the hope that, when I come, I may not have to deal severely with you, in the exercise of that authority which the Lord has given me to build up your faith, not to crush your spirits.

Finally, brethren, we wish you all joy. Perfect your lives, listen to the appeal we make, think the same thoughts, keep peace among yourselves; and the God of love and peace will be with you. Greet one another with the kiss of saints. All the saints send you their greeting. The grace of the Lord Jesus Christ, and the love of God, and the imparting of the Holy Spirit be with you all.

Third Missionary Journey
continued

He passed through all that region, and gave much encouragement; then he entered Greece.

Letter to the Romans

It is Paul who writes; a servant of Jesus Christ, called to be his apostle, and set apart to preach the gospel of God. That gospel, promised long ago by means of his prophets in the holy scriptures, tells us of his Son, descended, in respect of his human birth, from the line of David, but in respect of the sanctified spirit that was his, marked out miraculously as the Son of God by his resurrection from the dead—our Lord Jesus Christ. It is through him/we have received the grace of apostle

Paul uses the word 'power' to express the action he will take against the unrepentant. It is most probably both a formal act of excommunication (as passed on the incestuous man in 1 Cor. 5) and a miraculous infliction of some physical punishment, such as the blindness inflicted on Elymas in Cyprus (Acts 13, 8-11).

In Paul's final greeting he wishes them peace: union of mind and heart amid the dissension and division that was destroying the Corinthian church. The only source of such union is the one life possessed by Father, Son, and Holy Ghost. This was Jesus' last prayer for his Church, and it is Paul's last wish for Corinth.

From Philippi to Corinth 57 A.D.

Paul spent the months of October and November visiting Thessalonica and his other nearby foundations.

Salvation to All Who Believe

Paul Salutes the Roman Church. It was early December, the first of the winter months, when Paul came to Corinth. His Second Letter to the Corinthians had moved those erring brethren to repentance; he found all quiet and peaceful on his second visit to this port. This time he lodged with Caius (his former hosts, Aquila and Priscilla, had gone back to Rome, sailing from Ephesus about the same time as Paul left there for Philippi). While waiting out the winter months, before

ship; all over the world, men must be taught to honour his
name by paying him the homage of their faith, and you among
them, you, who are called to belong to Jesus Christ. I wish
to all those at Rome whom God loves and has called to be holy,
grace and peace from God our Father, and from the Lord
Jesus Christ.

And first, I offer thanks to my God through Jesus Christ
for all of you, you whose faith is so renowned throughout the
world. The God to whom I address the inner worship of my
heart, while I preach the gospel of his Son, is my witness how
constantly I make mention of you, never failing to ask, when
I am at my prayers, that somehow, in God's Providence, I
may be granted at last an opportunity of visiting you. I long
to see you, in the hope that I may have some spiritual gift to
share with you, so as to strengthen your resolve; or rather, so
that the faith we find in each other, you and I, may be an
encouragement to you and to me as well. I should be sorry,
brethren, if you were left in doubt that (although hitherto
I have always been prevented) I have often planned to visit
you, and to be able to claim some harvest among you, as I
can among the Gentiles elsewhere. I have the same duty to
all, Greek and barbarian, learned and simple; and for my own
part I am eager to preach the gospel to you in Rome as I
have to others.

I am not ashamed of this gospel. It is an instrument of
God's power, that brings salvation to all who believe in it,
Jew first and then Greek. It reveals God's way of justifying
us, faith first and last; as the scripture says, 'It is faith that
brings life to the just man.'

God's anger is being revealed from heaven; his anger against
the impiety and wrong-doing of the men whose wrong-doing

he could take ship back to Jerusalem, Paul's thoughts turned to Rome. His work in the East was now completed; all the major cities had flourishing churches. But Christ's kingdom had not yet been established in the West. Paul was thinking of the cities of Gaul and Spain; the obvious headquarters for this venture was the very capital of the Empire, the city of Rome.

Peter had founded the Roman church sixteen years before, and it had been a point of honour with Paul never to enter another man's field of labour (Rom. 15, 20). Even to write a letter to such a community was a new departure for him. It would seem then that Paul was asked to do so by Peter himself; that is why he does not bully the Romans, as he did the Corinthians, but treats them with reverence and ceremonious formality in his letter.

The expulsion of the Jews from Rome by the emperor Claudius in 50 A.D. had given the Gentile converts a majority in the Roman church. Even though the Jews had returned, the Gentile element was still uppermost. The friction between Jew and Gentile in the Christian churches was the outstanding internal problem of the time. Paul, as champion of Gentile freedom, was asked to write a treatise on this subject. So he called in Tertius, his secretary, and dictated this famous letter.

In the last five lines of this paragraph, Paul states his thesis: God's way of salvation for all men, both Jew and Gentile. He develops this in four main divisions. 1-4: the need of Christian faith. 5-8: the grounds of Christian hope. 9-11: the rejection of the Jewish people. 12-16: the practice of Christian charity.

Corruption of the Pagan World. In the first four chapters Paul demonstrates the need of faith in Jesus Christ, because

denies his truth its full scope. The knowledge of God is clear
to their minds; God himself has made it clear to them; from
the foundations of the world men have caught sight of his
invisible nature, his eternal power and his divineness, as they
are known through his creatures. Thus there is no excuse for
them; although they had the knowledge of God, they did not
honour him or give thanks to him as God; they became fantastic in their notions, and their senseless hearts grew be-
nighted; they, who claimed to be so wise, turned fools, and
exchanged the glory of the imperishable God for representa-
tions of perishable man, of bird and beast and reptile. That
is why God abandoned their lustful hearts to filthy practices
of dishonouring their own bodies among themselves. They
had exchanged God's truth for a lie, reverencing and worshipping the creature in preference to the Creator (blessed
is he for ever, Amen); and, in return, God abandoned them
to passions which brought dishonour to themselves. Their
women exchanged natural for unnatural intercourse; and the
men, on their side, giving up natural intercourse with women,
were burnt up with desire for each other; men practising vile-
ness with their fellow-men. Thus they have received a fitting
retribution for their false belief.

And as they scorned to keep God in their view, so God
has abandoned them to a frame of mind worthy of all scorn,
that prompts them to disgraceful acts. They are versed in
every kind of injustice, knavery, avarice, and ill-will; spiteful,
murderous, contentious, deceitful, depraved, backbiters, slanderers, God's enemies; insolent, haughty, vainglorious; inven-
tive in wickedness, disobedient to their parents; without
prudence, without honour, without love, without pity. Yet,
with the just decree of God before their minds that those who

of the failure of both Gentile and Jew to attain union with God. The great disaster for the human race was original sin; it darkened man's intellect, weakened his will, and inclined him to evil. Paul was no stranger to the pagan world; he had lived in many of its famous cities. Writing from Corinth, notorious for its degrading vices, he had only to look around him to see the sad fate to which pagans had been reduced.

Man is capable of union with God through the two faculties of intellect and will; his intellect seeks truth, his will seeks goodness. Paul proceeds to castigate the heathen for their abuse of these two faculties. The intellect is able to reason from the harmony and beauty of the created universe to the existence of an eternal, powerful, and divine Being. In theory they did arrive at this conclusion, but in practice they did not pay God the honour due to him; instead they made idolatrous images of God's creatures and served them.

The consequence of this abuse of their minds was that their wills did not seek goodness but evil. The pagan world had lost the art of right living. This was most apparent in the unnatural sexual vice which had not only become a part of their personal lives but was also practised as a religious act in their temples. It was not merely an act performed in a moment of passion that was in question, but a cold-blooded dedication to evil practices. Paganism had justly merited God's anger.

Paul lists 21 common sins obvious to any visitor to a pagan city such as Corinth. The entire life of a pagan was submerged in sinfulness. Two of these particularly characterized paganism, 'without love, without pity.' It was a cold, harsh world in which the heathen lived; slavery was an essential part of society, and slaves were regarded as so much merchandise, not

so live are deserving of death, they not only commit such acts,
but countenance those who commit them.

So, friend, if you can see your neighbour's faults, no excuse
is left you, whoever you are; in blaming him, you own
yourself guilty, since you, for all your blame, live the same
life as he. We know that God passes unerring judgment upon
such lives; and do you, friend, think to escape God's judgment, you who blame men for living thus, and are guilty
of the same acts yourself? Or is it that you are presuming on
that abundant kindness of his, which bears with you and waits
for you? Do you not know that God's kindness is inviting
you to repent? Whereas you, by the stubborn impenitence of
your heart, continue to store up retribution for yourself
against the day of retribution, when God will reveal the justice of his judgments. 'He will award to every man what his
acts have deserved'; eternal life to those who have striven for
glory, and honour, and immortality, by perseverance in doing
good; the retribution of his anger to those who are contumacious, rebelling against truth and paying homage to
wickedness.

There will be affliction then and distress for every human
soul that has practised wickedness, the Jew in the first instance, but the Gentile too; there will be glory and honour
and peace for everyone who has done good, the Jew in the
first instance, but the Gentile too. There are no human preferences with God. Those who have been sinners without
regard to the law will be doomed without regard to the law;
those who have been sinners with the law for their rule will
be judged with the law for their rule. To have heard the law
read out is no claim to acceptance with God; it is those who
obey the law that will be acquitted, on that day when God

as human beings with rights like other men. Charity alone can
unite men with each other and with God.

Impartial Judgment For All Men. 'The Pharisee stood upright, and made this prayer in his heart: "I thank you, God,
that I am not like the rest of men, who steal and cheat and
commit adultery." ' That parable of our Lord gives the exact
attitude of a Jew to the pagan world in which he lived; like
the Pharisee in the parable, the Jew had nothing but criticism
and condemnation for the heathen. If he would only turn his
critical eye on himself he would see that he himself was guilty
of many of the sins he condemned in the pagans. And that is
Paul's aim in this paragraph; he is proving that the unconverted Jew is no better off than the pagan. This will come to
light when God judges mankind.

In this and the next paragraph, Paul changes from the third
person to the second; he is addressing an imaginary audience.
He picks out one person; 'friend' is what he calls him. In the
next paragraph it is quite clearly an unconverted Jew that he
is talking to; but at this stage he does not wish to antagonize
such people, so he leaves uncertain the identity of the imaginary objector. This manner of approach has something of the
dramatic in it, like Nathan lulling David into a false security
with his story of the ewe lamb (2 Kings 12, 1-9), then at the
psychological moment pointing the finger at him with the
words: 'You are that man.'

Paul pictures the Jews listening to his condemnation of the
pagan world, nodding their heads in agreement. He proceeds
to focus their eyes on themselves. He takes their minds from
God's kindness to Israel throughout the course of their history,
and fixes it on the judgment scene at the end of time. Then
it will not be race that will count but how a man has observed

9*

(according to the gospel I preach), will pass judgment, through Jesus Christ, on the hidden thoughts of men. (As for the Gentiles, though they have no law to guide them, there are times when they carry out the precepts of the law unbidden, finding in their own natures a rule to guide them, in default of any other rule; and this shows that the obligations of the law are written in their hearts; their conscience utters its own testimony, and when they dispute with one another they find themselves condemning this, approving that.)

You claim Jewish blood; you rely on the law; God is all your boast; you can tell what is his will, discern what things are of moment, because the law has taught you. You have confidence in yourself as one who leads the blind, a light to their darkness; admonishing the fool, instructing the simple, because in the law you have the incarnation of all knowledge and all truth. Tell me, then, you who teach others, have you no lesson for yourself? Is it a thief that preaches against stealing, an adulterer that forbids adultery? Do you rob temples, you, who shrink from the touch of an idol? Your boast is in the law; will you break the law, to God's dishonour? 'The name of God,' says the scripture, 'has become a reproach among the Gentiles, because of you.'

Circumcision, to be sure, is of value, so long as you keep the law; but if you break the law, your circumcision has lost its effect. And if one who has never been circumcised observes the conditions of the law, does it not follow that he, though uncircumcised, will be reckoned as one who is circumcised? That he, who keeps the law, though uncircumcised in body, will be able to pass judgment on you, who break the law, though circumcised according to the letter of it? To be a Jew is not to be a Jew outwardly; to be circumcised is not to be circumcised outwardly, in the flesh. He is a Jew indeed who is

the law of God; Jews will be judged according to the Mosaic
law, Gentiles according to the natural law. The Jews have
God's revelation to guide them; this privileged position will
give them less excuse than the Gentiles for their sinful lives.
In actual fact, the ten commandments are their basic moral
code; with the exception of sabbath observance, these commandments are founded on the natural law, and so were
known to the Gentiles as well as the Jews.

The Test Of A True Jew.   In the Sermon on the Mount, our
Lord gave a simple test to determine whether a man is good or
bad: 'You will know them by the fruit they yield; the test of
the tree is in its fruit.' It is not what a man thinks that makes
him pleasing to God; it is how he lives. His own opinion of
himself does not count; the possession of knowledge and
truth, even the privileged status conferred on him by God, are
valueless if his behaviour does not conform to them.

The Jews of Paul's time, just like those in the Gospels, had
an entirely different test of their friendship with God. Paul is
careful not to deny their privileges; but he takes up two of
them, the Mosaic law and circumcision, and shows that the
Jews were unfaithful in observing the consequent obligations
of both these divine favours.

Paul chooses three commandments from the Mosaic law,
the seventh, sixth, and first (in that order). The Jews prided
themselves on their superiority over the Gentiles in these three
commandments. By robbing a pagan temple and stealing an
idol of silver or gold, they thought they were doing a favour
to God in that they were preventing idolatrous worship; in
reality they were offending God by stealing and by having an
idol in their possession. They were doubly transgressing God's
law.

one inwardly; true circumcision is achieved in the heart, according to the spirit, not the letter of the law, for God's, not for man's approval.

Of what use is it, then, to be a Jew? What value was there in circumcision? Much, I answer, in every respect; chiefly because the Jews had the words of God entrusted to them. Some, to be sure, showed unfaithfulness on their side; but can we suppose that unfaithfulness on their part will dispense God from his promise? It is not to be thought of; God must prove true to his word, though all men should play him false; so it is written, 'Your dealings were just, and if you are called in question, you have right on your side.' Thus our fault only serves to bring God's integrity to light. (Does that mean that God does wrong in punishing us for it? Impossible again, even according to our human standards; that would mean that God has no right to judge the world; it would mean that because my deceitfulness has promoted God's glory by giving scope to his truthfulness, I on my side do not deserve to be condemned as a sinner. If so, why should we not do evil so that good may come of it? That is what we are accused of preaching by some of our detractors; and their condemnation of it is just.)

Well then, has either side the advantage? In no way. Jews and Gentiles, as we have before alleged, are alike convicted of sin. Thus, it is written, 'There is not an innocent man among them, no, not one. There is nobody who reflects, and searches for God; all alike are on the wrong course, all are wasted lives; not one of them acts honourably, no, not one. Their mouths are gaping tombs, they use their tongues to flatter. Under their

Paul has a play on the meaning of circumcision. This mark of friendship with God was made by cutting with a knife; it is far more pleasing to God to cut out sin from one's life, than merely to cut the body.

Jewish Unfaithfulness Is Inexcusable. Another divine favour enjoyed exclusively by the Jews was the promise of a Redeemer to come, the Messias. The 140 Messianic promises contained in the Old Testament are here called by Paul, 'the words of God . . . his promise.' He probably intended to list a series of privileges possessed by the Jews (as he does in 9, 4-6); but he contents himself with just one, because it served to show up clearly the great sinfulness of the Jewish race.

By unfaithfulness he means the unbelief of the Jews in rejecting the Messias (our Lord Jesus Christ) when he did come to them; their crucifixion of Jesus was the culmination of a whole history of crime: 'There was not one of the prophets they did not persecute.'

The fact that it had a happy sequel (the admission of the Gentiles to the universal Church) does not excuse them; otherwise God would be unable to condemn any sinner, seeing that he can bring good from evil. Common sense leads to the same conclusion: all condemn the teaching that it is lawful to do evil to achieve good.

Human Sinfulness Is Universal. Paul has been arguing from hard realities, not from religious speculations. First of all he proved the need of the Gentile world for a redeemer by his devastating picture of pagan sinfulness. Then he proceeded with his indictment of the Jewish people; this he did most carefully by gradually building up his case from the observable behaviour of the Jews. They are even more guilty than the

lips the venom of asps is hidden. Their talk overflows with
curses and calumny. They run hot-foot to shed blood; havoc
and ruin follow in their path; the way of peace is unknown to
them. They do not keep the fear of God before their eyes.'
So the law says, and we know that the words of the law are
meant for the law's own subjects; it is determined that no one
shall have anything to say for himself, that the whole world
shall own itself liable to God's judgments. No human creature
can become acceptable in his sight by observing the law; what
the law does is to give us the full consciousness of sin.

But, in these days, God's way of justification has at last been
brought to light; one which was attested by the law and the
prophets, but stands apart from the law; God's way of justification through faith in Jesus Christ, meant for everybody that
has faith. There is no distinction; all alike have sinned, all
alike are unworthy of God's praise. And justification comes to
us as a free gift from his grace, through our redemption in
Jesus Christ. God has offered him to us as a means of reconciliation, in virtue of faith, ransoming us with his blood.
Thus God has vindicated his own holiness, showing us why
he overlooked our former sins in the days of his forbearance;
and he has also vindicated his holiness, here and now, as one
who is himself holy, and imparts holiness to those who take
their stand upon faith in Jesus. What has become, then, of
your pride? No room has been left for it. On what principle?
The principle which depends on observances? No, the principle
which depends on faith; our contention is, that a man is
justified by faith apart from the observances of the law. Is God
the God of the Jews only? Is he not the God of the Gentiles
too? Of the Gentiles too, assuredly; there is only one God, who

heathen, in that they possess a revealed code of conduct in the Mosaic law; the more divine favours they possess, the more will they have to answer for when God comes in judgment.

For the benefit of the Jewish reader, Paul now brings forward his final and decisive proof: God himself in the inspired writings of the Old Testament convicts all men, especially the Jews, of sin. The scripture quotation is a series of statements from five psalms and Isaias ('the law' here stands for the Old Testament in general). Such a testimony from the mouth of God is the final word on the sinfulness of Jew and Gentile alike.

Justification Through Faith In Christ. Just 28 years before in an eastern province of the Empire, outside the city walls of Jerusalem, a detachment of Roman soldiers crucified a Jewish criminal on orders from the governor. In heaven above, God the Father looked down with satisfaction on this scene; the victim crucified on Golgotha was his only Son, the Second Person of the Blessed Trinity, by that very act bringing back mankind to divine friendship. This plan of reconciliation had not been thought up by men; the initiative had come from God himself, a free gift of his divine grace.

This act was the most important ever to happen in the long history of the human race; the blood of Christ cried out more powerfully for pardon than the blood of Abel for vengeance. Jew and Gentile alike now had a means of approach to God. But God's friendship did not come automatically from Christ's death; man had to come in contact with the atoning sacrifice by faith; that was his contribution to God's way of justification. He could change from his sinful state to God's friendship by accepting Christ his redeemer, and surrendering his whole personality to the divine will in Christ Jesus. Faith

will justify the circumcised man if he learns to believe, and the
Gentile because he believes.

Does that mean that we are using faith to rob the law of its
force? No, we are setting the law on its right footing. What,
for instance, shall we say of Abraham, our forefather by human
descent? What kind of blessing did he win? If it was by observances that Abraham attained his justification, he, to be
sure, has something to be proud of. But it was not so in God's
sight; what does the scripture tell us? 'Abraham put his faith
in God, and it was reckoned virtue in him.' The reward given
to one who works to earn it is not reckoned as a favour, it is
reckoned as his due. When a man's faith is reckoned virtue in
him, it is not because of anything he does; it is because he has
faith, faith in the God who makes a just man of the sinner. So,
too, David pronounces his blessing on the man whom God ac-
cepts, without any mention of observances: 'Blessed are those
who have all their faults forgiven, all their transgressions buried
away; blessed is the man who is not a sinner in the Lord's
reckoning.' This blessing, then, does it fall only on those who
are circumcised, or on the uncircumcised as well? We saw that
Abraham's faith was reckoned virtue in him. And in what state
of things was that reckoning made? Was he circumcised or
uncircumcised at the time? Uncircumcised, not circumcised
yet. Circumcision was only given to him as a token; as the seal
of that justification which came to him through his faith while
he was still uncircumcised. And thus he is the father of all
those who, still uncircumcised, have the faith that will be
reckoned virtue in them too. Meanwhile, he is the father of
those who are circumcised, as long as they do not merely take
their stand on circumcision, but follow in the steps of that

in Christ was the first step in the process of becoming holy, of sharing in the divine life of sanctifying grace.

Abraham Was Justified By Faith. One day in Bethany a Jew asked our Lord: 'What must I DO to inherit eternal life?' That question represents the common Jewish outlook on how to gain God's friendship; it was entirely a matter of observing laws, of doing things set down in the Mosaic law. Circumcision was the first and most important of these acts by which a boy was initiated into God's chosen people. And now Paul was telling them that it was an interior disposition of soul, faith not observances, that made a man pleasing to God. To demonstrate that the new way of justification was not contrary to the old revelation, Paul here tells the story of Abraham.

Paul had already quoted the example of Abraham to the Galatians (3, 16-18). Every Jew prided himself on being a true son of Abraham, the father and founder of the chosen race; they could do no better than follow in his footsteps. To him was given the rite of circumcision, the mark and badge of the Jew distinguishing him and setting him above all other peoples. Paul freely admits this fact; it is narrated in Sacred Scripture (Gen. 17). But there is another incident in the Genesis story; it comes BEFORE (in chapter 15) Abraham was circumcised. And from this incident it is clear that Abraham was admitted to the friendship of God before he was circumcised.

The incident in Genesis that Paul refers to is this: God appeared to Abraham and told him that he would make his children as numerous as the stars in the heavens. A tremendous promise to a man who was nearing his century in age, and who had as yet no children at all. Abraham's reaction was an act of faith in the truth of God's promise. He accepted God

faith which he, our father Abraham, had before circumcision began.

It was not through obedience to the law, but through faith justifying them, that Abraham and his posterity were promised the inheritance of the world. If it is only those who obey the law that receive the inheritance, then his faith was ill founded, and the promise has been annulled. (The effect of the law is only to bring God's displeasure upon us; it is only where there is a law that transgression becomes possible.) The inheritance, then, must come through faith (and so by free gift); thus the promise is made good to all Abraham's posterity, not only that posterity of his which keeps the law, but that which imitates his faith. We are all Abraham's children; and so it was written of him, 'I have made you the father of many nations.' We are his children in the sight of God, in whom he put his faith, who can raise the dead to life, and send his call to that which has no being, as if it already were.

Abraham, then, believed, hoping against hope; and thus became the father of many nations; 'Like these,' he was told, 'your posterity shall be.' There was no wavering in his faith, even though he fully realized the want of life in his own body (he was nearly a hundred years old at the time), and the deadness of Sara's womb; he showed no hesitation or doubt at God's promise, but drew strength from his faith, confessing God's power, fully convinced that God was able to perform what he had promised. This, then, was reckoned virtue in him; and the words, 'It was reckoned virtue in him,' were not written of him only: they were written of us too. It will be reckoned virtue in us, if we believe in God as having raised our Lord Jesus Christ from the dead: handed over to death for our sins, and raised to life for our justification.

at his word, and in return 'it was reckoned virtue in him.' And when God says a man is virtuous, he is thereby made holy.

Abraham Father Of All Believers. The Jews laid an exclusive claim to Abraham: 'We have Abraham for OUR father.' But this was not what God had planned for him: 'I have made you the father of many nations.' The blood of Abraham did not run in the veins of the converts from paganism; in what way, then, could they be called the posterity of Abraham? There is only one way, says Paul, and that is by sharing in Abraham's faith. It was by faith that Abraham became God's friend; it is by faith that the Jew, no less than the Gentile, enters into the divine life in the Christian Church.

To Abraham and his posterity was promised 'the inheritance of the world'; this is the same as 'father of many nations.' If this promise was conditional on the carrying out of a law that did not come into existence until 430 years after Abraham (Gal. 3, 17), then not only was Abraham's faith ill-founded, but God was going back on his original promise. That such a thing is unthinkable is obvious from the role of the law; it was never meant to bring life and grace to men; by its positive commands and prohibitions it made men guilty not only of sin but of formal transgression as well.

When Abraham believed God's promise he had no children at all; a posterity as numerous as the stars in the sky could not come into being unless he had at least one son to carry on his name. Paul sees a hidden meaning in the manner of Isaac's birth; it was a rising to life from the dead. The womb of an eighty-year-old woman could be counted as powerless as a tomb to produce life. The birth of Isaac from such a place of death foreshadowed the resurrection of Christ from the dead on Easter Sunday.

Once justified, then, on the ground of our faith, we enjoy peace with God through our Lord Jesus Christ, as it was through him that we have obtained access, by faith, to that grace in which we stand. We are confident in the hope of attaining the glory of God; nay, we are confident even over our afflictions, knowing well that affliction gives rise to endurance, and endurance gives proof of our faith, and a proved faith gives ground for hope. Nor does this hope delude us; the love of God has been poured out in our hearts by the Holy Spirit, whom we have received. Were that hope vain, why did Christ, in his own appointed time, undergo death for us sinners, while we were still powerless to help ourselves? It is hard enough to find anyone who will die on behalf of a just man, although perhaps there may be those who will face death for one so deserving. But here, as if God meant to prove how well he loves us, it was while we were still sinners that Christ died for us. All the more surely, then, now that we have found justification through his blood, shall we be saved, through him, from God's displeasure. Enemies of God, we were reconciled to him through his Son's death; reconciled to him, we are surer than ever of finding salvation in his Son's life. And, what is more, we can boast of God's protection; always through our Lord Jesus Christ, since it is through him that we have attained our reconciliation.

[12]It was through one man that guilt came into the world; and, since death came owing to guilt, death was handed on to all mankind by one man. (All alike were guilty men; [13]there was guilt in the world before ever the law of Moses was given. Now, it is only where there is a law to transgress that guilt is imputed, [14]and yet we see death reigning in the world from Adam's time to the time of Moses, over men who were not themselves guilty of transgressing a law, as Adam was.) In this,

Our Life After Justification.   Our Lord described the purpose
of his coming, in the parable of the Good Samaritan. He himself is the Good Samaritan, mankind the wounded man by
the roadside. Jesus not only rescued him from his miserable
condition of original sin (Rom. 1-4), he also provided a home
(the Church) for man, where he could be nursed back to
health; there all the treasures of divine grace are provided for
him (Rom. 5-8).

This paragraph is the beginning of chapter 5; here Paul
begins a new section of his letter. In the first four chapters he
showed how a man comes into contact with the redeeming
death of Christ by faith; this first step in the Christian life,
from sin to grace, Paul calls justification. In the next four
chapters (5-8), his purpose is to show man how to live a
Christian life. His attention is now centred on his final goal,
glory with God in heaven for all eternity. This is what Paul
calls salvation; it is a sharing in Christ's life, which ultimately
is the divine life of the Blessed Trinity.

It is a long way from justification to salvation, and man has
to endure a life of afflictions. The Christian needs the virtue
of hope, by which he puts his confidence in divine goodness.
He has three motives for hope: the love of the Father, the
indwelling of the Holy Spirit, and the redemptive death of
the Son.

Grace Is Ours In Superabundance.   Paul here treats of original sin. Why did he not deal with it earlier in the letter? After
all, original sin was the basic cause of all evil in the world,
both heathen and Jewish. Most likely he left it till this chapter because he wanted to show how fortunate it was for man
that Adam sinned: the grace that came from the atoning death
of the Second Adam was out of all proportion to original sin.

Adam was the type of him who was to come. [15]Only, the grace which came to us was out of all proportion to the fault. If this one man's fault brought death on a whole multitude, all the more lavish was God's grace, shown to a whole multitude, that free gift he made us in the grace brought by one man, Jesus Christ. [16]The extent of the gift is not as if it followed one man's guilty act; the sentence which brought us condemnation arose out of one man's action, whereas the pardon that brings us acquittal arises out of a multitude of faults. [17]And if death began its reign through one man, owing to one man's fault, more fruitful still is the grace, the gift of justification, which bids men enjoy a reign of life through one man, Jesus Christ.

[18]Well then, one man commits a fault, and it brings condemnation upon all; one man makes amends, and it brings to all justification, that is, life. [19]A multitude will become acceptable to God through one man's obedience, just as a multitude, through one man's disobedience, became guilty. [20]The law intervened, only to amplify our fault; but, as our fault was amplified, grace has been more amply bestowed than ever; [21]that so, where guilt held its reign of death, justifying grace should reign instead, to bring us eternal life through Jesus Christ our Lord.

Does it follow that we ought to go on sinning, to give still more occasion for grace? God forbid. We have died, once for all, to sin; can we breathe its air again? You know well enough that we who were taken up into Christ Jesus by baptism have been taken up, all of us, into his death. In our baptism, we have been buried with him, died like him, that so, just as Christ was raised up by his Father's power from the dead, we too might live and move in a new kind of existence. We have to be closely fitted into the pattern of his resurrection, as we

Paul has three lines of thought. (1) In verses 13-14 he proves the existence of original sin (translated 'guilt' by Knox). His argument is historical: men died during the thousands of years between Adam and Moses; death is a punishment for disobedience to a positive law of God (Gen. 2, 17); but until the Mosaic law there were no such laws punishing disobedience by death; therefore men died because they were disobedient in the person of Adam, the representative man. (Death in vv. 12, 14 is bodily death, in vv. 15, 17, 21 it is spiritual.)

(2) Parallel between Adam and Christ, verses 12, 18, 19, 21. There is a close relation between Adam and Christ, in their manhood, the act each one did, and its result for mankind. One man Adam—disobedience—death upon all: One man Christ—obedience—life for all. Adam is a type of Christ in that in their different ways each is the head of the human race.

(3) Difference between Adam and Christ, verses 15, 16, 17, 20. First, the effects of Christ's atoning death far surpass what man would have possessed had Adam not fallen; the Incarnation brought God down to men, and raised them to an intimate sharing in the divine life. Second, Christ atoned not only for the one sin of Adam but for all the actual sins of mankind down the ages.

We Rise From Sin At Baptism. When John the Baptist baptized our Lord in the Jordan, he did not pour water over his head; he plunged him down into the water and drew him up again. And that is how baptism was carried out in the early Church—by immersion. This action of baptizing symbolized death; the sinner went down into the water, as if descending into his grave; there he left his old sinful nature, and rose up a new personality, with the new vital principle of sanctifying grace.

have been into the pattern of his death; we have to be sure of
this, that our former nature has been crucified with him, and
the living power of our guilt annihilated, so that we are the
slaves of guilt no longer. Guilt makes no more claim on a man
who is dead. And if we have died with Christ, we have faith
to believe that we shall share his life. We know that Christ,
now he has risen from the dead, cannot die any more; death
has no more power over him; the death he died was a death,
once for all, to sin; the life he now lives is a life that looks
towards God. And you, too, must think of yourselves as dead
to sin, and alive with a life that looks towards God, through
Christ Jesus.

You must not, then, allow sin to tyrannize over your perishable bodies, to make you subject to its appetites. You must not
make your bodily powers over to sin, to be the instruments of
harm; make yourselves over to God, as men who have been
dead and come to life again; make your bodily powers over to
God, to be the instruments of right-doing. Sin will not be able
to play the master over you any longer; you serve grace now,
not the law. And if it is grace, not the law, we serve, are we
therefore to fall into sin? God forbid. You know well enough
that wherever you give a slave's consent, you prove yourselves
the slaves of that master; slaves of sin, marked out for death, or
slaves of obedience, marked out for justification. And you,
thanks be to God, although you were the slaves of sin once, accepted obedience with all your hearts, true to the pattern of
teaching to which you are now engaged. Thus you escaped
from the bondage of sin, and became the slaves of right-doing
instead. I am speaking in the language of common life, because nature is still strong in you. Just as you once made over

By baptism a Christian is incorporated into the Mystical Body of Christ; the very process of receiving the sacrament symbolizes his sharing in the death and resurrection of his redeemer. Our Lord stated the same fact when he told his apostles after the Last Supper: 'I am the vine, you are its branches.'

Paul pictures Jesus dying on the cross on Calvary, his eyes closing on a sin-ridden world; when he opened them again on Easter Sunday morning, he saw only a world redeemed. And that is what baptism does for us; the old world atmosphere of sinfulness gives way to a life which is immersed in the person of Christ; the whole purpose of our lives is now turned Godwards.

Serve God Whole-Heartedly. The theme running through this paragraph is slavery. Paul keeps up a close parallel between man's life before and after justification, without any mention of the liberty of the sons of God. At the moment his thoughts are centred on the big decision each Christian has to make —either to serve God or sin. Our Lord put the same clear decision to his followers: 'A man cannot be the slave of two masters at once; either he will hate the one and love the other, or he will devote himself to the one and despise the other. You must serve God or money; you cannot serve both.'

Instead of money, Paul speaks of sin. It is a harsh, demanding master, a tyrant whose wages are spiritual death. Human nature, corrupted by the Fall, serves sin with all its powers and faculties; it has totally dedicated its whole life to sin; wickedness has become a second nature to unredeemed man. Paul has already given, in the first three chapters of the Romans, a gloomy picture of the life of mankind before the coming of Christ. It was based on his personal observance of

your natural powers as slaves to impurity and wickedness, till all was wickedness, you must now make over your natural powers as slaves to right-doing, till all is sanctified. At the time when you were the slaves of sin, right-doing had no claim upon you. And what harvest were you then reaping, from acts which now make you blush? Their reward is death. Now that you are free from the claims of sin, and have become God's slaves instead, you have a harvest in your sanctification, and your reward is eternal life. Sin offers death, for wages; God offers us eternal life as a free gift, through Christ Jesus our Lord.

You must surely be aware, brethren (I am speaking to men who have some knowledge of law), that legal claims are only binding on a man so long as he is alive. A married woman, for instance, is bound by law to her husband while he lives; if she is widowed, she is quit of her husband's claim on her; she will be held an adulteress if she gives herself to another man during her husband's lifetime, but once he is dead she is quit of the law's claim, and can give herself to another man without adultery. Well, brethren, you too have undergone death, as far as the law is concerned, in the person of Christ crucified, so that you now belong to another, to him who rose from the dead. We yield increase to God, whereas, when we were merely our natural selves, the sinful passions to which the law bound us worked on our natural powers, so as to yield increase only to death. Now we are quit of the law's claim, since we have died to that which hitherto held us bound, so that we can do service in a new manner, according to the spirit, not according to the letter as of old.

Does this mean that the law and guilt are the same thing? God forbid we should say that. But it was only the law that

people among whom he lived, and took on special vividness from the city in which he wrote the letter, Corinth the corrupt.

When the Christian died to sin in baptism, he pledged himself to a new life of service to God; from that moment he was a dedicated man. Holiness must become a second nature to him, just as evil had been before. To do this he must give over his entire nature to the guidance of Christ; his mind must be supernaturally enlightened by the teachings of our Lord. Obedience to this benign Master is rewarded by a gift out of all proportion to his services; this gift is eternal life.

We Are Quit Of The Law's Claim. The previous paragraph was directed mainly to the converts from paganism; in this paragraph Paul directs his words chiefly to the converts from Judaism. He repeats what he has already told the Galatians (3-4), that a Christian is freed from the Mosaic observances. But to the Romans he proves the fact of their freedom from the legal principle that death cancels all previous engagements. Rome was famous as a centre for the study of law; so Paul appeals to the legal-minded Romans in their own terminology.

He has already stated that a Christian dies with Christ at baptism; this frees him not only from sin but from the claims of the Mosaic law as well. In illustrating this truth, Paul takes the example of marriage legislation; a wife's obligations to her husband cease on his death; she is free to marry another man. The wife is a convert; the first husband is the Mosaic law, the second is Christ. In actual fact it is the wife who dies; but whoever dies, husband or wife, death cancels the bond.

The Law Only Gave Knowledge Of Sin. For the first time in Romans, Paul writes in the first person singular. The most

gave me my knowledge of sin; I should not even have known concupiscence for what it is, if the law had not told me, 'You shall not covet.' But the sense of sin, with the law's ban for its foothold, produced in me every sort of concupiscence. Without the law, the sense of sin is a dead thing. At first, without the law, I was alive; then, when the law came with its ban, the sense of sin found new life, and with that, I died. The ban, which was meant to bring life, proved death to me; the sense of sin, with the law's ban for its foothold, caught me unawares, and by that means killed me. The law, to be sure, is something holy; the ban is holy, and right, and good. A good thing, and did it prove death to me? God forbid we should say that. No, it was sin that produced death in me, using this good thing to make itself appear as sin indeed, sin made more sinful than ever by the ban imposed on it.

The law, as we know, is something spiritual; I am a thing of flesh and blood, sold into the slavery of sin. My own actions bewilder me; what I do is not what I wish to do, but something which I hate. Why then, if what I do is something I have no wish to do, I thereby admit that the law is worthy of all honour; meanwhile, my action does not come from me, but from the sinful principle that dwells in me. Of this I am certain, that no principle of good dwells in me, that is, in my natural self; praiseworthy intentions are always ready to hand, but I cannot find my way to the performance of them; it is not the good my will prefers, but the evil my will disapproves, that I find myself doing. And if what I do is something I have not the will to do, it cannot be I that bring it about, it must be the sinful principle that dwells in me. This, then, is what I find about the law, that evil is close at my side, when my will is to do what is praiseworthy. Inwardly, I applaud God's disposi-

common interpretation of this is that he takes up his own life before conversion as typical of the Jewish race before Christianity. First he speaks of his infancy, before he knew what sin was; then he came to the use of reason and began his first instruction in the Mosaic law. The ten commandments were his first introduction to what he was bound to do, and not to do. The law and the sense of sin came to him at the same time.

For a Jew every detail of life was regulated by the 613 prescriptions of the law; from the moment of waking till the end of the day not an action escaped the law. By telling men their duties without giving the grace to carry them out, the law only made its subjects more conscious of sin and brought them almost to despair. The law is holy because it comes from God; but it was never meant to bring man to union with God.

The Law Is Powerless Against Sin. Paul's change from past to present tense has led some authorities to hold the opinion that he now speaks of the inner struggle every Christian must make against the pull of his lower nature. But it is still Old Testament Judaism that he is visualizing. He is merely making his case more vivid and dramatic by presenting the struggle as something still happening, whose outcome he does not reveal till the very last words of this paragraph.

It is autobiographical only in that Paul himself, before his conversion, was a typical member of the chosen race: 'I am a Jew, a citizen of Tarsus; I was trained in exact knowledge of our ancestral law' (Acts 22, 3). The case presented by Paul is that of an individual Jew subject to temptation. Enlightened by the teachings of the Mosaic law his conscience tells him what is right and what is wrong; but such knowledge does not give him the power to do what he knows to be right. The

tion, but I observe another disposition in my lower self, which raises war against the disposition of my conscience, and so I am handed over as captive to that disposition towards sin which my lower self contains. Pitiable creature that I am, who is to set me free from a nature thus doomed to death? Nothing else than the grace of God, through Jesus Christ our Lord. If I am left to myself, my conscience is at God's disposition, but my natural powers are at the disposition of sin.

Well then, no judgment stands now against those who live in Christ Jesus. The spiritual principle of life has set me free, in Jesus Christ, from the principle of sin and death. There was something the law could not do, because flesh and blood could not lend it the power; and this God has done, by sending us his own Son, in the fashion of our guilty nature, to make amends for our guilt. He has signed the death-warrant of sin in our nature, so that we should be fully quit of the law's claim, we, who follow the ways of the spirit, not the ways of flesh and blood. To live the life of nature is to think the thoughts of nature; to live the life of the spirit is to think the thoughts of the spirit; and natural wisdom brings only death, whereas the wisdom of the spirit brings life and peace. That is because natural wisdom is at enmity with God, not submitting itself to his law; it is impossible that it should. Those who live the life of nature cannot be acceptable to God; but you live the life of the spirit, not the life of nature; that is, if the Spirit of God dwells in you. A man cannot belong to Christ unless he has the Spirit of Christ. But if Christ lives in you, then, although the body be a dead thing in virtue of our guilt, the spirit is a living thing, by virtue of our justification. And if the spirit of him who raised up Jesus from the dead dwells in you, he who raised up Jesus Christ from the dead will give life

law is something external to him, whereas sin is within him
as a result of the fall of Adam. This inner struggle can lead
to only one conclusion, the victory of sin.

It is this law-abiding soul, seeking good and doing evil, that
asks the final rhetorical question. It shows the longing and
need of Judaism for the coming of Christ. Through him alone
comes the power to win the victory: the law through Moses,
grace through Jesus Christ.

Living The Life Of The Spirit.   The path that leads to God
is not smooth and easy; it is blocked by many obstacles. Ever
since Paul embarked on his description of the way of salvation
(chapter 5), he has been concentrating his attention on these
obstacles. He has given most space to sin and law. Now that he
has disposed of the obstacles impeding the march of the Christian to union with God, he turns his thoughts to the positive
aspect—on living the Christian life.

He begins this paragraph with the familiar phrase, 'In Christ
Jesus.' It occurs on almost every page of his letters (actually
164 times in all). It expresses his doctrine of the incorporation
of the Christian into the Mystical Body of Christ. This is a
vital union (like that of branches with a vine), giving man access to the source of all supernatural life (sanctifying grace),
the life of God himself. Man so vivified thinks, wills, feels,
and acts with Christ; all his principles of conduct stem from
this organic union with Jesus Christ his Head.

This new Christian personality Paul calls 'the spirit.' He
contrasts it with 'nature . . . flesh and blood.' The latter is
man descended from Adam; the former is man vitalized by
the indwelling power of God, the Holy Spirit. The life of
Christ and the life of the Holy Spirit is the same, because it is
divine life, which is one. To help distinguish the functions of

to your perishable bodies too, through his Spirit who dwells in you.

Thus, brethren, nature has no longer any claims upon us, that we should live a life of nature. If you live a life of nature, you are marked out for death; if you mortify the activities of the body through the power of the Spirit, you will have life. Those who follow the leading of God's Spirit are all God's sons; the spirit you have now received is not, as of old, a spirit of slavery, to govern you by fear; it is the spirit of adoption, which makes us cry out, 'Abba, Father.' The Spirit himself thus assures our spirit, that we are children of God; and if we are his children, then we are his heirs too; heirs of God, sharing the inheritance of Christ; only we must share his sufferings, if we are to share his glory.

Not that I count these present sufferings as the measure of that glory which is to be revealed in us. If creation is full of expectancy, that is because it is waiting for the sons of God to be made known. Created nature has been condemned to frustration; not for some deliberate fault of its own, but for the sake of him who so condemned it, with a hope to look forward to; namely, that nature in its turn will be set free from the tyranny of corruption, to share in the glorious freedom of God's sons. The whole of nature, as we know, groans in a common travail all the while. And not only do we see that, but we ourselves do the same; we ourselves, although we have already begun to reap our spiritual harvest, groan in our hearts, waiting for that adoption which is the ransoming of our bodies from slavery. It must be so, since our salvation is founded upon the hope of something. Hope would not be hope at all if its object were in view; how could a man still hope for something which he sees? And if we are hoping for something still unseen, then

Christ and the Holy Spirit in the life of the Mystical Body, it is customary to call the Third Person of the Trinity the Soul (Christ is the Head) of the Body.

In addition to this vital metaphor, Paul has a legal metaphor as a secondary theme. Redeemed man, once at the mercy of corrupt nature, is freed now from the claim of sin and the law, because Christ has paid our debt. But instead of making us debtors, God has conferred sonship on us. When we say the Pater Noster (of which 'Abba' is the first word in the original Aramaic) we join our voices with the only true Son of God; by adoption we acquire that sonship which enables us to call on God not as slaves but as beloved children.

Our Bodies Long For The Resurrection. Adam's sin not only deprived man of sanctifying grace, it brought suffering and death as well. The redemption of Christ won back for man all that he lost in Adam's fall. Paul has just discussed the new life in Christ; but this only affects man's soul, not his body. It is only on the last day, at Christ's Second Coming, that he will receive bodily immortality; only then will man have received all that he lost when Adam fell.

With a poetic and mystical outlook such as that which we find so highly developed in St. Francis of Assisi, Paul sees in the material world around him a longing for better times. Plants and animals are subject to decay and death just as man is; this comes from the fact that all creation somehow has been dragged down with fallen man. With his ear to the ground Paul listens to their complaints of frustrated existence and interprets their expectancy as a yearning for the resurrection.

10

we need endurance to wait for it. Only, as before, the Spirit comes to the aid of our weakness; when we do not know what prayer to offer, to pray as we ought, the Spirit himself intercedes for us, with groans beyond all utterance: and God, who can read our hearts, knows well what the Spirit's intent is; for indeed it is according to the mind of God that he makes intercession for the saints.

Meanwhile, we are well assured that everything helps to secure the good of those who love God, those whom he has called in fulfilment of his design. All those who from the first were known to him, he has destined from the first to be moulded into the image of his Son, who is thus to become the eldest-born among many brethren. So predestined, he called them; so called, he justified them; so justified, he glorified them. When that is said, what follows? Who can be our adversary, if God is on our side? He did not even spare his own Son, but gave him up for us all; and must not that gift be accompanied by the gift of all else? Who will come forward to accuse God's elect, when God acquits us? Who will pass sentence against us, when Jesus Christ, who died, nay, has risen again, and sits at the right hand of God is pleading for us? Who will separate us from the love of Christ? Will affliction, or distress, or persecution, or hunger, or nakedness, or peril, or the sword? 'For your sake,' says the scripture, 'we face death at every moment, reckoned no better than sheep marked down for slaughter.' Yet in all this we are conquerors, through him who has granted us his love. Of this I am fully persuaded; neither death nor life, no angels or principalities, neither what is present nor what is to come, no force whatever, neither the height above us nor the depth beneath us, nor any other created thing, will

Just how the created universe will be integrated with man in his resurrected glory is uncertain. In some way all creation will share with man in his restoration; but the new heaven and new earth of the Apocalypse (21, 1) is probably not meant to be a literal description. The lesson Paul has for man in this valley of tears is patience under sufferings, and hope for bodily resurrection; this must be our constant prayer.

God's Love For Us In Christ. On Easter Sunday afternoon our Lord joined two disciples on the road to Emmaus; he explained to them the reason for his crucifixion: 'Was it not to be expected that the Christ should undergo these sufferings, and enter so into his glory?' Paul has the same lesson for the Christians of Rome; God's plan for each member of the Mystical Body is the same as his plan for the Head; we must all 'be moulded into the image of his Son.' Narrow and tortuous is the road that leads to life; it is a hard and stony path that the Christian must walk, just as the Master did.

The Christian will have nothing to fear at the final judgment, if he lives in accordance with God's plan for him. If he has lived his whole life in the shadow of the cross, the divine judge will have already acquitted him; and Jesus himself will be standing there to plead for him before the judgment seat of God.

Paul has enumerated four obstacles—sin, death, the law, and man's own corrupt nature. Maybe he has forgotten something? After all, he has not mentioned the angelic forces of evil ('angels or principalities'); possibly the Christians are thinking of some unknown danger, such as Men from Mars ('any other created thing'). So Paul will remove all such doubts in the minds of redeemed men; nothing can break the bond of love which was forged on Calvary and which unites each member

be able to separate us from the love of God, which comes to us in Christ Jesus our Lord.

I am not deceiving you, I am telling you the truth in Christ's name, with the full assurance of a conscience enlightened by the Holy Spirit, when I tell you of the great sorrow, the continual anguish I feel in my heart, and how it has ever been my wish that I myself might be doomed to separation from Christ, if that would benefit my brethren, my own kinsmen by race. They are Israelites, adopted as God's sons; the visible presence, and the covenants, and the giving of the law, and the Temple worship, and the promises, are their inheritance; the patriarchs belong to them, and theirs is the human stock from which Christ came; Christ, who rules as God over all things, blessed for ever. Amen.

And yet it is not as if God's promise has failed of its effect. Not all those who are sprung from Israel are truly Israelites; not all the posterity of Abraham are Abraham's children: 'It is through Isaac,' he was told, 'that your posterity shall be traced.' That is to say, God's sonship is not for all those who are Abraham's children by natural descent; it is only the children given to him as the result of God's promise that are to be counted as his posterity. It was a promise God made, when he said: 'When this season comes round again, I will visit you, and Sara shall have a son.' And not only she, but Rebecca too received a promise, when she bore two sons to the same husband, our father Isaac. They had not yet been born; they had done nothing, good or evil; and already, so that God's purpose might stand out clearly as his own choice, with no action of theirs to account for it, nothing but his will, from whom the call came, she was told: 'The elder is to be the servant of the

of the Mystical Body with its crucified Head, Christ Jesus our Lord.

The Problem Of Jewish Unbelief.   Paul here begins a new section of his letter; for the next three chapters (9-11) he discusses the sad fact of Israel's rejection of Jesus. The Jewish nation had been in training, during the whole period of their 2,000 years' existence, for the coming of their Redeemer; surely they, first of all other peoples, should have accepted Jesus without question. Did God's plan go astray somewhere? In answering this, Paul explores the mind of God, investigates the subject of human responsibility, and argues in detailed fashion from the words and persons of the Old Testament.

He does not deny the privileged position of the chosen people of God; instead, he lists nine privileges possessed by the Jews, and by no other peoples. They have Abraham, Isaac and Jacob (whose name was changed to Israel, and this name became God's own designation of his people) as their patriarchs; God has made covenants with them again and again, first with Abraham, then with Moses and David. He manifested his presence in a miraculous fashion under the form of a shining cloud during the whole forty years of the Exodus; he selected one place on earth, the temple at Jerusalem, where true worship could be offered to him. And finally, the Messias himself was a Jew; Jesus was born of king David's house in Bethlehem.

Paul begins his argument by investigating God's mode of action in the cases of Abraham and Isaac. He chose one son of each of these patriarchs to be the repository of his blessings. Isaac was chosen, Ishmael rejected; then Jacob was chosen, and Esau rejected. These selections were due solely to God's free choice; God picked his man before birth. This shows that

younger.' So it is that we read: 'I have been a friend to Jacob, and an enemy to Esau.'

What does this mean? That God acts unjustly? That is not to be thought of. 'I will show pity,' he tells Moses, 'on those whom I pity; I will show mercy where I am merciful'; the effect comes, then, from God's mercy, not from man's will, or man's alacrity. Pharao, too, is told in scripture: 'This is the very reason why I have made you what you are, so as to give proof, in you, of my power, and to let my name be known all over the earth.' Thus he shows mercy where it is his will, and where it is his will he hardens men's hearts. Hereupon you will ask, 'If that is so, how can he find fault with us, since there is no resisting his will?' Nay, but who are you, friend, to bandy words with God? Is the pot to ask the potter, 'Why have you fashioned me thus?' Is not the potter free to do what he wills with the clay, using the same lump to make two objects, one for noble and one for ignoble use? It may be that God has borne, long and patiently, with those who are the objects of his vengeance, fit only for destruction, meaning to give proof of that vengeance, and display his power at last; meaning also to display, in those who are the objects of his mercy, how rich is the glory he bestows, that glory for which he has destined them.

We are the objects of his mercy; we, whom he has called, Jews and Gentiles alike. That is what he says in the book of Osee: 'Those who were no people of mine, I will call my people; she who was unloved shall be loved. In places where they used to be told, "You are no people of mine," they will be called, now, sons of the living God.' And, where Israel is concerned, Isaias cries out: 'The number of the sons of Israel may

a vocation from God is something he gives; man does not earn it.

God's Purpose Served Even By Rebels.   There is no problem to the human mind in God's choosing Isaac and Jacob for his favours; the real difficulty is his justice in rejecting Ishmael and Esau. It is easy to see how the divine plan is carried out by those obedient to him; but how about those who rebel against him?

To illustrate this, Paul takes up a third character, the Pharao of the Exodus. This Egyptian king impeded God's plan at every turn; after each of the first nine plagues he promised to let Israel go, but when the plague ceased he went back on his word (Exod. 7-10). This does not mean that Pharao was frustrating God's purpose; unknowingly and unwillingly he was carrying out the divine plan, which is always fulfilled.

Just how this happens is best seen from the trade of pottery making. If the clay is suitable, the potter may produce a superb vessel fit to hold the most expensive perfume; if there is a flaw in the clay, the rejected article is not thrown away; it can serve some ignoble use (some ordinary household function). Pharao, the rejected vessel of clay, represents rebellious Israel. But they have not escaped the sovereignty of God; even the hard hearts of unrepentant Israel can be used by God.

God's Mercy To Jew And Gentile.   Alongside the divine plan of rejection there is his plan of election; there are the potter's vessels for noble as well as for ignoble uses. Paul's purpose in this paragraph is to show that the constitution of the Christian Church, the call of both Jew and Gentile, was not an after-thought; it was an integral part of his divine purpose right from the beginning of Jewish history, in Old Testament times.

be like the sand of the sea, but it is a remnant that will be left;
it is a short reckoning that the Lord will make upon earth.' So
Isaias had said earlier on: 'If the Lord of Hosts had not left
us a stock to breed from, we should have been like Sodom, we
should have gone the way of Gomorrah.'

What do we conclude, then? Why, that the Gentiles, who
never aimed at justifying themselves, attained justification,
that justification which comes of faith; whereas the Israelites
aimed at a disposition which should justify them, and never
reached it. Why was this? Because they hoped to derive their
justification from observance, not from faith. They tripped on
the stone which trips men's feet; so we read in scripture: 'Behold, I am setting down in Sion one who is a stone to trip
men's feet, a boulder to catch them unawares; those who believe in him will not be disappointed.'

Brethren, they have all the good will of my heart, all my
prayers to God, for their salvation. That they are jealous for
God's honour, I can testify; but it is with imperfect understanding. They did not recognize God's way of justification,
and so they tried to institute a way of their own, instead of submitting to his. Christ has superseded the law, bringing justification to anyone who will believe. The account which Moses
gives of that justification which comes from the law, is that a
man will find life in its commandments if he observes them.
But the justification which comes from faith makes a different
claim: 'Do not say, "Who will scale heaven for us?" ' (as if
we had to bring Christ down to earth), or, ' "Who will go
down into the depth for us?" ' (as if we had to bring
Christ back from the dead). 'No,' says the scripture, 'the
message is close to your hand, it is on your lips, it is in

By his use of the two phrases, 'no people of mine . . . un-loved,' Osee foreshadows the call of the heathen nations. The Gentiles with no membership in the chosen people, and out-side the influence of God's revealed religion in Old Testament times, now are welcomed into the Christian Church and the friendship of God.

Isaias is speaking of the Assyrian invasion of the eighth cen-tury B.C. (a century later than Osee). Israel will survive war and exile not as an entire nation but as a chosen few—the saved remnant. She will be partially saved, not totally destroyed as Sodom and Gomorrah were. That is why so many Gentiles and so few Jews make up the Christian Church; God foretold in the Scriptures who would accept and who would reject his Son, who is the stone (our Lord used the same metaphor of himself, Mt. 21, 44) which has tripped the feet of the mass of Israel.

Israel's Failure Her Own Fault. Up to this point Paul has been considering the problem of Israel's unbelief from God's point of view. From the Old Testament history he has shown that God has sovereign power to choose or reject whomever he will: his divine plan is carried out by both the obedient and the rebels. In this paragraph Paul examines the problem from man's point of view. His conclusion is that Israel herself is to blame; her failure to recognize that faith in Christ is the only way to justification is responsible for her exclusion from the Mystical Body of Christ.

The main line of his argument is again from the Old Testa-ment. He uses the wording of Deuteronomy 30, 12-14 to show that the New Testament approach by faith is less difficult than the Old Testament approach by observing the Mosaic law. The Jews thought they had to win God's friendship by

your heart'; meaning by that the message of faith, which
we preach. You can find salvation, if you will use your lips to
confess that Jesus is the Lord, and your heart to believe that
God has raised him up from the dead. The heart has only to
believe, if we are to be justified; the lips have only to make
confession, if we are to be saved. That is what the scripture
says, 'Anyone who believes in him will not be disappointed.'

There is no distinction made here between Jew and Gentile;
all alike have one Lord, and he has enough and to spare for all
those who call upon him. 'Every one who calls upon the name
of the Lord will be saved.' Only, how are they to call upon him
until they have learned to believe in him? And how are they
to believe in him, until they listen to him? And how can they
listen, without a preacher to listen to? And how can there be
preachers, unless preachers are sent on their errand? So we read
in scripture, 'How welcome is the coming of those who tell of
good news.' True, there are some who have not obeyed the call
of the gospel; so Isaias says, 'Lord, who has given us a faithful
hearing?' (See how faith comes from hearing; and hearing
through Christ's word.) But, tell me, did the news never come
to them? Why yes: 'The utterance fills every land, the message reaches the ends of the world.' And, tell me, was not Israel
warned of it? Why, there is a saying that goes back to Moses,
'I will make them jealous of a nation that is no nation at all;
I will put rivalry between them and a nation which has never
learned wisdom.' And Isaias speaks out boldly, 'Those who
never looked for me have found me; I have made myself
known to those who never asked for word of me'; and he says
of Israel, 'I have stretched out my hands all day to a people
that refuses obedience, and cries out against me.'

great deeds, like spacemen scaling the skies, or magicians bringing back the dead. That is unnecessary, says Paul, because God is not difficult to find; he came down on earth at the Incarnation, and rose from the tomb at the Resurrection. God has presented himself to us, without any effort on our part; all we have to do is to accept him by faith—internal assent of the mind and external profession.

The Gospel Has Been Preached Everywhere. This section is usually understood as a demonstration of the guilt of the Jews. They have no excuse at all, because the good news of salvation through Christ has been preached, by this time, all over the Mediterranean world; none of them can say that they have not heard of Christ. Paul's emphasis is on preachers because there were few books in those days; people did not find out about things from reading; it was preaching that was essential in spreading the belief in Christ.

But Mgr. Knox has an entirely different explanation. He holds that Paul is here treating of the call of the Gentiles; the unbelief of the Jews is only mentioned by way of contrast. Nationalism was so strong among the converts from Judaism that many of them thought the gospel should not be preached to the Gentiles at all; they had completely forgotten our Lord's express command to his followers: 'Preach the gospel to the whole of creation, making disciples of all nations.'

So Paul's objective is to prove that the admission of Gentiles to the Church was foretold in the Old Testament, that God always meant the true Israel to have a world-wide diffusion. In support of his claim, he goes right back to Moses; then he quotes king David, the prophet Joel, and his favourite Isaias (4 times).

Tell me, then, has God disowned his people? That is not to be thought of. Why, I am an Israelite myself, descended from Abraham; Benjamin is my tribe. No, God has not disowned the people which, from the first, he recognized as his. Do you not remember what scripture tells us about Elias? The complaint, I mean, which he made before God about Israel: 'Lord, they have killed your prophets, and overthrown your altars; I am the only one left, and my life, too, is threatened.' And what does the divine revelation tell him? 'There are seven thousand men I have kept true to myself, with knees that never bowed to Baal.' So it is in our time; a remnant has remained true; grace has chosen it. And if it is due to grace, then it is not due to observance of the law; if it were, grace would be no grace at all. What does it mean, then? Why, that Israel has missed its mark; only this chosen remnant has attained it, while the rest were hardened; so we read in scripture, 'God has numbed their senses, given them unseeing eyes and deaf ears, to this day.' David, too, says, 'Let their feasting be turned into a trap, a snare, a spring to recoil upon them; let their eyes be dim, so that they cannot see, keep their backs bowed down continually.'

Tell me, then, have they stumbled so as to fall altogether? God forbid; the result of their false step has been to bring the Gentiles salvation, and the result of that must be to rouse the Jews to emulate them. Why then, if their false step has enriched the world, if the Gentiles have been enriched by their default, what must we expect, when it is made good? (I am speaking now to you Gentiles.) As long as my apostolate is to the Gentiles, I mean to make much of my office, in the hope of stirring up my own flesh and blood to emulation, and saving some of them. If the losing of them has meant a world re-

A Believing Remnant Among The Jews. Paul's first contact with Christianity was the long sermon of Stephen, delivered on the day of his execution by the Jewish leaders. In this speech (Acts 7) Stephen traced the long history of rebellion against God by Israel; but there were always some true to the Lord, such as Abraham, Joseph, Moses, David. And this is the doctrine put forward here by Paul: there are Jews in the Christian Church, true followers of the Master. Peter and Paul, Mary the mother of Jesus, many bishops and missionaries engaged in spreading the faith, are members of the chosen race.

The doctrine of the Remnant, a percentage of the nation remaining true to the Lord, is developed in the Old Testament especially in the writings of Isaias. He used it to explain God's providence in the Babylonian exile; the exiles were the elect of God, they represented the true Israel. The teaching first appears in scripture in the story of Elias (ninth century B.C.). As he fled from the wrath of Achab and Jezabel, he complained to God that he was the only true worshipper left; but God told him there were 7,000 others who had not followed the idolatrous ways of the Jewish leaders; they were the remnant who remained true to the Lord.

The Church Not Meant For Gentiles Only. Up to this point Paul has been explaining the rejection of the Jews for the benefit of Jewish converts; now he is prophesying the return of the Jews, so as to keep the Gentile Christians in their place. Jewish Christians were a minority at Rome; there was danger of their being cold-shouldered by the Gentile majority. Probably Peter, the apostle of the Roman church, had asked Paul, as the champion of Gentile Christians, to put the Gentiles in their place, restore peace between the two communities, and make them live together in unity.

 conciled to God, what can the winning of them mean, but life risen from the dead?

When the first loaf is consecrated, the whole batch is consecrated with it; so, when the root is consecrated, the branches are consecrated too. The branches have been thinned out, and you, a wild olive, have been grafted in among them; share, with them, the root and the richness of the true olive. That is no reason why you should boast yourself better than the branches; remember, in your mood of boastfulness, that you owe life to the root, not the root to you. 'Branches were cut away,' you will tell me, 'so that I might be grafted in.' True enough, but it was for want of faith that they were cut away, and it is only faith that keeps you where you are; you have no reason for pride, rather for fear; God was unforgiving with the branches that were native to the tree, what if he should find occasion to be unforgiving with you too? There is graciousness, then, in God, and there is also severity. His severity is for those who have fallen away, his graciousness is for you, only so long as you continue in his grace; if not, you too shall be pruned away. Just so they too will be grafted in, if they do not continue in their unbelief; to graft them in afresh is not beyond God's power. Indeed, it was against nature when you were grafted on to the true olive's stock, you, who were native to the wild olive; it will be all the easier for him to graft these natural branches on to their own parent stock.

I must not fail, brethren, to make this revelation known to you; or else you might have too good a conceit of yourselves. Hardness has fallen upon a part of Israel, but only until the tale of the Gentile nations is complete; then the whole of Israel will find salvation, as we read in scripture: 'A deliverer

Paul reminds the Gentiles that the gospel was preached to them only when the Jews rejected the Christian missionaries; they should be grateful to the Jews for this opportunity of salvation. Will not this fact stir up the Jews to emulate the Gentiles, and eventually enter the Christian Church? Such a conclusion to history would be a wonderful surprise, something like Lazarus coming back from the grave (that seems to be the meaning of the disputed phrase, 'life risen from the dead').

In order to make it clear that the Gentiles are not to regard the temporary rejection of Israel as a compliment arranged for their personal benefit, Paul uses one of his best-known illustrations, that of an olive tree; instead of lording it over the Jews in arrogant fashion, the Gentiles should be humble and filled with a salutary fear of divine punishment.

Our Lord likened Israel to a fig-tree (Lk. 13, 6-9); in Isaias and the Psalms the image of a vine is used; in Osee and Jeremias we find Paul's figure of an olive tree. In the Mediterranean world the cultivated olive is the most familiar and widespread of all trees; it is the main source of cooking oil. Paul pictures a graft of wild branches on to a cultivated ('true olive') tree; this is contrary to normal procedure. And so is the Gentile influx into the Church; the Jews by all rights should have been the heirs to the Messianic promises made to the patriarchs (the root of the tree).

Final Conversion of the Jewish Race. Our Lord concluded his discourse in the temple on the Tuesday in Holy Week with these words: 'Believe me, you shall see nothing of me henceforward, until the time when you will be saying, "Blessed is he that comes in the name of the Lord." ' This seems to have

shall come from Sion, to rid Jacob of his unfaithfulness; and this shall be the fulfilment of my covenant with them, when I take away their sins.' In the preaching of the gospel, God rejects them, to make room for you; but in his elective purpose he still welcomes them, for the sake of their fathers; God does not repent of the gifts he makes, or of the calls he issues. You were once rebels, until through their rebellion you obtained pardon; they are rebels now, obtaining pardon for you, only to be pardoned in their turn. Thus God has abandoned all men to their rebellion, only to include them all in his pardon.

O depth of God's riches, his wisdom, and his knowledge! How inscrutable are his judgments, how undiscoverable his ways! 'Who has ever understood the Lord's thoughts, or been his counsellor? Who ever was the first to give, and so earned his favours?' All things find in him their origin, their impulse, and their goal; to him be glory throughout all ages, Amen.

And now, brethren, I appeal to you by God's mercies to offer up your bodies as a living sacrifice, consecrated to God and worthy of his acceptance; this is the worship due from you as rational creatures. And you must not fall in with the manners of this world; there must be an inward change, a remaking of your minds, so that you can satisfy yourselves what is God's will, the good thing, the desirable thing, the perfect thing. Thus, in virtue of the grace that is given me, I warn every man who is of your company not to think highly of himself, beyond his just estimation, but to have a sober esteem of himself, according to the measure of faith which God has apportioned to each. Each of us has one body, with many different parts, and not all these parts have the same function; just so we, though

been the revelation on which Paul bases his statement of the ultimate conversion of Israel. It was the unbelief of Israel that he announced to the Thessalonians (2 Thess. 2) as the obstacle in the way of the Second Coming. And it is generally understood in tradition that the end of the world will follow shortly on the conversion of the Jews. Probably the reason for Elias not undergoing death is so that he can come back before the end of time and convert the Jews (Mt. 17, 10-12). To do so there must be a Jewish nation still existing at the end of the world; this would seem to be the reason for the continued existence of Israel as a nation, despite all the vicissitudes of its history.

The entry of Israel into the Christian fold will be the final demonstration of God's mercy and wisdom; then it will be seen that the mystery of God's dealings with his chosen people was due to man's limited knowledge, not to any failure in divine Providence. All creation will fall on its knees in praise of the Trinity.

Harmony of Mind in the Mystical Body. Here begins part four of the Letter to the Romans. In the first three parts Paul has treated of man's need of redemption, the completeness of that salvation brought to man by Christ, and the problem of Israel's unbelief. Till now he has been concentrating on dogma, on teaching the Romans the truths of salvation; now he begins the moral section of his letter, the principles of right conduct which flow from truths already learnt.

The truths already set down by Paul in the first eleven chapters (this is chapter 12) demand a new outlook in the Christian; what Paul calls 'a remaking of your minds.' As rational creatures they are to give God a worship befitting their nature; their whole being, body and soul, must be dedi-

many in number, form one body in Christ, and each acts as the counterpart of another. The spiritual gifts we have differ, according to the special grace which has been assigned to each. If a man is a prophet, let him prophesy as far as the measure of his faith will let him. The administrator must be content with his administration, the teacher, with his work of teaching, the preacher, with his preaching. Each must perform his own task well; giving alms with generosity, exercising authority with anxious care, or doing works of mercy smilingly.

Your love must be a sincere love; you must hold what is evil in abomination, fix all your desire upon what is good. Be affectionate towards each other, as the love of brothers demands, eager to give one another precedence. I would see you unwearied in activity, aglow with the Spirit, waiting like slaves upon the Lord; buoyed up by hope, patient in affliction, persevering in prayer; providing generously for the needs of the saints, giving the stranger a loving welcome. Bestow a blessing on those who persecute you; a blessing, not a curse. Rejoice with those who rejoice, mourn with the mourner. Live in harmony of mind, falling in with the opinions of common folk, instead of following conceited thoughts; never give yourselves airs of wisdom.

Do not repay injury with injury; study your behaviour in the world's sight. Keep peace with all men, where it is possible, for your part. Do not avenge yourselves, beloved; allow retribution to run its course; so we read in scripture, 'Vengeance is for me, I will repay, says the Lord. Rather, feed your enemy if he is hungry, give him drink if he is thirsty; by doing this, you will heap coals of fire upon his head.' Do not be disarmed by malice; disarm malice with kindness.

cated to the service of the Lord. And since the Christian is not an isolated individual but a member of Christ's Mystical Body, he must think and live like Christ. This new life he is living is the life of the Head; all his thoughts and feelings, all his motives of conduct must be those of Christ.

The function of each individual is determined by the general good of the body; he must be content to carry out that function allotted to him in the Church, and not try to usurp the function of any other member. This body is an organism of delicately inter-related parts; the unity and peaceful working of the body depends on the harmonious working of all its members.

Paul is thinking of the jealousies and quarrels between the Jew and Gentile converts in Rome. He is directing his advice mostly to the Gentile majority, who were inclined to be proud and arrogant in their attitude to the less numerous Jewish converts.

Writing from Corinth, where spiritual gifts of all kinds flourished (1 Cor. 12-14), Paul illustrates his teaching on the need of harmony in the Mystical Body by choosing seven spiritual gifts. The function of the prophet, for example, is determined by the commission God has made to him, no more, no less.

Love of Neighbour and Civic Loyalty. Paul begins and ends this paragraph with an exhortation to practise charity. His words are addressed mainly to the Jewish Christians at Rome; and it is their conduct to the pagan neighbours that he has in mind. The Jews had been expelled from Rome by the emperor Claudius in 50 A.D. (Acts 18, 2). They had returned to their homes to find them looted; there was an atmosphere of tension and hostility in the neighbourhood; their loyalty as

Every soul must be submissive to its lawful superiors; authority comes from God only, and all authorities that hold sway are of his ordinance. Thus the man who opposes authority is a rebel against the ordinance of God, and rebels secure their own condemnation. A good conscience has no need to go in fear of the magistrate, as a bad conscience does. If you would be free from the fear of authority, do right, and you shall win its approval; the magistrate is God's minister, working for your good. Only if you do wrong, need you be afraid; it is not for nothing that he bears the sword; he is God's minister still, to inflict punishment on the wrong-doer. You must needs, then, be submissive, not only for fear of punishment, but in conscience. It is for this same reason that you pay taxes; magistrates are in God's service, and must give all their time to it. Pay every man his due; taxes, if it be taxes, customs, if it be customs; respect and honour, if it be respect and honour.

Do not let anybody have a claim upon you, except the claim which binds us to love one another. The man who loves his neighbour has done all that the law demands. (All the commandments, 'You shall not commit adultery, You shall do no murder, You shall not steal, You shall not covet,' and the rest, are resumed in this one saying, 'You shall love your neighbour as yourself.') Love of our neighbour refrains from doing harm of any kind; that is why it fulfils all the demands of the law.

Meanwhile, make no mistake about the age we live in; already it is high time for us to awake out of our sleep; our salvation is closer to us now than when we first learned to believe. The night is far on its course; day draws near. Let us abandon the ways of darkness, and put on the armour of light. Let us pass our time honourably, as by the light of day, not in

citizens was suspect by the pagans among whom they lived. Their natural reaction was to repay in like coin. That attitude is wrong, Paul tells them; they must repay injury by kindness. Such unexpected treatment will produce a salutary sense of discomfort ('coals of fire').

At the end of the paragraph, Paul presents charity as the Christian ideal, just as the Master himself showed by word and deed. The Christian who lives his life on the motive of love for the neighbour has no need to worry about commandments and obligations; he does not have to watch his step at every turn, because his charity will move him to act as he ought. Not only the fifth, sixth, seventh, ninth, and tenth commandments (which Paul lists here), but all laws and obligations are submerged in this new commandment of Christ.

Our Lord himself gave the principle by which a man can determine his obligations to God and the state, when he answered the question about tribute money: 'Give back to Caesar what is Caesar's, and to God what is God's.' Paul still has the Jewish converts in mind when he repeats the Master's lesson of obedience to authority. The Jews looked on the state as the empire of Satan; they were under Yahweh's direct rule (theocracy). In Palestine they were plotting the overthrow of Rome. The Christian attitude is different. The Church is catholic; its members must live as citizens of different governments; submission to lawful authority is a matter of conscience.

Christians the Light of the World.   This short section links up what Paul has just said with what is to follow. He has been speaking of the Christians' need to influence the pagan world around them; in the next section he goes on to a problem in the Roman church, the dispute between Jew and Gentile.

revelling and drunkenness, not in lust and wantonness, not in quarrels and rivalries. Rather, arm yourselves with the Lord Jesus Christ; spend no more thought on nature and nature's appetites.

Find room among you for a man of over-delicate conscience, without arguing about his scruples. Another man can, in conscience, eat what he will; one who is scrupulous is content with vegetable fare. Let not the first, over his meat, mock at him who does not eat it, or the second, while he abstains, pass judgment on him who eats it. God, after all, has found room for him. Who are you, to pass judgment on the servant of another? Whether he keeps his feet or falls, concerns none but his master. And keep his feet he will; the Lord is well able to give him a sure footing. One man makes a distinction between this day and that; another regards all days alike; let either have a clear conviction in his own mind. He who observes the day, observes it in the Lord's honour. Just so, he who eats does so in the Lord's honour; he gives thanks to God for it; and he who abstains from eating abstains in the Lord's honour, and he too thanks God. None of us lives as his own master, and none of us dies as his own master. While we live, we live as the Lord's servants, when we die, we die as the Lord's servants; in life and in death, we belong to the Lord. That was why Christ died and lived again; he would be Lord both of the dead and of the living. And who are you, to pass judgment on your brother? Who are you, to mock at your brother? We shall all stand, one day, before the judgment seat of God (so we read in scripture, 'As I live, says the Lord, there is no knee but shall bend before me, no tongue but shall pay homage to God'); and so each of us will have to give an account of himself before God. Let us cease, then, to lay down rules for one another, and make this

The metaphor of light shining in darkness is taken from our Lord's words. He himself is the light of the world (Jn. 8, 12); the Christian must be the same (Mt. 5, 12), since he is to live Christ's life over again.

We Must Practise Mutual Toleration. One of the big problems in the early Church was the relation between Jew and Gentile converts. Eight years before, a council had been held at Jerusalem to improve this situation. The Jerusalem decree read: 'You are to abstain from what is sacrificed to idols, from blood-meat and meat which has been strangled' (Acts 15, 29). Owing to the strict kosher regulations observed by Jews in eating, and the free use of all food by Gentiles, friction arose at every meal where Jew and Gentile sat down together. Each week the Agape (a banquet before Mass) brought the problem before the Christians. Paul had warned the Corinthians about their conduct at such a meal (I Cor. 11); he now gives some advice to the Romans.

The background of the convert Jew made him scrupulous about what he ate, and also he found it difficult to put aside strict sabbath observance. He knew that such laws were no longer binding on a Christian; but the habits of a lifetime left his conscience over-delicate. The Gentile convert was at a loss to understand such an outlook; he showed little sympathy or understanding and was inclined to poke fun at such trivial observances.

Paul lays down a principle to smooth out Jew-Gentile relations: A man must follow his individual conscience, even when it seems false and foolish to others. One man imitates our Lord by concentrating on his glorious life, his resurrection; another keeps his thoughts on the death of Jesus, his crucifixion. One feasts, the other fasts; one thinks of life, the other of death;

rule for ourselves instead, not to trip up or entangle a brother's conscience.

This is my assurance, this is what my conscience tells me in the name of our Lord Jesus, that there is nothing which is unclean in itself; it is only when a man believes a thing to be unclean that it becomes unclean for him. And if your brother's peace of mind is disturbed over food, it is because you are neglecting to follow the rule of charity. Here is a soul for which Christ died; it is not for you to bring it to perdition with the food you eat. You must not allow that which is a good thing for you to be brought into disrepute. The kingdom of God is not a matter of eating or drinking this or that; it means right-ness of heart, finding our peace and our joy in the Holy Spirit. Such is the badge of Christ's service which wins acceptance with God, and the good opinion of our fellowmen. Let our aim, then, be peace, and strengthening one another's faith. It is not for you to destroy God's work for the sake of a mouthful of food. Nothing is unclean; yet it goes ill with the man who eats to the hurt of his own conscience. You do well if you refuse to eat meat, or to drink wine, or to do anything in which your brother can find an occasion of sin, a cause for scandal or scruple. The good conscience that you have, keep it a matter between yourself and God; he is fortunate, who can make his own choice without self-questioning. He who hesitates, and eats none the less, is self-condemned; he acts in bad conscience, and wherever there is bad conscience, there is sin.

No, we who are bold in our confidence ought to bear with the scruples of those who are timorous; not to insist on having our own way. Each of us ought to give way to his neighbour,

but both are living the life of the Master, though in different ways. Each individual is responsible to God only for his own conduct.

Make Sacrifices for Peace and Unity.   This interminable bickering in the Roman community about what was lawful in the matter of eating and drinking placed a false emphasis on unimportant things and prevented the faithful from thinking on the lessons of conduct given them by our Lord. In reminding them of this, Paul possibly has in mind the advice of the Master to his followers: 'Do not fret, then, asking, "What are we to eat?" or "What are we to drink?" It is for the heathen to busy themselves over such things; you have a Father in heaven who knows that you need them all. Make it your first care to find the kingdom of God.' It is the supernatural life that really counts; the Romans were allowing themselves to be so taken up with material things that they were inclined to neglect true spiritual values.

There was also the danger of forcing a Jewish convert to eat food (such as pork), when his tender conscience considered it wrong. This is an offence against charity, and may cause the loss of a soul for whom Christ shed his blood on Calvary. But a sympathetic understanding on the part of the Gentiles could restore peace and harmony to the church at Rome.

At the Last Supper (Jn. 17), our Lord prayed for the unity of his Church; it would be a powerful motive attracting unbelievers. The want of unity and harmony among the Romans was a serious obstacle in the way of the conversion of the pagans.

Imitate Christ's Example of Unselfishness.   Writing five years later to the Philippians from Rome, Paul told them: 'Each of you must study the welfare of others, not his own. Yours

where it serves a good purpose by building up his faith. Christ, after all, would not have everything his own way: 'Was it not uttered against you,' says the scripture, 'the reproach I bore?' (See how all the words written long ago were written for our instruction; we were to derive hope from that message of endurance and courage which the scriptures bring us.) May God, the author of all endurance and all encouragement, enable you to be all of one mind according to the mind of Christ Jesus, so that you may all have but one heart and one mouth, to glorify God, the Father of our Lord Jesus Christ. You must befriend one another, as Christ has befriended you, for God's honour. I would remind those who are circumcised, that Christ came to relieve their needs; God's fidelity demanded it; he must make good his promises to our fathers. And I would remind the Gentiles to praise God for his mercy. So we read in scripture, 'I will give thanks to you for this, and sing your praise, in the midst of the Gentiles'; and again it says, 'You too, Gentiles, rejoice with his own people'; and again, 'Praise the Lord, all you Gentiles; let all the nations of the world do him honour'; and once more Isaias says, 'A root shall spring from Jesse, one who shall rise up to rule the Gentiles; the Gentiles, in him, shall find hope.'

May God, the author of our hope, fill you with all joy and peace in your believing; so that you may have hope in abundance, through the power of the Holy Spirit. It is not that I have any doubt of you, my brethren; I know that you are full of good will, knowing all you need to know, so that you can give advice to one another if need be; and yet I have written to you, here and there, somewhat freely, by way of refreshing your memory. So much I owe to the grace which God has given me, in making me a priest of Jesus Christ for the Gentiles, with

is to be the mind Christ Jesus showed.' And that is the lesson
he gives the Romans here. When the Second Person of the
Trinity was born in a stable at Bethlehem, he did not choose
the time and place for his own convenience; it was the welfare
of others that he had in mind. When crowds flocked round
him by the lake of Galilee so that he had no time to eat or
rest, he did not drive them away; it was not his own ease and
satisfaction that determined his course of action, but the
needs of others. The pain and agony of his death on the cross
was borne for the good of others. This is what Paul holds up
before the Romans; they must not insist on having their own
way; they must always consider the welfare of others, especially
the more timorous.

Such close imitation of the Head is essential for the unity
of the Body; there must be one mind directing and guiding the
action of all the members. Since the Gentile converts were
mainly responsible for the disunity of the Roman church, Paul
concludes his advice to them by four quotations from the scriptures. His purpose is to show how grateful the Gentiles should
be to God for his mercy to them. If Christ had been interested only in what was to his own advantage, he would never
have given up so much to win eternal life for the Gentiles.

Why Paul Wrote to the Romans. The main body of the
Letter to the Romans has been completed. It was an ambitious
effort on Paul's part; also it was the first and only time that
he ventured to write to a church unknown to him personally.
Just as he began his letter (1, 8-13) with an explanation of
why he presumed to address the community at Rome, so he
again takes up the subject with further elaboration.

Paul had plenty of problems to occupy all his time among
the churches he had personally founded. He humbly pictures

God's gospel for my priestly charge, to make the Gentiles an offering worthy of acceptance, consecrated by the Holy Spirit. I have, then, through Christ Jesus, some reason for confidence in God's sight. It is not for me to give you any account of what Christ has done through agents other than myself to secure the submission of the Gentiles, by word and action, in virtue of wonders and signs, done in the power of the Holy Spirit. My own work has been to complete the preaching of Christ's gospel, in a wide sweep from Jerusalem as far as Illyricum. It has been a point of honour with me to preach the gospel thus, never in places where Christ's name was already known; I would not build on the foundation another man had laid, but follow the rule of scripture, 'He shall be seen by those who had had no tidings of him, he shall be made known to those who had never heard of him.'

This was the chief reason which prevented me from visiting you. But now I can find no further scope in these countries, and I have been eager, these many years past, to find my way to you; as soon, then, as I can set out on my journey to Spain, I hope to see you in passing; and you shall put me on my way, when you have done something to gratify this longing of mine. As I write, I am making a journey to Jerusalem, with an errand of relief to the saints there. You must know that Macedonia and Achaia have thought fit to give those saints at Jerusalem who are in need some share of their wealth; they have thought fit to do it, I say, and indeed, they are in their debt. The Gentiles, if they have been allowed to share their spiritual gifts, are bound to contribute to their temporal needs in return. When that is done, and I have seen this revenue safely in their hands, you shall be a stage on my journey to Spain; and I am

himself going about preaching the gospel in those places the other Christian missionaries had not had time to evangelize; he never put his sickle in another man's harvest. It seems most likely, then, that Peter, the founder of the Roman church, had asked Paul to write to his community in Rome. Paul does not mention Peter by name, but that may have been for reasons of security; it would not be prudent to have Peter's name in black and white when persecution started against the Christians.

Paul's basic claim to teach the Romans came from the Master himself; the grace of apostolate to the Gentiles had been conferred on him by Jesus on the Damascus Road (Acts 22, 21). Rome was predominantly a Gentile church, and so a special charge of the apostle of the Gentiles. It was Paul's official function to present the Gentile sacrifice as an offering to God.

Paul Hopes to Visit Rome Soon. Eight years earlier, Paul had probably intended going to Rome. This was during the course of his Second Missionary Journey. He left Thessalonica (Acts 17, 10-15), and proceeded along the Egnatian Way towards Dyrrachium. Knox suggests that he actually set sail for Brindisi, and was shipwrecked; had he landed at Brindisi, on the Italian mainland, he would have gone on to Rome; in actual fact he wound up at Corinth (Acts 18).

Now that his work in the East is completed, his eyes turn to the West. Possibly Jewish opposition to him has become so strong in the countries he has evangelized that it would be better for the Christians if Paul removed himself elsewhere. He knew that he was looked on as an apostate in Jerusalem; he even asks the Romans to pray for his safety. Actually he is in for a lot of trouble when he does arrive at Jerusalem at the

well assured that when I visit you, I shall be able to visit you in the fulness of Christ's blessing. Only, brethren, I entreat you by our Lord Jesus Christ, and by the love of the Spirit, to give me the help of your prayers to God on my behalf. Pray that I may be kept safe from those who reject the faith in Judea, and that my mission to Jerusalem may be well received by the saints there; so that I may reach you, God willing, glad at heart, and make holiday with you. May God, the author of peace, be with you all. Amen.

I commend our sister Phoebe to you; she has devoted her service to the church at Cenchrae. Make her welcome in the Lord as saints should, and help her in any business where she needs your help; she has been a good friend to many, myself among them. My greetings to Prisca and Aquila, who have worked at my side in the service of Christ Jesus, and put their heads on the block to save my life; not only I but all the churches of the Gentiles have reason to be grateful to them. My greetings, also, to the congregation which meets at their house; to my dear Epaenetus, the first offering Asia made to Christ, and to Mary, who has spent so much labour on you. My greetings to Andronicus and Junias, kinsmen and fellow-prisoners of mine, who have won repute among the apostles that were in Christ's service before me. My greetings to Amplias, whom I love so well in the Lord; to Urbanus, who helped our work in Christ's cause, and to my dear Stachys; to Apelles, a man tried in Christ's service; and those of Aristobulus' household; to my kinsman Herodion, and to such of Narcissus' household as belong to the Lord. My greetings to Tryphaena and Tryphosa, who have worked for the Lord so well; and dear Persis, too; she has been long in the Lord's

end of his Third Missionary Journey (Acts 21).

There is an early tradition written down by the fourth pope, Clement, about thirty years after Paul's death. It says that Paul 'went to the confines of the west.' This is usually interpreted as Spain, in the light of Paul's words to the Romans. Actually Britain is further west than Spain, but it had only just been conquered (15 years before), and would hardly have been contemplated by Paul as a field for his missionary activities.

Greetings to Friends at Rome.   There were no post offices in Paul's time; letters were sent by personal messenger. That is why Paul mentions Phoebe here; she was to carry his letter to Rome. Cenchrae (pronounced Kenkray) was the eastern port of Corinth.

Paul greets 28 people in his list of Roman friends; a rather surprising fact, seeing that he has never visited Rome. The most probable explanation is that most were Jews exiled from Rome by Claudius eight years earlier in 50 A.D. (Acts 18, 2); they had met Paul, chiefly at Corinth and Ephesus, during their exile; they were now living at Rome again. Practically all the names in the list are Greek or Latin; but it was normal procedure for Jews living outside Palestine to adopt Greek names; Paul did this when he changed his Hebrew name, Saul. There is another theory that this list was originally part of the Letter to the Ephesians, not an authentic part of Romans at all; Paul spent three years at Ephesus, and so would know many people there.

This list gives us an insight into Paul's genius for friendship; like the Master he was the most approachable of men. Undoubtedly his most intimate friends were Aquila and Priscilla

service. My greetings to Rufus, a chosen servant of the Lord, and his mother, who has been a mother to me; to Asyncritus, Phlegon, Hermas, Patrobas, Hermes, and the brethren who are with them; to Philologus and Julia, Nereus and his sister, Olympias, and all the saints who are of their company. Greet one another with the kiss of saints; all the churches of Christ send you their greeting.

Brethren, I entreat you to keep a watch on those who are causing dissension and doing hurt to consciences, without regard to the teaching which has been given you; avoid their company. Such men are no servants of Christ our Lord; their own hungry bellies are their masters; but guileless hearts are deceived by their flattering talk and their pious greetings. You are renowned all over the world for your loyalty to the gospel, and I am proud of you; but I would wish to see you circumspect when there is a good end to be served, innocent only of harmful intent. So God, who is the author of peace, will crush Satan under your feet before long. May the grace of our Lord Jesus Christ be with you.

Timothy, who works at my side, sends you his greeting; so do my kinsmen, Lucius and Jason and Sosipater. (I, Tertius, who have committed this letter to paper, greet you in the name of the Lord.) Greetings to you from my host, Caius, who is the host, too, of the whole church; from Erastus, treasurer of the city, and your brother Quartus.

There is one who is able to set your feet firmly in the path of that gospel which I preach, when I herald Jesus Christ; a gospel which reveals the mystery, hidden from us through countless ages, but now made plain, through what the prophets have written, now published, at the eternal God's command, to all the nations, so as to win the homage of their

(Prisca); he had lived with them during his first stay at Corinth, and then later at Ephesus (they remind us of Jesus' intimate friends at Bethany, the household of Martha, Mary and Lazarus). Another interesting person is Rufus, probably the son of Simon of Cyrene, who carried Jesus' cross (Mk. 15, 21); he had a brother Alexander, and his mother was well known to Paul; she is only one of the eight women on his list.

Final Warning Against False Teachers.   Unlike the letters to the Corinthians and Galatians, Romans is lacking in personalities; it is rather a thesis, a closely reasoned dogmatic treatment of fundamental principles of the faith. It is surprising, then, to find Paul warning his readers against false teachers. There is no agreement among commentators as to the identity of these men; some think that Paul is only giving a general warning to the Romans to be on the lookout in case such teachers as disturbed Corinth and Galatia should turn up in Rome. About the only clue to their identity is the dissension over eating, treated in Romans 14 15; possibly Paul is afraid that his defence of Jewish customs might lead to a revival of the Judaizing problem that troubled many of his other foundations.

On the day that Paul came to the end of his letter, there was a group of eight Christians around him in the house of Caius. Paul mentions them all, beginning with his most trusted disciple, Timothy. Three of them he describes as kinsmen (there are another three in the Roman list); this probably means that they were of the same tribe as Paul, the tribe of Benjamin.

Paul has seemed to end this letter so many times that it is not surprising to find a final doxology. He took the pen from Tertius and added a postscript with his own hand. It is a summary of his doctrinal thesis, but this time the emphasis is on

11

faith. To him, to God who alone is wise, glory be given from age to age, through Jesus Christ, Amen.

Third Missionary Journey
continued

When he had stayed three months there, he was meaning to take ship for Syria; but, finding that the Jews were plotting against him, he resolved to go back again through Macedonia. He was accompanied by Sopater, son of Pyrrhus, from Beroea, Aristarchus and Secundus from Thessalonica, Gaius from Derbe, Timothy, and two friends from Asia, Tychicus and Trophimus. These went on first, and waited for us at Troas. As soon as the time of unleavened bread was over, we set sail from Philippi, and took five days to reach them at Troas, where we spent seven days.

When the new week began, we had met for the breaking of bread, and Paul was preaching to them; he meant to leave them next day, and he continued speaking till midnight. There were many lamps burning in the upper room where we had met; and a young man called Eutychus, who was sitting in the embrasure of the window, was overcome by deep sleep. As Paul still went on preaching, sleep weighed him down, and he fell from the third storey to the ground, where he was taken up dead. Paul went down, bent over him, and embraced him; then he said, 'Do not disturb yourselves; his life is yet in him.' And so he went up again and broke bread and ate; afterwards he talked with them for some time until dawn came, when he left. And the boy was taken home alive, to their great comfort.

the call of the Gentiles, not the rejection of the Jews. The entry of all nations into the Mystical Body is God's great mystery.

From Corinth to Jerusalem 58 A.D.

Raising of Eutychus at Troas. The seven companions of Paul mentioned here were delegates of the various churches entrusted with the collections made for the needy Christians of Jerusalem. Paul's intention was that all proceed together by sea from Corinth, arriving in time for Easter at Jerusalem. He changed his plans when he learnt of a plot to assassinate him on board the pilgrim ship to Jerusalem. Keeping probably only one disciple as companion he went overland to Philippi, sending the others by sea to Troas to await his arrival there. In this way he outwitted his enemies.

Easter fell on 28 March in 58 A.D. Paul's evasion tactics delayed him so that he was still in Philippi when Easter ('the time of unleavened bread') came. Luke joined the party there (he had been appointed bishop of Philippi eight years before by Paul); he narrates the rest of the journey to Jerusalem in the first person (this is the second of the three 'we-sections' of the Acts).

Paul had been at Troas twice before. Apart from the young man mentioned in this paragraph, we know only one other Christian of that city, Carpus (2 Tim. 4, 13). Mass ('the breaking of bread') was celebrated in the early hours of Sunday morning; the Christians assembled on Saturday evening, and kept vigil throughout the night; this was the common practice in the early Church.

For ourselves, we took ship and sailed to Assos, where we were to take Paul on board; he had arranged this, because he himself meant to go across by land. So at Assos we met him, and took him on board, and journeyed to Mitylene. Sailing thence, we reached a point opposite Chios the following day; on the next, we put in at Samos, and arrived on the third at Miletus. Paul had made up his mind to sail past Ephesus, for fear of having to waste time in Asia; he was eager, if he found it possible, to keep the day of Pentecost at Jerusalem. From Miletus he sent a message to Ephesus, summoning the presbyters of the church there. And when they had come out to him, he said to them: 'You yourselves can testify, how I have lived among you, since the first day when I set foot in Asia, serving the Lord in all humility, not without tears over the trials which beset me, through the plots of the Jews; and how I have never failed you, when there was any need of preaching to you, or teaching you, whether publicly or house by house. I have proclaimed both to Jew and to Greek repentance before God and faith in our Lord Jesus.

'Now, a prisoner in spirit, I am going up to Jerusalem, knowing nothing of what is to befall me there; only, as I go from city to city, the Holy Spirit assures me that bondage and affliction await me. I care nothing for all that; I do not count my life precious compared with my work, which is to finish the course I run, the task of preaching which the Lord Jesus has given me, in proclaiming the good news of God's grace. Here, then, I stand, feeling sure that you will not see my face again; you, among whom I came and went, preaching the kingdom. And I ask you to bear me witness today that I have no man's blood on my hands; I have never shrunk from revealing to you the whole of God's plan. Keep watch, then, over yourselves, and over God's Church, in which the Holy Spirit

Paul's Farewell to the Ephesian Elders. *It is rather surprising that Luke makes no mention of Titus among the companions of Paul, seeing that Titus was appointed to take up the collection at Corinth. Possibly the Corinthians were not yet ready with their contribution, and Titus was still making the rounds of the churches of Achaia. Another explanation is that Titus was actually among the delegates to Jerusalem, but Luke refrained from mentioning him. Tradition has it that Titus was Luke's brother; it was considered bad form to mention relatives in writings of that period. In point of fact Titus is never mentioned in the Acts.*

Paul himself walked the 20 miles across the peninsula from Troas to Assos, while his disciples made the voyage by sea. He did this either to have more time with the Christians at Troas or, as is more likely, to visit some friends along the road. Coastal vessels put in to land for the night, and travelled only by day; so Paul had plenty of time to join his ship at Assos, since it would not be sailing until the following day.

It was about 20 April by the time the ship arrived at Miletus. This slow rate of travel was due mostly to contrary winds; the loading of cargo at various ports also slowed the ship's progress. Ephesus was not among the ports of call of this particular ship; so Paul used the quickest means of summoning the elders from Ephesus; he sent messengers, probably Tychicus and Trophimus, by the land route 30 miles up the coast from Miletus. He was anxious to be in Jerusalem for the feast of Pentecost in the middle of the month of May.

Paul's tearful farewell to the Ephesian elders is full of sentiments paralleled in his letters. In it he quotes a saying of our Lord not found in the Gospels (the only other authentic addition to the four Gospels is Luke's account of the Ascension in

has made you bishops; you are to be the shepherds of that flock which he won for himself at the price of his own blood. I know well that ravening wolves will come among you when I am gone, and will not spare the flock; there will be men among your own number who will come forward with a false message, and find disciples to follow them. Be on the watch, then; do not forget the three years I spent, instructing every one of you continually, and with tears. Now, as then, I commend you to God, and to his gracious word, that can build you up and give you your allotted place among the saints everywhere. I have never asked for silver or gold or clothing from any man; you will bear me out, that these hands of mine have sufficed for all that I and my companions needed. Always I have tried to show you that it is our duty so to work, and be the support of the weak, remembering the words spoken by the Lord Jesus himself: "It is more blessed to give than to receive." '

When he had said this, he knelt down and prayed with them all. They all wept abundantly, and embraced Paul and kissed him, grieving most over what he had said about never seeing his face again. And so they escorted him to the ship.

When we tore ourselves away from them, and at last put out to sea, we made a straight course, sailing to Cos, and next day to Rhodes, and thence to Patara. There, finding a ship crossing to Phoenicia, we went on board and set sail. We sighted Cyprus, but passed it on our left, and held on for Syria, where we landed at Tyre, the port for which the vessel had shipped her cargo. Here we enquired for the brethren, and made a stay of seven days with them; they, by revelation, warned Paul not to go up to Jerusalem, but when the time

the first chapter of the Acts of the Apostles). This saying of
Jesus expresses the essential of Paul's pastoral ministry—*giving*
rather than *receiving*. Luke calls the group from Ephesus
'presbyters'; Paul calls them 'bishops.' At this early stage of
the Church's history the distinction of names was not as
exact as it is today; bishop was an office distinct from both
priest and laity, but the name was used generally for those in
charge (the word means overseer) of a church; the whole group
is best called elders.

Both here at Miletus and earlier at Troas Paul spoke long
and affectionately to the Christian communities, because he
felt that he would never meet them again; he had a premonition of death at the end of his journey. In actual fact this
premonition was false; he was eventually freed from his first
imprisonment in Rome and travelled again through Greece
and Asia, stopping at both Ephesus (1 Tim. 1, 3) and Miletus
(2 Tim. 4, 20). This journey took place after the mission to
Spain, six or seven years after the farewell recorded here. Paul's
prediction was based on human calculation alone; the Holy
Spirit told him only that he would be imprisoned. Luke's
account in the Acts is inspired, not Paul's speech; Luke's
inspiration guarantees that Paul spoke the words attributed to
him.

The Return to Jerusalem. This is Paul's fifth visit to Jerusalem in the twenty-eight years since his conversion. And on this
final visit to Jerusalem, his attitude resembles that of the
Master himself on his last journey to Jerusalem: 'The Holy
Spirit assures me that bondage and affliction await me.' Paul's
thirteen years of missionary labour correspond to our Lord's
Galilean ministry; he has laid the foundations of the Church
in the Mediterranean world, and now his face is set towards
Jerusalem where he is to begin his passion.

came to an end, we left them and continued our journey. All of them, with their wives and children, escorted us until we were out of the city; and so we knelt down on the beach to pray; then, when farewells had been made on either side, we went on board the ship, while they returned home.

The end of the voyage brought us from Tyre to Ptolemais, where we greeted the brethren and stayed one day with them; the day after, we left them and arrived at Caesarea, where we went to the house of Philip the evangelist, one of the seven, and lodged with him. He had four daughters, who possessed the gift of prophecy. During our stay of several days there, a prophet named Agabus came down from Judea. When he visited us, he took up Paul's girdle, and bound his own hands and feet with it; then he said, 'Thus speaks the Holy Spirit: "The man to whom this girdle belongs will be bound, like this, by the Jews at Jerusalem, and given over into the hands of the Gentiles." '

At hearing this, both we and our hosts implored Paul not to go up to Jerusalem. To which he answered: 'What do you mean by lamenting, and crushing my spirits? I am ready to meet prison and death as well in Jerusalem for the name of the Lord Jesus.'

Finding that he would not take our advice, we composed ourselves and said: 'The Lord's will be done.'

When the time came to an end, we made all ready, and went up to Jerusalem. Some of the brethren from Caesarea went with us, to take us to the house of a Cypriot called Mnason, one of the first disciples, with whom we were to lodge. When we reached Jerusalem, the brethren received us with joy. The next day Paul took us with him to see James; all the presbyters had gathered; and he greeted them, and told them point by point of all that God had done among the Gentiles through his ministry.

All Paul's friends tried to persuade him to abandon his return to Jerusalem; the same foreboding and fear had also taken possession of Jesus' followers: 'And now they were on the way going up to Jerusalem; and still Jesus led them on, while they were bewildered and followed him with faint hearts' (Mk. 10, 32). The Master could relive his passion only in the persons of the members of his Mystical Body; Paul was filled with the same courage that Jesus showed in the face of danger. His one concern was to follow closely in the footsteps of the Master in carrying out the will of the Father.

The end of the sea voyage came at Caesarea, the Roman capital of Judea and the seaport for the final stage by road to Jerusalem, sixty miles away in the hills to the southeast. Paul had been in Caesarea twice before, on his way to Tarsus (Acts 9, 30) and after his second missionary journey. Before the end of May he will be back there, a prisoner for two years.

The stay at Caesarea was a busy and interesting time for Luke, the author of the Acts; it was probably his first visit to the Holy Land. He undoubtedly got his vivid account of Philip and the Ethiopian (Acts 8) from Philip himself. Men like Agabus and Mnason must have provided him with much valuable material on the early days of the church in Palestine. He had a genius for listening to the stories of eyewitnesses and then setting down his own authentic narrative. Most of the material for his Gospel was also gathered at this time.

Paul had met Agabus at Antioch, fourteen years earlier (Acts 11, 28). On that occasion he had foretold a famine in Palestine; Paul and Barnabas had carried to the needy in Jerusalem the first gift of alms from the Gentile churches. Now Paul was returning to Jerusalem with large sums of money from his Gentile foundations. Agabus' symbolic act reminds us of the prophets of the Old Testament; they commonly

11*

They praised God for the news he gave, and said: 'Brother, you can see for yourself how many thousands of the Jews have learned to believe, and they are all zealous supporters of the law. And this is what has come to their ears about you; that you teach all the Jews in Gentile parts to break away from the law of Moses, telling them not to circumcise their children, and not to follow the tradition. What will happen? Why, a crowd of them will assuredly gather round you, hearing that you have come. Follow our advice, then, in this; we have four men here who are under a vow; if you will take these with you, and join in their purification and defray the cost for the shaving of their heads, then all will see clearly that the report they have heard about you has no substance, and that you do follow the observance of the law like other men. As for the Gentile believers, we have already written to them; we laid it down that they must abstain from what is sacrificed to idols, and from blood-meat and meat which has been strangled, and from fornication.'

Arrest and Imprisonment

So, next day, Paul took the men with him, and began going to the temple, publicly fulfilling the days of purification, until the time came for each to have sacrifice made on his behalf. And when the seven days were all but at an end, the Jews from Asia saw him in the temple. Whereupon they threw the whole crowd into an uproar, and laid hands on him, crying out: 'Men of Israel, come to the rescue; here is the man who goes about everywhere, teaching everybody to despise the people, and our law, and this place. He has brought Gentiles into the Temple,

added such actions to the message they had to deliver from the Lord.

Paul must have been disappointed at the cool reception he received from the Christian leaders in Jerusalem. In effect he was asked to perform a public penance for his outspoken championship of freedom from the Mosaic law. He showed his greatness by submitting to the demands of James, bishop of Jerusalem and cousin of our Lord. He expressed the principle that guided him when he wrote to the Corinthians: 'With the Jews I lived like a Jew, to win the Jews, with those who keep the law, as one who keeps the law (though the law had no claim on me), to win those who kept the law.' He joined four Christian Jews who had taken the Nazirite vow (Num. 6, 13-21); his motive was Christian unity and peace. He was not abandoning his stand for Gentile liberty, as defended in his Letters to the Galatians and Romans; it was customary for Jerusalem Christians to keep Jewish observances.

Jerusalem and Caesarea 58-60 A.D.

The Riot and Rescue in the Temple. In the eyes of the Jews, Paul was a renegade; he had abandoned the Jewish faith, in which he had been born and educated, and embraced a new religion. Had he remained true to the faith of his fathers, he would now have been one of the leaders in Israel; he had been one of the most promising students ever to study in Jerusalem's rabbinical school. But instead of being a champion he was now the greatest enemy of Judaism; and they hated him with a fierce, unreasoning hatred. Like the Master before

too, profaning these sacred precincts.' They had seen Trophimus, who was from Ephesus, in the city with him, and it was
he whom they suspected Paul of introducing into the temple.
The whole city was in a commotion, and the common folk
ran up from all sides. They seized Paul and dragged him out of
the temple, upon which the gates were shut; and they were
preparing to kill him, when word came to the captain of the
garrison that the whole of Jerusalem was in an uproar. He at
once summoned his troops, with their officers, and swept down
upon them; and at the sight of the captain with his troops they
left off beating Paul.

The captain came up and arrested him, giving orders that he
should be bound with a double chain; then he asked him who
he was, and what he had done. But some of the crowd were
shouting this and some that, and it was impossible to find out
the truth amidst the clamour; so he gave orders that Paul
should be taken to the soldiers' quarters. When he reached
the steps, he had to be carried by the soldiers because of the
crowd's violence; a rabble of the common people kept following behind, with cries of, 'Put him to death.'

And just as he was being taken into the soldiers' quarters,
Paul asked the centurion, 'May I have a word with you?'

At which he said, 'What, can you talk Greek? You are not,
then, that Egyptian, that raised a band of four thousand cut-
throats, some time back, and led them out into the wilderness?'

'I am a Jew,' said Paul, 'a citizen of Tarsus in Cilicia, no
mean city; my request of you is that you would let me speak to
the people.'

And so, having obtained his leave, Paul stood there on the
steps, and made a gesture with his hand to the people. There

him, Paul was disowned by his own people: 'He came to what was his own, and they who were his own gave him no welcome.'

It was the time of the morning sacrifice when Paul made his way into the temple for the final ceremonies of the Nazirite vow. The temple was divided into two sections by a low stone wall separating the outer Court of the Gentiles from the inner courts; no Gentile was permitted beyond this barrier (called Soreg): 'No stranger is permitted to cross this barrier into the holy place; the penalty is death.' Even the Roman soldiers respected the sacredness of the inner enclosure.

At the times of great festivals the Roman garrison in fortress Antonia, in the northwest corner of the temple area, was strengthened to meet any emergency. This occasion was the feast of Pentecost, and the Roman guard was on the look-out for any disturbance among the pilgrims thronging the temple courts. The riot started in the Men's Court; the temple police quickly forced the fighting crowd outside the sanctuary proper into the Gentiles' Court to avoid profanation of the holy place; they then closed the big bronze doors of the Beautiful Gate.

Captain Lysias lost no time in getting to the scene of the disturbance; his soldiers knew just how to handle an oriental mob. He wasted no time in questioning the rioters but took Paul immediately into the barracks at the top of the steps leading into fortress Antonia. Lysias felt quite sure that he had at last captured the dangerous rebel, an Egyptian Jew who had been causing much trouble to the Jerusalem garrison (he had escaped into the desert country east of Olivet). This Egyptian is also mentioned by the contemporary historian Josephus.

Paul's Account of His Own Conversion. As Paul stood at the top of the Antonia steps looking down at the hostile faces of

was deep silence, and he began addressing himself to them in Hebrew: 'Brethren and fathers, listen to the defence I am putting before you.' (And now they gave him even better audience, finding that he spoke to them in Hebrew.) 'I am a Jew, born at Tarsus in Cilicia and brought up in this city; I was trained, under Gamaliel, in exact knowledge of our ancestral law, as jealous for the honour of God as you are, all of you, today. I persecuted this Way to the death, putting men and women in chains and handing them over to the prisons. The chief priests and all the elders will bear me out in that; it was from them that I was carrying letters to their brethren, when I was on my way to Damascus, to make fresh prisoners there and bring them to Jerusalem for punishment. While I was on my journey, not far from Damascus, about midday, this befell me; all at once a great light from heaven shone about me, and I fell to the ground, and heard a voice saying to me, "Saul, Saul, why do you persecute me?"

' "Who are you, Lord?" I answered.

'And he said to me, "I am Jesus of Nazareth, whom Saul persecutes."

'My companions saw the light, but could not catch the voice of him who spoke to me. Then I said, "What must I do, Lord?"

'And the Lord said to me, "Rise up, and go into Damascus; there you shall be told of all the work that is destined for you."

'The glory of that light had blinded me, and my companions were leading me by the hand when I came into Damascus. There a certain Ananias, a man well known among his Jewish neighbours for his pious observance of the law, came and stood beside me, and said, "Brother Saul, look up and see." And at that instant I looked up into his face. Then he said to me,

the crowd in the Court of the Gentiles, his mind must have gone back 28 years to a similar scene, when Stephen stood on trial for his life in this same temple of Jerusalem. He surely sent up a prayer to Stephen, the man who first brought him into contact with the risen Christ, the source of all grace and truth. At Stephen's trial, Paul was a prominent persecutor; but now he himself is on trial for his own life.

He follows an approach similar to that of Stephen. But instead of tracing the history of the Jewish people, Paul gives an autobiographical sketch of his own conversion. He speaks in Aramaic (called Hebrew by Luke), the mother tongue of Jews living in Palestine. He could have spoken in Greek and been understood by all; he chose Aramaic for the same reason that Peter did on Pentecost Sunday. It was an appeal to patriotism and national sentiment, and at once established an intimacy with the audience not shared by the Roman soldiers standing by, who would understand only an occasional word of Aramaic.

Once Paul began to speak, he felt sure of himself. He recalls the situation leading to his conversion; the details were well known to the Jewish leaders listening to him; many of them were his own contemporaries. His purpose is to show that he is no enemy of the Jewish religion. The Jews were familiar from their history with the intervention of the Lord God in their lives; the Old Testament was full of such incidents. As to the prophets of old, God himself had spoken directly to Paul; the divine will was made clear to him in no uncertain terms. What else could he do but obey God?

In Acts 9 Luke gives an account of Paul's conversion; Paul himself will repeat the story before Agrippa at Caesarea (Acts 26). There are minor variations in the three accounts. The only detail that needs clarification is the seeming contradiction

"The God of our fathers has made choice of you to know his will, to have sight of him who is Just, and hear speech from his lips; and what you have seen and heard, you shall testify before all men. Come then, why are you wasting time? Rise up, and receive baptism, washing away your sins at the invocation of his name."

'Afterwards, when I had gone back to Jerusalem, and was at prayer in the temple, I fell into a trance, and saw the Lord there speaking to me; "Make haste," he said, "leave Jerusalem with all speed; they will not accept your witness of me here."
' "But Lord," I said, "it is within their own knowledge, how I used to imprison those who believed in you, and scourge them in the synagogues; and when the blood of Stephen, your martyr, was shed, I too stood by and gave my consent, and watched over the garments of those who slew him."
'And he said to me, "Go on your way; I mean to send you on a distant errand, to the Gentiles." '

Up to this point, they listened to his speech; but then they cried aloud, 'Away with such a fellow from the earth; it is a disgrace that he should live.' So, when he saw them raising shouts and throwing down their garments and flinging dust into the air, the captain had Paul taken into the soldiers' quarters, telling them to examine him under the lash; thus he would find out the cause of the outcry against him. And they had already tied Paul down with thongs, when he said to the centurion who was in charge, 'Have you the right to scourge a man, when he is a Roman citizen, and has not been sentenced?'

The centurion, as soon as he heard this, went to the captain and told him of it; 'What are you about?' he said. 'This man is a Roman citizen.'

as to what Paul's companions heard. Acts 9, 7 says that they heard the voice speak; in this paragraph Paul says they 'could not catch the voice of him who spoke to me.' The simplest explanation is that the other members of Paul's party heard a voice (like the heavenly voice in the temple, Jn. 12, 29), but were unable to pick up the actual words spoken.

The Crowd Interrupts Paul's Speech.   Since Paul was such a devoted son of the law, why did he not return to Jerusalem and preach the gospel there? It is to answer this unasked question which must have been in the minds of his listeners that Paul now tells of a vision in the temple that commanded him to preach to the Gentiles. His mission was not to the Jews but to the pagans scattered throughout the vast Roman Empire. At the mention of the hated Gentiles, all the anger of the crowd rose again to the surface; their outcry put an end to Paul's defence.

As a point of chronology, Paul did not return to Jerusalem immediately after his conversion; he spent three years in retreat in the Arabian desert (Gal. 1, 18). In Acts 9, 29 Luke says that the reason for Paul's departure from Jerusalem on the occasion of his first visit was a plot against his life, not a revelation from the Lord. So Knox thinks Paul is not referring to the first visit, three years after his conversion, but to his second visit, fourteen years after conversion. It was only a year after this second visit that Paul's mission to the Gentiles really began, with his first missionary journey in the company of Barnabas. It was this vision in the temple that initiated the Gentile mission.

Paul was taken for scourging into the barracks, where Jesus had been scourged by Pilate. He was no stranger to the lash; already he had suffered it at least eight times (2 Cor. 11, 24-

So the captain came and asked him, 'What is this? You are a Roman citizen?'

'Yes,' he said.

'Why,' answered the captain, 'it cost me a heavy sum to win this privilege.'

'Ah,' said Paul, 'but I am a citizen by birth.'

Upon this, the men who were to have put him to the question moved away from him; and the captain himself was alarmed, to find out that this was a Roman citizen, and he had put him in bonds.

So, the next day, determined to discover the truth about the charge the Jews were bringing against him, he released him, summoned a meeting of the chief priests and the whole Council, and brought Paul down to confront them with him. Paul fastened his eyes on the Council, and said, 'Brethren, all my life I have behaved myself with full loyalty of conscience towards God.' At this, the high priest Ananias bade those who were standing near smite him on the mouth. Then Paul said to him, 'It is God that will smite you, for the whitened wall you are; you are sitting there to judge me according to the law, and will you break the law by ordering them to smite me?'

'What,' said the bystanders, 'would you insult God's high priest?'

And Paul said, 'Brethren, I could not tell that it was the high priest; to be sure, it is written, "You shall not speak ill of him who rules your people." ' And now, finding that there were two factions among them, one of the Sadducees and the other of the Pharisees, Paul cried out in the Council, 'Brethren, I am a Pharisee, and my fathers were Pharisees before me. And I am standing on my trial because I am one

25). This was surely Paul's great opportunity to suffer like the Master and relive in his own body the sufferings of the Head. The reason he refused to suffer scourging was probably that he was not being subjected to torture for Christ's sake, but owing to the mistaken impression that he was the Egyptian impostor.

The claim to Roman citizenship was never made falsely, because if untrue such a claim was punishable by death. It was a rare privilege in the provinces; probably Paul's family in Tarsus had won this coveted privilege by some service rendered to an earlier emperor.

Paul Before the Council. The Romans were always puzzled by the feeling shown by the Jews over religious matters. Captain Claudius Lysias was determined to get to the bottom of the Jewish hostility to Paul; so he summoned the Jewish leaders to meet him. This meeting took place, it is most likely, in some room in the fortress Antonia, not in the council chamber, which was in the Priests' Court; Lysias and his Roman soldiers would not have been permitted to enter that place. The high priest, Ananias, did not preside (otherwise Paul could not have mistaken his identity), nor were witnesses called; this meant that it was not a regular Jewish trial but an enquiry conducted under the presidency of Lysias.

A blow on the face was a grievous insult to a Jew; it signified his exclusion from the chosen people. Paul lost his temper, and reacted so quickly that the blow was probably never delivered. Our Lord's calmness in a similar situation is in contrast to Paul's anger. Paul's outburst soon subsided, and he apologized for his offensive words to the high priest. His apology took the form of a quote from Exodus; the rabbi in Paul shows in the apt manner in which he could find a text for every purpose.

who hopes for the resurrection of the dead.'

When he said this, a dissension arose between the Pharisees and the Sadducees and the assembly was in two minds. The Sadducees will have it that there is no resurrection, that there are no angels or spirits, whereas the Pharisees believe in both. So that a great clamour followed; and some scribes of the Pharisees' party came forward to protest; 'We cannot find any fault in this man,' they said. 'Perhaps he has had a message from a spirit, or an angel.' Then dissension rose high; and the captain, who was afraid that they would tear Paul in pieces, ordered his troops to come down and rescue Paul from their midst, and bring him safe to the soldiers' quarters.

On the next night, the Lord came to his side, and told him, 'Do not lose heart; you have done with bearing me witness in Jerusalem, and now you must carry the same witness to Rome.' When day came, the Jews held a conclave, and bound themselves under a solemn curse that they would not eat or drink until they had killed Paul; more than forty of them joined in this conspiracy. So they went to the chief priests and elders, and told them, 'We have bound ourselves under a solemn curse not to take food until we have killed Paul. Your part, then, is to signify to the captain your wish and the Council's, that he would bring him down before you, as if you meant to examine his cause more precisely; and we are ready to make away with him before he reaches you.' Paul's sister had a son who heard of this ambush being laid; and he went to the soldiers' quarters and gave news of it to Paul. Whereupon Paul had one of the centurions brought to him, and said, 'Take this young man to the captain; he has news to give him.'

So he bade him follow, and took him to the captain; 'The prisoner Paul,' he said, 'had me summoned and asked me to

Paul was soon master of the situation; he led the discussion onto his own ground. Possibly a chance remark on Paul's apt quotation from the scriptures decided him in bringing up the question of the Resurrection. He would divide the Pharisees and Sadducees on this famous disputed question (for the Sadducees' opinion see the case of the woman with seven husbands, Mt. 22, 23-33). Also, the Resurrection was the key doctrine in Christian apologetic; so that Paul was not distracting the Council from the real reason of their opposition to him. It was the basic apologetic of both Peter and Paul in their recorded sermons in the Acts (chapters 2 and 13).

Paul Sent Under Guard to Caesarea. It was in this same fortress Antonia that Peter had been imprisoned 14 years earlier. At that time the whole Christian Church had sent up prayer to God for his release (Acts 12). But the Christian community in Jerusalem had been rather cool in their attitude to Paul; he felt sad and dejected as he sat in his prison cell that night. He had come back from years of missionary activity in pagan lands only to end his career alone and unwanted in prison.

He could not help contrasting his conduct on the previous day with that of the Master who had been condemned and gone to his death from this same building. Instead of suffering and dying like the Master, Paul had lost his temper, and argued his way out of the danger in which he had found himself. He had often spoken of being crucified with Christ; and when the opportunity came, he had not been equal to the sacrifice. As he meditated long into the night on the disparity between his own life and the Master's, sleep came to his troubled mind; and in his sleep, Jesus stood by his side. He calmed Paul's fears, and brought new hope for the future: Paul had work to do for the Lord in Rome.

take this young man into your presence; he has a message for you.'

And the captain, taking him by the hand and drawing him aside, asked, 'What is the news you bring me?'

'The Jews,' he said, 'have formed this design; they will ask you to bring Paul down before the Council tomorrow, as if they meant to examine his cause more precisely. Do not listen to them; some of them will be lying in ambush for him, more than forty in number. They have sworn not to eat or drink until they have made away with him; even now they are in readiness, only waiting for your consent.'

Thereupon the captain dismissed the young man, warning him not to let anyone know that he had revealed this secret to him. Then he summoned two of the centurions, and told them, 'You are to have two hundred men from the cohort ready to march to Caesarea, with seventy horsemen and two hundred spearmen; they will set out at nine o'clock tonight. And you must provide beasts, so that they can mount Paul and take him safely to the governor, Felix.' He also wrote a letter, with these contents: 'Claudius Lysias, to his excellency Felix, the governor, sends greeting. Here is a man whom the Jews seized, and set about killing him; but I came up with my men and rescued him, learning that he was a Roman citizen. Since I had a mind to discover what complaint it was they had against him, I took him down into the presence of their Council; but I found that the accusation was concerned with disputes about their own law, and that he was charged with nothing that deserved death or imprisonment. And now, since I have information of a plot which they have laid against him, I am sending him to you, telling his accusers at the same time that they must plead their cause before you. Farewell.'

The soldiers, obeying their orders, took Paul with them,

The future of the infant Church from now on was to develop within the framework of the Roman Empire; the break with Judaism was only a matter of time. Paul had written of this in Romans 13. The Master had now made Paul's position clear: freedom would not come by submitting to Jewish law and justice, but by taking Christianity out into the Roman world order. It was this vision that ultimately decided Paul to appeal to Caesar two years later when he was in prison at Caesarea.

The trial on the previous day had been held in the Roman fortress; the Jews now proposed that Paul should be sent down into the temple to the council chamber. This would mean that he would be separated from the Roman guard and be an easy target for the assassin's knife. It is not known whether or not Paul's nephew was a Christian, or how he heard of this plot to kill his uncle; it seems likely that he would have better opportunities to overhear, or discover, the plot if he was not a Christian. We know nothing of Paul's family apart from this casual mention of his sister. Possibly she was married to some official who handed on the information; the nephew was sent to the barracks so as not to arouse suspicion.

Lysias was taking no chances, with his 470 soldiers (though Knox suggests that the text originally read only 270) to guard Paul on the twelve hours' night march to Caesarea. Once they arrived at Antipatris, they were away from the hill country, and there was little danger of ambush. The cavalry would be adequate for the rest of the journey across the plain of Sharon. The infantry were recalled to Jerusalem because the feast of Pentecost was still on, and there might be trouble there.

There is an authentic touch in Claudius' letter to Felix. He makes his case better by falsely claiming that he rescued Paul because he knew he was a Roman citizen (actually he had not

and conducted him, travelling all night, to Antipatris. Next day they left the horsemen to accompany him, and went back to their quarters. The horsemen, upon reaching Caesarea, delivered the letter to the governor, and brought Paul, too, into his presence. So the governor read the letter, and asked from what province he came, and was told, 'From Cilicia'; then he said, 'I will give you a hearing when your accusers, too, are present.' And he gave orders that he should be kept safe in Herod's palace.

Five days later the high priest Ananias came down, accompanied by some of the elders and by an advocate named Tertullus; these appeared before the governor against Paul. So, when Paul had been summoned, Tertullus began his indictment thus: 'Such is the peace you have enabled us to enjoy, so many wrongs have been righted for this nation through your wisdom, that always and everywhere, most noble Felix, we are ready to acknowledge it with grateful hearts. But I must not weary you with more of this; what we ask of your courtesy is no more than a brief audience. Here is a man who is known to us as a pestilent mover of sedition among Jews all over the world, a ringleader of the sect of the Nazarenes, who has not scrupled to attempt a violation of the temple. We arrested him; interrogate him yourself, and you will be able to learn the truth about all the accusations we bring against him.' And the Jews, for their part, supported the indictment, alleging that all this was the truth.

Then the governor made a sign to bid Paul speak, and he answered: 'I am the more emboldened to make my defence, because I know well that you have been a judge over this nation for many years. You have the means of assuring yourself that it is only twelve days since I came to Jerusalem, to worship there. They have never found me raising controversy,

discovered this fact till later). Also he makes no mention of his attempt to torture Paul; this could have got the captain into trouble.

Paul's birthplace, Tarsus, was in the Roman province of Cilicia; this was an imperial, not a senatorial province, and so Felix was competent to try the case. Paul was lodged in prison in the governor's residence; it had been built originally by Herod the Great.

Paul Before Felix. Within a week of Paul's arrival at Caesarea, a Jewish delegation under the leadership of the high priest arrived from Jerusalem. Their purpose was to obtain Paul's condemnation from the Roman governor, as they had obtained that of our Lord himself. To present their case they engaged a Roman barrister, Tertullus; he would be more familiar than a Jewish lawyer with Roman procedure, which was entirely different from the Jewish manner of trying a prisoner.

Tertullus presented three indictments against Paul; each of the three was a crime punishable by death according to Roman law. They bear a striking resemblance to the crimes with which the Master had been charged. Paul was accused of sedition, of being a ringleader of a religion ('sect') which was illegal in the empire, and of violating the temple (presumably by taking Trophimus into the sanctuary, beyond the Soreg).

Paul's reply is factual. The crimes alleged against him must all have happened in Jerusalem during the past fortnight. So he tells Felix just what happened during his brief visit to the holy city. He dismisses the charge of sedition by his statement that no one can produce the slightest evidence that he ever gathered a crowd about him, or addressed any body of men, anywhere in Jerusalem. He explains his presence in the temple;

or bringing a crowd together, either in the temple, or in the synagogues, or in the open city; nor can they produce any proof of the charges they bring against me. But this I admit to you, that in worshipping the God of our fathers, I follow what we call the Way, and they call a sect. I put my trust in all that is written in the law and the prophets, sharing before God the hope they have too, that the dead will rise again, both just and unjust. To that end I, like them, am at pains to keep my conscience clear of offence towards God or man, at all times. After some years' absence I came up to bring alms to the men of my own race, and certain offerings. It was when I had just made these offerings and had been purified in the temple, that I was found there, no crowd about me, no rioting, by whom? By some Jews from Asia, who ought to be here, standing in your presence, if they had any quarrel with me. In default of that, it is for those who are here to give their account of what blame they found in me, when I stood before the Council; unless it were over one single utterance, when I cried out, standing there among them, "If I am on my trial before you today, it is because of the resurrection of the dead." '

Felix, who had full information about the Way, reserved judgment; 'I will give you a hearing,' he said, 'when Lysias, the captain, has come down here.' And he gave orders to the centurion that Paul was to be kept safely, but left at his ease, and that any of his friends should be given liberty to minister to him. And some days afterwards, when Felix was there with his wife Drusilla, who was a Jewess, he sent for Paul, and listened to his message about faith in Jesus Christ. When he spoke of justice, and continence, and of the judgment that is to come, Felix was terrified; 'No more of this for the present,' he said, 'I will send for you when I can find leisure.'

he brought alms to his own people, and offered sacrifices just as any good Jew would do. It was not he, Paul, that caused the riot in the temple, but the false accusations of some Asian Jews; and they were not present at Felix's tribunal to undergo questioning.

The charge of belonging to a sect (the Nazarenes as distinct from the Jews) was probably the most dangerous to the Christian cause. Rome protected Judaism as a state-approved religion; the Christians enjoyed the rights of Jews, since they were not at this time regarded as a separate political body. Paul's purpose is to guard this protected status; he argues that the dispute between himself and the Council is purely a domestic matter within the framework of Judaism. Like the Jews themselves he believes in the Old Testament ('the law and the prophets'). The resurrection of the dead is not a purely Christian belief; it is held by the majority of the Jews themselves. So Paul denies the charge of being a sect distinct from Judaism; rather, Christianity is the fulfilment and completion of the Old Testament; in reality Christians are the true Israel of God.

Felix was governor of Judea from 52 to 60 A.D., when he was recalled on account of complaints by the Jews against his harsh rule. He was originally a slave; he was a cruel and dissolute ruler. He should have concluded Paul's trial by acquittal; he temporized because he was afraid of Jewish reaction, and also because he hoped to receive a bribe for Paul's release.

Some authorities think that Paul spent part of his two years' captivity at Caesarea working out the plan of his Letter to the Hebrews. Though the evidence favours its publication about 65 A.D., when Paul was in Rome after his journey to Spain, it is probably better to read it at this point when the

At the same time, he hoped that Paul would offer him a bribe, and for that reason sent for him often, and courted his company. So two years passed; then Porcius Festus came as successor to Felix; and Felix, who wished to ingratiate himself with the Jews, left Paul in prison.

And Festus, three days after entering his province, went up from Caesarea to Jerusalem. Here the high priest and the leaders of the Jews put before him their case against Paul, and were urgent with him, asking as a favour, that he would summon Paul to Jerusalem; meanwhile they were preparing an ambush, so as to make away with him on the journey. But Festus answered that Paul was in safe keeping at Caesarea; he himself would be removing there as soon as possible; 'Let those of you who are men of influence,' he said, 'travel down with me, and bring your charges against this man, if you have anything against him.'

So, when he had spent a week with them, or ten days at most, he went down to Caesarea; and next day, sitting on the judgment seat, he gave orders for Paul to be brought in. When he appeared, there were the Jews who had come down from Jerusalem, standing round him and bringing many grave accusations against him, which they could not prove; while Paul said in his defence, 'I have committed no crime against the Jewish law, or against the temple, or against Caesar.'

But Festus had a mind to ingratiate himself with the Jews, so he answered Paul thus, 'Are you ready to go up to Jerusalem, and meet these charges before me there?'

Upon which Paul said, 'I am standing at Caesar's judgment seat, where I have a right to be tried. As for the Jews, I have done them no wrong, as you know well enough. If I am guilty, if I have done something which deserves death, I

atmosphere is right for an appreciation of its message. Almost certainly Luke was busy at this time visiting places and people, gathering information for the writing of his Gospel, which he finished during Paul's Roman captivity.

Paul Appeals to Caesar. Governor Festus was a Roman nobleman, an official of the old school; he was a firm and honest administrator. He arrived at Caesarea in August, 60 A.D., to find his province of Palestine in a state of unrest. His predecessor, Felix, had put down a riot between Greeks and Jews in Caesarea by a large-scale massacre of Jews; for his savagery he had been recalled in disgrace. Festus had been briefed on the difficulty of the Palestinian situation and the fanaticism of the Jews. His policy was to become friendly with the local leaders and not to antagonize them.

That is why he made an immediate visit to the Jewish headquarters at Jerusalem. A new high priest, Ishmael, had come into office; he was aware of Festus' desire to win Jewish support, and so asked as a favour that Paul be tried in Jerusalem. Knowing of the attempted ambush during the governorship of Felix, Festus was taking no risks; he decided to keep Paul at Caesarea. Accordingly a trial was arranged before the governor at Caesarea. Just as at the previous trial two years before, the Jews could prove none of their charges.

At the conclusion of this trial, Festus asked Paul if he was willing to be tried in Jerusalem. This sudden change of mind on Festus' part was probably brought about by his fear at seeing the fierce, violent Jewish hatred of Paul, and the conviction that the case was a matter for a Jewish court rather than a Roman. Paul saw that Festus was unequal to dealing with the Jewish leaders, and that there was no possibility that his case

do not ask for reprieve; if their charges are without substance, no one has a right to make them a present of my life. I appeal to Caesar.'

Then Festus conferred with his council, and answered, 'Have you appealed to Caesar? To Caesar you shall go.'

Some days later, king Agrippa and Bernice came to Caesarea, to give Festus their greeting, and, since he was spending several days there, Festus put Paul's case before the king: 'There is a man here,' he said, 'whom Felix left behind in prison; and when I went to Jerusalem the chief priests and elders of the Jews denounced him to me, asking for his condemnation. I replied that it is not the Roman custom to make a present of any man's life, until the accused man has been confronted with his accusers, and been given the opportunity to clear himself of the charge. So they came here with me, and I did not keep them waiting; the next day, sitting on the judgment seat, I gave orders for the man to be brought in. His accusers, as they stood round him, could not tax him with any criminal offence, such as I had expected; their controversies with him were concerned with scruples of their own, and with a dead man called Jesus, whom Paul declared to be alive. For myself, I hesitated to enter upon the discussion of such matters; so I asked whether he was willing to go to Jerusalem, and meet these charges there. Upon which Paul appealed to have his case reserved for the emperor's cognizance; and I gave orders that he should be kept safe until I can send him to Caesar.'

Then Agrippa said to Festus, 'I have often wished, myself, to hear this man speak.'

'You shall hear him,' said he, 'tomorrow.'

So, on the next day, Agrippa and Bernice came with great pomp, and made their entry into the hall of judgment, at-

could be brought to a speedy conclusion here at Caesarea. Guided, too, by his vision of the Lord at Jerusalem, he decided that this was the time to appeal to the supreme court, to Rome itself. This was the most coveted privilege possessed by a Roman citizen.

Festus Puts Paul's Case to Agrippa. This young king, Herod Agrippa II, was the last of the house of Herod. His father, Agrippa I, had died suddenly here at Caesarea in 44 A.D. (Acts 12). Agrippa II had been educated in Rome, and was more Roman than Jewish in outlook. In 53 A.D. he had been appointed ruler of northern Palestine, with his capital at Caesarea Philippi. He was also authorized to inspect the temple at Jerusalem; he spent much of his time in Jerusalem, and was engaged in repairing and renovating the temple courts at this time. He was unmarried; his sister Bernice acted as his queen. Another, younger sister, Drusilla, was the wife of the former governor Felix; she was in Rome at this time; she was eventually to perish in the eruption of Vesuvius.

There must have been many visitors to see Paul during the course of his two years' imprisonment at Caesarea. Philip the deacon was undoubtedly a constant visitor; many of Paul's disciples came to report, and went out on various missions. But Luke makes no mention of any of them; instead he gives practically the whole of his narrative to an account of Paul's trial and defence before the Roman authorities. He wrote the Acts in Rome while Paul was waiting to be tried before the emperor Nero. This was to be a test case for the right to preach Christianity throughout the Roman world; it would be a precedent in Roman law for all missionaries to follow in Paul's footsteps. Festus' report on Paul's case was probably lost in the shipwreck on the island of Malta during the voyage to Rome; Luke took great care in his presentation of the

tended by the captains and all the eminent persons of the
city; and Paul, at Festus' command, was brought in. Then
Festus said, 'King Agrippa, and all you who are present, you
see before you a man over whom the whole Jewish body has
been petitioning me, not only here but at Jerusalem, crying
out that he must not be allowed to live a day longer. For myself, I was satisfied that he had not done anything deserving
of death; but, since he has appealed to the emperor, I have
thought it best to send him, and now, writing to my sovereign
lord, I have no clear account to give of him. That is why I
have brought him before you, and before you especially, king
Agrippa, so that the examination may afford material for my
letter. It would be unreasonable, I conceive, to remit a prisoner
for trial without putting on record the charges that lie against
him.'

Then Agrippa said to Paul: 'You are free to give an account
of yourself.'

And Paul, stretching out his hand, began his defence: 'King
Agrippa, I count myself fortunate today, to be defending
myself against all the accusations of the Jews in your presence.
No one is more familiar than you with the customs of the
Jews, and their controversies; and this makes me bold to ask
you for a patient audience. What my life was like when boyhood was over, spent from the first among my own people and
in Jerusalem, all the Jews know; their earliest memory of me,
would they but admit it, is of one who lived according to the
strictest tradition of observance we have, a Pharisee. And if
I stand here on my trial, it is for my hope of the promise God
made to our fathers. Our twelve tribes worship him cease-
lessly, night and day, in the hope of attaining that promise
and this is the hope, my lord king, for which the Jews call me
to account. Why should it be beyond the belief of men such

defence, so that the authorities could read in detail just what Paul said, and what the local rulers had to say about his case.

Throughout the Acts, Luke emphasizes how well the Christian cause was received by the imperial authorities in the provinces. In Cyprus, the governor Sergius Paulus listened to Paul and Barnabas and 'learned to believe' (Acts 13, 7-12). At Philippi, a Roman colony, the magistrates at first scourged and imprisoned Paul and Silas, but afterwards they apologized for this injustice, and Paul and Silas parted with them on good terms (Acts 16). At Corinth, proconsul Gallio refused to listen to the Jews, and set Paul free (Acts 18). At Ephesus, 'the delegates of Asia' were his friends; the town clerk there pointed out that Paul had done nothing to cause such a riot (Acts 19).

Paul's Speech Before Agrippa. No royal family had such close contact with our Lord and his Church as the Herods. Herod the Great, great-grandfather of Agrippa II, had put the Innocents to death in an attempt to kill Jesus (Mt. 2); his son Antipas had John the Baptist beheaded (Mk. 6), and mocked our Lord during his Roman trial (Lk. 23); his grandson Agrippa I killed James the Greater, and tried to kill Peter too (Acts 12). In face of such a history, Paul was optimistic in thinking that the last of the Herod dynasty would be favourable to the Christian cause. But at least Agrippa II was familiar with both the Jewish and the Christian background of Paul's case. Paul could talk to him in language that would be understood.

First of all Paul establishes his right to be regarded as a true Jew. He traces his early life, particularly his student days in Jerusalem. Like all the Jews he had had as his main religious interest the expectation of the Messiah who was to come and

12

as you are, that God should raise the dead?

'Well then, I thought it my duty to defy, in many ways, the name of Jesus the Nazarene. And that is what I did, at Jerusalem; it was I, under powers granted me by the chief priests, who shut up many of the faithful in prison; and when they were done to death, I raised my voice against them. Often have I tried to force them into blaspheming, by inflicting punishment on them in one synagogue after another; nay, so unmeasured was my rage against them that I used to go to foreign cities to persecute them. It was on such an errand that I was making my way to Damascus, with powers delegated to me by the chief priests, when, journeying at midday, I saw, my lord king, a light from heaven, surpassing the brightness of the sun, which shone about me and my companions. We all fell to the ground, and I heard a voice which said to me, in Hebrew, "Saul, Saul, why do you persecute me? This is a thankless task of yours, kicking against the goad."

' "Who are you, Lord?" I asked.

'And the Lord said, "I am Jesus, whom Saul persecutes. Rise up, and stand on your feet; I have shown myself to you, that I may single you out to serve me, as the witness of this vision you have had, and other visions you will have of me. I will be your deliverer from the hands of your people, and of the Gentiles, to whom I am now sending you. You shall open their eyes, and turn them from darkness to light, from the power of Satan to God, so that they may receive, through faith in me, remission of their sins and an inheritance among the saints."

'Whereupon, king Agrippa, I did not show myself disobedient to the heavenly vision. First to those in Damascus,

redeem Israel. This hope had been realized in the person of Jesus Christ; God himself had raised Jesus from the dead, providing the authentic guarantee of the truth of Jesus' claim to be the Redeemer. Paul's point in bringing up this fundamental claim of Christianity is to show that it is the fulfilment of all Jewish hopes, that the Christian religion is not something alien to Judaism but its final completion.

For the third time in Acts (chapters 9, 22, 26) Paul recounts his conversion on the road to Damascus. Without this incident Paul's career has no meaning; it was the turning point in his life. He did not willingly change his way of life; the risen Christ personally appeared to him and commanded his allegiance. Paul had been waging an inner struggle against the grace of God; he had been like an ox kicking against a sharp-pointed goad; but the more he struggled to escape, the more determined God was to win him to the Christian cause.

By that vision on the Damascus Road, Paul became an apostle of Jesus Christ. An apostle is one who is sent; Paul had been sent to preach the gospel to both Jew and Gentile. It was particularly his mission to the Gentiles that annoyed the Jews and made him a renegade from Israel. But for Paul this was his greatest privilege: 'Of making known to the Gentiles the unfathomable riches of Christ.' The audience listening to Paul in the palace at Caesarea was mostly Gentile; the words he spoke would eventually be sent to Rome. The religion Paul was preaching to them would ultimately spread throughout the Roman Empire, and it would be the vitality infused by the Christian faith which would save this civilization from total destruction.

Paul Tries to Convert Agrippa. Paul never missed an opportunity to win souls to the cause of Christ. At dead of night,

then in Jerusalem, then to all the country of Judea, then to the heathen, I preached repentance, bidding them turn to God, and so act as befits men who are penitent. That is why the Jews, when they caught me in the temple, tried to murder me. But, thanks to God's help, I still stand here today, bearing my witness to small and great alike. Yet there is nothing in my message which goes beyond what the prophets spoke of, and Moses spoke of, as things to come; a suffering Christ, and one who would show light to his people and to the Gentiles by being the first to rise from the dead.'

When Paul had proceeded so far with his defence, Festus said in a loud voice, 'Paul, you are mad; they are driving you to madness, these long studies of yours.'

But Paul answered, 'No, most noble Festus, I am not mad; the message which I utter is sober truth. The king knows about all this well enough; that is why I speak with such confidence in his presence. None of this, I am sure, is news to him; it was not in some secret corner that all this happened. Do you believe the prophets, king Agrippa? I am well assured you do believe them.'

At this, Agrippa said to Paul, 'You would have me turn Christian with very little ado.'

'Why,' said Paul, 'it would be my prayer to God that, whether it were with much ado or little, both you and all those who are listening to me today should become such as I am, chains and all.'

Then the king rose, and so did the governor, and Bernice, and all those who sat there with them. When they had retired, they said to one another, 'This man is guilty of no fault that deserves death or imprisonment.' And Agrippa said to Festus, 'If he had not appealed to Caesar, this man might have been set at liberty.'

after the earthquake at Philippi (Acts 16), he instructed and baptized the gaoler and his family. And here in Caesarea, as he watches Agrippa's keen interest in his speech, he directs his words towards gaining the soul of the king. Whether the man is unimportant (like the gaoler) or a royal person ('small and great alike') makes no difference to Paul's zealous interest. He is all things to all men, to win them to Christ.

This talk of repentance, of obedience to God's grace, of the truth of the Christian message in view of its conformity to the Old Testament revelation, and the fact of Christ's resurrection struck a responsive chord in the Jewish soul of Agrippa. But such considerations passed completely over the head of Festus; they bore no resemblance to the facts of daily life that he had to deal with. He blamed it all on Paul's constant reading of the Sacred Scriptures: 'These long studies of yours.' But Paul was not directing his message to Festus on this occasion; he disregards the interruption and appeals personally to Agrippa. Moved and somewhat shaken, Agrippa tries to extricate himself from this uncomfortable situation. A jest, a piece of irony, is the best way of turning aside a too personal interest in one's life. And that is just what Agrippa tries to do; he attempts to pass it off with a pleasantry, as Pilate did at the trial of Jesus, with the phrase, 'What is truth?'

It was a dramatic moment, as the insignificant prisoner raised his manacled hands to the assembly. The chains did not fetter his soul, they only identified him the more with his crucified Master. Luke concludes his account of this episode of Paul's life by emphasizing again that he was declared innocent of any crime worthy of death. He does the same in his account of Jesus' trial (Lk. 23); three times Pilate stated the fact of our Lord's innocence.

Letter to the Hebrews

In old days, God spoke to our fathers in various partial ways and in many figurative ways, through the prophets; now at last in these times he has spoken to us, with a Son to speak for him; a Son, whom he has appointed to inherit all things, just as it was through him that he created this world of time; a Son, who is the radiance of his Father's splendour, and the full expression of his being; all creation depends, for its support, on his enabling word. Now, making atonement for our sins, he has taken his place on high, at the right hand of God's majesty, superior to the angels in that measure in which the name he has inherited is more excellent than theirs. Did God ever say to one of the angels, 'You are my Son, I have begotten you this day'? And again, 'He shall find in me a Father, and I in him a Son'? Why, when the time comes for bringing his first-born into the world anew, then, he says, 'Let all the angels of God worship before him.'

What does he say of the angels? 'He will have his angels be like the winds, the servants that wait on him like a flame of fire.'

And what of the Son? 'Your throne, O God, stands firm for ever and ever; the sceptre of your kingship is a rod that rules true. You have been a friend to right, an enemy to wrong; and God, your own God, has given you an unction to bring you pride, as none else of your fellows.' And elsewhere: 'Lord, you have laid the foundations of the earth at its beginning, and the heavens are the work of your hands. They will perish, but you will remain; they will all be like a cloak that grows threadbare, and you will fold them up, like a garment, and change them as one changes his cloak; but you are he who never changes, your years will not come to an end.'

Christ's Priesthood and Sacrifice

Christ Is Superior to the Angels. *This letter alone does not carry Paul's name on the letter-head; the other thirteen letters all begin with a greeting in his name. Paul's characteristic broken, spoken style, with its sudden changes of thought, gives way in Hebrews to a calm, placid, written style that flows smoothly. Writing in the third century, Origen, a great Christian critic of Paul, gave an explanation of the difference between Hebrews and the other Pauline letters which is still the most commonly accepted: 'If I may give my own opinion, I would say that the thoughts are the thoughts of the Apostle, but the phraseology and the composition are of someone who is giving the teaching of the Apostle.'*

'Hebrews' is generally understood to refer to Christian converts from Judaism; judging from the emphasis in this letter on the temple and its sacrifices, it is reasonable to conclude that Paul has in mind the Christian Jews of Jerusalem. With the help of inspiration from the Holy Spirit, he was moved to set down his thoughts on the position of Jewish converts in relation to the Jewish religion; his two years in prison at Caesarea, in close contact with the church at Jerusalem, is the most likely setting for such an undertaking. It is likely that one of his disciples edited and amplified Paul's original draft into the document we now possess. Probably it was not published until after the death of James, bishop of Jerusalem, in 62 A.D. When James was killed by the Jews it must have been obvious to all Christians that the Church could not persist in its ties with Judaism.

The theme of Hebrews is the superiority of the New Testament over the Old, particularly in the worship of God; Christ in his person and the sacrifice he offered on Calvary is shown

Did he ever say to one of the angels, 'Sit on my right hand, while I make your enemies a footstool under your feet'? What are they, all of them, but spirits apt for service, whom he sends out when the destined heirs of eternal salvation have need of them?

More firmly, then, than ever must we hold to the truths which have now come to our hearing, and run no risk of drifting away from them. The old law, which only had angels for its spokesmen, was none the less valid; every transgression of it, every refusal to listen to it, incurred just retribution; and what excuse shall we have, if we pay no heed to such a message of salvation as has been given to us? One which was delivered in the first instance by the Lord himself, and has been guaranteed to us by those who heard it from his own lips? One which God himself has attested by signs and portents, manifesting his power so variously, and distributing the gifts of his Holy Spirit wherever he would?

We are speaking of a world that is to come; to whom has God entrusted the ordering of that world? Not to angels. We are assured of that, in a passage where the writer says, 'What is man, that you should remember him? What is the son of man, that you should care for him? Man, whom you have made a little lower than the angels, whom you have crowned with glory and honour, setting him in authority over the works of your hands? You have made all things subject at his feet.' Observe, he has subjected all things to him, left nothing unsubdued. And what do we see now? Not all things subject to him as yet. But we can see this; we can see one who was made a little lower than the angels, I mean Jesus, crowned, now, with glory and honour because of the death he underwent; in God's gracious design he was to taste death, and taste it on behalf of all. God is the last end of all things, the first beginning of all

to be superior to the priests and sacrifices of the Old Law. Paul begins with an elaborate portrait of the Incarnate Son of God from his Incarnation to his Ascension. The key idea he wants to impress on his readers is the unique position of Jesus Christ in history: he is the only true Son of God; he alone of all men has the same divine nature as God the Father.

With a series of seven quotations from the Old Testament, mostly psalms, Paul shows his Jewish readers that the scriptures testify to the superiority of the Son over the angelic hosts. He begins with the angels, as God's highest creatures; they are associated with Judaism by assisting in the giving of the Mosaic law on Sinai (a Jewish tradition not found in the Old Testament). There were no hosts of angels ushering in the Christian sacrifice; Christ died on Calvary without this spectacular display from the heavens; but what display could add to the glory of the Father's eternal son?

Christ Became Man to be Our Representative. As Paul read through his Old Testament, picking out texts to show the superiority of Christ over the angels, he noted one psalm which seemed to contradict his thesis. It was Psalm 8: 'Man, whom you have made a little lower than the angels.' So he deals with this scriptural objection in this paragraph. Angels are immortal; man is subject to suffering and death, as a penalty for the sin of our first parents. That is the point Paul concedes in discussing man's inferiority to angels.

Paul understands Psalm 8 as Messianic; that is, he takes it as referring directly to the person of our Lord, not to mankind in general. The situation he visualizes is that of Jesus in agony in the garden of Gethsemani. In the darkest moment of his inner sufferings and struggle against the thought of his impending death, God sends him an angel: 'And he had sight

12*

things; and it befitted his majesty that, in summoning all those sons of his to glory, he should crown with suffering the life of that Prince who was to lead them into salvation. The Son who sanctifies and the sons who are sanctified have a common origin, all of them; he is not ashamed, then, to own them as his brethren. 'I will proclaim your renown,' he says, 'to my brethren; with the church around me I will praise you'; and elsewhere he says, 'I will put my trust in him,' and then, 'Here stand I, and the children God has given me.' And since these children have a common inheritance of flesh and blood, he too shared that inheritance with them. By his death he would depose the prince of death, that is, the devil; he would deliver those multitudes who lived all the while as slaves, made over to the fear of death. After all, he does not make himself the angels' champion, no sign of that; it is the sons of Abraham that he champions. And so he must needs become altogether like his brethren; he would be a high priest who could feel for us and be our true representative before God, to make atonement for the sins of the people. It is because he himself has been tried by suffering, that he has power to help us in the trials we undergo.

Brethren and saints, you share a heavenly calling. Think, now, of Jesus as the apostle and the high priest of the faith which we profess, and how loyal he was to the God who had so appointed him; just as Moses was loyal in all the management of God's house. In any household, the first honours are reserved for him who founded it; and in that degree, Jesus has a prouder title than Moses. Every household has its founder, and this household of creation was founded by God. Thus the loyalty of Moses in the management of all God's house was the loyalty of a servant; he only bore witness to what was to be

of an angel from heaven, encouraging him.' This surely shows Jesus in an inferior position to the comforting angel. How is it possible, then, to uphold the superiority of Jesus Christ over the angels? The evidence is all to the contrary.

Paul concedes that Jesus, as man mortal and passible, was inferior in nature to the angels during his earthly life. But after his death upon Calvary and his consequent glorification at the right hand of the Father, even as man he is above all the angels. In his glorified life, God 'has made all things subject at his feet.' And that, of course, includes angels.

This state of exaltation and supremacy now enjoyed by our Lord is due to his passion and death; it is the reward and result of suffering. To become our representative before God, he had first to become a member of suffering humanity, to become one of us. It was men, not angels, that he came to redeem. As a true high priest he had to bring men into union with God; he could unite us to God because he was the Second Person of the Trinity; and as man he could represent and champion us.

Christ is Superior to Moses. The metaphor of the church as a house is best known from our Lord's promise: 'You are Peter, and it is upon this rock that I will build my church.' Paul includes Old Testament Israel and the New Testament Church under his image of a house; it is the same one building brought into being and kept in existence by the care of God.

Moses as the mediator of the Old Testament on Sinai and Jesus as the mediator of the New Testament on Calvary are here compared. There is a double comparison: (1) The house has an owner (its builder). Christ is superior to Moses

revealed later on; whereas Christ's was the loyalty of a Son
over a household which is his own. What is that household?
We are, if only we will keep unshaken to the end our confidence, and the hope which is our pride.

Come, then, the Holy Spirit says, 'If you hear his voice speaking to you this day, do not harden your hearts, as they were
hardened once when you provoked me, and put me to the test
in the wilderness. Your fathers put me to the test, made trial
of me, and saw what I could do, all those forty years. So I became the enemy of that generation; "These," I said, "are ever
wayward hearts, these have never learned my lessons." And I
took an oath in my anger, "They shall never attain my rest." '
Take care, brethren, that there is no heart among you so
warped by unbelief as to desert the living God. Each day, while
the word Today has still a meaning, strengthen your own resolution, to make sure that none of you grows hardened; sin has
such power to cheat us. We have been given a share in Christ,
but only on condition that we keep unshaken to the end our
first confidence. That is the meaning of the words, 'If you hear
his voice speaking to you this day, do not harden your hearts,
as they were hardened once when you provoked me.' Who was
it that provoked him? Was it not all those whom Moses rescued
from Egypt? Who was it, during all those forty years, that
incurred his enmity? Those who sinned; it was their corpses
that lay scattered in the wilderness. To whom did he swear
that they should never attain his rest? Those who refused to
obey him. We see, then, the consequences of unbelief; this it
was that denied them entrance.

The promise, therefore, still holds good, that we are to attain God's rest; what we have to be afraid of, is that there may

because he is God, the owner (creator) of the house, whereas Moses is a part (a member) of the house. (2) The house has a manager to run it. Christ is the Son-manager, whereas Moses is only a servant in the house.

Israel's Fate a Warning Against Apostasy. From a comparison of Christ and Moses, Paul passes smoothly to a comparison of the people each of these led and instructed. God spoke to Israel through Moses during the forty years of their wandering in the desert on their way to the promised land. The essential of God's plan for the entry of the Jews into Palestine was belief in his divine power to protect and guard them and lead them in the conquest of the land. But when they came to the southern border of Palestine, and were told that the land was ready to fall into their hands, they replied: 'It is a powerful race that dwells in it, with strong walled cities; we cannot attack such a people as this; they are too strong for us' (Num. 14, 29, 32).

Because they refused to believe in God's promises to them, he kept them out of Palestine for forty years, until all those who had disobeyed him had died in the desert. And even during these forty years they were still unbelieving. In Psalm 94 (which Paul is quoting throughout this paragraph) two incidents are chosen to show Israel's lack of faith in God; these were famous occasions when God was 'put to the test.' On both occasions, one at the beginning (Exod. 17, 1-7), the other towards the end of the forty years (Num. 20, 1-13), the Jews bitterly complained to Moses that God had led them out into this barren wilderness only to let them die of thirst; in both cases a miracle relieved their needs.

Psalm 94 quotes God's words to the Israelites, 1300 years

be someone among you who will be found to have missed his chance. The promise has been proclaimed to us, just as it was to them. The message which came to them did them no good, because it was not met by belief in those who heard it, and this rest is only to be attained by those.who, like ourselves, have learned to believe; that is why he said, 'I took an oath in my anger, "They shall never attain my rest."' God's rest, from what? From labours which were over and done with, as soon as the world was founded; in another passage he has said of the sabbath, 'God rested on the seventh day from all his labours'; and yet in this passage he is still saying, 'They shall not attain my rest.' It is still left for some, then, to attain it, and meanwhile, those to whom the message first came have been excluded by their disobedience. So he fixes another day, Today, as he calls it; in the person of David, all those long years afterwards, he uses the words I have already quoted, 'If you hear his voice speaking this day, do not harden your hearts.' (Joshua cannot have brought them their rest, or God would not still be talking of a fresh Today, long afterwards.) You see, therefore, that God's people have a sabbath of rest still in store for them; to attain his rest means resting from human labours, as God did from divine.

We must strive eagerly, then, to attain that rest; none of you must fall away into the same kind of disobedience. God's word to us is something alive, full of energy; it can penetrate deeper than any two-edged sword, reaching the very division between soul and spirit, between joints and marrow, quick to distinguish every thought and design in our hearts. From him, no creature can be hidden; everything lies bare, everything is brought face to face with him, this God to whom we must give our account.

earlier. But that does not mean these words have no meaning for Christians today. God's word is different from men's; his word is 'alive'; it is meant for all times. If Christians do not continue true to the faith they received when they learnt to believe in Jesus Christ and his divine message, then they too will be disowned and punished by God. To bring home his point, Paul analyzes two words from Psalm 94, 'Today' and 'Rest,' and shows that God is addressing his warning to Christians even more directly than to the Jews of the Exodus. His argument is based on chronology. When David wrote Psalm 94, the Jews had enjoyed the rest of the promised land for over 300 years (ever since their conquest of Palestine under Joshua); yet God is still speaking of a rest yet to be attained. Such 'Rest' cannot be Palestine; it must be a sharing of God's own rest in heaven.

Paul's emphasis on rest is due to the fact that he was writing in a time of unrest; he was warning the Christians that they should not expect beatitude in this life, only in the next. Even before 60 A.D. there were signs of the coming Jewish rebellion against Rome, which was to end in the destruction of Jerusalem in 70 A.D. (just forty years after the Crucifixion). If this Letter was not published till about 65 A.D., then all the more would Paul's warning against the danger of apostasy be needed. The Jewish Christians, especially in Jerusalem, were under pressure from the unconverted Jews to join the forces of liberation; they were being lured away from their Christian faith by the powerful appeal of nationalism. Even secret membership in such underground movements (with a pretended loyalty to Christianity) could not be kept hidden from God: 'He reads every thought and design of our hearts.' A return to Judaism is a denial of Christ.

Let us hold fast, then, by the faith we profess. We can claim a great high priest, and one who has passed right up through the heavens, Jesus, the Son of God. It is not as if our high priest was incapable of feeling for us in our humiliations; he has been through every trial, fashioned as we are, only sinless. Let us come boldly, then, before the throne of grace, to meet with mercy, and win that grace which will help us in our needs.

The purpose for which any high priest is chosen from among his fellow men, and made a representative of men in their dealings with God, is to offer gifts and sacrifices in expiation of their sins. He is qualified for this by being able to feel for them when they are ignorant and make mistakes, since he, too, is all beset with humiliations, and, for that reason, must needs present sin-offerings for himself, just as he does for the people. His vocation comes from God, as Aaron's did; nobody can take on himself such a privilege as this. So it is with Christ. He did not raise himself to the dignity of the high priesthood; it was God that raised him to it, when he said, 'You are my Son, I have begotten you this day,' and so, elsewhere, 'You are a priest for ever, in the line of Melchisedech.' Christ, during his earthly life, offered prayer and entreaty to the God who could save him from death, not without a piercing cry, not without tears; yet with such piety as won him a hearing. Son though he was, he learned obedience in the school of suffering, and now, his full achievement reached, he wins eternal salvation for all those who render obedience to him. A high priest in the line of Melchisedech, so God has called him.

Of Christ as priest we have much to say, and it is hard to make ourselves understood in the saying of it, now that you have grown so dull of hearing. You should, after all this time,

Our Lord is a Sympathetic High Priest.   *Christ has already entered into this Rest, which is the goal of all Christians.* He is in a position to help those Jewish Christians in Jerusalem, now struggling against pressure from unconverted Jews and in danger of falling into the sin of despair. He is our high priest, the link between men and God; the whole purpose of the existence of a priest is to be a mediator, a representative of sinful men before the throne of grace; the fact that he himself has suffered and been humiliated during his earthly life, in their own city of Jerusalem, makes him sympathetic to the cause of his fellow sufferers there.

Every priest must be called by God, that is he must have a divine vocation. Paul begins here his treatment of the priesthood of Christ, and so he mentions Aaron, as the founder of the Jewish priesthood, with which he will contrast Christ's Melchisedechian priesthood (mainly in chapter 7). The fact of Aaron's vocation is narrated in Leviticus 8; that Christ was also called to be a priest is obvious from Psalms 2 and 109.

Undoubtedly the key idea Paul develops in this paragraph is the sympathy of our Lord. The scene that he chooses from Jesus' life is the Agony in the garden of Gethsemani (he mentions two details, 'a piercing cry . . . tears,' not found in the Gospels). Any Jew in the holy city has only to look out his window across the Kedron valley to the olive grove at the foot of mount Olivet and remember what happened there on the night before the great high priest offered his sacrifice on Golgotha. Christians can approach such a priest without fear.

The Fearful State of an Apostate.   The faithful in Jerusalem have now enjoyed the blessings of Christianity for thirty years; they are no longer catechumens; they should be far past the

have been teachers yourselves, and instead of that you need to be taught; taught even the first principles on which the oracles of God are based. You have gone back to needing milk, instead of solid food. Those who have milk for their diet can give no account of what holiness means; how should they? They are only infants. Solid food is for the full-grown; for those whose faculties are so trained by exercise that they can distinguish between good and evil.

We must leave on one side, then, all discussion of our first lessons in Christ, and pass on to our full growth; no need to lay the foundations all over again, the change of heart which turns away from lifeless observances, the faith which turns towards God, instructions about the different kinds of baptism, about the laying on of hands, about resurrection of the dead, and our sentence in eternity. Such will be our plan, if God permits it. We can do nothing for those who have received, once for all, their enlightenment, who have tasted the heavenly gift, partaken of the Holy Spirit, known, too, God's word of comfort, and the powers that belong to a future life, and then fallen away. How can they attain a fresh repentance, while they crucify the Son of God a second time, hold him up to mockery a second time, for their own ends?

No, a piece of ground which has drunk in, again and again, the showers which fell upon it, has God's blessing on it, if it yields a crop answering the needs of those who tilled it; if it bears thorns and thistles, it has lost its value; a curse hangs over it, and it will feed the bonfire at last.

Beloved, of you we have better confidence, which does not stop short of your salvation, even when we speak to you as we are speaking now. God is not an injust God, that he should

kindergarten stage. There can be no middle course for a Christian; he must accept the faith in its entirety or else stand condemned. Reprobation follows necessarily from the neglect of divine blessings, just as a piece of ground will bear thorns and thistles if it fails to produce its crop of wheat. Many of the Christians in Jerusalem still clung too literally to the Old Testament, and so failed to see its fulfilment in Jesus Christ, the true mediator.

Paul speaks only in a general way of the blessings which a Christian squanders when he abandons the faith; this makes their identification uncertain. He refers probably to Baptism ('enlightenment'), and the Eucharist ('the heavenly gift'); 'God's word' is the Sacred Scriptures, the spiritual nourishment of the Christian mind; 'the powers that belong to a future life' are a summary of the miraculous powers, particularly the spiritual gifts of the early Church (I Cor. 12-14).

An apostate abandons all these divine treasures; such a person puts himself in a situation from which it is difficult to win him back to the faith. Paul uses a terrifying picture of the state of an apostate by likening his act of denial to that of the Jews who crucified the Master. (It would have a powerful appeal to the Christians of Jerusalem, with Calvary there to remind them continually of the Crucifixion.) Such an act denies the very source of grace, since it makes of no account the redemptive death: 'What of the man who has trampled the Son of God under foot, who has reckoned that blood which sanctified him as a thing unclean?' (Heb. 10, 29).

Encouragement To Hope As Abraham Did. With one of those sudden changes Paul is noted for, he abandons his sombre tone of warning and presents a brighter side of the picture;

forget all you have done, all the charity you have shown towards his name, you who have ministered, and still minister, to the needs of his saints. But our great longing is to see you all showing the same eagerness right up to the end, looking forward to the fulfilment of your hope; listless no more, but followers of all those whose faith and patience are to bring them into possession of the good things promised them.

Such was Abraham. God made him a promise, and then took an oath (an oath by himself, since he had no greater name to swear by), in the words, 'More and more I will bless you, more and more I will give you increase'; whereupon Abraham waited patiently, and saw the promise fulfilled. Men, since they have something greater than themselves to swear by, will confirm their word by oath, which puts an end to all controversy; and God, in the same way, eager to convince the heirs of the promise that his design was irrevocable, pledged himself by an oath. Two irrevocable assurances, over which there could be no question of God deceiving us, were to bring firm confidence to us poor wanderers, bidding us cling to the hope we have in view, the anchorage of our souls. Sure and immovable, it reaches that inner sanctuary beyond the veil, which Jesus Christ, our escort, has entered already, a high priest, now, eternally with the priesthood of Melchisedech.

It was this Melchisedech, king of Salem, and priest of the most high God, who met Abraham and blessed him on his way home, after the defeat of the kings; and to him Abraham gave a tenth of his spoils. Observe, in the first place, that his name means, the king of justice; and further that he is king of Salem, that is, of peace. That is all; no name of father or mother, no pedigree, no date of birth or of death; there he stands, eternally, a priest, the true figure of the Son of God. Consider how great

he shows his tender affection for the Hebrews in the trials they are undergoing by addressing them as 'beloved' (the only time he does so in this letter). He recalls the charitable manner in which they distributed the vast alms he brought to Jerusalem from the Gentile churches; the deacons went about their ministration of this kindly service in a most edifying way. If only they would suffer their trials patiently, their hope in Christ's help and protection would be further strengthened; their minds would be centred on the graces that come to them rather than on their problems.

Hope follows on faith; it aspires to God, relying on his power and goodness. As in Romans 4 and Galatians 3, Paul illustrates from the father of all believers, Abraham. The scene he considers is the sacrifice of Isaac (Gen. 22). When Abraham successfully endured this trial from God, he was promised greater blessings still; these blessings were to be fulfilled in Abraham's posterity, in his most illustrious son, Jesus Christ. God's own word, and his oath as well, give adequate guarantee that he will not go back on the promise made to Abraham. The hope which looks to heaven is compared to an anchor which holds firm in the midst of a violent storm; it leads to Christ, who has entered into God's presence and will bring there all those who put their confidence in him.

Melchisedech Foreshadows Christ's Priesthood. Just three verses of Genesis (14, 18-20) is all that is given to Melchisedech in the story of the patriarchs. But he is a most important name in Paul's demonstration of the superiority of the Christian priesthood over the Jewish, because he is a type of Christ. Tradition emphasizes the bread and wine he offered in sacrifice; it foreshadows the Eucharist. But that is not Paul's line of thought. He is interested in the absence of a genealogy for

·a man was this, to whom the patriarch Abraham himself gave a tenth part of his chosen spoil. The descendants of Levi, when the priesthood is conferred on them, are allowed by the provisions of the law to take tithes from God's people, though these, like themselves, come from the privileged stock of Abraham; after all, they are their brothers; here is one who owns no common descent with them, taking tithes from Abraham himself. He blesses him, too, blesses the man to whom the promises have been made; and it is beyond all question that blessings are only given by what is greater in dignity to what is less. In the one case, the priests who receive tithe are only mortal men; in the other, it is a priest (so the record tells us) who lives on. And indeed, there is a sense in which we can say that Levi, who receives the tithe, paid tithe himself with Abraham; as the heir of Abraham's body, he was present in the person of his ancestor, when he met Melchisedech.

Now, there could be no need for a fresh priest to arise, accredited with Melchisedech's priesthood, not with Aaron's, if the Levitical priesthood had brought fulfilment. And it is on the Levitical priesthood that the law given to God's people is founded. When the priesthood is altered, the law, necessarily, is altered with it. After all, he to whom the prophecy relates belonged to a different tribe, which never produced a man to stand at the altar; our Lord took his origin from Juda, that is certain, and Moses in speaking of this tribe, said nothing about priests. And something further becomes evident, when a fresh priest arises to fulfil the type of Melchisedech, appointed, not to obey the law, with its outward observances, but in the power of an unending life; ('You are a priest in the line of Melchisedech,' God says of him, 'for ever'). The old observance is abrogated now, powerless as it was to help us; the law had

Melchisedech. The Levitical priests received their priesthood by descent; their power to offer sacrifice came from their genealogy. Melchisedech stands alone, like our Lord; his priesthood is from God.

That fact demonstrates the essential difference between Melchisedechian and Levitical priesthood. Paul now shows that the former is superior. His argument is from tithes and blessing. A tithe is a tenth part of income paid to a master; a blessing is always given by a superior to an inferior. Levi does not come into Genesis 14; but his great-grandfather Abraham does. Paul regards Levi as paying tithes to Melchisedech, because Levi was a descendant of Abraham, and was seminally present in Abraham's body. It might be objected that Christ also was Abraham's descendant. St. Thomas Aquinas answers by quoting the virginal conception of Jesus; all his human nature he got from Mary; he had no human father.

Old Priesthood And Old Law Superseded. Moses and Aaron were brothers, both sons of Levi, one of the twelve sons of Jacob (Israel) who made up the chosen people of God. The key incident in the lives of Moses and Aaron, and of the people they represented before the Lord, was the giving of the law and the priesthood on mount Sinai. It was through Moses that God promulgated his law for the Jewish nation, and it was to Aaron, the first high priest of the new religious institution, that he entrusted the priestly work of divine worship.

Law and priesthood are joined intimately as parts of one religious system; if one is abrogated, the other must go with it. Paul has proved in both Romans and Galatians that the law was abrogated by Christ; here he proves that the priesthood was superseded by the one, eternal high-priesthood of

nothing in it of final achievement. Instead, a fuller hope has been brought into our lives, enabling us to come close to God. And this time there is a ratification by oath; none was taken when those other priests were appointed, but the new priest is appointed with an oath, when God says to him, 'The Lord has sworn an irrevocable oath, "You are a priest for ever" '; all the more solemn, then, is that covenant for which Jesus has been given us as our surety. Of those other priests there was a succession, since death denied them permanence; whereas Jesus continues for ever, and his priestly office is unchanging; that is why he can give complete salvation to those who through him make their way to God, he lives on still to make intercession for them. Such was the high priest that suited our need, holy and guiltless and undefiled, not reckoned among us sinners, lifted high above all the heavens; one who has no need to do as those other priests did, offering a twofold sacrifice day by day, first for his own sins, then for those of the people. What he has done he has done once for all; and the offering was himself. The law makes high priests of men, and men are frail; promise and oath, now, have superseded the law; our high priest, now, is that Son who has reached his full achievement for all eternity.

And here we come to the very pith of our argument. This high priest of ours is one who has taken his seat in heaven, on the right hand of that throne where God sits in majesty, ministering, now, in the sanctuary, in that true tabernacle which the Lord, not man, has set up. After all, if it is the very function of a priest to offer gift and sacrifice, he too must needs have an offering to make. Whereas, if he were still on earth, he would be no priest at all; there are priests already, to offer the gifts.

the Son of God himself. His approach is different, but it has the same conclusion.

It is clear from history that our Lord came from the tribe of Juda, not Levi (these two were brothers); his priesthood must then be something distinct and apart from the Levitical. As a priest, Christ brings men into close union with God; it is a spiritual relationship deep in the soul of man. The Levitical priesthood conferred only external, outward purity, without removing sin from the souls of those who lived under its regime.

Our Lord's superiority as priest over the Levitical priesthood is shown chiefly from the Melchisedechian Psalm 109, especially the two words 'oath' and 'forever.' God made no oath when inaugurating Aaron as high priest; his priesthood was transitory, Christ's is eternal; an oath makes the divine act permanent and irrevocable (it cannot be destroyed by man's unworthiness). The Levitical priests were sinful men subject to death; their priesthood was continued only by a series of replacements. Christ alone needs no successor; he possesses his priesthood forever. Such a sinless high priest, with his one completely satisfactory sacrifice, fulfils all the needs of mankind.

Superiority Of New Sanctuary And Covenant. The main work of a priest is to offer sacrifice; this is the essential act of his office. For the next three chapters (Heb. 8-10) Paul deals with the superiority of Christ's sacrifice, his death on Calvary. If our Lord were still on earth he would be a priest without an offering to make to God the Father; that is why he had to die; otherwise he would have no sacrifice to offer for sinful men. Actually the scene of his priestly activity is now in heaven.

which the law demands, men who devote their service to the
type and the shadow of what has its true being in heaven.
(That is why Moses, when he was building the tabernacle, received the warning, 'Be sure to make everything in accordance
with the pattern that was shown to you on the mountain.') As
it is, he has been entrusted with a more honourable ministry,
dispenser as he is of a nobler covenant, with nobler promises
for its sanction. There would have been no room for this second covenant, if there had been no fault to find with the first.
But God, you see, does find fault; this is what he tells them:
'Behold, says the Lord, a time is coming when I will ratify a
new covenant with the people of Israel, and with the people of
Juda. It will not be like the covenant which I made with their
fathers, on the day when I took them by the hand, to rescue
them from Egypt; that they should break my covenant, and I
(says the Lord) should abandon them. No, this is the covenant
I will grant the people of Israel, the Lord says, when that time
comes. I will implant my law in their innermost thoughts, engrave it in their hearts; I will be their God, and they shall be
my people. There will be no need for citizen to teach fellow
citizen, or brother to teach brother, the knowledge of the Lord;
all will know me, from the highest to the lowest. I will pardon
their wrong-doing; I will not remember their sins any more.'
In speaking of a new covenant, he has superannuated the old.
And before long the superannuated, the antiquated, must
needs disappear.

The former covenant, to be sure, had its own ceremonial observances, its own earthly sanctuary. There was an outer tabernacle, which contained the lampstand and the table of the
loaves set out before God; sanctuary was the name given to
this; and then, beyond the second veil, the inner sanctuary, as

Paul emphasizes this because he is contrasting the place where the Jewish high priest offers sacrifice with that where Jesus, the Christian high priest, offers his.

Instead of comparing the temple courts in Jerusalem with the heavenly sanctuary, Paul considers the tabernacle of the Exodus. This he does because his mind is still on Aaron and Moses, not on the reigning high priest in Jerusalem. The scene of Aaron's high-priestly ministry was the tabernacle built at Sinai and carried by the Jews during their forty years' wandering; it was used as the place of sacrifice until the temple was built by Solomon as a more permanent structure. The importance of the tabernacle came from its divine origin; it was designed in heaven, where Jesus, the priest of the new covenant, dwells now in divine glory (Apoc. 4-5).

Both the old and the new covenant were inaugurated by sacrifices; the superiority of Christ's sacrifice is clear from the greater efficacy of the new covenant (even the name 'old' indicates that it is near its demise). Paul quotes Jeremias 31 to prove that Christ's covenant on Calvary is superior to that inaugurated by Moses on Sinai. (1) The old was written on stone, the new on the mind and heart; the old was outside man, the new is personal and spiritual. (2) The old compelled men to observe a code of laws; the new is grace and love. (3) The old gave only ritual cleanness; the new brings complete reconciliation with God by forgiving man's sins.

Heaven Opened Through Blood Of Christ. Paul still continues to speak of the tabernacle in the time of Moses and Aaron, though his words are just as applicable to the temple at Jerusalem, frequented by the Jewish Christians at the moment of his writing. The tabernacle was composed of two

it is called, with the golden altar of incense, and the ark of the covenant, gilded all round. In the ark rested the golden urn with the manna in it, Aaron's staff that budded, and the tablets on which the covenant was inscribed; above were the Cherubim, heralds of the divine glory, spreading their wings over the throne of mercy. We have no time to treat of these more particularly, but this was the general fashion of it. Into the outer tabernacle the priests made their way at all times, in the perfomance of their duties; into this other, only the high priest, once a year, and even then not without an offering of blood, for the faults which he and the people had committed unknowingly. The Holy Spirit meant us to see that no way of access to the true sanctuary lay open to us, as long as the former tabernacle maintained its standing. And that allegory still holds good at the present day; here are gifts and sacrifices being offered, which have no power, where conscience is concerned, to bring the worshipper to his full growth; they are but outward observances, connected with food and drink and ceremonial washings on this occasion or that, instituted to hold their own until better times should come.

Meanwhile, Christ has taken his place as our high priest, to win us blessings that still lie in the future. He makes use of a greater, a more complete tabernacle, which human hands never fashioned; it does not belong to this order of creation at all. It is his own blood, not the blood of goats and calves, that has enabled him to enter, once for all, into the sanctuary; the ransom he has won lasts for ever. The blood of bulls and goats, the ashes of a heifer sprinkled over men defiled, has power to hallow them for every purpose of outward purification; and shall not the blood of Christ, who offered himself, through his eternal spirit, as a victim unblemished in God's sight, purify

small rooms, the first room being known as the holy place, and the second or inner room as the holy of holies; it is this latter room that is important for Paul's purpose in this paragraph. The essential furniture of the holy of holies was the ark of the covenant; this was God's mercy throne, where he dwelt among his people; for the Jews it represented the presence of God. It was as close to heaven as they could come.

On only one day each year could anyone enter this inner sanctuary; this was the tenth day of the month Tishri, five days before the feast of Tabernacles; and it was the high priest alone who could enter. With the blood of a goat, sacrificed for the sins of the people, he went right into the presence of God and poured out the blood on the lid of the ark of the covenant (Lev. 16). Paul chooses the Day of Atonement (10 Tishri), because the sacrifice offered on that day was the most solemn function of the Jewish liturgy, and it was offered by the most important man in Israel, the high priest.

When our Lord died on the cross, a significant happening occurred in the temple: 'And all at once, the veil of the sanctuary was torn this way and that from the top to the bottom.' It was a symbol of the changed conditions of man's relationship to God; there was no longer a barrier, a veil holding mankind back from the divine presence; heaven was now open to all without distinction. What the sacrifices of the old law could not accomplish Jesus obtained through the shedding of his blood on the cross. Even the solitary act of entry of the high priest could win only ceremonial, ritual purity for the people; whereas the blood of Jesus cleansed man's soul from sin and won for all men access to the divine presence.

With a sudden change, Paul calls Christ's body a taber-

our consciences, and set them free from lifeless observances, to
serve the living God?

Thus, through his intervention, a new covenant has been
bequeathed to us; a death must follow, to atone for all our
transgressions under the old covenant, and then the destined
heirs were to obtain, for ever, their promised inheritance.
Where a bequest is concerned, the death of the testator must
needs play its part; a will has no force while the testator is
alive, and only comes into force with death. Thus the old
covenant, too, needed blood for its inauguration. When he
had finished reading the provisions of the law to the assembled
people, Moses took blood, the blood of calves and goats, took
water, and scarlet-dyed wool, and hyssop, sprinkled the book
itself, and all the people, and said: 'This is the blood of the
covenant which God has prescribed to you.' The tabernacle,
too, and all the requisites of worship he sprinkled in the same
way with blood; and the law enjoins that blood shall be used
in almost every act of purification; unless blood is shed, there
can be no remission of sins.

And if such purification was needed for what was but a rep-
resentation of the heavenly world, the heavenly world itself will
need sacrifices more availing still. The sanctuary into which
Christ has entered is not one made by human hands, is not
some adumbration of the truth; he has entered heaven itself,
where he now appears in God's sight on our behalf. Nor does
he make a repeated offering of himself, as the high priest, when
he enters the sanctuary, makes a yearly offering of the blood
that is not his own. If that were so, he must have suffered again
and again, ever since the world was created; as it is, he has been
revealed once for all, at the moment when history reached its
fulfilment, annulling our sin by his sacrifice. Man's destiny is

nacle through which we come to God; just as the Jew had to enter God's presence through the tabernacle, so the Christian comes to heaven through Christ.

Necessity And Finality of Christ's Death.   Death is a decisive moment in every man's career, because it seals his eternal destiny; it is final and irrevocable. The death of Christ was equally decisive, not only for our Lord himself but for all mankind; by it they came into their eternal inheritance. For his followers the death of the Master had been a great disaster; it was the end of all their hopes: 'We had hoped that it was he who was to deliver Israel' (Lk. 23, 21). For the Hebrews it was still a difficulty that needed explanation. That is why Paul proves that Jesus had to die; without his death the New Testament would never have existed.

Paul's argument is based on death as the necessary condition for a last will and testament to become a valid legal document. The word covenant in Greek has two meanings: a contract between two parties (its significance elsewhere in practically all sacred scripture), and a bequest. It is this second meaning that is considered here. A will or testament becomes a final and irrevocable document only on the death of the testator. This means the Hebrews are not at liberty to set it aside.

There is a parallel between the old and the new testaments in that both required the shedding of blood (which means death) for their inauguration. But more important is the contrast between the two: the transitory, temporal nature of the old which made it so far inferior to the new with its one, final, eternal sacrifice. To illustrate this, Paul returns to the Day of Atonement. This time it is the annual repetition of the same animal sacrifices that he contrasts with the one death of Christ on the cross. It is impossible to imagine our Lord

to die once for all; nothing remains after that but judgment; and Christ was offered once for all, to take a world's sins upon himself; when we see him again, sin will play its part no longer, he will be bringing salvation to those who await his coming.

What the law contains is only the shadow of those blessings which were still to come, not the full expression of their reality. The same sacrifices are offered year after year without intermission, and still the worshipers can never reach, through the law, their full growth. If they could, must not the offerings have ceased before now? There would be no guilt left to reproach the consciences of those who come to worship; they would have been cleansed once for all. No, what these offerings bring with them, year by year, is only the remembrance of sins; that sins should be taken away by the blood of bulls and goats is impossible. As Christ comes into the world, he says: 'No sacrifice, no offering was your demand; you have endowed me, instead, with a body. You have not found any pleasure in burnt sacrifices, in sacrifices for sin. "See then," I said, "I am coming to fulfil what is written of me, where the book lies unrolled; to do your will, O my God." ' First he says, 'You did not demand victim or offering, the burnt sacrifice, the sacrifice for sin, nor have you found any pleasure in them'—in anything, that is, which the law has to offer—and then he adds, 'See, I am coming to do your will.' He must clear the ground first, so as to build up afterwards. In accordance with this divine will we have been sanctified by an offering made once for all, the body of Jesus Christ.

One priest after another must stand there, day after day, offering again and again the same sacrifices, which can never

coming back repeatedly to die; he is not only priest, he is victim as well; a victim can die only once. The blood of the Old Testament victims did not take away sin; these sacrifices only foreshadowed the one, final, decisive sacrifice of Christ, which won eternal life for men.

Christ's One Sacrifice Remits Sin Once For All. Morning and evening, day after day, sacrifice was offered in the temple at Jerusalem; this was the daily liturgy, the official, public sacrifice of the nation to God. During the day other private sacrifices were offered by the priests on the altar of burnt offerings; the blood of sheep and oxen was poured out continually, and their carcasses were burnt before the Lord in his holy temple. It is these sacrifices, repeated day after day, that Paul considers in this last paragraph on Christ's sacrifice and its superiority over the Levitical priests' sacrifices. For most of his treatment of our Lord's sacrificial death, in the three previous paragraphs (chapters 8-9), he has been writing of the high priest and his annual sacrifice on the Day of Atonement; but here he comes back to the existing conditions in the temple, no longer the tabernacle in the wilderness of the Exodus.

To prove his thesis, Paul again argues from the scriptures; this time he uses Psalm 39. The Second Person of the Blessed Trinity became a priest at the moment of his Incarnation; so it is the Annunciation of Gabriel to our Lady that is the gospel background of this psalm. But instead of giving the angel's words, or Mary's reply, the psalmist gives our Lord's own attitude at the moment of his Incarnation. The essential priestly act of Jesus from the first moment of his human existence to the very end of his life, his sacrificial death, was his obedience to God the Father; at the moment of his entry into the world

13

take away our sins; whereas he has offered for our sins a sacrifice that is never repeated, and taken his seat for ever at the right hand of God. He only waits, until all his enemies are made a footstool under his feet; by a single offering he has completed his work, for all time, in those whom he sanctifies. And here the Holy Spirit adds his testimony. He has been saying, 'This is the covenant I will grant them, the Lord says, when that time comes; I will implant my laws in their hearts, engrave them in their innermost thoughts.' And what follows? 'I will not remember their sins and their transgressions any more.' Where they are so remitted, there is no longer any room for a sin-offering.

Why then, brethren, we can enter the sanctuary with confidence through the blood of Christ. He has opened up for us a new, a living approach, by way of the veil, I mean, his mortality. A great priest is ours, who has dominion over God's house. Let us come forward with sincere hearts in the full assurance of the faith, our guilty consciences purified by sprinkling, our bodies washed clean in hallowed water. Do not let us waver in acknowledging the hope we cherish; we have a promise from one who is true to his word. Let us keep one another in mind, always ready with incitements to charity and to acts of piety, not abandoning, as some do, our common assembly, but encouraging one another; all the more, as you see the great day drawing nearer.

If we go on sinning wilfully, when once the full knowledge of the truth has been granted to us, we have no further sacrifice for sin to look forward to; nothing but a terrible expectation of judgment, 'a fire that will eagerly consume the rebellious.' Let a man be convicted by two or three witnesses of defying the law of Moses, and he dies, without hope of mercy. What of

he accepted his death on the cross.

The superior efficacy of Christ's redemptive death over the daily Jewish sacrifices is shown in this paragraph by three contrasts. (1) The Jewish sacrifices were animals, mainly bulls, goats, and sheep; our Lord offered his human body, with the full obedience of his human will. (2) The continual, daily repetition of Jewish sacrifices shows they were imperfect and unsatisfactory; Christ's sacrifice was perfect and complete. (3) Animal sacrifices gave only legal purity; the sacrifice of Christ atoned for all our sins, once for all. Christ's death on the cross made all other sacrifices unnecessary.

Divine Judgment On Sin Of Apostasy. In practically all Paul's letters he gives his doctrine first of all, and then applies it to the lives of his readers. He has now finished his thesis on the superiority of Christ's priesthood and sacrifice over the Levitical priesthood and the Old Testament sacrifices. At this point he begins the moral section of his letter: Christianity is a way of life as well as a system of beliefs. So he exhorts the Christians of Jerusalem to persevere in the faith, to continue firmly to hope in the Lord's goodness, and to practise charity to all among whom they live.

For a Jew there was no distinction between church and state; religion and nationalism were closely bound together. That is why they never accepted the rule of a foreign power; they were waiting for the day when Rome would be driven out of the holy land. Even before 60 A.D. they were planning the revolt that eventually broke out in 66 and ended with the destruction of Jerusalem in 70 A.D. Naturally enough, some of the Christian Jews were involved in the underground movement against Rome; and pressure was brought to bear on those

the man who has trampled the Son of God under foot, who has reckoned the blood of the covenant, that blood which sanctified him, as a thing unclean, mocked at the Spirit that brought him grace? Will not he incur a punishment much more severe? It is one we know well, who has told us, 'Vengeance is for me, I will repay'; and again, 'The Lord will judge his people.' It is a fearful thing to fall into the hands of the living God.

Remember those early days, when the light first came to you, and the hard probation of suffering you went through. There were times when you yourselves were publicly exposed to calumny and persecution; there was a time when you took part with those who had the same path to tread. You showed your sympathy with those who were in bonds; and when you were robbed of your goods you took it cheerfully, as men who knew that a higher, a more lasting good was yours. Do not throw away that confidence of yours, with its rich hope of reward; you still need endurance, if you are to attain the prize God has promised to those who do his will. 'Only a brief moment, now, before he who is coming will be here; he will not linger on the way. It is faith that brings life to the man whom I accept as justified; if he shrinks back, he shall win no favour with me.' Not for us to shrink away, and be lost; it is for us to have faith, and save our souls.

What is faith? It is that which gives substance to our hopes, which convinces us of things we cannot see. It was this that brought credit to the men who went before us. It is faith that lets us understand how the worlds were fashioned by God's word, so that the world we see did not simply arise out of matter. It was in faith that Abel offered a sacrifice richer than Cain's, and was proved thereby to be justified, since God recog-

who held aloof. In such close association with unconverted
Jews, there was the danger that their nationalism would lead
them back to the practice of Judaism; their sympathy for their
fellow Jews made them lax in the practice of Christianity. Paul
gives them solemn warning of the great danger they are in; to
deny the faith is to apostatize; it is a sin that will bring eternal
punishment from the divine judge.

He contrasts their present flirting with danger to the earlier
years of persecution for the faith, when they stored up merit
which they now propose to throw away. Almost certainly the
persecution he is thinking of is that in which he himself
played a leading role: 'Saul, with every breath he drew, still
threatened the disciples of the Lord with massacre.' This was
the most important of the several attempts made by the Jews
to exterminate the new religion. It began with Stephen's execution, at which Paul was in charge; it ended dramatically with
the conversion of Paul himself.

Throughout this paragraph Paul keeps on reminding the
Hebrews of God's judgment. The early Christians were in
constant expectation of the Second Coming of Christ at the
general judgment (this is clear from the Letters to the Thessalonians); so that the thought came naturally to Paul's mind.
He may also have been thinking of Jesus' prediction of the
destruction of Jerusalem.

The Faith Of Our Fathers. By his death on the cross, our
Lord atoned for the sins of mankind, and so won for them
the right to enter God's presence, the sanctuary where he now
dwells, heaven itself. But Christ's death on Calvary was an
event that happened thirty years before, and heaven comes
only in the future, after death. What the Christians of Jerusalem saw before their eyes day after day was the temple with

nised his offering; through that offering of his he still speaks in
death. When Enoch was taken away without the experience
of death, when God took him and no more was seen of him,
it was because of his faith; that is the account we have of him
before he was taken, that he pleased God; and it is impossible
to please God without faith. Nobody reaches God's presence
until he has learned to believe that God exists, and that he re-
wards those who try to find him. When Noah received a warning about dangers still unseen, it was faith that made him take
alarm, and build an ark to preserve his family. Thus he proved
the whole world wrong, and was left heir to the justification
which comes through faith. Abraham, when he was called,
showed faith when he left his home, obediently, for the country
which was to be his inheritance; left it without knowing where
his journey would take him. Faith taught him to live as a
stranger in the land he had been promised for his own, en-
camping there with Isaac and Jacob, heirs with him of a common hope; looking forward all the while to that city which has
true foundations, which is God's design and God's fashioning.
It was faith that enabled Sara to conceive offspring, although
she was past the age of child-bearing; she believed that God
would be faithful to his word. Here is one man, a man for
whom life is already over; and from him springs a race whose
numbers rival the stars of heaven, or the uncounted grains of
sand on the sea shore. It was faith they lived by, all of them,
and in faith they died; for them, the promises were not fulfilled, but they looked forward to them and welcomed them at
a distance, owning themselves no better than strangers and
exiles on earth. Those who talk so make it clear enough, that
they have found their home. Did they regret the country they
had left behind? If that were all, they could have found oppor-

its sacrificial smoke rising up to God. Paul had been showing the superiority of Christ's sacrifice over the temple sacrifices, but it was an argument that could be seen only with the eyes of faith, not with ordinary human observation. The natural instinct of the Christian Jew was to follow the habits of a lifetime and the daily experience of his senses; this was the real world for him, the substantial things around him.

Faith is a virtue exercised by both intellect and will. It makes the absent object present to the will; that is, it makes heaven real. It brings conviction to the intellect of the existence of the unseen world. To the Christian Jew of Jerusalem it proves that the heavenly sanctuary of Jesus the high priest is just as certain as the earthly sanctuary of the temple in Jerusalem; it gives him the supernatural power to see what is not observable by human vision alone. Both the future and the unseen are made to exist now, by the virtue of faith.

Throughout the Letter to the Hebrews, Paul has argued continually from the scriptures. For a Jew the scriptural argument could not be contradicted; it was the word of God. For the whole of this paragraph (chapter 11), he illustrates the gift of faith from the Old Testament; it is ninety-five per cent scriptural. He begins with the first chapter of the Book of Genesis and works his way through to the Second Book of Machabees. From the first five books (the Pentateuch) he selects nine names and gives incidents to show how these persons exercised the virtue of faith; he then mentions six persons by name from the later books without giving any incidents from their lives. In his final section he gives a general summary, without identifying any persons; they are mostly prophets.

The first three examples of men of faith are Abel, Enoch, and Noah. Abel's faith is attested by the fact that his sacrifice

tunities for going back to it. No, the country of their desires is a better, a heavenly country. God does not disdain to take his title from such names as these; he has a city ready for them to dwell in.

Abraham showed faith, when he was put to the test, by offering up Isaac. He was ready to offer up an only son, this man who had made the promises his own, and received the assurance, 'It is through Isaac that your posterity shall be traced.' God, he argued, had the power to restore his son even from the dead; and indeed, in a hidden sense, he did so recover him. It was by faith that Isaac, in blessing Jacob and Esau, foretold what was to come; by faith that Jacob, on his death-bed, made reverence to the top of Joseph's staff, as he blessed his two sons in turn; by faith that Joseph, when he, too, came to the end of his life, spoke of the Israelites' escape from Egypt, and gave orders for the removal of his bones. The parents of Moses showed faith, in making light of the king's edict, and hiding their child away for three months, when they saw what a fine child he was. And Moses showed faith, when he grew up, by refusing to pass for the son of Pharaoh's daughter. He preferred ill usage, shared with the people of God, to the brief enjoyment of sinful pleasures; all the wealth of Egypt could not so enrich him as the despised lot of God's anointed; he had eyes, you see, for nothing but the promised reward. It was in faith that he left Egypt behind, defying the royal anger, made strong as if by the very sight of him who is invisible; in faith that he performed the paschal rite, and the sprinkling of the blood, to leave Israel untouched by the angel that destroyed the first-born; in faith that they crossed the Red Sea as if it had been dry land, whereas the Egyptians, when they ventured into it, were drowned. Faith pulled down the walls of Jericho, after seven days spent in marching round them;

was accepted by God (a man is not pleasing to God without faith). Enoch, like Elias, was taken away from the earth by God; God would not have taken him unless he was a holy man, which means that he must have had faith. It is uncertain just what has happened to Elias and Enoch, and where they live at the present time; some have suggested that they are the two witnesses (Apoc. 11, 4), and that they will return to convert the Jews before the end of the world. The third person, Noah, showed his faith by believing God when he told him of the flood; he began to build the ark, even though the flood was not to come for over a hundred years.

Undoubtedly the hero among all these men of the Bible was Abraham, not only a man of faith in his own life but also a model for our true Christian faith. In his own life he showed his faith by leaving his home and country at God's command, by believing God's promise of a numerous posterity when he had no children of his own, and by being ready to sacrifice his only son at God's order. But for Paul's purpose it is the object of Abraham's faith that is important, Abraham looked forward to 'that city which has true foundations, which is God's design and God's fashioning.' This is not Palestine, where he was then living, but 'a better, a heavenly country.' What buoyed Abraham up in all his difficulties was a belief that 'God's people have a sabbath of rest still in store for them.' Although heaven was not open until Christ died, Abraham longed for that blessed peace and eternal happiness with God; and that is what the readers of this Letter to the Hebrews should be looking forward to. Their faith should be centred on their heavenly home, not the earthly sanctuary of the temple in Jerusalem.

With a brief mention of Isaac, Jacob, and Joseph, Paul passes on to the second book in the Bible, Exodus. To his

13*

faith saved Rahab, the harlot, from sharing the doom of the disobedient, because she had given the spies a peaceable welcome.

What need is there to say more? Time will fail me if I try to go through all the history of Gedeon, of Barac, of Samson, of Jephte, of David and Samuel and the prophets. Theirs was the faith which subdued kingdoms, which served the cause of right, which made promises come true. They shut the mouths of lions, they quenched raging fire, swords were drawn on them, and they escaped. How strong they became, who till then were weak, what courage they showed in battle, how they routed invading armies! There were women, too, who recovered their dead children, brought back to life. Others, looking forward to a better resurrection still, would not purchase their freedom on the rack. And others experienced mockery and scourging, chains, too, and imprisonment; they were stoned, they were tortured, they were cut in pieces, they were put to the sword; they wandered about, dressed in sheepskins and goatskins, amidst want, and distress, and ill usage; men whom the world was unworthy to contain, living a hunted life in deserts and on mountain sides, in rock-fastnesses and caverns underground. One and all gave proof of their faith, yet they never saw the promise fulfilled; for us, God had something better in store. We were needed, to make the history of their lives complete.

Why, then, since we are watched from above by such a cloud of witnesses, let us rid ourselves of all that weighs us down, of the sinful habit that clings so closely, and run, with all endurance, the race for which we are entered. Let us fix our eyes on Jesus, the origin and the crown of all faith, who, to win his prize of blessedness, endured the cross and made light of its shame, Jesus, who now sits on the right of God's throne. Take

treatment of Abraham he allowed eleven verses (out of the 40 in Hebrews 11); Moses comes second in importance with an allotment of seven verses. Paul is interested in the faith of Moses only as showing that 'he preferred ill usage, shared with the people of God . . . the despised lot of God's anointed.' He could have stayed in Egypt, at the royal court, living a life of ease and wealth; but he chose to throw in his lot with the persecuted and despised chosen people and live a life of exile from Egypt. There is a valuable lesson for the Christian Jews in this: with faith in the divine promise of a yet unseen reward, they must be prepared to leave the shelter of Jewish nationalism (the equivalent of Old Testament Egypt) and expose themselves to bitter persecution.

At this stage, Paul must have realized that it would take too much space to deal with the rest of the Bible in detail. In one of the finest poetic passages in the Pauline Letters he summarizes the rest of Jewish history, emphasizing the perils these men of faith overcame, the persecution they endured, the unbelievable torments they suffered. Daniel ('lions'), David ('battles, armies'), the Seven Machabees ('rack'), Eliseus ('mockery'), Jeremias ('scourging, imprisonment'), Zacharias ('stoned'), Isaias ('cut in pieces'), all had faith in a heavenly reward, even though heaven was closed in their day; the death of Christ was needed to complete their lives.

Let Us Fix Our Eyes On Jesus. There are only two chapters in the history book of the human race; the first is headed B.C., the second A.D. It is the Incarnation that divides these two chapters of world history. The lives of faith of the Old Testament heroes, the first chapter, is incomplete until the final chapter of Christian faith and endurance is added. Paul picturesquely visualizes all the Old Testament heroes seated

your standard from him, from his endurance, from the enmity
the wicked bore him, and you will not grow faint, you will not
find your souls unmanned.

Your protest, your battle against sin, has not yet called for
bloodshed; yet you have lost sight, already, of those words of
comfort in which God addresses you as his sons: 'My son, do
not undervalue the correction which the Lord sends you, do
not be unmanned when he reproves your faults. It is where he
loves that he bestows correction; there is no recognition for
any child of his without chastisement.' Be patient, then, while
correction lasts; God is treating you as his children. Was there
ever a son whom his father did not correct? No, correction is the
common lot of all; you must be bastards, not true sons, if you
are left without it. We have known what it was to accept correction from earthly fathers, and with reverence; shall we not
submit, far more willingly, to the Father of a world of spirits,
and draw life from him? They, after all, only corrected us for
a short while, at their own caprice; he does it for our good, to
give us a share in that holiness which is his. For the time being,
all correction is painful rather than pleasant; but afterwards,
when it has done its work of discipline, it yields a harvest of
good dispositions, to our great peace. Come then, stiffen the
sinews of drooping hand, and flagging knee, and plant your
footprints in a straight track, so that the man who goes lame
may not stumble out of the path, but regain strength instead.

Your aim must be peace with all men, and that holiness
without which no one will ever see God. Take good care that
none of you is false to God's grace, that no poisonous shoot is
allowed to spring up, and contaminate many of you by its influence. None of you must be guilty of fornication, none of
you earthly-minded, as Esau was, when he sold his birthright

in a vast amphitheatre, watching the Christian warriors performing the final act of the drama. From the height of their heavenly blessedness, they watch intently as the Christians are put to the test; by their example and prayers they will help those now undergoing the same contest they themselves underwent long ago.

As a model, and as a motive for Christians to strive manfully, Paul gives the example of our Lord. In the garden of Gethsemani he had to fight against his repugnance for suffering and death; by fixing his thoughts on his heavenly Father he was able to accept the divine will. He underwent suffering and death and now sits in glory with the Father. The Christian Jews will win the grace and strength to endure the persecution of the unconverted Jews of Jerusalem if they look to our Lord and imitate his passion. No one is crowned unless he strives courageously.

The doctrine of the cross is clear and inevitable from both our Lord's life and his words: 'If any man has a mind to come my way, let him renounce self, and take up his cross, and follow me.' Paul does not dwell on this; he takes for granted that it is familiar teaching to the Christians who now live in the city where Jesus suffered and died. What he does dwell on is the notion of sonship. As usual in Hebrews, he quotes a passage from scripture as the basis for his message; this time it is two verses from the Book of Proverbs. Discipline is essential to family life, for God's family as well as every human family; sinful man is in need of continual correction; hardship and suffering are part of God's plan for the good of the human race. It is a father's office to train his family by corrective discipline; he would be wanting in true affection if he neglected it.

Paul concludes on a note of warning. He quotes the example of Jacob's brother Esau. It was because Esau thought only of

for a single dish of food; afterwards, you may be sure, he was eager enough to have the blessing allotted to him, but no, he was rejected. He pleaded for it in tears, but no second chance was given him.

What is the scene, now, of your approach to God? It is no longer a mountain that can be discerned by touch; no longer burning fire, and whirlwind, and darkness, and storm. No trumpet sounds; no utterance comes from that voice, which made those who listened to it pray that they might hear no more (daunted by the command, that if even a beast touched the mountain it should die by stoning. Moses said, in terror at the sight, 'I am overcome with fear and trembling'). The scene of your approach now is mount Sion, is the heavenly Jerusalem, city of the living God; here are gathered thousands upon thousands of angels, here is the assembly of those first-born sons whose names are written in heaven, here is God sitting in judgment on all men, here are the spirits of just men, now made perfect; here is Jesus, the spokesman of the new covenant, and the sprinkling of his blood, which has better things to say than Abel's had.

Beware of excusing yourselves from listening to him who is speaking to you. There was no escape for those others, who tried to excuse themselves when God uttered his warnings on earth; still less for us, if we turn away when he speaks from heaven. His voice, even then, made the earth rock; now, he has announced to us that it shall happen again: 'Only once again and I will shake earth and heaven too.' Only once again— that means that what is shaken, this created universe, will be removed; only the things which cannot be shaken are to stand firm. The kingdom we have inherited is one which cannot be shaken; in gratitude for this, let us worship God as he would

his own pleasure and satisfaction that God rejected him; and the rejection was final. This should be a lesson to the Hebrews not to presume on God's mercy; apostates will not win God's pardon.

Mosaic Sinai and Christian Sion.   Throughout the Letter to the Hebrews Paul is showing the superiority of Christianity over Judaism as a religious system. Both began as a covenant inaugurated by a sacrifice to God. The scene of both covenants was a mountain; Sinai with its thunder and lightning was a terrifying sight; Sion with its atoning death of the Son of God raises the minds of Christians to a merciful God in heaven; it suggests thoughts of peace and rest. Sinai symbolizes the fear of divine punishment in the Old Testament; everyone was afraid to come near that mountain. Sion symbolizes the joy of the New Testament; access to the divine presence is easy and is open to all Christians. By Sion (another name for Jerusalem) Paul means the Church, the Mystical Body of Christ; it is a heavenly city, because its head sits at the right hand of the Father; while living on earth the Christian is in reality a citizen of heaven. It is far superior to the earthly city of stone with its temple, priests, and sacrifices; the heavenly Jerusalem has our Lord Jesus Christ as its high priest, and a sacrifice that cries to God for pardon.

When God spoke at Sinai, the earth shook. This reminds Paul of another shaking of both heaven and earth predicted by the prophet Aggaeus. This is a metaphorical way of speaking of divine intervention in human affairs; it refers to the founding of the Church on earth, not to any event connected with the end of the world. The intervention of God at Sinai had only a local and temporal effect; his second intervention is

have us worship him, in awe and reverence; no doubt of it,
our God is a consuming fire.

Let brotherly love be firmly established among you; and do
not forget to show hospitality; in doing this, men have before
now entertained angels unawares. Remember those who are in
prison, as if you were prisoners too; those who endure suffering,
since you have mortal bodies of your own. Marriage, in every
way, must be held in honour, and the marriage bed kept free
from stain; over fornication and adultery, God will call us to
account. The love of money should not dwell in your thoughts;
be content with what you have. God himself has told us, 'I will
never forsake you, never abandon you'; so that we can say
with confidence, 'The Lord is my champion; I will not be
afraid of what man can do to me.'

Do not forget those who have had charge of you, and
preached God's word to you; contemplate the happy issue of
the life they lived, and imitate their faith. What Jesus Christ
was yesterday, and is today, he remains for ever. Do not be
carried aside from your course by a maze of new doctrines;
what gives true strength to a man's heart is gratitude, not observances in the matter of food, which never yet proved useful
to those who followed them. We have an altar of our own,
and it is not those who carry out the worship of the tabernacle
that are qualified to eat its sacrifices. When the high priest
takes the blood of beasts with him into the sanctuary, as an
offering for sin, the bodies of those beasts have to be burned
away from the camp; and thus it was that Jesus, when he
would sanctify the people through his own blood, suffered
beyond the city gate. Let us, too, go out to him away from
the camp, bearing the ignominy he bore; we have an everlasting city, but not here; our goal is the city that is one day to be.

universal and eternal in its effects. The Church is God's final
revelation to man on earth; it is an unchangeable kingdom.

Go Out To Jesus Beyond The City Gate.   Paul's usual custom in his letters is to close with some practical advice on
Christian conduct. First of all, he recommends the practice
of charity, purity, and detachment. The motive he gives for
the practice of charity is in keeping with the scriptural background of Hebrews; it is the story of Abraham entertaining
three angels (Gen. 18). The advice on detachment is based
on the Providence of God; it is the same lesson our Lord gave
to his apostles when he sent them out to preach the gospel
(Mt. 10).

All the rest of Paul's letters were addressed to Gentile converts; the moral problems of converted pagans were more numerous than those of converted Jews; the Jewish moral code
protected them from many of the grosser pagan vices. So Paul
has very little moral advice for the Hebrews; almost his only
concern is the danger of apostasy. And he returns to that subject after his opening lines on charity, purity, and detachment.

He quotes the example of those Christian leaders who have
lived and died for the faith in Jerusalem. They should serve as
models in these hazardous times when there is danger of deny-
ing the faith. Stephen the deacon was the first to shed his
blood for the Christian cause (Acts 7); then James the brother
of John was slain by Agrippa to please his Jewish subjects
(Acts 12). Both of these gave their lives for Christ in the city
of Jerusalem. If this Letter was written after 62 A.D., then
James the Less, a cousin of Jesus and bishop of Jerusalem, had
also been killed by the Jews. The Christians should take heart
from these champions and hold firm to the faith.

It is through him, then, that we must offer to God a continual sacrifice of praise, the tribute of lips that give thanks to his name. Meanwhile, you must remember to do good to others and give alms; God takes pleasure in such sacrifices as this.

Obey those who have charge of you, and yield to their will; they are keeping unwearied watch over your souls, because they know they will have an account to give. Make it a grateful task for them: it is your own loss if they find it a laborious effort.

Pray for us; we trust we have a clear conscience, and the will to be honourable in all our dealings. And I make this request the more earnestly, in the hope of being restored to you the sooner. May God, the author of peace, who has raised our Lord Jesus from the dead, that great shepherd, whose flock was bought with the blood of an eternal covenant, grant you every capacity for good, to do his will. May he carry out in us the design he sees best, through Jesus Christ, to whom glory belongs throughout all ages, Amen. I entreat you, brethren, bear patiently with all these words of warning; it is but a brief letter I am sending you. You must know that our brother Timothy has been set at liberty; if he comes soon, I will bring him with me when I visit you. Greet all those who are in authority, and all the saints. The brethren from Italy send you their greetings. Grace be with you all, Amen.

The Voyage to Rome

And now word was given for the voyage to Italy, Paul being handed over, with some other prisoners, to a centurion called Julius, who belonged to the Augustan cohort. We embarked

Even though these Christian leaders were killed, the object of their faith remains unchangeable. Jesus Christ does not die; he remains the same for ever. And it is this ever-living, crucified Master that Paul takes as his main motive for the conduct of his Hebrew audience. Jesus consummated his life outside the gates of the city of Jerusalem. This means that his sacrifice did not take place in the temple, the sanctuary of the Jewish people; he had to go outside Jerusalem to offer his atoning death to his Father. The Jewish Christians must do the same: they must go outside the shelter of Judaism, leave the sanctuary of the old covenant. From now on their lives are integrated with a new society, the Mystical Body of Christ; this is the Church, a new, everlasting city far better than the old city of Jerusalem. They must break completely with the Jewish religious system; they are now an autonomous Christian community.

Possibly the last 16 lines are a postscript added in Paul's own hand; they contain the only personal details found in the letter. The body of the letter may have been composed at Caesarea by Paul, then put into its present literary form by one of his disciples; it was sent to Paul for approval, and he added the last few lines. By this time he was back in Rome after his journey to Spain, five years later than his Caesarean captivity. It seems that Paul never came back to Palestine; these are his last words to the Christians of Jerusalem.

From Caesarea to Rome 60-63 A.D.

The Voyage As Far As Crete. Luke here begins his third and final 'we-section' of the Acts; this means he accompanied Paul on his voyage to Rome. Another disciple, Aristarchus,

on a boat from Adrumetum which was bound for the Asiatic ports, and set sail; the Macedonian, Aristarchus, from Thessalonica, was with us. Next day we put in at Sidon; and here Julius showed Paul courtesy by allowing him to visit his friends and be cared for. Then, setting sail, we coasted under the lee of Cyprus, to avoid contrary winds, but made a straight course over the open sea that lies off Cilicia and Pamphylia, and so reached Myra, in Lycia. There the centurion found a boat from Alexandria which was sailing for Italy, and put us on board. We had a slow voyage for many days after this; we made Gnidus with difficulty, and then, with the wind beating us back, had to sail under the lee of Crete by way of Salmone. Here we were hard put to it to coast along as far as a place called Fair Havens, near the city of Lasea. Much time had now been wasted, and sailing had become dangerous; the fast was already over; and Paul gave them this advice: 'Sirs,' he said, 'I can see plainly that there is no sailing now, without injury and great loss, not only of our freight and of the vessel, but of our own lives too.' The centurion, however, paid more attention to the helmsman and the master than to Paul's advice. The harbour was not well placed for wintering in; so that more of them gave their voices for sailing further still, in the hope of making Phoenix and wintering there; it is a harbour in Crete, which faces in the direction of the Southwest and Northwest winds.

A light breeze was now blowing from the South, so that they thought they had achieved their purpose; they weighed anchor and sailed close along the coast of Crete. But it was not long before a gale of wind from the land struck the ship, the wind called the Northeaster; she was carried out of her course, and

completed the party of Christians. These two were permitted to travel with Paul, the Roman citizen, as his slaves. There were 276 people on the ship for Rome. Some of them were political prisoners, others condemned criminals on their way to fight and die in the Circus Maximus for the sport of Roman crowds.

From Caesarea to Rome is 1,500 miles by sea; the direct course is in a westerly direction. Since no ship sailing direct to Rome was available, Julius had to take a ship north to the Galatian coast. As they passed close to Cyprus, Paul's thoughts went back to his first missionary journey to that island in company with Barnabas. That was 15 years before; but it seemed like yesterday. They put in at Myra, a port not far from where Paul had landed from Cyprus to begin his conquest of Galatia; his thoughts must have gone far over the Taurus mountains to Pisidian Antioch, Iconium, and Lystra; in all these places there were flourishing Christian communities.

It was late in September when the ship sailed from Caesarea; the prevailing northwest wind had slowed down the progress of the ship, so that it was now well into the month of October. Things did not improve when the party boarded a second ship sailing direct to Italy; instead of heading west to Cape Malea, on the southern tip of Greece, the ship was forced south of Crete by northwest winds. It was now late in October; the Day of Atonement ('the fast') fell on 28 October in 60 A.D.

Storm At Sea And Shipwreck. With the month of November, the Mediterranean world is in the grip of winter; after the dry summer months rain begins to fall. This means that the sky is clouded over, and the mariner cannot be guided by sight of sun or stars. This was most important in those days

could make no head against the wind, so we gave up and let
her drive. We now ran under the lee of an island named
Cauda, where we contrived, with difficulty, to secure the ship's
boat. When it had been hoisted aboard, they strengthened the
ship by passing ropes round her; then, for fear of being driven
on to the Syrtis sands, they let down the sea-anchor, and so
drifted. On the next day, so violently were we tossed about in
the gale, they lightened ship, and on the third, they deliber-
ately threw the spare tackle overboard.

For several days we saw nothing of the sun or the stars, and
a heavy gale pressed us hard, so that we had lost, by now, all
hope of surviving: and we were much in want of food. And
now Paul stood up in their presence, and said, 'Sirs, you
should have taken my advice; if you had not put out from
Crete, you would have saved all this injury and damage. But
I would not have you lose courage, even now; there is to be no
loss of life among you, only of the ship. An angel stood before
me last night, sent by the God to whom I belong, the God
whom I serve, and said, "Have no fear, Paul, you are to stand
in Caesar's presence; and behold, God has granted you the
safety of all your fellow-voyagers." Have courage, then, sirs; I
trust in God, believing that all will fall out as he has told me.
Only we are to be cast up on an island.'

On the fourteenth night, as we drifted about in the Adriatic
sea, the crew began to suspect, about midnight, that we were
nearing land; so they took soundings, and made it twenty
fathoms; then they sounded again, a short distance away, and
made it fifteen fathoms. Afraid, therefore, that we might be
cast ashore on some rocky coast, they let down four anchors
from the stern, and fell to wishing it were day. And now the
sailors had a mind to abandon the ship, and lowered the boat
into the sea, pretending that they meant to lay out anchors

before the invention of the compass; it was the main reason why all traffic in the Mediterranean stopped by November at the latest. There was the added peril of gale-force winds, and the difficulty of life on board ship in the cold of winter.

The ship had left Lasea, against Paul's advice, and was coasting along the southern shore of Crete in a westerly direction; its objective was the port of Phoenix, about 50 miles distant. The hurricane struck the ship without warning, rushing down from the 7,000-ft. high mountains of Crete. Within a matter of minutes, the ship was forced to turn and run with the wind. Driven in a southwesterly direction, it was heading for the dreaded Syrtis quicksands on the north coast of Africa; to slow down the rate of drift, a heavy sail was dragged behind the ship as a sea-anchor.

As Crete was blotted out by the storm, Paul would hardly have had the thought that he would come back one day to this mountainous island. But in fact he did come back, about five years later, with his disciple Titus, whom he left on Crete as its first bishop. But at this moment his thoughts were completely taken up with the problem of survival aboard the tossing ship.

Most of the grain ships from Egypt were about 300 tons. The greater part of the wheat used by Rome came from the Nile delta in this type of ship. Ordinarily in good weather those on board slept and cooked their meals on deck; but in gale conditions they would be battened down in one of the holds, safe at least from the danger of being washed overboard. Morale was undoubtedly low among the 276 seasick, scared, and starving passengers. Among them moved Paul, the ship's chaplain, and Luke, the ship's doctor; there was plenty of work for both.

As a guide to his conduct, Paul had two storm scenes from

from the bows. But Paul told the centurion and the soldiers, 'These must stay on board, or there is no hope left for you'; whereupon the soldiers cut the boat's ropes away and let it drop.

As day began to break, Paul entreated them all to take some food; 'Today,' he said, 'is the fourteenth day you have been in suspense, and all that time gone hungry, neglecting to eat; pray take some food, then; it will make for your preservation; not a hair of anyone's head is to be lost.' And with that he took bread, and gave thanks to God before them all, and broke it, and began to eat. Thereupon they all found courage, and themselves took a meal. The whole number of souls on board was two hundred and seventy-six. So all ate till they were content; and afterwards they began to lighten the ship, throwing the wheat into the sea.

When day broke, they found that the coast was strange to them. But they sighted a bay with a sloping beach, and made up their minds, if it should be possible, to run the ship ashore there. They cast off the anchors and left them in the sea, at the same time unlashing the tiller; then they hoisted the foresail to the breeze, and held on for the shore. But now, finding they were running into a cross sea, they grounded the ship where they were. The bows, which were stuck fast, felt no movement, but the stern began falling to pieces under the violence of the waves; whereupon the soldiers would have killed the prisoners, for fear that any of them should dive overboard and escape, but the centurion balked them of their will, because he had a mind to keep Paul safe. He gave orders that those who could swim should go overboard first, and make their way to land; of the rest, some were ferried across on planks, and some on the ship's wreckage. So it was that all reached land in safety.

the life of the Master. Just as Jesus had comforted and strengthened the panic-stricken crew of a fishing boat on the lake of Galilee, so Paul brought new faith and confidence to the despairing passengers drifting in the Mediterranean. He had often told his converts in letter after letter that a Christian is a member of Christ, that the Master shows his love for men by working through human instruments. During this fortnight of darkness and despair, Paul passed from man to man in the closed hold of the ship bringing that grace and light which only Jesus Christ can bestow on men.

Malta lies 600 miles to the west of Crete; this means that the hurricane must have shifted round to the east soon after the ship was driven away from Crete towards the African coast. Since it took a fortnight to cover the distance, the drift rate was about two miles an hour; this is normal for a helpless ship. Luke calls the central Mediterranean the Adriatic (not to be confused with the modern name for the sea lying between Italy and Yugoslavia). The ship was grounded on a sandbank offshore; this meant a swim of some hundreds of yards for the passengers and crew. It was the possibility of their escape which made the soldiers decide to kill the prisoners; they were responsible for these captives with their own lives. It was only Paul's presence that saved the prisoners' lives; this is a remarkable tribute to the power that Paul had over men, pagan as well as Christian.

The documents sent by Festus concerning Paul's case must surely have perished in the shipwreck off the coast of Malta. This explains why Luke wrote the Acts while Paul was in Rome; it would be the main documentary evidence at his trial before the Imperial Court. That is why he stresses the favourable impression Paul made on Roman authorities at Caesarea and elsewhere, during the course of his missionary journeys.

When we were safe on land, we found that the island was called Malta. The kindness which the natives showed to us was beyond the ordinary; they welcomed us all by making a fire for us, because rain was coming on, and it was cold. Paul had collected a bundle of faggots and had just put them on the fire, when a viper, coming out to escape the heat, fastened on his hand; and the natives, when they saw the beast coiled round his hand, said to one another, 'This must be some murderer; he has been rescued from the sea, but divine vengeance would not let him live.' He, meanwhile, shook the beast into the fire, and was none the worse. They still waited to see him swell up, or fall down dead on a sudden; but when they had waited a long time, and found that there was nothing amiss with him, they changed their minds, and declared that he must be a god. Among the estates in that part were some which belonged to the leading citizen on the island, a man named Publius, who took us in and for three days entertained us hospitably; and it so happened that Publius' father had taken to his bed, laid up with fever and dysentery. Paul, who had gone to visit him, laid his hands upon him with prayer, and healed him; whereupon all the other folk in the island who were suffering from infirmities came to him and found a cure. These paid us great honour, and when we embarked they loaded us with all the supplies we needed.

It was at the end of three months that we sailed, in a ship from Alexandria which had wintered at the island; its sign was Castor and Pollux. We put in at Syracuse, where we waited for three days; then we coasted round the further shore, and so arrived at Rhegium. When we had spent a day there, a South wind came on, and we made Puteoli on the second day out. Here we found some brethren, who prevailed on us to stay with

From Malta To Rome. The warm welcome given to Paul by the Maltese was repaid by God with the gift of faith, a prized possession which this Catholic island has never lost. They have erected a statue to St. Paul on the site of his providential shipwreck and celebrate the event annually with great enthusiasm. A local tradition also credits Paul with banishing snakes forever from their island. Possibly there never were any snakes native to the island; the viper of the Acts may have come to Malta as a stowaway on one of the Egyptian grain ships.

Malta belonged to the Roman province of Sicily; Publius was the local representative of the Sicilian governor. His family were probably the first Christian converts on the island. With Jesus' power to heal the sick, Paul won an entry into this influential family. The receptive Maltese flocked to him with their sick; by the time the three winter months had passed, a large part of the population had heard the Christian message. Publius was ordained by Paul and put in charge of the flock.

By the end of February, an Egyptian ship like the one that had been shipwrecked was ready to put to sea again; centurion Julius went aboard it with all his passengers. After passing through the Straits of Messina, the Castor and Pollux landed its passengers at Puteoli, a suburb of Naples. There was no smoking Vesuvius to look at in those days; eighteen years would pass before the famous eruption was to take place.

The delay at Naples gave time for the news of Paul's arrival to reach the Christians in Rome. While he was making the week's journey by land from Naples to Rome, his Roman friends decided to come out and meet him along the road and escort him into the city. In his Letter to the Romans, written three years before from Corinth, he greeted 28 people by name; some of these were the nucleus of the welcoming com-

them for a week. And so we ended our journey at Rome. The brethren there, who had heard our story, came out as far as Appius' Forum, and on to the Three Taverns, to meet us; Paul gave thanks to God and took courage when he saw them.

Once we were in Rome, Paul was allowed to have his own residence, which he shared with the soldier who guarded him. It was three days later that he called a meeting of the leading men among the Jews. When they had assembled, he told them: 'Brethren, I am one who has done nothing to the prejudice of our people, or of our ancestral customs; yet, in Jerusalem, they handed me over to the Romans as a prisoner. These, when they had examined me, had a mind to release me, since no capital charge lay against me; but the Jews cried out against it, and I was forced to appeal to Caesar, though it is not as if I had any fault to find with my own nation. That is why I have asked for the opportunity of seeing you and speaking to you. It is because I hope as Israel hopes, that I wear this chain.'

At this they said to him: 'We have not received any letter about you from Judea, nor has any of the brethren come here with any ill report or hard words about you. We ask nothing better than to hear what your opinions are; all we know of this sect is, that it is everywhere decried.'

So they made an appointment with him, and met him at his lodging in great numbers. And he bore his testimony and told them about the kingdom of God, trying to convince them from Moses and the prophets of what Jesus was, from dawn till dusk. Some were convinced by his words, others refused belief; and they took their leave still at variance among themselves, but not till Paul had spoken one last word: 'It was a

mittee. Probably his two great personal friends, Aquila and Priscilla, were among the first to greet him on the Appian Way. Paul was filled with happiness as he entered the capital of the Empire.

Paul Interviews The Jewish Leaders. Eleven years earlier, in 50 A.D., the Jews had been expelled from Rome by the emperor Claudius; but they had gradually found their way back to the capital, particularly after the accession of the emperor Nero in 54 A.D. At the time of Paul's arrival in March 61 A.D. they were about 25,000 in number; probably a half of these were already converted to Christianity. The unconverted Jews had thirteen synagogues in the city of Rome and were powerful at the Roman court of Nero. This is the reason why Paul so speedily summoned them to his prison-residence; they could cause him much trouble in his forthcoming trial. So he would explain his case and sound them out on their attitude to him. He must have been relieved to hear that no evidence had yet come from Jerusalem concerning his case; it was too soon after winter for any letters to have come across the Mediterranean.

At a later meeting, Paul had a religious discussion with these same Jewish leaders. Undoubtedly his argument was the usual scriptural approach: he would prove that the crucifixion of Jesus was an essential part of the divine plan; and then he would show the divinity of Jesus from his resurrection. But the majority still refused belief, and Paul was forced to quote the terrible words of Isaias, just as the Master himself had done (Mt. 13, 14). It only confirmed Paul's often expressed conviction that the Church's future lay with the Gentiles.

Two years was the legal period of detention during which the accusers had to bring their charge against the prisoner. It

true utterance the Holy Spirit made to your fathers through the prophet Isaias: "Go to this people, and tell them, 'You will listen and listen, but for you there is no understanding; you will watch and watch, but for you there is no perceiving.' The heart of this people has become dull, their ears are slow to listen, and they keep their eyes shut, so that they may never see with those eyes, or hear with those ears, or understand with that heart, and turn back to me, and win healing from me." Take notice, then, that this message of salvation has been sent by God to the Gentiles, and they, at least, will listen to it.'

And for two whole years he lived in a lodging hired at his own expense, and welcomed all who came to visit him, proclaiming God's kingdom, and teaching them the truths which concern our Lord Jesus Christ, boldly enough, without let or hindrance.

Letter to the Ephesians

Paul, by God's will an apostle of Jesus Christ, to those saints, the faithful in Jesus Christ, who dwell at Ephesus, grace and peace be yours from God, our Father, and from the Lord Jesus Christ. Blessed be that God, the Father of our Lord Jesus Christ, who has blessed us, in Christ, with every spiritual blessing, higher than heaven itself. He has chosen us out, in Christ, before the foundation of the world, to be saints, to be blameless in his sight; in his love marking us out beforehand (such was his loving design) to be his adopted children through Jesus Christ. Thus he would manifest the splendour of that grace by which he has taken us into his favour in the person of his beloved Son. It is in him and through his blood

seems that none of the Jews pursued the case against Paul, and he was freed at the end of two years without a formal trial. Julius would give his report, and Paul's case would be presented to the judge in Luke's Acts. While waiting for his freedom, Paul lived in a house in the Jewish quarter near the Tiber. A soldier was on guard all the time; the guard changed frequently, and many of these men were converted by Paul.

Peter and his disciple Mark were probably frequent visitors during Paul's imprisonment. His close friend Timothy also returned from the mission field. Tychicus, Epaphroditus, Demas, Justus, and Onesimus are the names of other visitors who came to Paul at this time. The house by the Tiber now became the headquarters of Paul's vast mission to the Gentiles scattered far and wide throughout the far distant provinces of the Empire.

The Church Is the Body of Christ

A Hymn Of Our Redemption.   Towards the end of Paul's Roman captivity, he wrote four letters: Ephesians, Colossians, Philemon, and Philippians. The first three are a group, addressed to the Church in Asia; of these the most important is Ephesians. It has been called 'the crown of Paul's writings, one of the divinest compositions of man.' It is more in the style of a meditation than a letter; its solemn and majestic tone is manifest from this opening paragraph, which is one long sentence of 202 words in the original Greek.

In the other three Letters, Timothy's name is joined to Paul's; it is missing from Ephesians, which is surprising, in view of the fact that Timothy was with Paul in Rome and was

that we enjoy redemption, the forgiveness of our sins. So rich is God's grace, that has overflowed upon us in a full stream of wisdom and discernment, to make known to us the hidden purpose of his will. It was his loving design, centred in Christ, to give history its fulfilment by resuming everything in him, all that is in heaven, all that is on earth, summed up in him.

In him it was our lot to be called, singled out beforehand to suit his purpose (for it is he who is at work everywhere, carrying out the designs of his will); we were to manifest his glory, we who were the first to set our hope in Christ; in him you too were called, when you listened to the preaching of the truth, that gospel which is your salvation. In him you too learned to believe, and had the seal set on your faith by the promised gift of the Holy Spirit; a pledge of the inheritance which is ours, to redeem it for us and bring us into possession of it, and so manifest God's glory.

Well then, I too play my part; I have been told of your faith in the Lord Jesus, of the love you show towards all the saints, and I never cease to offer thanks on your behalf, or to remember you in my prayers. So may he who is the God of our Lord Jesus Christ, the Father to whom glory belongs, grant you a spirit of wisdom and insight, to give you fuller knowledge of himself. May your inward eye be enlightened, so that you may understand to what hopes he has called you, how rich in glory is that inheritance of his found among the saints, what surpassing virtue there is in his dealings with us, who believe. Measure it by that mighty exercise of power which he showed when he raised Christ from the dead, and bade him sit on his right hand above the heavens, high above all princedoms and powers and virtues and dominations, and

well known at Ephesus. Another unexpected feature is the absence of personal greetings to Paul's many friends at the end of the letter. The words 'at Ephesus' are missing from two of the most important Greek MSS. These facts have led most commentators to hold that Ephesians was a circular letter sent to the Asian churches; it became known as Ephesians because that city was the capital of the province, and a copy was preserved there.

This opening paragraph has been called Paul's Magnificat. It shows that God's plan from all eternity was the redemption of man in time; all history is centred on the most important event that has taken place on this earth. Paul looks on the human race as beheaded in Adam and given a new head in Christ. From the depths of the Blessed Trinity, the Second Person creates a new human race in his blood; individuals long divided by sin are now united in the person of Christ; through faith they are made one body under the headship of Christ.

The Church Completes Christ. Paul wrote Ephesians towards the end of five years' imprisonment (58-63 A.D.), first at Caesarea and then at Rome. During these years he had much time to think and meditate. The Judaizing crisis of Galatians and Romans had passed; the battle he had waged against enemies of his apostolic authority in 1 and 2 Corinthians had died down. In Ephesians Paul was thinking more of post-war reconstruction, of building up the full Christian life. Probably his observation of the social unity of the Empire turned his thoughts to the idea of the Christian Church as the one organism destined by God for all mankind; in it individuals are united in the one body, animated by one and the same Spirit, under the authority of one head, Christ.

14

every name that is known, not in this world only, but in the world to come. He has put everything under his dominion, and made him the supreme head to which the Church is joined, so that the Church is his body, the completion of him who everywhere and in all things is complete.

He found you dead men; such were your transgressions, such were the sinful ways you lived in. That was when you followed the fashion of this world, when you owned a prince whose domain is in the lower air, that spirit whose influence is still at work among the unbelievers. We too, all of us, were once of their company; our life was bounded by natural appetites, and we did what corrupt nature or our own calculation would have us do, with God's displeasure for our birthright, like other men. How rich God is in mercy, with what an excess of love he loved us! Our sins had made dead men of us, and he, in giving life to Christ, gave life to us too; it is his grace that has saved you; raised us up too, enthroned us too above the heavens, in Christ Jesus. He would have all future ages see, in that clemency which he showed us in Christ Jesus, the surpassing richness of his grace. Yes, it was grace that saved you, with faith for its instrument; it did not come from yourselves, it was God's gift, not from any action of yours, or there would be room for pride. No, we are his design; God has created us in Christ Jesus, pledged to such good actions as he has prepared beforehand, to be the employment of our lives.

Remember, then, what you once were, the Gentiles, according to all outward reckoning; those who claim an outward circumcision which is man's handiwork call you the uncircumcised. In those days there was no Christ for you; you were outlaws from the commonwealth of Israel, strangers to every

In his other letters, Paul wrote frequently of the Mystical Body of Christ; in Ephesians it is his theme. In this paragraph he uses a new expression to illustrate the relation between Christ and his Church; it is the word 'completion' (in Greek, pleroma). It is a nautical expression, possibly suggested to Paul from his many sea voyages, or even picked up by him as a boy in the seaport of Tarsus; it means the ship's crew, the complement.

Without the Church, Christ would in a sense be incomplete; it is part of God's plan that the Incarnation of his Son should be continued in time and place by means of the Church. The head cannot express itself except through the organs and limbs of the body; the ship cannot put to sea unless it has a crew to sail it. This must not be understood as implying imperfection in our Lord's humanity; it is purely from God's own design that he has permitted mankind to share in the work of redemption by becoming his Mystical Body; it is a divine favour conferred on men.

It is the risen Christ who is head of the body. Paul emphasizes this because the Church is raised up to the level of its head; just as Jesus now dwells in the glory of the Trinity in heaven, so the Church's true life is a sharing in that of Father, Son, and Holy Ghost. Christ is far above all angelic powers (a point discussed more fully in Colossians); as his members, Christians must rise from their subjection to sin and Satan ('a prince whose domain is in the lower air'); the life of grace must show itself in good actions.

Jews And Gentiles United In The Church. All the Asian churches were predominantly Gentile; Christianity was Jewish in origin. That is why Paul addresses his readers as 'you Gentiles,' but includes himself among the Jews by the use of 'we.' He begins by describing the pitiable state of the pagan

covenant, with no promise to hope for, with the world about
you, and no God. But now you are in Christ Jesus; now,
through the blood of Christ, you have been brought close, you
who were once so far away. He is our bond of peace; he has
made the two nations one, breaking down the wall that was
a barrier between us, the enmity there was between us, in his
own mortal nature. He has put an end to the law with its
decrees, so as to make peace, remaking the two human creatures as one in himself; both sides, united in a single body,
he would reconcile to God through his cross, inflicting death,
in his own person, upon the feud. So he came, and his message was of peace for you who were far off, peace for those
who were near; far off or near, united in the same Spirit, we
have access through him to the Father. You are no longer
exiles, then, or aliens; the saints are your fellow-citizens, you
belong to God's household. Apostles and prophets are the
foundation on which you were built, and the chief corner-
stone of it is Jesus Christ himself. In him the whole fabric is
bound together, as it grows into a temple, dedicated to the
Lord; in him you too are being built in with the rest, so that
God may find in you a spiritual dwelling-place.

With this in mind, I fall on my knees; I, Paul, of whom
Jesus Christ has made a prisoner for the love of you Gentiles.
You will have been told how God planned to give me a special
grace for preaching to you; how a revelation taught me the
secret I have been setting out briefly here; briefly, yet so as
to let you see how well I have mastered this secret of Christ's.
It was never made known to any human being in past ages,
as it has now been revealed by the Spirit to his holy apostles
and prophets, and it is this: that through the gospel preaching the Gentiles are to win the same inheritance, to be made

world before the coming of Christ; they did not enjoy God's revelation made to the Jews in the Old Testament.

Their exclusion from the divine benefits conferred by God on Israel was symbolized by the 'wall' that separated the Court of the Gentiles from the inner courts of the temple at Jerusalem. It was only four feet six inches high, but no Gentile dared pass through it into the presence of God; it was called Soreg by the Jews. Within its enclosure they were a race apart, holding fanatically to their privileged position. This was the barrier that Jesus removed by his death on the cross. He raised both Jew and Gentile to a new plane of existence by making them one; not one people, but one person through membership in his Mystical Body, the Church.

Blood divides races on the face of the earth; the blood of Christ flowed on Calvary to reunite them. The Gentiles now have access to God the Father; they can enter God's presence because they are members of his household. Since Paul's mind is on the temple of Jerusalem, he finally pictures Jew and Gentile as two walls joined together by Jesus Christ himself as the corner-stone; they are living stones in God's own building.

Paul's Commission To Promulgate The Secret. Paul's thoughts are on the temple in Jerusalem; it was there the trouble began which led to his present imprisonment. As a further link with the letter he is now writing, it was an Ephesian, who had accompanied him on his return to Jerusalem, that was the cause of all the trouble. This man was Trophimus, a Gentile Christian whom the unconverted Jews in the temple precincts accused of entering the inner enclosure, beyond the Soreg. This accusation had led to Paul's arrest and his consequent five years in prison at Caesarea and Rome.

part of the same body, to share the same divine promise, in Christ Jesus. With what grace God gives me (and he gives it in all the effectiveness of his power), I am a minister of tha gospel; on me, least as I am of all the saints, he has bestowed this privilege, of making known to the Gentiles the un fathomable riches of Christ, of publishing to the world the plan of this mystery, kept hidden from the beginning of time in the all-creating mind of God. The principalities and power: of heaven are to see, now, made manifest in the Church, the subtlety of God's wisdom; such is his eternal purpose, centred in Christ Jesus our Lord, who gives us all our confidence, bids us come forward, emboldened by our faith in him. Let there be no discouragement, then, over the affliction I undergo on your behalf; it is an honour done to you.

With this in mind, then, I fall on my knees to the Father, that Father from whom all fatherhood in heaven and on earth takes its title. May he, out of the rich treasury of his glory, strengthen you through his Spirit with a power that reaches your innermost being. May Christ find a dwelling-place, through faith, in your hearts; may your lives be rooted in love, founded on love. May you and all the saints be enabled to measure, in all its breadth and length and height and depth, the love of Christ, to know what passes knowledge. May you be filled with all the completion God has to give. He whose power is at work in us is powerful enough, and more than powerful enough, to carry out his purpose beyond all our hopes and dreams; may he be glorified in the Church, and in Christ Jesus, to the last generation of eternity. Amen.

Here, then, is one who wears chains in the Lord's service, pleading with you to live as befits men called to such a voca-

As Paul looks at his chains, he is reminded of these distant happenings in Jerusalem; but he does not complain. He falls on his knees to thank God the Father for the great privilege of permitting him to undergo such afflictions on behalf of the Gentiles; for this is his great vocation in life. Ever since the day, thirty-three years before, when Jesus appeared to him on the Damascus Road, Paul has gloried in the commission given him to be the apostle of the Gentiles: 'Go on your way; I mean to send you on a distant errand, to the Gentiles.'

This is the secret hidden from all eternity in the divine plan for the human race: the Gentiles are to become members of the Mystical Body of Christ with all the rights and privileges of the chosen race. Even the angels were not told of this great secret of the incorporation of mankind under the headship of Christ. Although it was hinted at by our Lord during his earthly life (notably in his parables: the tramps brought into the marriage feast signify the call of the Gentiles; likewise the eleventh-hour labourers in the vineyard, and the return of the prodigal to the Father's house) it was left to Paul to make it known in clear terms, and to put it into execution by his mission to the Gentile world.

Jews usually prayed standing; Paul expresses the intensity of his prayer by falling on his knees, like Jesus in Gethsemani. He is transported out of himself by the thought of what incorporation in Christ does for men; it raises them to the life of the Blessed Trinity; they are sons of the Father, indwelt by the Holy Spirit, the love of Christ the Redeemer poured out upon them.

Full Spiritual Growth In Christ.   The vocation of all Christians, both Jew and Gentile, is to live in unity. This is what

tion as yours. You must be always humble, always gentle; patient, too, in bearing with one another's faults, as charity bids; eager to preserve that unity the Spirit gives you, whose bond is peace. You are one body, with a single Spirit; each of you, when he was called, called in the same hope; with the same Lord, the same faith, the same baptism; with the same God, the same Father, all of us, who is above all things, pervades all things, and lives in all things.

But each of us has received his own special grace, dealt out to him by Christ's gift. (That is why we are told, 'He has mounted up on high; he has captured his spoil; he has brought gifts to men.' The words, 'He has gone up,' must mean that he had gone down to the lower regions of earth. And he who so went down is no other than he who has gone up, high above all the heavens, to fill creation with his presence.) Some he has appointed to be apostles, others to be prophets, others to be evangelists, or pastors, or teachers. They are to order the lives of the faithful, minister to their needs, build up the frame of Christ's body, until we all realize our common unity through faith in the Son of God, and fuller knowledge of him. So we shall reach perfect manhood, that maturity which is proportioned to the completed growth of Christ; we are no longer to be children, no longer to be like storm-tossed sailors, driven before the wind of each new doctrine that human subtlety, human skill in fabricating lies, may propound. We are to follow the truth, in a spirit of charity, and so grow up, in everything, into a due proportion with Christ, who is our head. On him all the body depends; it is organized and unified by each contact with the source which supplies it; and thus, each part receiving the active power it needs, it achieves its natural growth, building itself up through charity.

Christ has won for them by his redemptive death; but they must maintain it by a life of charity. Christians are taken from all walks of life; there is bound to be friction in the daily problem of living together; humble, patient charity in putting up with the faults of others is essential to Christian unity. It is not a quality that comes naturally to men; it is a sharing in the life of the Blessed Trinity. 'That they should all be one, as we are one,' was our Lord's final prayer for his Church at the Last Supper.

But unity does not mean uniformity. This is clear from the diversity of functions ('special grace') in the teaching ministry of the Church; some go to new missions among the pagans ('apostles'), others preach the gospel in established communities; and in this latter group there is a division of work, some reading the secrets of hearts ('prophets'), others telling the gospel story ('evangelists'), others instructing converts and teaching children. All these offices are given by Christ the conqueror, who has won the right to bestow his gifts on men; although he now reigns in heaven, he won his victory on earth as the Incarnate Son of God (the six lines in brackets prove this by a quotation from Psalm 67).

Our Lord did not intend his Church to be static; its nature is to grow and develop; it is his Mystical Body, and a body is a vital organism. The different organs and limbs of a body grow in proportion to the head; it is the exemplar and standard of growth. The unity of the Church comes from its conformity to its head; the more each Christian is identified with Jesus by his knowledge and love, the more the Church grows to its full stature, and the more closely are its members united to each other. Charity is the vital force that flows from the head to the body and brings it to maturity.

14*

This, then, is my message to you; I call upon you in the Lord's name not to live like the Gentiles, who make vain fancies their rule of life. Their minds are clouded with darkness; the hardness of their hearts breeds in them an ignorance, which estranges them from the divine life; and so, past all feeling, they have given themselves up to incontinence, to selfish habits of impurity. This is not the lesson you have learned in making Christ your study, if you have really listened to him. If true knowledge is to be found in Jesus, you will have learned in his school that you must be quit, now, of the old self whose way of life you remember, the self that wasted its aim on false dreams. There must be a renewal in the inner life of your minds; you must be clothed in the new self, which is created in God's image, justified and sanctified through the truth.

Away with falsehood, then; let everyone speak out the truth to his neighbour; membership of the body binds us to one another. 'Do not let resentment lead you into sin'; the sunset must not find you still angry. Do not give the devil his opportunity. The man who was a thief must be a thief no longer; let him work instead, and earn by his own labour the blessings he will be able to share with those who are in need. No base talk must cross your lips; only what will serve to edify others as opportunity arises, and bring a grace to those who are listening; do not distress God's holy Spirit, whose seal you bear until the day of your redemption comes. There must be no trace of bitterness among you, of passion, resentment, quarrelling, insulting talk, or spite of any kind; be kind and tender to one another, each of you generous to all, as God in Christ has been generous to you. As God's favoured children, you must be like him. Order your lives in charity, upon the model of that charity which Christ showed to you, when he gave himself up on our behalf, a sacrifice breathing out fragrance as he offered it to God.

Model Your Lives On Christ.   *It is* difficult to lay aside the way of thought and the habits of a lifetime. Most of Paul's converts in Ephesus and the other cities of Asia had lived in an atmosphere of superstition and magic during their pagan days. Seven years before, the converts of Ephesus had made a bonfire and burnt all their books of black magic (Acts 19, 19); but many of their superstitious beliefs had lingered on in the background of their minds; helped along by the false teachers who flourished at this time in Asia, a number of the converts were falling back into pagan ways. So Paul warns them of the danger; there can be no compromise between paganism and Christianity; the old self cannot coexist with the new self, man regenerated by grace.

The Mystical Body of Christ must learn from its head, Jesus himself, how it is to think and how to live; its attitude and conduct towards those around them must be the same as those our Lord taught both by word and example. Pagan thinking must give way to Christian thinking; that is what Paul means by 'a renewal in the inner life of your minds.' They must look at men with the eyes of Christ, see everything as he saw it related to the will of his Father in heaven; their standard of conduct must be the Sermon on the Mount.

In the second part of this paragraph, Paul lists five common failings that the Asian churches are to pay particular attention to. They are lying, anger, thieving, base talk, and uncharitableness; these are sins which destroy the unity and harmony of the Mystical Body, cause friction and opposition among the members who are bound so closely to each other through their common union with the head. As in 1 Corinthians 13, it is particularly charity Paul insists on. And the motive is Christ's love for us by his death on the cross, his sacrificial offering that ascends like incense to the Father.

As for debauchery, and impurity of every kind, and covetousness, there must be no whisper of it among you; it would ill become saints; no indecent behaviour, no ribaldry or smartness in talk; that is not your business, your business is to give thanks to God. This you must know well enough, that nobody can claim a share in Christ's kingdom, God's kingdom, if he is debauched, or impure, or has that love of money which makes a man an idolater. Do not allow anyone to cheat you with empty promises; these are the very things which bring down God's anger on the unbelievers; you do ill to throw in your lot with them. Once you were all darkness; now, in the Lord, you are all daylight. You must live as men native to the light; where the light has its effect, all is goodness, and holiness, and truth; your lives must be the manifestation of the Lord's will. As for the thankless deeds men do in the dark, you must not take any part in them; rather, your conduct must be a rebuke to them; their secret actions are too shameful even to bear speaking of. It is the light that rebukes such things and shows them up for what they are; only light shows up. That is the meaning of the words, 'Awake, you that sleep, and arise from the dead, and Christ shall give you light.'

See then how carefully you have to tread, not as fools, but as wise men do, hoarding the opportunity that is given you, in evil times like these. No, you cannot afford to be reckless; you must grasp what the Lord's will is for you. Do not besot yourselves with wine; that leads to ruin. Let your contentment be in the Spirit; your tongues unloosed in psalms and hymns and spiritual music, as you sing and give praise to the Lord in your heart.

Give thanks continually to God, who is our Father, in the name of our Lord Jesus Christ; and, as you stand in awe of

Christians The Light Of The World. In the previous paragraph, Paul pointed out sins that were destroying the unity of the Church. He was considering the relations of Christians to one another. Here he is concerned with the need to give good example to the pagan world; it is the Church's mission to convert the heathen.

They cannot do this if they live as the heathen do. It would seem that the heresy known later as Gnosticism was beginning its growth among the Asian churches; this taught that the high graces of Christianity put its members above the moral law. So Paul warns that such vices as impurity and drunkenness debase the Christian name, and will bring down God's anger.

Impurity and drunkenness are sins especially of the night, 'when evils are most free.' In those times night was more a time of darkness than it is nowadays; there was no adequate lighting; lamps gave off more smoke than light. Consequently the rising of the sun each morning was an event that meant much more to the ancients than it does to us. It was under this image of the sun coming to shine in a darkened world that Simeon welcomed the Messiah: 'This is the light which shall give revelation to the Gentiles.' And our Lord used the same image when he called himself 'the light of the world.'

The Mystical Body has the same function as its head; it reflects the light which belongs to it from its union with Jesus. It is a luminous body in the midst of the darkness of paganism. Even the ceremony of baptism reminded a Christian of this; in the early Church it was called 'enlightenment' (Heb. 6, 4); that is why Paul quotes from an early baptismal hymn.

The Christian Home. So far Paul's teaching on how to live the Christian life in the unity of the Mystical Body has been

Christ, submit to each other's rights. Wives must obey their husbands as they would obey the Lord. The man is the head to which the woman's body is united, just as Christ is the head of the Church, he, the Saviour on whom the safety of his body depends; and women must owe obedience at all points to their husbands, as the Church does to Christ. You who are husbands must show love to your wives, as Christ showed love to the Church when he gave himself up on its behalf. He would hallow it, purify it by bathing it in the water to which his word gave life; he would summon it into his own presence, the Church in all its beauty, no stain, no wrinkle, no such disfigurement; it was to be holy, it was to be spotless. And that is how husband ought to love wife, as if she were his own body; in loving his wife, a man is but loving himself. It is unheard of, that a man should bear ill-will to his own flesh and blood; no, he keeps it fed and warmed; and so it is with Christ and his Church; we are limbs of his body; flesh and bone, we belong to him. 'That is why a man will leave father and mother and will cling to his wife, and the two will become one flesh.' Yes, those words are a high mystery, and I am applying them here to Christ and his Church. Meanwhile, each of you is to love his wife as he would love himself, and the wife is to pay reverence to her husband.

You who are children must show obedience in the Lord to your parents; it is your duty: 'Honour your father and your mother'—that is the first commandment which has a promise attached to it—'so it shall go well with you, and you shall live long to enjoy the land.' You who are fathers, do not rouse your children to resentment; the training, the discipline in which you bring them up must come from the Lord. You who are slaves, give your human masters the obedience you owe to Christ, in anxious fear, single-mindedly; not with that show

directed to all Christians. In this paragraph he restricts himself to one element of society, the family. In God's plan, from the creation of the human race, the family was intended to be the basic unit of society. Paul goes a step further; he treats the family as the Church in miniature; he likens the relations of members of a family to those existing between Christ and the Church. In a family of Paul's time there were three elements: husband and wife, parents and children, masters and slaves. Paul has something to say to each category; he deals first with the weaker member, then with the stronger. His main teaching is: love on the part of superiors, obedience on the part of inferiors.

It is especially in his teaching on the relations between husband and wife that Paul's doctrine had such an influence on Christian living. The position of a wife in pagan society, and to a lesser extent in Jewish, was not much better than that of a slave; in most cases her true position in the home was not recognized. She was regarded as a fickle, unreliable person unworthy of trust or a position of authority: 'One thing I ever longed to find, and found never, a true woman. One true man I might find among a thousand, but a woman never' (Ecclesiastes 7, 29). By restoring woman to her original position intended by God in creating Adam and Eve, and by supernaturalizing the love of husband and wife, Paul raised the status of the wife in a Christian family.

The model for the husband in his love for his wife is none other than Christ himself. Just as the members of Christ's Mystical Body, the Church, are united to him by the sacrament of baptism, so the marriage service unites husband and wife in a holy bond. That is what Paul is alluding to in his 'bathing in the water'; the marriage ceremony in those days resembled baptism in that a ceremonial bath was given to the

of service which tries to win human favour, but in the character of Christ's slaves, who do what is God's will with all their heart. Yours must be a slavery of love, not to men, but to the Lord; you know well that each of us, slave or free, will be repaid by the Lord for every task well done. And you who are masters, deal with them accordingly; there is no need to threaten them; you know well enough that you and they have a Master in heaven, who makes no distinction between man and man.

I have no more to say except this; draw your strength from the Lord, from that mastery which his power supplies. You must wear all the weapons in God's armoury, if you would find strength to resist the cunning of the devil. It is not against flesh and blood that we enter the lists; we have to do with princedoms and powers, with those who have mastery of the world in these dark days, with malign influences in an order higher than ours. Take up all God's armour, then; so you will be able to stand your ground when the evil time comes, and be found still on your feet, when all the task is over. Stand fast, your loins girt with truth, the breastplate of justice fitted on, and your feet shod in readiness to publish the gospel of peace. With all this, take up the shield of faith, with which you will be able to quench all the fire-tipped arrows of your wicked enemy; make the helmet of salvation your own, and the sword of the spirit, God's word. Use every kind of prayer and supplication; pray at all times in the spirit; keep awake to that end with all perseverance; offer your supplication for all the saints. Pray for me too, that I may be given words to speak my mind boldly, in making known the gospel revelation, for which I am an ambassador in chains; that I may have boldness to speak as I ought. If you would know more

bride on the eve of her wedding. There is something deep and beyond human comprehension ('a high mystery') in God's creating man and woman capable of the highest form of human love in the married state; it takes on a more profound meaning still when seen as a sharing in Christ's love for his Church.

A family prayer: 'Jesus, dearest Master, who lived and died for love of us, may our love for each other help us understand your deep, personal love for us; and please let it lead us to love you more and more.'

The Soldier of Christ. Paul was a prisoner in his hired house in Rome; a Roman soldier stood on guard night and day. A chain hung on the wall; at night, and whenever Paul left the house during the day, he was chained to the soldier on duty. It was the armour of this ever-present guard that suggested to Paul his illustration of what a Christian should wear in his fight against his spiritual enemies.

The devil is the principal enemy a Christian has to fight against; his power is far greater than that of any human enemies ('flesh and blood'), such as unconverted pagans and Jews who oppose and persecute Christians. The Master himself demonstrated this when he met Satan in battle at the very beginning of his Public Ministry (see Mt. 4, 1-11). Jesus came to destroy Satan's empire; but the devil does not give up without a struggle; he will do all in his power to win men away from their allegiance to Christ the Redeemer.

In listing the weapons a Christian must use in this spiritual warfare against Satan and his diabolical army, Paul picks out six items of a Roman soldier's armour: belt ('loins girt'), breastplate, shoes ('feet shod'), shield, helmet and sword. As he points out the significance of each of these parts of a soldier's equipment, he probably asked for and was given technical

of my circumstances, my occupations, you may learn all that from Tychicus, my dearly loved brother and faithful servant in the Lord; that is the reason why I have sent him, to let you have news of me, and to bring courage to your hearts. Peace to the brethren, and love joined with faith, from God the Father and our Lord Jesus Christ. Grace be with all those who love our Lord Jesus Christ with an immortal love.

Letter to the Colossians

From Paul, by God's purpose an apostle of Jesus Christ, and Timothy who is their brother, to the saints at Colossae, our brethren who believe in Christ, grace be yours and peace from God our Father. We give thanks to God, the Father of our Lord Jesus Christ, continually in our prayers for you, when we are told of your faith in Jesus Christ, and the love which you show to all the saints; such hope have you of what awaits you in heaven. Hope was the lesson you learned from that truth-giving message of the gospel which has reached you, which now bears fruit and thrives in you, as it does all the world over, since the day when you heard of God's grace and recognized it for what it is. Your teacher was Epaphras, for us, a well-loved fellow bondsman, and for you a loyal minister of Christ; and it is he who has told us of this love which you cherish in the Spirit. So, ever since the news reached us, we have been praying for you in return, unceasingly. Our prayer is, that you may be filled with that closer knowledge of the Lord's will which brings all wisdom and all spiritual insight with it. May you live as befits his servants, waiting continually on his pleasure; may the closer knowledge of God bring you

assistance by the stolid Roman guard standing by. The belt, or girdle, was drawn tight around the waist so that the soldier would be ready for action; 'justice' here means sanctifying grace by which the whole person is protected; 'God's word' is the divine message delivered by Christ, who made known God's final revelation to men.

Christ the King

Paul's Prayer for the Colossians. The man responsible for this letter was Epaphras, the founder of the church at Colossae in Asia. He was probably well known to Paul from his long stay of three years at Ephesus. Colossae was only 100 miles east of Ephesus, just off the main road to Antioch; although Paul had often been along this highway, he had never visited Colossae.

Paul greeted his fellow missionary with warmth; he was delighted at this unexpected visit from far-off Asia. The two sat down for a talk on the state of the Church in Epaphras' field of labour. All was not well at Colossae; the Christians there were showing an unhealthy interest in the world of spirits; they were engaged in dreaming and useless subtleties; their fantastic and extravagant theorizing on angels and demons was leading them to minimize the part played by Christ in their redemption and sanctification.

From his prison in Rome, Paul dictated this letter, Epaphras standing by to prompt and explain as Paul developed his reply to this first appearance of the heresy that later became known as Gnosticism. He begins with a prayer that is rather long and involved, as though he was having trouble in coming to grips

fruitfulness and growth in all good. May you be inspired, as
his glorious power can inspire you, with full strength to be
patient and to endure; to endure joyfully, thanking the Father
for making us fit to share the light which saints inherit, for
rescuing us from the power of darkness, and transferring us
to the kingdom of his beloved Son.

In the Son of God we find the redemption that sets us free
from our sins. He is the true likeness of the God we cannot
see; his is that first birth which precedes every act of creation.
Yes, in him all created things took their being, heavenly and
earthly, visible and invisible; what are thrones and dominions,
what are princedoms and powers? They were all created
through him and for him; he takes precedency of all, and in
him all subsist. He too is that head whose body is the Church;
it begins with him, since his was the first birth out of death;
thus in every way the primacy was to become his. It was God's
good pleasure to let all completeness dwell in him, and through
him to win back all things, whether on earth or in heaven,
into union with himself, making peace with them through
his blood, shed on the cross.

You, too, were once estranged from him; your minds were
alienated from him by a life of sin; but now he has used Christ's
natural body to win you back through his death, and so to
bring you into his presence, holy, and spotless, and unreproved. But that means that you must be true to your faith,
grounded in it, firmly established in it; nothing must shift
you away from the hope you found in the gospel you once
listened to. It is a gospel which has been preached to all creation under heaven, and I, Paul, have been brought into its
service.

with the problem; possibly he is somewhat diffident in rebuking a church that he himself did not found. He praises their faith, hope, and charity; then he wishes them a deeper knowledge, wisdom, and spiritual insight, without which they cannot understand the mysteries of the faith.

The Primacy of Christ. Gnosticism comes from the Greek word 'gnosis,' which means knowledge of the invisible God. According to the Gnostics, contact with God was made through intermediary spiritual beings, 'thrones, dominions, princedoms, and powers.' They put Christ in this category, among these angelic beings.

In refuting this pagan approach to God, Paul states the pre-eminent dignity of Christ both as creator and redeemer. The Gnostic idea that God has no interest in the material things of this world is completely wrong; he himself created it through his 'true likeness,' Christ the Second Person of the Trinity. Even these angelic beings were created by Christ; they came into existence through him who lives for all eternity.

Far from being apart and aloof from men, God himself has become a man like them; by shedding his blood on the cross Christ has won them from the power of sin, and brought them under his sovereignty. And after his resurrection, Christ has not left mankind alone; he still lives on as the vital power of the Church, the head from which the body draws all its spiritual strength, and by which it shares in God's own life. It is not necessary for the Colossians to go outside Christ to obtain contact with the God we cannot see; through him they have access to all the divine treasures of grace.

Even as I write, I am glad of my sufferings on your behalf, as, in this mortal frame of mine, I help to pay off the debt which the afflictions of Christ leave still to be paid, for the sake of his body, the Church. When I entered its service, I received a commission from God for the benefit of you Gentiles, to complete the preaching of his word among you. This was the secret that had been hidden from all the ages and generations of the past; now, he has revealed it to his saints, whom he wished to publish among the Gentiles the manifold splendour of this secret—Christ among you, your hope of glory. Him, then, we proclaim, warning every human being and instructing every human being as wisely as we may, so as to exhibit every human being perfect in Christ. It is for this that I labour, for this that I strive so anxiously; and with effect, so effectually does his power manifest itself in me.

And indeed, I must let you know what anxiety I feel over you, and the Laodiceans, and those others who have never seen me in person. I would bring courage to their hearts; I would see them well ordered in love, enriched in every way with fuller understanding, so as to penetrate the secret revealed to us by God: Christ, in whom the whole treasury of wisdom and knowledge is stored up. I tell you this, for fear that somebody may lead you astray with high-flown talk. In person, I am far away from you, but I am with you in spirit; and I rejoice to see how well disciplined you are, how firm is your faith in Christ. Go on, then, ordering your lives in Christ Jesus our Lord, according to the tradition you have received of him. You are to be rooted in him, built up on him, your faith established in the teaching you have received, overflowing with gratitude. Take care not to let anyone cheat you with his philosophizings, with empty phantasies drawn from

The Afflictions of Christ. The Roman guard at the door and the chain dragging on the wall were a constant reminder to Paul of the afflictions he was was suffering for Christ. They were a link with the Gentile churches of Asia, because it was on their account that he was now imprisoned; his arrest at Jerusalem, and the hostility of the Jews, came from his teaching that there was no longer any distinction between Jew and Gentile in the Church, the Mystical Body of Christ.

The essential event in our Lord's life was his passion and death; the members of his Mystical Body must live the same life as their thorn-crowned head. In his natural body Christ can suffer no more; it is only through his members, such as Paul, that he can continue his sufferings. It was a privilege for Paul to endure so much because it united him both to Christ and Christians.

The Incarnation and Redemption. At the Last Supper, the apostle Philip made this request of Jesus: 'Lord, let us see the Father; that is all we ask.' To which Jesus replied: 'Whoever has seen me, has seen the Father.' The outlook of the Colossian Christians was similar to that of Philip; they wanted contact with the Deity; they were seeking to penetrate the secrets of God. But they sought it through the world of spiritual beings, from philosophy, from mysticism and empty phantasies. They had forgotten the lesson they should have remembered from Bethlehem: God himself, 'the whole plenitude of Deity,' had come down in human form; in Christ 'the whole treasury of wisdom and knowledge is stored up.' By the Incarnation, God became accessible to men; the earthly life of Jesus in Palestine brought God close to his human creatures. They have only to study Jesus Christ to see what God himself is like.

human tradition, from worldly principles; they were never Christ's teaching. In Christ the whole plenitude of Deity is embodied, and dwells in him, and it is in him that you find your completion; he is the fountain head from which all dominion and power proceed. In him you have been circumcised with a circumcision that was not man's handiwork. It was effected by the despoiling of our sinful nature, by the circumcision of Christ; you, by baptism, have been united with his burial, united, too, with his resurrection, through your faith in that exercise of power by which God raised him from the dead. And in giving life to him, he gave life to you too, when you lay dead in your sins, with nature all uncircumcised in you. He condoned all our sins; cancelled the deed which excluded us, the decree made to our prejudice, swept it out of the way, by nailing it to the cross; and the dominions and powers he robbed of their prey, put them to an open shame, led them away in triumph, through him.

So no one must be allowed to take you to task over what you eat or drink, or in the matter of observing feasts, and new moons, and sabbath days; all these were but shadows cast by future events, the reality is found in Christ. You must not allow anyone to cheat you by insisting on a false humility which addresses its worship to angels. Such a man takes his stand upon false visions; his is the ill-founded confidence that comes of human speculation. He is not united to that head of ours, on whom all the body depends, supplied and unified by joint and ligament, and so growing up with a growth which is divine. If, by dying with Christ you have parted company with worldly principles, why do you live by these prescriptions, as if the world were still your element? Prescriptions against touching, or tasting, or handling those creatures which vanish

All religious systems have an initiation ceremony. With Judaism it was circumcision; with Christianity it is baptism. In those early days, baptism was by immersion; the person being baptized was plunged down into the water and raised up again. This always reminds Paul of Christ's death and resurrection; just as our Lord went down into the tomb and rose up again, so the Christian dies to his sins and his old corrupt nature and rises to a new life in Christ Jesus.

Paul often saw victory parades in the streets of Rome; every time a victorious general returned from a campaign he was given a triumphal procession. In a final, vivid scene he presents Christ's way of the cross as such a triumph. As a trophy of war he carried, as a title on his cross, the conquered Mosaic law (the deed which excluded the Gentiles from God's kingdom); in his train marched the angel custodians ('dominions and powers') of the Old Covenant, prisoners won in battle.

The Reality is Found in Christ. The Gnostics at Colossae were not content with mere speculation on the mediatorship of angels, they also adopted a number of ascetical practices in their daily lives. Their observance of the sabbath indicates that at least some of these practices were borrowed from Judaism; 'feasts and new moons' probably refers to the Jewish annual festivals of Passover, Pentecost, Tabernacles, and Dedication, as well as the celebration of the first day of each month (the new moon) as a special feast day. Their scruples about eating may also have been based on the Jewish kosher food laws. Paganism provided a number of superstitious bodily mortifications which made up the ascetical programme of the Gnostic false visionaries.

Paul lumps all these practices together as 'worldly prin-

altogether as we enjoy them, all based on the will and the word of men? They will win you, no doubt, the name of philosophers, for being so full of scruple, so submissive, so unsparing of your bodies; but they are all forgotten, when nature asks to be gratified.

Risen, then, with Christ, you must lift your thoughts above, where Christ now sits at the right hand of God. You must be heavenly-minded, not earthly-minded; you have undergone death, and your life is hidden away now with Christ in God. Christ is your life, and when he is made manifest, you too will be made manifest in glory with him. You must deaden, then, those passions in you which belong to earth, fornication and impurity, lust and evil desire, and that love of money which is an idolatry. These are what bring down God's vengeance on the unbelievers, and such was your own behaviour, too, while you lived among them. Now it is your turn to have done with it all, resentment, anger, spite, insults, foul-mouthed utterance; and do not tell lies at one another's expense. You must be quit of the old self, and the habits that went with it; you must be clothed in the new self, that is being refitted all the time for closer knowledge, so that the image of the God who created it is its pattern. Here is no more Gentile and Jew, no more circumcised and uncircumcised; no one is barbarian, or Scythian, no one is slave or free man; there is nothing but Christ in any of us.

You are God's chosen people, holy and well beloved; the livery you wear must be tender compassion, kindness, humility, gentleness and patience; you must bear with one another's faults, be generous to each other, where somebody has given grounds for complaint; the Lord's generosity to you must be the model of yours. And, to crown all this, charity; that is the

ciples.' They are without effect in the struggle man has to wage against his sinful nature; they fail in the attempt at union with God. That comes only from the union of the members of the Mystical Body with their Head; he is the reality for which men are groping.

Christ is Your Life. By baptism a Christian enters into membership of the Mystical Body of Christ; not only is his conduct patterned on the life of the Head, but his spiritual vitality flows from his union with Christ. When the Christian went down into the baptismal water, he was imitating Christ's burial in the tomb at Calvary; he was dead to his former way of life; all his sinful habits ('the old self') were to be laid aside like an old cloak. He rose from the water, as Christ rose from the tomb, a new man; from now on he lived with the power which came to him from Christ.

The false asceticism practised by the Colossians was probably based on the belief that some material things were evil. Paul points out that sin is in the will, not in things external to man. True mortification consists in overcoming vice and practising virtue; it is in conquering impure desires and avarice that a Christian shows true asceticism, not by beating his body or abstaining from certain foods.

In the second list of five sins, Paul seems to be visualizing some kind of divisions and quarreling among the Colossians; they were moved to anger, uncharitable remarks, and even lying about one another. Possibly national and class distinctions of Jew and Gentile, slave and free man, had flared up ('Scythian' means Russian, the most uncivilized people of that time). Paul's solution of the situation at Colossae is the practice of true mortification; he lists nine virtues which must be the uniform of true Christians, obliterating all distinctions

bond which makes us perfect. So may the peace of Christ, the very condition of your calling as members of a single body, reign in your hearts. Learn, too, to be grateful. May all the wealth of Christ's inspiration have its shrine among you; now you will have instruction and advice for one another, full of wisdom, now there will be psalms, and hymns, and spiritual music, as you sing with gratitude in your hearts to God. Whatever you are about, in word and action alike, invoke always the name of the Lord Jesus, offering your thanks to God the Father through him.

Wives must be submissive to their husbands, as the service of the Lord demands; and you, husbands, treat your wives lovingly, do not grow harsh with them. Children must be obedient to their parents in every way; it is a gracious sign of serving the Lord; and you, parents, must not rouse your children to resentment, or you will break their spirits. You who are slaves, give your human masters full obedience, not with that show of service which tries to win human favour, but single-mindedly, in fear of the Lord. Work at all your tasks with a will, reminding yourselves that you are doing it for the Lord, not for men; and you may be sure that the Lord will give the portion he has allotted you in return. Be slaves with Christ for your Master. Whoever does wrong will be requited for the wrong done; there are no human preferences with God. And you who are masters, give your slaves just and equitable treatment; you know well enough that you, too, have a Master in heaven.

Persevere in prayer, and keep wakeful over it with thankful hearts. Pray, too, for us; ask God to afford us an opening for preaching the revelation of Christ, which is the very cause of my imprisonment, and to give me the right utterance for

and uniting them in the person of Christ. Most important of all in the Christian uniform is the virtue of charity; it is the belt ('the bond') which keeps all the rest of the Christian clothing in place.

Paul concludes with a description of how the Mystical Body functions in peace and harmony when Christ is allowed to take possession of his members; it becomes a shrine in which all the inspiration of right living comes from Christ himself.

Be Slaves with Christ for Your Master. The type of oriental mysticism that was flourishing at Colossae multiplied new observances borrowed from Judaism and paganism and emphasized severe bodily mortifications. In the previous paragraph, Paul pointed out that true asceticism is found in combating vice and practising virtue. Here he continues the lesson by his insistence on sound family life as the basis of a good Christian life; the two virtues of obedience and charity are the main foundations of a healthy family life.

In the similar passage to the Ephesians, he gave most of his advice to husband and wife; here he concentrates on the life slaves should lead. He is probably still thinking of the spurious mortifications of the Colossians who wanted to win a name for holiness. They forgot that, as slaves of Christ, they should not try to please men; all their efforts should be directed to the only Master whose approval is worth having.

News from a Roman Prison. Prayer bridges all distances; the members of the Mystical Body can help each other, wherever they are, in all parts of the Empire. Like the Master himself, Paul emphasizes the importance of perseverance in prayer. He

making it known. Be prudent in your behaviour towards those who are not of your company; it is an opportunity you must eagerly grasp. Your manner of speaking must always be gracious, with an edge of liveliness, ready to give each questioner the right answer. You will hear how things go with me from Tychicus, my dearly loved brother and faithful servant, my fellow bondsman in the Lord; that is the reason why I have sent him, to let you have news of us, and to bring courage to your hearts; from Onesimus, too, a brother faithful and well beloved, who is of your own number; they will tell you how things stand here.

Greetings to you from my fellow prisoner Aristarchus, and from Mark, the kinsman of Barnabas, about whom you have been given instructions; if he visits you, make him welcome; from Jesus, too, whom they call Justus. These are the only Jews who have helped me to preach God's kingdom; they have been a comfort to me. Your own fellow countryman Epaphras sends you his greeting, a servant of Jesus Christ who ever remembers you anxiously in his prayers, hoping that you will stand firm in the perfect achievement of all that is God's will for you; I can vouch for him as one who is greatly concerned over you, and those others at Laodicea and Hierapolis. Greetings from my beloved Luke, the physician, and from Demas. Greet the brethren at Laodicea, and Nymphas, with the church that is in his household. When this letter has been read out to you, see that it is read out to the Laodicean church too, and that you read the letter they have received at Laodicea. Give this message to Archippus: 'Be careful to fulfil the duty which has been committed to you in the Lord's service.' Here is a greeting for you from Paul in his own hand; do not forget that he is a prisoner. Grace be with you.

asks the Colossians for their prayers to help him in his apostolate of preaching Christ to all men. They too have the same obligation of spreading the gospel among those with whom they live; all Christians must be ready to give a charitable answer about any point of the faith to any questioner.

It is clear from Philippians 1, 15-17 that some Jewish Christians in Rome preached 'Christ from wrong motives, just because they hope to make my chains gall me worse.' In Paul's list of people who sent greetings to Colossae, three of the eight people, Aristarchus, Mark, and Jesus Justus, were the only Jewish Christians then in Rome who co-operated with Paul in preaching the gospel. Evidently the Jewish converts were unsympathetic to Paul because of his championing of the Gentiles.

The other five people who sent greetings were all of Gentile origin. Tychicus, an Ephesian disciple, was the bearer of this letter, as well as of Ephesians and Philemon. Onesimus was the convert slave about whom Paul wrote the Letter to Philemon, a wealthy Colossian Christian. Luke was the author of the Third Gospel; Demas later deserted Paul, 'falling in love with this present world.' Epaphras was the apostle of Colossae; it was he who brought to Paul in Rome the details of how some Colossians had gone over to the false doctrines and superstitious practices of Gnosticism. If he is to be identified with Epaphroditus (Phil. 2, 25-30), he stayed a little longer with Paul before returning via Philippi.

Archippus was probably in charge of the Colossian church during the absence of Epaphras. The Letter to Laodicea is identified by some with Ephesians; others regard it as an otherwise unknown and now lost letter. Nymphas is the only name we know from Laodicea, a church that is sternly rebuked by St. John (Apoc. 2, 14).

Letter to Philemon

Paul, a prisoner of Jesus Christ, and Timothy, who is their brother, to the well beloved Philemon, who shares our labours, and to all the church that is in his household, to our dear sister Appia, Archippus, who fights the same battle with ourselves, and the rest; grace and peace be yours from God, our Father, and from the Lord Jesus Christ.

I give thanks to my God at all times, remembering you in my prayers; such accounts I hear of the love and faith you show towards the Lord Jesus and towards all the saints. May your sharing in the faith become effective, in the fuller knowledge of all the good that is in us in Christ. It has been a happiness and a comfort to me to hear of your charity, brother, and of the refreshment you have brought to the hearts of the saints. And now, though I might well make bold in Christ to prescribe a duty to you, I prefer to appeal to this charity of yours. Who is it that writes to you? Paul, an old man now, and in these days a prisoner, too, of Jesus Christ; and I am appealing to you on behalf of Onesimus, the child of my imprisonment. He did you an ill service once; now, both to you and to myself, he can be serviceable, and I am sending him back to you; make him welcome, for my heart goes with him. I would sooner have kept him here with me, to attend, as your deputy, on a prisoner of the gospel, but I would do nothing without your leave; your generosity should be exercised freely, not from lack of choice. Perhaps, after all, the very purpose of your losing him for a time was that you might have him always by you. Do not think of him any longer as a slave; he is something more than a slave, a well loved brother, to me in a special way; much more, then, to you, now that both nature and Christ make him your own. As you value your fellowship with me, make him welcome as you would

Onesimus the Slave

The best place for a fugitive from justice to hide in is a big city; the further it is from the scene of the crime and the people to whom he is known, the better. That is why Onesimus wound up at Rome, a thousand miles away from his master Philemon of Colossae. The money he had stolen from Philemon was soon used up; freedom has its drawbacks when a man is hungry and cold and finds it almost impossible to get work. At this stage, Onesimus went to Paul's lodging for help. Though not a Christian himself, he had often heard Philemon, his wife, Appia, and son, Archippus, speaking of Paul's charity and sympathy for all mankind (they had been converted by Paul during his long three years at Ephesus, 54-57 A.D.). Drawn by Paul's magnetism, he came back again and again. Paul gave him more than financial assistance; as he spoke to Onesimus of the crucified Jesus, grace entered Onesimus' soul and he received the gift of faith.

Christianity does not change a man's social position; even though baptized, Onesimus was still a slave. To have freed slaves would have meant a civil war in the Empire, and worse conditions for the slaves than before; also it would have led to false conversions to the Christian faith. Paul decided to send Onesimus back with Tychicus, who was carrying the Letters to the Ephesians and Colossians. He wrote a third Letter, this little gem of tact and urbanity which is an excellent illustration of his literary art; it shows a finesse of word selection that is not surpassed in any of Paul's longer and more famous letters.

Onesimus means profitable; it was a name probably given by Philemon when he bought him in the slave market, a real bargain. The name seemed to have been badly chosen when Onesimus robbed his master and ran away to Rome. That is

myself; if he has wronged you, or is in your debt, make me
answerable for it. Here is a message in Paul's own hand; I
will make it good. Not to remind you that you owe me a
debt already, yourself. And now, brother, let me claim your
services in the Lord; give comfort in Christ to my anxious
heart. I write to you counting on your obedience, well assured that you will do even more than I ask. Be prepared,
meanwhile, to entertain me; I hope, through your prayers, to
be restored to you. Greetings to you from Epaphras, my fellow prisoner in Christ Jesus; from Mark, Aristarchus, Demas
and Luke, who share my labours. The grace of the Lord Jesus
Christ be with your spirit. Amen.

Letter to the Philippians

Paul and Timothy, the servants of Jesus Christ, to all the
saints in Christ Jesus that are at Philippi, with their pastors
and deacons; grace and peace be yours from God who is our
Father, and from the Lord Jesus Christ. I give thanks to my
God for all my memories of you, happy at all times in all the
prayer I offer for all of you; so full a part have you taken in
the work of Christ's gospel, from the day when it first reached
you till now. Nor am I less confident, that he who has inspired this generosity in you will bring it to perfection, ready
for the day when Jesus Christ comes. It is only fitting that I
should entertain such hopes for you; I am close to your heart,
and I know that you all share with me this grace in being a
prisoner, and being able to defend and assert the truth of the
gospel. God knows how I long for you all, with the tenderness
of Christ Jesus himself. And this is my prayer for you; may

not so, says Paul. It has led to the conversion of Onesimus, and now his return to his master, surely a most profitable bargain to all concerned. Instead of a slave, Philemon now has a brother: 'No more slave and freeman; you are all one person in Jesus Christ.' That is how Christianity elevates slaves, by obliterating all distinctions through membership in the Mystical Body. Paul prefers to appeal to Philemon's well-known charity, rather than put him under an obligation. But he gently reminds Philemon of the debt he owes him for the gift of faith that came through Paul's instructions. Philemon owes Paul the enormous debt of his own self; whereas Onesimus only stole a sum of money. But one act of forgiveness will square the accounts.

Joy to You in the Lord

A Thankful Prayer. Thirteen years before, Paul had a vision at Troas; he saw a Philippian appealing to him, 'Come over into Macedonia, and help us.' At Philippi on this occasion he converted a wealthy widow, Lydia, a possessed girl, and the gaoler and his family (Acts 16). The city was a Roman colony of old soldiers, and most of the congregation were from these army families. They were Paul's most loyal church, contributing to his material needs many times throughout the course of his missionary journeys. They had sent a sum of money by Epaphroditus to help him over his imprisonment and to defray the costs of his coming trial. They also sent a message of sympathy to him in his chains, showing their solidarity with their beloved apostle in his sufferings for Christ.

The primary purpose of this letter is to thank them for their kindness and thoughtfulness. Philippi was Paul's favourite

your love grow richer and richer yet, in the fullness of its knowledge and the depth of its perception, so that you may learn to prize what is of value; may nothing cloud your conscience or hinder your progress till the day when Christ comes; may you reap, through Jesus Christ, the full harvest of your justification to God's glory and praise.

I hasten to assure you, brethren, that my circumstances here have only had the effect of spreading the gospel further; so widely has my imprisonment become known, in Christ's honour, throughout the praetorium and to all the world beyond. And most of the brethren, deriving fresh confidence in the Lord from my imprisonment, are making bold to preach God's word with more freedom than ever. Some of them, it is true, for no better reason than rivalry or jealousy; but there are others who really proclaim Christ out of goodwill. Some, I mean, are moved by charity, because they recognize that I am here to defend the gospel, others by party spirit, proclaiming Christ from wrong motives, just because they hope to make my chains gall me worse. What matter, so long as either way, for private ends or in all honesty, Christ is proclaimed? Of that I am glad now; yes, and I shall be glad hereafter; I am well assured that this will make for my soul's health, with you to pray for me, and Jesus Christ to supply my needs with his Spirit. This is my earnest longing and my hope, that I shall never be put to the blush; that I shall speak with entire freedom, and so this body of mine will do Christ honour, now as always, in life or in death. For me, life means Christ; death is a prize to be won. But what if living on in this mortal body is the only way to harvest what I have sown? Thus I cannot tell what to choose; I am hemmed in on both sides. I long to have done

church, and this is his tenderest letter. Their sympathy moves him to thank God for such love and affection, and to pray for the welfare of his devoted Philippians. Paul's reaction to sympathy was as spontaneous and deep as that of the Master himself; when he was dying on the cross a word of consolation from the Good Thief was rewarded by Jesus with eternal life.

Paul's Imprisonment All for the Best. It was near the end of Paul's fifth year in prison. His converts at Philippi felt sorry for him, and depressed at the thought of their beloved apostle languishing so long in chains. Paul had been imprisoned when he first arrived at Philippi; the gaoler there, one of Paul's converts, knew how depressing prison life could be; he was most unhappy to see Paul subjected for so long a period to the rigours and sufferings of imprisonment.

Paul tries to cheer them up by pointing out that the notoriety of his case was good publicity for the gospel; the faith was spreading more rapidly because of this than if he were free to resume his missionary journeys. The Lord inspired many of the timid Christians of Rome with zeal and courage to preach the gospel. The motives of others were not so good, but Christ was being preached just the same. These latter seem to have been Jewish Christians who were opposed to Paul because of his championing of the Gentiles' cause. They were eagerly trying to win over their Jewish brethren to the faith, so that the Roman church would not be swamped by Gentile converts. They made an all-out effort to win more converts than the Gentile Christians while the Gentile's champion was locked up and unable to compete with them.

Though Paul knew (possibly by revelation) that he would be freed at his coming trial, he was indifferent to life or death.

with it, and be with Christ, a better thing, much more than a better thing; and yet, for your sakes, that I should wait in the body is more urgent still. I am certain of that, and I do not doubt that I shall wait, and wait upon you all, to the happy furtherance of your faith. Yes, you shall be prouder of me than ever in Christ Jesus, when I come once again to visit you.

Only, you must play a part worthy of Christ's gospel; whether I come to see you, or only hear about you at a distance, this must be my news of you, that you are standing fast in a common unity of spirit, with the faith of the gospel for your common cause. Show a bold front at all points to your adversaries; that is the seal of their perdition, of your salvation, and it comes from God; the grace that has been granted you is that of suffering for Christ's sake, not merely believing in him. Your battle is my own battle; you saw how I fought it once, and you have heard how I am fighting it now.

If anything is meant by encouragement in Christ, by loving sympathy, by common fellowship in the spirit, by feelings of tenderness and pity, fill up my cup of happiness by thinking with the same mind, cherishing the same bond of charity, soul knit to soul in a common unity of thought. You must never act in a spirit of factiousness, or of ambition; each of you must have the humility to think others better men than himself, and study the welfare of others, not his own. Yours is to be the same mind which Christ Jesus showed. His nature is, from the first, divine, and yet he did not see, in the rank of Godhead, a prize to be coveted; he dispossessed himself, and took the nature of a slave, fashioned in the likeness of men, and presenting himself to us in human form; and then he lowered his own dignity, accepted an obedience which brought him death, death on a cross. That is why God has raised him to such a height, given

For Paul 'life means Christ.' This is the union with Jesus by
membership in the Mystical Body: 'I am the way, I am truth
and life.' Bodily death opens the way to the perfect union
of the beatific vision; this is the goal of all men. But the
Mystical Body can only be built up by labouring for Christ
here on this earth; that is why Paul is content to remain alive.

Humility of the Incarnation. The most practical way the
Philippians can console Paul is by reforming their lives. They
were worried and anxious about his imprisonment; so he tells
them that the only thing which can make him unhappy is to
see them proud, uncharitable, and wanting in that harmony
and unity so essential to the Mystical Body of Christ. Later
(4, 2) he makes mention of a squabble going on between two
ladies of the congregation; it may have been more widespread,
judging by the way he urges them to give up personal rights.

Paul has taken the thoughts of the Philippians off himself
to fix their minds on their own lives. The second step is to
get them thinking of Christ our Lord: 'He is that head of
ours, on whom all the body depends, supplied and unified by
joint and ligament, and so growing up with a growth that is
divine.' The scene Paul presents to the Philippians is the birth
of Christ at Bethlehem. When the Second Person of the
Blessed Trinity became man, he laid aside the glory that right-
fully belonged to him as God; there were no courtiers to bow
the knee in worship; his creatures on earth saw in the baby
at Bethlehem a being like themselves, not the Creator of the
universe. He was not even born a prince in a palace, where
some honour would have been paid him; his parents were
ordinary folk, and he was born in a stable. His babyhood
made him so dependent on others that his status resembled
that of a slave rather than of a prince.

him that name which is greater than any other name; so that everything in heaven and on earth and under the earth must bend the knee before the name of Jesus, and every tongue must confess Jesus Christ as the Lord, to the glory of God the Father.

Beloved, you have always shown yourselves obedient; and now that I am at a distance, not less but much more than when I am present, you must work to earn your salvation, in anxious fear. Both the will to do it and the accomplishment of that will are something which God accomplishes in you, to carry out his loving purpose. Do all that lies in you, never complaining, never hesitating, to show yourselves innocent and single-minded, God's children, bringing no reproach on his name. You live in an age that is twisted out of its true pattern, and among such people you shine out, beacons to the world, upholding the message of life. Thus, when the day of Christ comes, I shall be able to boast of a life not spent in vain, of labours not vainly undergone. Meanwhile, though your faith should prove to be a sacrifice which cannot be duly made without my blood for its drink-offering, I congratulate myself and all of you over that; on your side, you too must congratulate yourselves and me.

It is my hope in the Lord Jesus that I shall be sending Timothy to visit you before long; then I shall be able to refresh myself with news of you; I have no one else here who shares my thoughts as he does, no one who will concern himself so unaffectedly with your affairs; one and all have their own interest at heart, not Christ's; his worth is well tried, you must know that he has shared my task of preaching the gospel like a son helping his father. Him, then, I hope to send without

The Philippians are not to insist on their rights and privileges; they are to cast them aside, humiliate themselves by giving in to the opinions of others. It is only by waiving their rights that they can imitate the divine outlook at the Incarnation. Paul could have (it may have come to his mind as he wrote) reminded them of how he did not take the opportunity of claiming Roman citizenship when he was arrested and flogged in Philippi (Acts 16); it was because he was thinking of Christ that he did not claim his privileged status.

The Incarnation was an act of humility for Christ as God, the Crucifixion an act of humility for Christ as Man. There were no half measures with our Lord; he would humiliate himself to the extreme limit of a slave's death on the cross. As members of Christ's Mystical Body, the Christians of Philippi must not be cast down by sufferings; it is a necessary part of their life to be subject to opposition and persecution from the world around them; by their imitation of the humiliated Master they 'shine out, beacons to the world.' Paul's absence should not be a barrier to their spiritual advancement; it is to Jesus that they should turn as the centre of their lives, because he is God.

News of Timothy and Epaphroditus. When he wrote to the Colossians, Paul sent greetings from nine of his disciples; now, in this letter, there were only two of them left with him. This means that the inactivity of the winter months had passed, and Paul's disciples had taken to the road once more to visit the churches scattered throughout the provinces; it must have been about the month of April 63 A.D.

Timothy had been a disciple of Paul for thirteen years;

15*

delay, when I have had time to see how I stand; and I am
persuaded in the Lord that I myself shall be coming to you
before long.

Meanwhile, here is Epaphroditus, my brother, my companion in so many labours and battles, your own delegate, who
has provided for my needs. I felt that I must send him to you,
so great was his longing to see you, and his distress that you
should have heard about his illness. Ill he certainly was, and in
near danger of death; but God had pity on him, and not only
on him but on me too; he would not let me have anxiety
added to anxiety. So I am hastening to send him back to you;
it will be a happiness for you to see him again, and I shall be
anxious no longer. Welcome him, then, in the Lord gladly,
and do honour to such a man as he is; one who came close to
death's door on Christ's errand, risking life itself to do me that
kindness, which was all your kindness left to be desired.

And now, brethren, joy to you in the Lord. I find no difficulty
in always writing the same message to you, and it is your safeguard. Beware of these prowling dogs, beware of their evil
practices, of their disfigurement. As for circumcision, it is we
who practise it, we who worship by the Spirit of God, and
take pride in Jesus Christ, instead of putting our trust in outward observances. Not that I have no outward claims to give
me confidence; if others put their trust in outward claims, I
can do so with better reason. I was circumcised seven days
after I was born; I came from the stock of Israel, from the tribe
of Benjamin, Hebrew-speaking as my parents were before me.
Over the law, I was a Pharisee; to prove my loyalty, I persecuted the Church; in observing what the law commands, I was
beyond reproach. And all this, which once stood to my credit, I
now write down as loss, for the love of Christ. For that matter,

he was his most trusted lieutenant. Since he could not come to Philippi himself, Paul would send Timothy to set their minds at rest; he would be able to give first-hand news that Paul was not pining away in prison; and so a great source of worry would be removed from the minds of the anxious Philippians.

Epaphras and Epaphroditus are two forms of the same name (like Silas and Silvanus); they probably refer to the one person. He came from Colossae to report on the Asian churches; on his way overland he passed through Philippi. They took the opportunity of sending a gift of money by him to Paul at Rome. At the moment Epaphroditus was recovering from a severe bout of Roman fever; but Paul felt he would be well enough to make the journey along the Appian Way and the Egnatian Way, and carry the Letter to the Philippians with him.

A Warning Against the Judaizers. At this point of the letter, Paul most unexpectedly introduces the subject of the Judaizers. It is abrupt even for Paul, well known though he is for sudden changes of topic and for mental gymnastics. There may have been a day's break in his letter writing, and some fresh item of news of the evil the Judaizers were causing, possibly in Rome itself, moved Paul to set down his warning against this danger. Philippi had no large colony of Jews; it did not even have a synagogue. Possibly the nearby Thessalonian Jews were causing trouble in Philippi; maybe the people of Philippi needed warning because of its position on the Egnation Way; among the travellers passing through would be a good number belonging to the Judaizers.

Paul had battled fiercely in his Letter to the Galatians for the freedom of Christians from the Mosaic law; he produced

there is nothing I do not write down as loss compared with the high privilege of knowing Christ Jesus, my Lord; for love of him I have lost everything, treat everything else as refuse, if I may have Christ to my credit. In him I would render my account, not claiming any justification that is my own work, given me by the law, but the justification that comes from believing in Jesus Christ, God's gift on condition of our faith. Him I would learn to know, and the virtue of his resurrection, and what it means to share his sufferings, moulded into the pattern of his death, in the hope of achieving resurrection from the dead.

Not that I have already won the prize, already reached fulfilment. I only press on, in hope of winning the mastery, as Christ Jesus has won the mastery over me. No, brethren, I do not claim to have the mastery already, but this at least I do; forgetting what I have left behind, intent on what lies before me, I press on with the goal in view, eager for the prize, God's heavenly summons in Christ Jesus. All of us who are fully grounded must be of this mind, and God will make it known to you, if you are of a different mind at present. Meanwhile, let us all follow the same rule, according to the progress we have made. Be content, brethren, to follow my example, and mark well those who live by the pattern we have given them; I have told you often, and now tell you again with tears, that there are many whose lives make them the enemies of Christ's cross. Perdition is the end that awaits them, their own hungry bellies are the god they worship, their own shameful doings are their pride; their minds are set on the things of earth; whereas we find our true home in heaven. It is to heaven that we look expectantly for the coming of the Lord Jesus Christ to save us; he will form this humbled body of ours anew, moulding it into

a more studied statement of the case in his Letter to the Romans. The subject had exercised his mind and kept him alert throughout his missionary life, so that he wrote easily and spontaneously of it. Here he takes his own life as a typical example of how Christ frees a Christian from Judaism; Paul was a Jew to his finger tips, the rabbi who found Christ and gave up his national inheritance. Christ is his life, all else is mere refuse; he is prepared to lose everything to gain Christ. It is especially by suffering that Paul shares in the life of Jesus; the Christian must first die with Christ so that he can enjoy the glory of the resurrection.

Victory Not Won Yet. Membership in the Mystical Body is not a guarantee of the enjoyment of God's presence in heaven; a Christian still has to attain this goal by running the race of life like an athlete. Christ takes possession of the Christian at baptism, and the whole purpose of the Christian's life from then on is to win Christ for himself; the beatific vision is a prize to be won by living a good Christian life.

Paul presents this in the first person. He is thinking of how Christ mastered him on the road to Damascus (like Francis Thompson's 'Hound of Heaven'); just as Christ pursued and overtook Paul, so Paul is now striving to take possession of Christ by faith and love.

It seems that Paul has forgotten the Judaizers. Here he is thinking rather of those false Christians who considered that Christian freedom put them above even the moral law; their avarice ('hungry bellies') and incontinence ('shameful doings') were leading them to perdition, not to Christ. Worldly thoughts and desires are unbecoming to a Christian whose true life is to share Christ's life. Christ came from heaven to earth, and he returned there at the Ascension; he will come

the image of his glorified body, so effective is his power to make all things obey him.

Then, O my brethren, so greatly loved and longed for, all my delight and prize, stand firmly in the Lord, beloved, as I bid you. I call upon you, Evodia, and I call upon you, Syntyche, to make common cause in the Lord. Yes, and I ask you, who share the yoke so loyally, to take part with them; they have worked for the gospel at my side, as much as Clement and those other fellow labourers of mine, whose names are recorded in the book of life.

Joy to you in the Lord at all times; once again I wish you joy. Give proof to all of your courtesy. The Lord is near. Nothing must make you anxious; in every need make your requests known to God, praying and beseeching him, and giving him thanks as well. So will the peace of God, which surpasses all our thinking, watch over your hearts and minds in Christ Jesus. And now, brethren, all that rings true, all that commands reverence, and all that makes for right; all that is pure, all that is lovely, all that is gracious in the telling; virtue and merit, wherever virtue and merit are found—let this be the argument of your thoughts. The lessons I taught you, the traditions I handed on to you, all you have heard and seen of my way of living—let this be your rule of conduct. Then the God of peace will be with you.

It has been a great happiness to me in the Lord that your remembrance of me should have blossomed out afresh. It has flowered late, but then, you had never forgotten me; it was only that you lacked the opportunity. I am not thinking of my own want; I have learned by now to be content with my circumstances as they are. I know what it is to be brought low,

back from heaven to confer eternal glory on our bodies. Surely heaven is the true home of a Christian.

Concord, Joy and Peace. It has been suggested that Evodia and Syntyche were members of Lydia's household, and that Paul was addressing her in the phrase, 'you who share the yoke so loyally.' But the Greek words that underlie the phrase are masculine; so they must indicate a man. Some suggest Luke, who may have returned to Philippi before this letter was written; others think that the phrase should not be translated, that it is really a proper name, Syzygus; he may have been in charge of the church at Philippi as its bishop.

Paul repeats the word 'joy' eleven times in this letter. It is not a virtue, but it is the atmosphere in which virtue thrives, the light by which it sees. Paganism had lost all knowledge of true happiness; it could only grope blindly in a degenerate culture. Christianity goes to the Lord, the source of all joy; it is only from the heart of God that true happiness flows.

Christian joy embraces everything that is good in the world; it is in league with everything that is true, good, noble, and beautiful; it absorbs and makes its own what is best in the surrounding culture. Paul shows a fine delicacy and sensitivity in his selection of these eight phrases, the Magna Charta of artists.

Final Acknowledgment of Alms. The main reason for writing this letter was to thank the Philippians for their generous gift of money. Right at the beginning of the letter, Paul did make mention of their generosity; but here he thanks them in a more formal fashion. He seems to have been rather embarrassed at receiving such gifts; that is why he assumes a playful tone

and what it is to have abundant means; I have been apprenticed to everything, having my fill and going hungry, living in plenty and living in want; nothing is beyond my powers, thanks to the strength God gives me. No, but it was kindness in you to share my hardships in this way. You remember, Philippians, as well as I do, that when I left Macedonia in those early days of gospel preaching, yours was the only church whose sympathy with me meant alms given and received; not once but twice, when I was at Thessalonica, you contributed to my needs. It is not that I set store by your alms; I set store by the rich increase that stands to your credit. I am content, more than content; I am fully endowed, ever since Epaphroditus brought me your gift, a sacrifice that breathes out fragrance, winning favour with God. So will he, the God I serve, supply every need of yours; he has treasures of glory laid up in Jesus Christ. Glory to God, who is our Father, for ever and ever, Amen.

Greet all the saints in Christ Jesus. The brethren who are with me send you their greeting; greeting, too, from all the saints, especially those who belong to the Emperor's household. The grace of the Lord Jesus Christ be with your spirit, Amen.

Letter to Titus

It is Paul who writes; God's servant, sent out as an apostle of Jesus Christ, with the faith of God's elect for his care; they were to acknowledge that truth which accords with holiness, and fix their hopes on eternal life. It had been promised to us long ages since by the God who cannot fail us; and now, in due

in this paragraph. He is trying to hide his real, deep feelings under facetiousness and humour.

He has two vivid illustrations of their almsgiving. Their thoughtfulness for him is like the sudden flowering of a tree (since he is writing at the end of winter, this image may have been suggested to him by the blossoming trees outside his window). The second illustration is from the incense of sacrifice; their gift goes up to God like the smoke of incense, winning his favour.

In 2 Corinthians 11, 9 Paul related that the Philippians sent him money at Corinth, as well as on the two occasions mentioned in this paragraph. It is quite likely that there were other occasions during the course of his missionary journeys. The person mainly responsible for these gifts was undoubtedly the wealthy widow Lydia; she seems to have been a forceful character, who successfully overcame Paul's scruples about taking money from the churches he had founded.

'The Emperor's household' probably refers to the soldiers guarding Paul; they were members of the Pretorian guard, which was part of the Imperial household; no doubt Paul had already converted some of them.

The Church in Crete

Worthy Priests and False Teachers. A few months after Paul wrote to the Philippians, an imperial messenger knocked on the door of his hired house in Rome. His case had been dismissed; he was now a free man. The chain hanging on the wall was removed, and Paul no longer had a guard at the door.

time, he has made his meaning clear to us, through the preaching with which God, our Saviour, has seen fit to entrust me. To Titus, my own son in the faith we share, grace and peace from God the Father, and from Christ Jesus our Saviour.

If I left you behind me in Crete, it was to put all in order, where order is still needed. It is for you to appoint presbyters, as I enjoined, in each city, always looking for a man who is beyond reproach, faithful to one wife; one whose children hold the faith, not accused of reckless living, not wanting in obedience. A bishop, after all, since he is the steward of God's house, must needs be beyond reproach. He must not be an obstinate or quarrelsome man, one who drinks deep, or comes to blows, or is grasping over money. He must be hospitable, kindly, discreet, upright, unworldly and continent. He must hold firmly to the truths which have tradition for their warrant; able, therefore, to encourage sound doctrine, and to show the wayward their error.

There are many rebellious spirits abroad, who talk of their own fantasies and lead men's minds astray; those especially who hold by circumcision; and they must be silenced. They will bring ruin on entire households by false teaching, with an eye to their own base profits. Why, one of themselves, a spokesman of their own, has told us, 'The men of Crete were ever liars, venomous creatures, all hungry belly and nothing besides'; and that is a true account of them. Be strict, then, in taking them to task, so that they may be soundly established in the faith, instead of paying attention to these Jewish fables, these rules laid down for them by human teachers who will not look steadily at the truth. As if anything could be unclean for those who have clean hearts! But for these men, defiled as they are by want of faith, everything is unclean; defilement has entered their very thought, their very consciences. They profess

Word soon spread among the Christians, and a continual stream of Paul's converts kept coming to the house to congratulate him.

Soon after his liberation, Paul was on the march again. He had promised Philemon that he would come and stay with him at Colossae; also he was anxious to visit his churches in the East. He probably went along the Appian Way, crossed the Adriatic Sea from Brindisi to Dyrrachium, and made for Philippi, where he picked up his disciple, Timothy. From there he journeyed by sea to Ephesus, and then inland to Philemon's house at Colossae.

For some time Paul had intended to visit Spain. It was probably in 64 A.D., about a year after his liberation from his Roman prison, that he went on board a ship at Ephesus bound for Marseilles; from there he went to Spain. Most likely Timothy was one of his companions, and Rufus, the son of Simon of Cyrene, whom he left in charge of the church at Tortosa in Spain.

The next year Paul returned via Rome to Ephesus, where he picked up Titus, and together they took ship for the island of Crete. Titus had proved himself an able diplomat in his handling of a difficult situation in Corinth some seven years earlier (see 2 Corinthians); so Paul could safely leave him to set the Cretan church in order. After a month or so Paul left Crete for Ephesus; there he appointed Timothy to be his legate while he himself made his way north again to Philippi. It was from this city that he wrote the Letter to Titus in Crete.

There had been Jews from Crete at Jerusalem when the Holy Spirit came down on Pentecost Sunday, thirty-five years earlier. They probably brought Christianity to the island. It had been a neglected outpost, and was now in need of reform. This letter is meant to encourage Titus to carry out the instructions Paul had given him before he left Crete. He is

recognition of God, but their practice contradicts it; it is they who are abominable, who are disloyal, who are ill qualified for the practice of any true virtue.

Yours is to be a different message, with sound doctrine for its rule. Teach the older men to be sober, decent, orderly, soundly established in faith, in charity, in patience. The older women, too, must carry themselves as befits a holy calling, not given to slanderous talk or enslaved to drunken habits; teaching others by their good example. From them the younger women must learn orderly behaviour, how to treat their husbands and their children lovingly, how to be discreet, modest, busy about the house, kindly, submissive to their own husbands; the preaching of God's word must not be brought into disrepute. Encourage the young men, too, to live orderly lives. Let them find in all you do the model of a life nobly lived; let them find you disinterested in your teaching, worthy of their respect, your doctrine sound beyond all cavil; so that our adversaries may blush to find that they have no opportunity for speaking ill of us. Slaves must be submissive to their own masters, so as to content them in every way; no arguing, no pilfering; they must give good proof of utter fidelity, every action of theirs bringing credit to the teaching which God, our Saviour, has revealed.

The grace of God has dawned, salutary to all men alike, schooling us to forgo irreverent thoughts and worldly appetites, and to live, in this present world, a life of order, of justice, and of holiness. We were to look forward, blessed in our hope, to the day when there will be a new dawn of glory, the glory of our great God and Saviour Jesus Christ; who gave

to appoint worthy ministers throughout the island and silence the false teachers. These latter seem to have been Judaizers; they gave a dangerous emphasis to the teachings of the Mosaic law, with its prescriptions as to clean and unclean food.

Christians Must Exercise Self-Restraint. While Paul was away in Spain, the city of Rome was almost completely destroyed by fire; that was in July 64 A.D., a little more than a year before this Letter to Titus. The Christians were falsely blamed for the fire and were subjected to the first great persecution by the emperor Nero. Throughout the Empire Christians had a bad name; they were now looked on as the worst of criminals; they were living in most perilous times.

This changed situation explains why Paul here tells the Christians of Crete not to give an opportunity to their enemies of speaking ill of them. He is not setting forth the ideal of Christian conduct but prescribing the minimum of good exterior behaviour required to avoid giving scandal to the world around them. That is why he emphasizes such things as intemperance.

Paul usually addresses his Christians as a family group: husband and wife, parents and children, masters and slaves. Here, for the first time, he divides them into age groups. The reason may be that the Church was now 35 years old, and gray hairs were more noticeable; also Paul, now old, was more conscious of age groups.

God's Kindness: Christmas. A persecuted people is naturally inclined to retaliate. Why should they be loyal to a government that regards them as outlaws? They engage in criticism, lose their tempers, and pick quarrels with their pagan neighbours. Paul knows that they need a powerful motive to overcome their natural human reactions. And in this paragraph

himself for us, to ransom us from all our guilt, a people set apart for himself, ambitious of noble deeds. Be this your message, lending all authority to your encouragement and your reproof. Let no man lightly esteem you.

Remind them that they have a duty of submissive loyalty to governments and to those in authority, of readiness to undertake any kind of honourable service. They are not to speak injuriously of anyone, or pick quarrels; they must be considerate, and lose no opportunity of showing courtesy to the world around them. We, after all, were once like the rest of them, reckless, rebellious, the dupes of error; enslaved to a strange medley of desires and appetites, our lives full of meanness and of envy, hateful, and hating one another. Then the kindness of God, our Saviour, dawned on us, his great love for man. He saved us; and it was not thanks to anything we had done for our own justification. In accordance with his own merciful design he saved us, with the cleansing power which gives us new birth, and restores our nature through the Holy Spirit, shed on us in abundant measure through our Saviour, Jesus Christ. So, justified by his grace, we were to become heirs, with the hope of eternal life set before us.

It is well said, and I would have you dwell on it, that 'Those who have learned to trust in God should be at pains to find honourable employment.' That is their duty, and the world will benefit by it. But take no part in vain researches into pedigrees, and controversies that wrangle over points of the law; they are useless folly. Give a heretic one warning, then a second, and after that avoid his company; his is a perverse nature, you may be sure, and his fault has been admitted on his own confession.

When I send for you by Artemas or Tychicus, make haste

he appeals to the great kindness of God in sending Christ to
free us from sin. A Christian must show the same consideration for the world around him. The Incarnation has changed
him completely; he can no longer live as he did before baptism. Christ will come a second time to reward him for a life
well lived.

Paul uses the word 'dawn' three times in this paragraph; the
sun rising over a darkened world is a vivid picture of the Incarnation. Our Lord spoke of himself as 'the light of the
world.' Maybe Paul had been reading the Gospel of Luke
(it was published during his Roman captivity); it is there
that the details of our Lord's birth at night in Bethlehem are
set down: 'In the same country there were shepherds living
out in the fields, keeping night-watches over their flocks.'

Two of the Epistles for Christmas Day Masses are taken
from this paragraph; so that Christians down the centuries
have been reading these words in the same atmosphere in
which they were written. Though Christmas was not kept as a
special Feast until the fourth century, the early Christians must
have known at what time of the year our Lord was born; this
letter was written only a few months before the anniversary of
Christ's birth.

Christians Must Find Honourable Employment. Probably
the situation which led to this command was the same as that
of the Second Thessalonians: Christians were sitting around
idle, waiting for the Second Coming. Their stopwork attitude
was giving Christianity a bad name among the pagans. Paul
here recalls them to reality and strikes a note of sound common sense.

Paul sent this letter by Zenas and Apollo (who figured
prominently in the Corinthian letters); they were passing
through Crete on their way elsewhere, their destination prob-

and come to meet me at Nicopolis; I have decided to spend the winter there. Make careful provision for Zenas, the lawyer, and Apollo on their journey; they must not be left wanting for anything. It would be well if our brethren would learn to find honourable employment, so as to meet what necessity demands of them, instead of having nothing to contribute. All those who are with me send their greeting to you. Greet all those who are our friends in the common faith. Grace be with you all.

First Letter to Timothy

Paul, an apostle of Jesus Christ by the appointment of God our Saviour, and of Jesus Christ who is our hope, to Timothy, my own son in the faith, grace be yours, and mercy, and peace, from God the Father and from our Lord Jesus Christ, as you fulfil the charge I gave you, when I passed on into Macedonia, to stay behind at Ephesus. There were some who needed to be warned against teaching strange doctrines, against occupying their minds with legends and interminable pedigrees, which breed controversy, instead of building up God's house, as the faith does. The end at which our warning aims is charity, based on purity of heart, on a good conscience and a sincere faith. There are some who have missed this mark, branching off into vain speculations; who now claim to be expounding the law, without understanding the meaning of their own words, or the subject on which they pronounce so positively. The law? It is an excellent thing, where it is applied legitimately; but it must be remembered that the law is not meant for those who live innocent lives. It is meant for the lawless and the refractory; for the godless and the sinner, the unholy and the profane;

ably Alexandria in Egypt, where Apollo came from. Titus is asked to give them financial assistance for the remainder of their journey; situations such as this show the need for prosperous members of the flock, as opposed to idlers. Paul eventually sent Artemas to replace Titus (2 Tim. 4, 11). When Artemas arrived, Titus was to take the first ship and come to Paul's winter quarters at Nicopolis; this was a port not far up the Adriatic coast from Corinth.

The Church at Ephesus

Safeguard True Doctrine. As the winter months wore on at Nicopolis, Paul's thoughts went frequently to Timothy at Ephesus. Eight months had passed since he had left this most trusted disciple to straighten out the problems that had arisen in the Ephesian church. As well as his own personal knowledge of the Ephesian church, Paul had a short note from Timothy giving an account of how he was getting on there; this letter arrived at Nicopolis about the same time as Titus did, just before winter stopped travel. As Paul talked over the Cretan problems with Titus, this letter to Timothy began to take form; he decided to let Timothy share Titus' experience in dealing with a like situation.

In his Letter to the Ephesians, three years earlier, Paul had warned them of the danger of Gnostic speculations. In this Letter to Timothy, the warning is more urgent. These false teachers are of the same type as those he rebuked in his Letter to Titus; they seem to have been Jewish in origin. Like the Judaizers of the Galatian crisis, and Apollo in his teaching at Corinth, they put a false emphasis on the Old Testament.

for those who lay violent hands on father or mother, for mur-
derers, for those who commit fornication or sin against nature,
the slave-dealer, the liar, the perjurer. All this and much else
is the very opposite of the sound doctrine contained in the
gospel I have been entrusted with, that tells us of the blessed
God and his glory.

How I thank our Lord Jesus Christ, the source of all my
strength, for showing confidence in me by appointing me his
minister, me, a blasphemer till then, a persecutor, a man of
violence, author of outrage, and yet he had mercy on me, because I was acting in the ignorance of unbelief. The grace of
the Lord came upon me in a full tide of faith and love, the love
that is in Christ Jesus. How true is that saying, and what a welcome it deserves, that 'Christ Jesus came into the world to
save sinners.' I was the worst of all, and yet I was pardoned,
so that in me first of all Christ Jesus might give the extreme
example of his patience; I was to be the pattern of all those
who will ever believe in him, to win eternal life. Honour and
glory through endless ages to the king of all the ages, the immortal, the invisible, who alone is God. Amen.

This charge, then, I give into your hands, my son Timothy,
remembering how prophecy singled you out, long ago. Serve,
as it bade you, in this honourable warfare, with faith and a
good conscience to aid you. Some, through refusing this duty,
have made shipwreck of the faith; among them, Hymenaeus
and Alexander, whom I have made over to Satan, till they are
cured of their blasphemy.

This first of all, I ask; that petition, prayer, entreaty and
thanksgiving should be offered for all mankind, especially for
kings and others in high station, so that we can live a calm and

Seemingly they embellished the scriptures with all kinds of fantastic legends and interpretations. Instead of appealing to Christian tradition, they looked to the Mosaic law. Paul reminds them that the law was meant to keep men conscious of their sinful nature; the gospel teaching emphasizes man's close relation to God by the bond of charity.

Paul's Vocation and Timothy's.   Paul has not to search far for an illustration of how grace comes to men through Christ, not through study of the Mosaic law; he himself is a perfect example. His thoughts go back to that crisis of his life on the Damascus Road: Saul the Pharisee, the devoted student of the Old Testament, was suddenly changed into Paul the convert; he experienced 'the love that is in Christ Jesus.' Paul's case is typical of God's dealings with men: He is patient with sinners, his grace pursues them till they find faith in Christ.

It is Paul's vocation in life to proclaim salvation to all mankind in Christ Jesus. Timothy has a like vocation. Jesus told his apostles: 'It was not you that chose me, it was I that chose you.' It was not Timothy's choice that made him a minister of the gospel; it was a call from God expressed through a member of the church at Lystra. That is what Paul is referring to in the phrase, 'prophecy singled you out.' This was one of the spiritual gifts discussed in 1 Corinthians 12-14.

From a comparison with 1 Corinthians 5, 5 it seems that Paul excommunicated Hymenaeus and Alexander; they had fallen into heresy 'by contending that the resurrection has come about already' (2 Tim. 2, 18).

The Duty of Public Prayer.   Before the year 66 A.D. was out, the Jews in Palestine would be in open revolt against Rome; for the past few years it had been working up to a climax.

tranquil life, as dutifully and decently as we may. Such prayer is our duty, it is what God, our Saviour, expects of us, since it is his will that all men should be saved, and be led to recognize the truth; there is only one God, and only one mediator between God and men, Jesus Christ, who is a man, like them, and gave himself as a ransom for them all. At the appointed time, he bore his witness, and of that witness I am the chosen herald, sent as an apostle (I make no false claims, I am only recalling the truth) to be a true and faithful teacher of the Gentiles.

It is my wish that prayer should everywhere be offered by the men; they are to lift up hands that are sanctified, free from all anger and dispute. So, too, with the women; they are to dress themselves modestly and with restraint in befitting attire; no plaited hair, no gold ornaments, or pearls, or rich clothes; a virtuous life is the best adornment for women who lay claim to piety. Women are to keep silence, and take their place, with all submissiveness, as learners; a woman shall have no leave from me to teach, and issue commands to her husband; her part is to be silent. It was Adam that was created first, and Eve later, nor was it Adam that went astray; woman was led astray, and was involved in transgression. Yet woman will find her salvation in the Child-bearing, if they will but remain true to faith and love and holy living.

It is well said, 'When a man aspires to a bishopric, it is no mean employment that he covets.' The man who is to be a bishop, then, must be one with whom no fault can be found; faithful to one wife, sober, discreet, well behaved, hospitable, experienced in teaching, no lover of wine or of brawling, courteous, neither quarrelsome nor grasping. He must be one

The Roman authorities did not distinguish Jews from Christians, so that the Christian name was in bad repute throughout the Empire. Added to this was the blame for the burning of Rome in 64 A.D. and the consequent persecution of Christians by Nero. Paul knew how to deal with the situation: the best way to combat persecution is to convert the persecutor (after all, he himself had been a persecutor and had been converted). The Church is not in opposition to the State; the two must work together, each in its proper sphere. Christians must pray for secular rulers, and for the whole pagan world; Christ's Redemption, like God's Fatherhood, is world-wide.

Christians stretched out their hands to God in prayer, like Jesus on the cross. It is public prayer, the social act of the community, that Paul has in mind. And that is why he forbids women to take part; they have no official status in public worship. He dealt with the same problem in 1 Corinthians 11, 3-16 and 14, 34; he still stands by his decision that women must be silent.

Most commentators hold that Paul tells women their vocation is motherhood ('child-bearing'). But the Greek definite article refers to one famous Child-bearing, the birth of our Lord at Bethlehem. Just as Eve brought shame on womanhood by her transgression, so Mary has re-established the glorious position of woman by her obedience; it was she who bore the Redeemer.

Qualifications for the Ministry. During the eighteen months of our Lord's Galilean ministry, his chief concern was the selection and training of his twelve apostles. He spent the night, before he made the final choice, in prayer on the mountainside overlooking the lake; next to his Passion and Death it was the most important act of his earthly life. Paul shows a similar

who is a good head to his own family, and keeps his children
in order by winning their full respect; if a man has not learned
how to manage his own household, will he know how to govern
God's church? He must not be a new convert, or he may be
carried away by vanity, and incur Satan's doom. He must bear
a good character, too, in the world's eyes; or he may fall into
disrepute, and become a prey to the False Accuser.

Deacons, in the same way, must be men of decent behaviour, men of their word, not given to deep drinking or to
money-getting, keeping true, in all sincerity of conscience, to
the faith that has been revealed. These, in their turn, must
first undergo probation, and only be allowed to serve as deacons if no charge is brought against them. The women-folk,
too, should be modest, not fond of slanderous talk; they must
be sober, and in every way worthy of trust. The deacon must be
faithful to one wife, good at looking after his own family and
household. Those who have served well in the diaconate will
secure for themselves a sure footing, and great boldness in proclaiming that faith, which is founded on Christ Jesus. So much
I tell you by letter, although I hope to pay you a visit before
long; so that, if I am slow in coming, you may be in no doubt
over the conduct that is expected of you in God's household.
By that I mean the Church of the living God, the pillar and
foundation upon which the truth rests.

No question of it, it is a great mystery we worship: 'Revelation made in human nature, justification won in the realm of
the Spirit; a vision seen by angels, a mystery preached to the
Gentiles; Christ in this world, accepted by faith, Christ, on
high, taken up into glory.'

We are expressly told by inspiration that, in later days,
there will be some who abandon the faith, listening to false

concern for a worthy clergy in the advice he here gives Timothy. The candidates must have a good name among the people with whom they have to live; their conduct in the past, especially in governing their own household, is the best guide to their suitability in ruling God's household. Paul warns Timothy of Satan's watchfulness to do harm to the Church; he must take care of his selection of ministers so that no foothold is given to the Enemy.

In his advice to Titus, Paul used the word 'presbyter' in exactly the same sense as he here uses 'bishop.' It seems clear from Acts 20, 17-38 that the two names were synonyms. It was not until the early part of the second century that bishop came to be used in its present meaning of one with episcopal powers in charge of a diocese. It is clear that both Titus and Timothy had episcopal powers (they are told to ordain), but they went from place to place as Paul decided; they were legates of Paul with a roving commission.

Celibacy of the clergy was not of obligation at this period; probably the bulk of converts were already married; it would have been impossible to get enough priests from among the unmarried Christians. 'Faithful to one wife' may be a prohibition on a widower's remarrying, or it might mean the exclusion of those who had two wives living; divorce was widely practised among the heathen.

Christ the Test of Orthodoxy. Paul begins by quoting from what is probably an early Christian hymn. Its subject is the Incarnation, the central mystery of Christianity. The hymn is rather cryptic; it is a series of three contrasts. This is how Mgr. Knox explains it: 'Christ manifested to the world in his humanity, yet redeeming us through the dignity of his divine Person; the Resurrection, a sight only witnessed by angels, yet

inspirations, and doctrines taught by the devils. They will be deceived by the pretensions of impostors, whose conscience is hardened as if by a searing-iron. Such teachers bid them abstain from marriage, and from certain kinds of food, although God has made these for the grateful enjoyment of those whom faith has enabled to recognize the truth. All is good that God has made, nothing is to be rejected; only we must be thankful to him when we partake of it, then it is hallowed for our use by God's blessing and the prayer which brings it. Lay down these rules for the brethren, and you will show yourself a true servant of Jesus Christ, thriving on the principle of that faith whose wholesome doctrine you have followed.

Leave foolish nursery tales alone, and train yourself, instead, to grow up in holiness. 'Training of the body avails but little; holiness is all-availing, since it promises well both for this life and for the next'; how true is that saying, and what a welcome it deserves! It is for this that we toil and struggle, our hope in a living God, who is the Saviour of mankind, and above all of those who are faithful in his service.

Such is the charge, such is the doctrine you are to deliver. Do not let anyone think the less of you for your youthfulness; make yourself a model of speech and behaviour for the faithful, all love, all faith, all purity. Reading, preaching, instruction, let these be your constant care while I am absent. A special grace has been entrusted to you; prophecy awarded it, and the imposition of the presbyters' hands went with it; do not let it suffer from neglect. Let this be your study, these your employments, so that all may see how well you are doing. Two things claim your attention, yourself and the teaching of the faith; spend your care on them; so will you and those who listen to you achieve salvation.

published throughout the world; Christ still making his power felt here below, through the faith of his Church, although he has ascended into heaven.'

It is this twofold aspect of Christ's life, his earthly existence and his heavenly existence, his human nature and his divine nature, that is neglected by the false teachers at Ephesus. Paul's own teaching was always of Christ, but these men look elsewhere for the doctrine they are teaching. If Timothy applies this infallible test to them, he will see that they are impostors; their pretensions to holiness are based on a false asceticism that derives from paganism and Judaism.

Grow Up In Holiness. The best way to prove the truth of orthodox doctrine is not so much by argument as by example; if Timothy's personal piety and holiness of life surpasses that of the false teachers, then it will be obvious to all that his gospel is that of Christ. This was the very test our Lord himself gave: 'It is by their fruit that you will know them.' The ascetical practices of the Ephesian false teachers were mostly concerned with the body; Paul reminds Timothy that holiness is in the soul, in the practice of virtue.

Timothy must have been in his early thirties at this time; he had been with Paul for sixteen years (50-66 A.D.). But Paul still thinks of him as the youth he ordained at Lystra. Possibly Timothy was timid by nature; so Paul is trying to bolster up his courage in dealing with a difficult situation among a clergy that was much older than he. In Timothy's favour is the fact that he has been selected by the Holy Spirit as a ruler of the flock; this divine vocation more than compensates for the absence of gray hair. He must not forget his twofold obligation to preach the truth and live a holy life.

16

Instead of finding fault, appeal to an older man as if he were your father, to younger men as your brothers, to the older women as mothers, to the younger (but with all modesty) as sisters. Give widows their due, if that name really belongs to them; if a widowed woman is left with children or grandchildren, they must be warned that their own flesh and blood has the first claim on their piety. They must make due returns to those who gave them birth; that is what God asks of them. The woman who is indeed a widow, bereft of all help, will put her trust in God, and spend her time, night and day, upon the prayers and petitions that belong to her state; one who lives in luxury would be alive and dead both at once. Warn them of this, too, or they will bring themselves into disrepute; the man who makes no provision for those nearest him, above all his own family, has contradicted the teaching of the faith, and indeed does worse than the unbelievers do.

If a woman is to be put on the list of widows, she must have reached, at least, the age of sixty, and have been faithful to one husband. She must have a name for acts of charity; has she brought up children? Has she been hospitable? Has she washed the feet of the saints? Has she helped those who were in affliction? Has she attached herself to every charitable cause? Have nothing to do with younger widows; they will live at their ease at Christ's expense, and then be for marrying again, thus incurring the guilt of breaking the promise they have made. Meanwhile, they learn habits of idleness as they go from house to house, nor are they merely idle, they gossip and interfere, and say what they have no right to say. So I would have the younger women marry and bear children and have households to manage; then they will give enmity no handle for speaking ill of us. Already there are some who have turned aside, to follow Satan. Meanwhile, if a believer has any widows depending

On the Position of Widows. Paul was an expert in dealing with people; his genius for friendship, his long years of experience, had give him an understanding and skill that has never been surpassed. He gently reminds Timothy that gentleness and charity are far more effective than sternness and fault-finding; the atmosphere he should cultivate is that of a family; he will find a way to their hearts by familiarity and friendliness.

From the earliest times the Christians made it a special duty to look after destitute widows; the order of deacons was established for this purpose (Acts 6, 1). Probably the nucleus of the first group of widows was that band of holy women who accompanied our Lord and his apostles during the public ministry; we find them with the apostles and disciples in the Cenacle awaiting the coming of the Holy Spirit (Acts 1, 14).

By the time Paul wrote this Letter to Timothy, the widows seem to have formed a religious community which gave most of its time to charitable works. His main concern in this paragraph is to see that unsuitable candidates do not enter the community of widows. He reminds Timothy that the obligation of providing for widows belongs primarily to the family not the church. Even when these ladies do pass the means test, Paul still requires that Timothy conduct a searching enquiry into the life and virtues of the candidates.

Under paganism woman's place was in the home, where she was under the absolute power of her husband. By its teaching on the indissolubility of marriage, and also by opening up the life of celibacy to women, Christianity gave new hope to women, and an opportunity for charitable activity never known before. Owing to their lack of training for such work, they were in need of advice to help them avoid pitfalls, and to protect the good name of the Christian community. That Paul did permit women to embark on this new career,

on him, he should undertake their support, leaving the church free to support the widows who are really destitute.

Presbyters who have acquitted themselves well of their charge should be awarded double consideration; those especially, who bestow their pains on preaching and instruction: there is a passage in scripture which tells us not to muzzle the ox while it is threshing grain, and the labourer has a right to expect his maintenance. Do not take cognizance of any charge made against a presbyter, unless there are two witnesses or more. Give a public rebuke to those who are living amiss, and thus put fear into the rest. I adjure you in the sight of God and of Jesus Christ, and the angels he has chosen, to observe these rules without rash judgment, without yielding to partiality. As for the imposition of hands, do not bestow it inconsiderately, and so share the blame for the sins of others. Keep yourself clear of fault. (No, do not confine yourself to water any longer; take a little wine to relieve your stomach, and your frequent attacks of illness.) Some men have faults that are plain to view, so that they invite question; with others, discovery follows upon the heels of enquiry; so it is, too, with their merits; some are plain to view, and where they are not, they cannot long remain hidden.

Those who are bound to slavery must treat their masters as entitled to all respect; otherwise God's name and our doctrine will be ill spoken of. And those whose masters belong to the faith must not think the less of them, for being their brethren; they should render all the better service, when those who benefit by their good will are believers, worthy of their love. Teach them, and encourage them, so to act.

despite the dangers, entitles him to rank among the great liberators of women.

On the Restoration of Church Discipline.

It would seem that Timothy had started a purge among the Ephesian clergy. Whether the cause of the scandals among these presbyters was doctrinal or moral, or both, is not sure; probably most of the false teachers rebuked by Paul in the Pastoral Epistles were members of the clergy. Timothy may have been a little uncertain how far to go, and so appealed to Paul for advice. Paul tells him to reward those who have remained true to Christian principles, and to punish, after a fair trial, those who have deviated from true doctrine or Christian standards. He also warns him against ordaining ('the imposition of hands') any candidate not suitable for the ministry.

Paul is reminded of another question of Timothy's, probably by the word 'fault.' In this matter Timothy is at fault, and should correct it at once. He was under doctor's orders to take wine with his meals; he had disregarded this medical advice, probably with the intention of giving a good example to some of his clergy who were inclined to drink too much. Not being sure that he was acting rightly, he submitted the case to the decision of his old master in the spiritual life. Paul became so engrossed in other matters that he almost forgot to answer this question; he did so in a footnote.

Mgr. Knox suggests that the slaves mentioned in the final paragraph of this section were presbyters; this would fit perfectly in the context. It is not unlikely that some of the Christian slaves received ordination to the priesthood. Timothy may have asked if they should be set free by their Christian masters.

Is there some rival teacher, who refuses assent to the sound principles which are the principles of our Lord Jesus Christ, to the doctrine which accords with holiness? Then it is because he is puffed up with vanity; knowledge he has none, but an itch for speculation and controversy. What comes of it? Only jealousy, quarrelling, recriminations and base suspicions, all such encounters as must arise between men with corrupted minds who have lost track of the truth. Religion, they think, will provide them with a living. And indeed, religion is ample provision for life, though no more than a bare sufficiency goes with it. Empty-handed we came into the world, and empty-handed, beyond question, we must leave it; why, then, if we have food and clothing to last us out, let us be content with that. Those who would be rich fall into temptation, the devil's trap for them; all those useless and dangerous appetites which sink men into ruin here and perdition hereafter. The love of money is a root from which every kind of evil springs, and there are those who have wandered away from the faith by making it their ambition, stabbing themselves with many a sorrow.

It is for you, servant of God, to shun all this; to aim at right living, holiness, and faith, and love, and endurance, and kind forbearance. Fight the good fight of faith, lay your grasp on eternal life, that life you were called to, when you asserted the great claim before so many witnesses. I adjure you before the God who gives life to all things, before Jesus Christ who bore witness to that great claim when he stood before Pontius Pilate, to fulfil your charge without stain of reproach until the day when our Lord Jesus Christ appears. God will reveal him in due time, the blessed God who alone enjoys dominion; he is King of kings, and Lord of lords; to him alone immortality belongs, his dwelling is in unapproachable light; no hu-

The Root of All Evil. *The subject that occupies most of the First Letter to Timothy is that of false teachers.* These men were not Jewish or pagan adversaries but members of the Ephesian church; for the most part they were members of the clergy, for whom Timothy was personally responsible. They were not teaching heresy but were indulging in idle speculation and controversy; they had wandered far from the sound doctrine of the gospel preached to them by Paul; they disputed and quarrelled over the most trivial and unimportant matters.

In the pagan world around them, religion and finance were closely associated. The great temple of Diana at Ephesus was as much a bank as a place of worship. Brought up with such a background, many of the Ephesian clergy looked upon the priesthood as a source of financial security; they became so intent on making money that they forgot this was not their real vocation. Possibly the smallness of their stipends as priests led them into temptation; in their eagerness to possess an adequate income they became greedy for money and seized every opportunity of getting their hands on it.

That money is a dangerous commodity is clear from our Lord's teaching. At the end of his parable on the Dishonest Steward, he gave this warning: 'No servant can be in the employment of two masters at once; either he will hate the one and love the other, or he will devote himself to the one and despise the other. You must serve God or money; you cannot serve both.'

In contrast to this false way of life, Timothy is to stand forth as the champion of Christian principles. To do this he must have courage. Paul appeals to his youthful and timid disciple by reminding him of the profession of faith in Christ and his teachings that he made at his ordination ('the great claim'). He must continue to bear witness to the truth just

man eye has seen or can ever see him; to him be glory and everlasting empire, Amen.

Warn those who are rich in this present world not to think highly of themselves, not to repose their hopes in the riches that may fail us, but in God, who bestows on us so richly all that we enjoy. Let them do good, enrich their lives with charitable deeds, always ready to give, and to share the common burden, laying down a sure foundation for themselves in time to come, so as to have life which is true life within their grasp. It is for you, Timothy, to keep safe what has been entrusted to you, avoiding these empty, intruding forms of speech, this quibbling knowledge that is knowledge only in name; there are those who profess them, and in professing them have shot wide of the mark which faith sets us. Grace be with you.

Second Letter to Timothy

Paul, sent as an apostle of Jesus Christ by the will of God, in furtherance of that promise of life which is given us in Christ Jesus, to Timothy, his well beloved son, grace and mercy and peace from God the Father, and from Christ Jesus our Lord. It is with gratitude to that God, whom I worship with a clear conscience in the way my fathers taught me, that I make mention of you continually, day and night, in my prayer. I keep the memory of your tears, and long to see you again, so as to have my fill of joy when I receive fresh proof of your sincere faith. That faith dwelt in your grandmother Lois, and in your mother, Eunice, before you; I am fully persuaded that it

as the Master himself bore witness before Pilate: 'What I was born for, what I came into the world for, is to bear witness of the truth.' It is this same Lord and Master who will appear at the Second Coming to reward those who have stood true to him through the struggles and difficulties of life.

It is a common error for the rich to rest content with their wealth; Paul warns them that the only way they can lay hold on that 'life which is true life' is by using their money for charitable purposes. True riches are stored up in the deposit of faith, that sum of truths handed on by Jesus Christ to his Church. These are the riches which Timothy has in his keeping, and which he must guard securely. He is to enrich his Ephesian charges by sharing with them this deposit of truth, and so protecting them from the errors of the false teachers.

Last Will and Testament

Paul Once More a Prisoner. At the first sign of spring, in March 66 A.D., Paul was once more on the road to revisit his many foundations. He had promised Timothy, in his First Letter to him, that he would come and see him soon. He left Nicopolis and made his way either by land or sea to Corinth, 100 miles distant. After a few months in Corinth, Paul departed by sea for Miletus, leaving behind him his disciple Erastus (4, 20); a second disciple, Trophimus, was too ill to go on with Paul (4, 20), so that he probably arrived alone at Ephesus. Here he hoped to meet Timothy, but he had already left that city.

16*

dwells in you too. That is why I would remind you to fan the
flame of that special grace which God kindled in you, when my
hands were laid upon you. The spirit he has bestowed on us is
not one that shrinks from danger; it is a spirit of action, of love,
and of discipline. Do not blush, then, for the witness you bear
to our Lord, or for me, who am his· prisoner; share all the
tribulations of the gospel message as God gives you strength.
Has he not saved us, and called us to a vocation of holiness?
It was not because of anything we had done; we owe it to his
own design, to the grace lavished on us, long ages ago, in Christ
Jesus. Now it has come to light, since our Saviour Jesus Christ
came to enlighten us; now he has annulled death, now he has
shed abroad the rays of life and immortality, through that gospel which I have been appointed to herald, as an apostle and
a teacher of the Gentiles. This is what I have to suffer as the
result; but I am not put to the blush. He, to whom I have
given my confidence, is no stranger to me, and I am fully persuaded that he has the means to keep my pledge safe, until
that day comes.

With all the faith and love you have in Christ Jesus, keep to
the pattern of sound doctrine you have learned from my lips.
By the power of the Holy Spirit who dwells in us, be true to
your high trust. In Asia, as you know, all have treated me
coldly, Phigellus and Hermogenes among them. May the Lord
grant mercy to the household of Onesiphorus; often enough he
revived my spirits. Instead of being ashamed of a prisoner's
acquaintance, he sought me out when he was in Rome, and
succeeded in finding me. The Lord grant that he may find
mercy with his Lord when that day comes; what he did for me
in Ephesus I have no need to tell you.

Paul was destined not to see Timothy on this occasion. He had not been long in Ephesus when a Roman guard came to his lodging (probably at the house of Onesiphorus), and took him prisoner. The persecution begun by Nero, after the burning of Rome two years earlier, was now intensified; leading Christians were being arrested even in the provinces. Added to this was the Jewish revolt against Roman administration in Palestine. It had just broken out, and an important Jew like Paul was under suspicion by the authorities.

The Christians at Ephesus, with the one exception of Onesiphorus, were afraid to come to Paul's assistance. He was chained to a soldier and marched northwards along the road to Troas. Here he left his cloak and his books of the scriptures (4, 12); he had no need of a winter cloak in midsummer, and he was afraid that his precious books would be lost or destroyed on the way to Rome.

When Paul arrived in Rome this time he was a criminal in chains. He was sent to the dank Mamertine prison, from which he wrote to Timothy; Luke was with him, and acted as Paul's secretary in writing this letter. It is the final farewell of an old warrior for Christ to his favourite disciple. In his loneliness Paul's mind goes back to those happy early days of their first meeting at Lystra; Timothy has much to be thankful for in his good home background, and the vocation from God to be a priest and a minister of Christ. Paul needs courage, and so too does Timothy; they both must go to the source of all strength, to the Master himself. Paul has staked his all on Christ; he has given up everything to follow him. He knows that suffering is an essential part of his life, as it was of Jesus'; he knows too that the Master will reward him for his life of labour for the cause of Christ.

Take strength, my own son, from the grace which dwells in Christ Jesus. You have learned, from many who can witness to it, the doctrine which I hand down; give it into the keeping of men you can trust, men who will know how to teach it to others besides themselves. Then, like a good soldier of Christ Jesus, take your share of hardship. The soldier on service, if he would please the captain who enlisted him, will refuse to be entangled in the business of daily life; the athlete will win no crown, if he does not observe the rules of the contest; the first share in the harvest goes to the labourer who has toiled for it. Grasp the sense of what I am saying; the Lord will give you quick insight wherever it is needed. Fix your mind on Jesus Christ, sprung from the race of David, who has risen from the dead; that is the gospel I preach, and in its service I suffer hardship like a criminal, yes, even imprisonment; but there is no imprisoning the word of God. For its sake I am ready to undergo anything; for love of the elect, that they, like us, may win salvation in Jesus Christ, and eternal glory with it. It is well said, 'We are to share his life, because we have shared his death; if we endure, we shall reign with him, if we disown him, he in his turn will disown us. If we play him false, he remains true to his word; he cannot disown himself.'

Bring this back to men's thoughts, pleading with them earnestly in God's name; there must be no wordy disputes, such as can only unsettle the minds of those who are listening. Aim first at winning God's approval, as a workman who does not need to be ashamed of his work, one who knows how to handle the claims of the truth like a master. Keep your distance from those who are bringing in a fashion of meaningless talk; they will go far to establish neglect of God, and their influence eats

A Good Soldier of Christ Jesus. From the moment when our Lord claimed Paul for his own on the road to Damascus, Paul's whole life was centred on Jesus. From the start he grasped the essential of following in the footsteps of Christ: 'If any man has a mind to come my way, let him renounce self, and take up his cross, and follow me.' It is the same message that the Lord delivered to Ananias, when he sent him to heal Paul of his blindness after the vision on the Damascus Road: 'I have yet to tell him, how much suffering he will have to undergo for my name's sake.'

During his second imprisonment in Rome Paul was not permitted to reside in his own lodgings; he was a common criminal in chains in the underground dungeon of the Mamertine prison, near the Roman forum. It was a most trying experience for an old man worn out in the service of Christ. But Paul is thinking more of Timothy than of himself. He appeals to him to remember his teaching, which comes from our Lord himself, that hardship is the lot of Christ's soldier. A soldier must practise detachment from worldly preoccupation. Paul continues with his advice to Timothy, but now changes the metaphor; like an athlete he must keep the rules to win the prize; like a farmer he must work hard for the harvest.

A Warning to Avoid Fanciful Speculations. During our Lord's Roman trial, he made this statement to Pilate: 'What I was born for, what I came into the world for, is to bear witness of the truth.' Pilate brushed this statement aside as of no importance by his reply: 'What is truth?' A pagan believed and worshipped because it was convenient, or to his own personal advantage, not because he thought any religion was true. Christianity was the first religion to demand belief

in like a cancer. Such are Hymenaeus and Philetas, who have missed the true mark, by contending that the resurrection has come about already, to the overthrow of the faith in some minds. But God's foundation-stone stands firm, and this is the legend on it, 'The Lord acknowledges none but his own'; and again, 'Let everyone who names the Lord's name keep far from iniquity.'

A great house, besides its plate of gold and silver, contains other objects made of wood and earthenware; those for noble, these for ignoble uses; it is by keeping himself separate from these that a man will prove the object of his Lord's regard, hallowed, and serviceable, and fit for all honourable employment. Shun these youthful ardours I speak of; aim at right living, faith, and love, and fellowship with all those who call on the name of the Lord with a pure heart. Leave these foolish, ill-conceived disputes alone; be very sure, they breed nothing but quarrels. A servant of the Lord has no business with quarrelling; he must be kindly towards all men, persuasive and tolerant, with a gentle hand for correcting those who are obstinate in their errors. It may be that God will enable them to repent, and acknowledge the truth; so they will recover their senses, and shake off the snare by which the devil, till now, has held them prisoners to his will.

Be sure of this, that in the world's last age there are perilous times coming. Men will be in love with self, in love with money; boastful, proud, abusive; without reverence for their parents, without gratitude, without scruple, without love, without peace; slanderers, incontinent, strangers to pity and to kindness; treacherous, reckless, full of vain conceit, thinking rather of their pleasures than of God. They will preserve all

because it was true. This difference of outlook keeps cropping
up in Paul's letters. His converts from paganism found it hard
to put off their pagan upbringing; they showed more interest
in argument and discussion than in following the truth that
came from Christ's revelation. That is why he warns Timothy
and Titus so often in these three letters.

Judaism was almost as bad as paganism in its fanciful speculations about trivialities and its useless distinctions about
things that did not matter. The big danger of these mental
gymnastics was that they could easily lead inexperienced young
theologians into error and heresy. Hymenaeus is mentioned
as such a one, but with a different companion, in 1 Timothy
1, 20. He probably explained the resurrection away as only a
spiritual rebirth in baptism. Such men are heretics, and so
unworthy of admission into that building which excludes them
by the inscription on its foundation stone.

The figure of a building ('a great house') had been tradi-
tional imagery for the church ever since our Lord told Peter,
'Upon this rock I will build my Church.' Paul pictures its
members as furniture in the house; those who follow true
doctrines are pure gold and silver, those who indulge in vain
fancies are only second-best furniture, utensils put to more
common use in the house.

Perilous Times Are Coming. The scriptures pictured God
coming in judgment at a time when evil seemed to reign
supreme: 'The charity of most men will grow cold, as they
see wickedness abound everywhere.' The persecution of Nero
was now reaching its peak of ferocity; all around Paul the
Christians of Rome were being subjected to all kinds of
barbaric torments. It reminded Paul of the scriptural predic-

the outward form of religion, although they have long been strangers to its meaning. From these, too, turn away. They count among their number the men that will make their way into house after house, captivating weak women whose consciences are burdened by sin; women swayed by shifting passions, who are for ever inquiring, yet never attain to recognition of the truth. Moses found rivals in Jannes and Jambres; just so the men I speak of set themselves up in rivalry against the truth, men whose minds are corrupt, whose faith is counterfeit; yet they will come to little, they will soon be detected, like those others, in their rash folly.

Not such was the schooling, the guidance, you had from me; in firm resolve, in faith, in patience, in love, in endurance; all my persecutions and sufferings, such as those which befell me at Antioch, Iconium, and Lystra; what persecutions I underwent! And yet the Lord brought me through them all safely. And indeed, all those who are resolved to live a holy life in Christ Jesus will meet with persecution; while the rogues and the mountebanks go on from bad to worse, at once impostors and dupes.

It is for you to hold fast by the doctrine handed on to you, the assurance imparted to you; you know well, from whom that tradition came; you can remember the holy learning you have been taught from childhood upwards. This will train you up for salvation, through the faith which rests in Christ Jesus. Everything in the scripture has been divinely inspired, and has its uses; to instruct us, to expose our errors, to correct our faults, to educate us in holy living; so God's servant will become a master of his craft, and each noble task that comes will find him ready for it.

tions of the Second Coming.

It seems that Paul is thinking of the pagan world in the first seven lines; from then on he seems to have the Christian world in mind. Possibly he is thinking of his Ephesian converts disowning him when he was arrested there on his arrival from Nicopolis (1, 15-18). The mention of Jannes and Jambres (the two magicians who opposed Moses at Pharao's court) seems to indicate that many Ephesian Christians had fallen back into their magical practices (Acts 19, 18-19). The defection of one of his own disciples, Demas (4, 9), put the final touches on this depressing picture of disaster.

Live a Holy Life in Christ Jesus. Persecution was nothing new to Paul: 'I have spent longer days in prison, been beaten so cruelly, so often looked death in the face. Five times the Jews scourged me; three times I was beaten with rods, once I was stoned' (2 Cor. 11). Here he mentions what took place at Timothy's birthplace, Lystra, where Paul was stoned, dragged outside the city, and left for dead (Acts 14, 18). At nearby Iconium, the people turned against Paul and threatened to stone him. Paul was often at Antioch, the main base for his missionary journeys, but we have no record in the Acts of any persecution there. In these trials, the Lord looked after Paul; he will likewise guard and bring Timothy safely through the persecution now raging.

To carry out his office as Paul's son and heir, Timothy must hold fast to the true doctrine handed down to him. There are two sources from which he must learn—tradition and scripture. The first comes from our Lord through his apostles; the second is the inspired word of God set down in the holy writings. God is as much the author of the revelation

I adjure you in the sight of God, and of Jesus Christ, who is to be the judge of living and dead, in the name of his coming, and of his kingdom, preach the word, dwelling upon it continually, welcome or unwelcome; bring home wrong-doing, rebuke the sinner, comfort the waverer, with all the patience of a teacher. The time will surely come, when men will grow tired of sound doctrine, always itching to hear something fresh; and so they will provide themselves with a continuous succession of new teachers, as the whim takes them, turning a deaf ear to the truth, bestowing their attention on fables instead. It is for you to be on the watch, to accept every hardship, to employ yourself in preaching the gospel, and perform every duty of your office.

As for me, my blood already flows in sacrifice; the time has nearly come when I can go free. I have fought the good fight; I have finished the race; I have redeemed my pledge; I look forward to the prize that is waiting for me, the prize I have earned. The Lord, the judge whose award never goes amiss, will grant it to me when that day comes; to me, yes, and all those who have learned to welcome his appearing.

Make haste, and come quickly to me. Demas has fallen in love with this present world; he has deserted me, and gone to Thessalonica. Crescens has gone to Galatia, Titus to Dalmatia, and Luke is my only companion. Join company with Mark, and bring him here with you; he can help me with the exercise of his ministry now that I have sent Tychicus away to Ephesus. When you come, bring with you the cloak which I left in Carpus' hands at Troas; the books, too, and above all the rolls of parchment. I have had much ill usage from Alexander, the coppersmith. As for what he has done, the Lord will judge him

given to man in the Old Testament as he is of that given through Jesus Christ. Both have the same purpose: to educate men in holy living. This statement of Paul's is the classic text on Biblical Inspiration.

An essential of a bishop's office is to preach and teach his flock. It is not only important that he know the truth; he must be prepared to impart it to others. Paul is most insistent that Timothy fulfil this function completely. Undoubtedly it was the errors of false teachers that moved him to emphasize this point. All through the Pastoral Letters, Paul's theme is the evil being done by false doctrine in the churches he has founded. Once heresy destroys the truth, the whole fabric of Christian living is destroyed.

It is for Timothy to keep the faith alive; the time has come for Paul to hand over to him the responsibility for his converts. He knows that he will not be freed from prison this time; the life he has lived for Christ is soon to be changed to eternal glory. Characteristically Paul uses two metaphors from athletics to describe his life: he has always been a fighter; he has run the race with his eyes fixed on Christ Jesus.

Paul's Loneliness. In time of trial there is comfort in human friendship. During the Agony in the Garden our Lord came back three times to his sleeping disciples in search of consolation. Paul, who followed so closely in Jesus' footsteps, felt the same abandonment as he awaited death. As winter came on, and the cold seeped into his bones, he thought of his beloved disciple Timothy; in his distress he sent out a pathetic appeal that we hope was answered in time.

Tychicus may have carried this letter to Ephesus, which was Timothy's headquarters; he was to find Timothy and send

for it; only do you, too, be on your guard against him; he has been a great enemy to our preaching.

At my first trial, no one stood by me; I was deserted by everybody; may it be forgiven them. But the Lord was at my side; he endowed me with strength, so that through me the preaching of the gospel might attain its full scope, and all the Gentiles might hear it; thus I was brought safely out of the jaws of the lion. Yes, the Lord has preserved me from every assault of evil; he will bring me safely into his heavenly kingdom; glory be to him through endless ages, Amen.

My greetings to Prisca and Aquila, and to the household of Onesiphorus. Erastus has stayed on at Corinth; Trophimus fell ill, and I left him behind at Miletus. Make haste, and come to me before winter. Eubulus and Pudens and Linus and Claudia and all the brethren send you their greeting. The Lord Jesus be with your spirit. Grace be with you all.

him at once to Rome. Timothy was to come to Rome via Troas, so that he could pick up the cloak and Bible ('parchment') that Paul had been forced to leave there on his way to Rome in chains. Perhaps Alexander was the renegade Christian of 1 Timothy 1, 20, and possibly the same person mentioned in Acts 19, 33. He was now living at Ephesus. He may have been Paul's betrayer in Asia, a second Judas; possibly he had gone to Rome as a witness against Paul at his trial there.

Paul had already been tried once during his present imprisonment; this was probably shortly after his arrival in Rome. Just as in Asia, where he had been arrested, all the Christians abandoned him through fear; but unaided by man Paul had made a brilliant defence that saved him from death for the time being. The second time, in the following year 67 A.D., he would be condemned to death, taken a few miles outside the city and beheaded. At long last his life was complete in Christ Jesus.

CHRONOLOGY OF PAUL'S LIFE

DATE	MAIN PAULINE EVENTS	PAGE	S. S. REFERENCES	CONTEMPORARY EVENTS
30	Descent of Holy Spirit at Pentecost	2	Acts 2,1–36	Caiphas H.P. (18–36)
30	Infant Church at Jerusalem	6	Ac. 2,37–5,42	Pilate (26–36)
30	Ss. Stephen and Philip and the other Deacons	24	Ac. 6–8	Herod Antipas + 39
30	CONVERSION OF PAUL: Damascus, Arabia, Damas.	40	Ac. 9; Gal. 1,15–17; 2 Cor. 11,32–33	
31	Conversion of Cornelius, Caesarea ..	46	Ac. 10,1–11,18	Tiberius Emp. (14–36)
33	Paul at Jerusalem (1st visit), Tarsus	44	Ac. 9,26–30; Gal. 1,18–24	Caligula Emp. (37–41)
43–44	Paul at Antioch, Jerusalem (2nd visit)	56	Ac. 11,25ff.;12,2,5;22,17ff.; Gal. 2,1–10; 2 Cor. 12,2ff.	Claudius Emp. (41–54)
43–44	Persecution by Agrippa; Apostles disperse	58	Ac. 12	Herod Agrippa I (41–44)
45–47	FIRST MISSIONARY JOURNEY: Cyprus and Galatia	62	Ac. 13–14	
48	Paul rebukes Peter, Antioch	78	Gal. 2,11–14	Aramaic Gospel of St. Mt. (c44)
49	GALATIANS, from Antioch	74	Gal. 1,6	
49	Council of Jerusalem (Paul's 3rd visit)	96	Ac. 15; Gal. 2	
50–52	SECOND MISSIONARY JOURNEY: Syria, Cilicia, Galatia, Macedonia, Achaia, back by sea	100	Ac. 15,36–18,22; Rom. 15,19	

From Antioch to Corinth (50–51)	100	Ac. 15,36–18,11	Jews banished from Rome (50)
			Gallio Proconsul of Achaia (51–52)
Early 51	1 THESSALONIANS, from Corinth	116	1 Thess. 3,1ff.
Late 51	2 THESSALONIANS, from Corinth	128	2 Thess. 2,1ff.
	From Corinth to Jerusalem (52) ...	134	Ac. 18,12–22
53–58	THIRD MISSIONARY JOURNEY: Galatia, Asia, Macedonia, Achaia, Maced., back by sea	136	Ac. 18,22–21,16
			Herod Agrippa II (53–93)
	From Antioch to Ephesus (53–57) ..	136	Ac. 18,23–19,22
April 57	1 CORINTHIANS, from Ephesus	140	1 Cor. 16,5ff.
			Nero Emp. (54–68)
	From Ephesus to Philippi (57)	202	Ac. 19,23–20,1
Oct. 57	2 CORINTHIANS, from Philippi	204	2 Cor. 2,13; 7–8
			Ananias H.P. (47–59)
	From Philippi to Corinth (Oct.–Dec. 57)	244	Ac. 20,2
Early 58	ROMANS, from Corinth	244	Rom. 15,25–26; 16,1–2
			Felix (53–60)
	From Corinth to Jerusalem (Easter-Pent. 58)	308	Ac. 20,3–21,25
			Festus (60–62)
58–60	ARREST in Jerusalem, IMPRISONMENT in Caesarea	316	Ac. 21,26–26,32
60	HEBREWS, DRAFTED at Caesarea	344	Heb. 13,23–25
			Gospel of St. Mark (Rome: 53–60)

DATE	MAIN PAULINE EVENTS	PAGE	S. S. REFERENCES	CONTEMPORARY EVENTS
60–61	VOYAGE TO ROME, winter at Malta	388	Ac. 27,1–28,15	Epistle of St. James (Jerus.: c61)
61–63	FIRST ROMAN CAPTIVITY	398	Ac. 28,16–31	
Early 63	EPHESIANS, from Rome	400	Eph. 3,1	Gospel of St. Luke (Rome: c63)
Early 63	COLOSSIANS, from Rome	420	Col. 4,3ff.;4,18	
Early 63	PHILEMON, from Rome	434	Philemon	1st Ep. of St. Peter (Rome: c63)
April 63	PHILIPPIANS, from Rome	436, 443	Phil. 1,1.12ff.;4,15	
62–63	Luke writes ACTS OF THE APOSTLES, at Rome	401	Ac. 16,10ff.; 28,30–31 Col. 4,14; 2 Tim. 4,9–11	
63–66	LAST JOURNEYS	453, 475	(Not in "ACTS")	Epistle of St. Jude (Syria: c63)
	From Rome to Ephesus and Colossae (63)	453	Philemon 22	
	From Ephesus to Spain (April 64–April 65)	453	Rom. 15,24–28	
	From Spain (via Rome: HEBREWS PUBLISHED) to Ephesus, Crete, Eph., Philippi (65)	453, 389	Tit. 1,5; 1 Tim. 1,3	
Sept. 65	TITUS, from Philippi	450	Tit. 1,4–5	Great earthquake at Pompeii (63) (Destruction: 79)

Feb. 66	1 Timothy, from Nicopolis	458	1 Tim. 1,3; Tit. 3,12	
	From Nicopolis to Corinth, Miletus and Ephesus (ARREST)	475, 486	2 Tim. 4,20	Great Fire of Rome (July 64) begins Nero's Persecution
	JOURNEY TO ROME, SECOND ROMAN CAPTIVITY	477, 484	2 Tim. 4,13	Jewish War begins (66)
Oct. 66	2 Timothy, from Rome	474, 484–6	2 Tim. 4,13–21	2nd Ep. of St. Peter (Rome: c66)
67	Death of Ss. Peter and Paul, Rome	487		

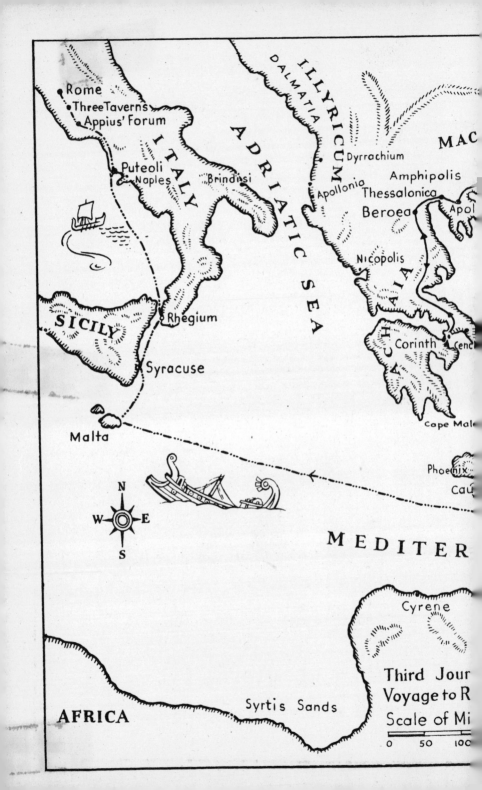